Argumentation Methods for Artificial Intelligence in Law

Douglas Walton

Argumentation Methods for Artificial Intelligence in Law

With 28 Figures

Springer

Professor Dr. Douglas Walton
University of Winnipeg
Department of Philosophy
Winnipeg, Manitoba R3B 2E9
Canada
d.walton@uwinnipeg.ca

ISBN-10 3-540-25187-1 Springer Berlin Heidelberg New York
ISBN-13 978-3-540-25187-3 Springer Berlin Heidelberg New York

Library of Congress Control Number: 2005927861

Springer is a part of Springer Science+Business Media

springeronline.com

Printed in Germany

Hardcover-Design: Erich Kirchner, Heidelberg

SPIN 11402756 64/3153-5 4 3 2 1 0 – Printed on acid-free paper

For Karen
With Love

Contents

Introduction

During a recent visit to China to give an invited lecture on legal argumentation I was asked a question about conventional opinion in western countries. If legal reasoning is thought to be important by those both inside and outside the legal profession, why does there appear to be so little attention given to the study of legal logic? This was a hard question to answer. I had to admit there were no large or well-established centers of legal logic in North America that I could recommend as places to study. Going through customs in Vancouver, the customs officer asked what I had been doing in China. I told him I had been a speaker at a conference. He asked what the conference was on. I told him legal logic. He asked whether there was such a thing.[1] He was trying to be funny, but I thought he had a good point. People will question whether there is such a thing as "legal logic", and some recent very prominent trials give the question some backing in the common opinion. But having thought over the question of why so little attention appears to be given to legal logic as a mainstream subject in western countries, I think I now have an answer. The answer is that we have been looking in the wrong place. We have traditionally looked to formal deductive and inductive models of legal reasoning, and the results, while far from insignificant, especially as a starting point, have just not taken us far enough to deal effectively with the kind of reasoning that is fundamental to law. This is defeasible reasoning, the kind of reasoning in which a rule or generalization that is subject to exceptions is applied to a single case, producing a plausible inference that can fail in some cases, yet can still provide evidence to support a conclusion.

This book moves to a different model, and a different set of methods, that show great promise in dealing more effectively with defeasible reasoning. In this book, tools for argument analysis and evaluation that have been developed in informal logic and refined in artificial intelligence are applied to some central problems of defeasible reasoning in law. These methods were originally developed in argumentation studies and informal logic in order to provide tools to help students think more critically, for example when trying to analyze and evaluate controversial arguments of the kind typically studied in a philosophy course. They proved to be especially successful in analyzing arguments of the kind associated with traditional informal fallacies, like appeal to expert opinion. Such arguments were problematic in the past because they are defeasible, and thus prone to failure in some

---

1 The question can be taken in various ways. It could be taken as suggesting that the kind of argumentation used in trials, especially famous ones reported in the press, is not logical. This could be taken as a negative comment on the current state of law, or even on the methods used by trial lawyers. On the other hand, there is a legal tradition that there is no such thing as legal logic. Thayer (1889, p. 142) suggested that there are no special rules of logical inference unique to law when he wrote, "there is no law for reasoning other than what is found in the laws of thought". Thus the phrase 'legal logic' may seem to be an oxymoron even to many lawyers and judges.

instances, even though they can provide support for a conclusion in other instances. Meantime, the field of computing, especially artificial intelligence, became centrally preoccupied with such defeasible arguments. Hence the next development was that some in the computing field started to take an interest in these new methods, and to start trying to refine them into forms precise enough that they could help with problems in artificial intelligence. This synergy between the two fields led to collaboration and cross-fertilization of results. Now artificial intelligence is regarded as the main area of application of argumentation theory.

This book proceeds with the hypothesis that the next most important test bed for argumentation is legal reasoning. Argumentation is based on a pragmatic approach in which the use of an argument is studied in a dialogue context. An argument is seen not just as an arbitrarily selected set of premises and a single conclusion, but also as taking part in an orderly conversational exchange between two parties in which one is offering reasons to support a conclusion the other has doubts about, or needs to be convinced to accept. This approach sees an argument not only as a set of propositions, but as such a set used for some purpose in a dialogue context. Thus the approach can be called pragmatic in that it sees an argument as used in some context. This approach can be immediately seen to fit legal argumentation naturally and extremely well, if one thinks of the kind of argumentation typically found in a trial setting. There are two sides, there is a conflict of opinions, and each of them presents arguments to support its side and raise doubts about the argument put forward by the other side. Of course, there is more going on in a trial than this. There are many participants and there are specific procedural rules that vary from one jurisdiction to another. Still, once you start to think of it, law is a natural and highly promising field for the pragmatic approach to argumentation. Not only does law stand to profit greatly from this new approach, but the field of argumentation can find lots of highly interesting and important examples and case studies of arguments, like those found in famous trials.

Following up this line of thinking, I ventured to write a pioneering book (Walton, 2002) that tried the experiment of applying argumentation tools then being developed to a central field of law, that of evidence. Although legal reasoning had often been thought important as a field of study, especially as applied to rules of evidence, this field had never seemed to attain much status, or come up with important results, in the way, for example, social studies of witness testimony had done. Wigmore diagrams have never been fashionable in law, despite Wigmore's status as a scholar of evidence in law, and deductive and inductive models of argument, the dominant ones in logic for so long, didn't apply to legal reasoning in a way that was turning out to be all that useful in leading to powerful techniques for the evaluation of evidence. The wave of unjust conviction cases led some critics to conclude that evidence law was "adrift" (Damaska, 1997). The entry point for argumentation was this central notion in law that at trial evidence is admitted as relevant and then evaluated through the trial process. These methods were under development both in artificial intelligence and argumentation research, during and after the period the book (Walton, 2002) was being written and published. These new developments have advanced the analysis of legal argumentation in several ways indicated by the topics covered in this book.

One tool is a set of argumentation schemes representing common forms of argument that are presumptive and defeasible. A second is the software system *Araucaria* for argument diagramming that enables a user to mark up and save a diagram displaying a chain of reasoning in a case. The third tool is the classification system for different types of dialogue in which argumentation is commonly put forward. Chapter 1 introduces these methods and shows how to apply them to typical cases of legal argumentation of the kind common in evidence law. Chapter 2 goes on to show how the role of generalizations in reasoning in evidence law can be analyzed using these new tools. Suppose a suspect is charged with theft, and the police search his apartment. Among his possessions is found an unusual object that can be positively identified as the one stolen. Such a finding constitutes legal evidence, a kind of evidence based on an inference that is, in turn, based on a generalization. The generalization asserts that any item found in the possession of a theft suspect that appears to be the same as the one stolen is evidence that the suspect stole it. Generalizations of this kind support inferences that are extremely common in legal argumentation, especially in evidence law.

In chapter 3, the same tools are applied to the problem of analyzing and evaluating defeasible arguments of the kind so often used as evidence in law. One such tool is the argumentation scheme, which represents the form of a defeasible argument, and is accompanied by a set of appropriate critical questions. The schemes studied include argument from witness testimony, argument from expert opinion, argument from ignorance, and abductive reasoning. It is shown how defeasible arguments are best analyzed in a dialogue model of rational argumentation, of the kind used in logic to study fallacies, and now used to study legal argumentation in the new field of computational dialectics, a branch of artificial intelligence. According to Lodder (2000, p. 255), the term 'computational dialectics' first appeared when Ron Loui and Tom Gordon organized an AAAI workshop with Johanna Moore and Katya Sycara under the name Computational Dialectics in Seattle in 1994. The call for papers for the workshop (Loui and Gordon, 1994) described the field of computational dialectics as the study of structured dialogues used in multi-agent communication systems in which agents reach agreement to achieve common goals through rational interaction leading to an outcome in a fair and effective way. Such dialogues contain a blend of adversarial argumentation, so that each agent has an individual goal, and is an advocate, but at the same time the procedure is collaborative and works only because the agents also share a common goal. Thus the workshop invitation used the expression "communal standards" when describing such computational models of deliberation, negotiation and discussion.

The problem of epistemic closure is that of finding the criterion for closing a search in a knowledge base so a conclusion can be drawn that has been established by the evidence found. Sometimes not finding anything after such a search can represent evidence. Paradoxically, the lack of evidence found is a sort of evidence. In such cases, a failure to find some proposition in a knowledge base is a premise supporting an argument that the proposition sought for is false. In chapter 3, the problem of how to identify and evaluate lack of evidence arguments of this form is studied, and linked to the problem of epistemic closure, with special reference to legal argumentation and burden of proof. It is argued that a proper evaluation of such arguments needs, in addition to a consideration of the semantic form of the argument, a consideration of its dialectical context, representing the stage of progress of an investigation towards closure.

Relevance is a central concept in trial rules used to ensure that a trial introduces and sticks to the right kind of evidence needed to bring the trial to a successful outcome of resolving the conflict of opinions that set it into motion in the first place. In chapter 4, argument diagramming is used to provide a model of relevance of the kind defined in Rule 401(a) of the Federal Rules of Evidence. By assigning values to the nodes in the diagram, the method is extended so that it represents probative weight of evidence, a notion central to the definition of relevance given in the Federal Rules. But the notion of relevance has always been highly problematic and elusive in the past. One of the central and most puzzling enigmas is the notion of conditional relevance. This notion means that an item of evidence can be introduced even if it is not relevant yet in the trial, at the stage reached so far, but it may become relevant at some future point as more and more evidence is presented. This notion has always been puzzling and controversial, as it seems to give a lawyer a kind of blank check to promise he will show something is relevant later on. Even so, sometimes using the notion of conditional relevance can help to move a trial along. But how could such a notion be defined, logically speaking? In chapter 4, the two techniques of the argument diagram and the framework of dialogue are combined to provide an analysis of the concept of conditional relevance.

Use of argumentation methods applied to legal argumentation is a relatively new field of study. Many vitally important problems of evidence in law can be formulated in light of these new methods, and even if these problems cannot be solved within the scope of any single monograph on the subject, some indications can be given on which direction for further research to take. Chapter 5 is a survey of several of these leading problems, with brief indication of how future research using argumentation-based methods might proceed. One set of problems concerns the analysis of different kinds of evidence that are mainly used in law – witness testimony, circumstantial evidence, forensic evidence and character evidence are all included. Two new tools for analyzing these kinds of evidence are introduced – abductive reasoning and examination dialogue. In the last section, a summary is given of the general methodology of how to evaluate evidence.

The next new tool introduced is a dialectical theory of explanation, an essential component in analyzing abductive reasoning as inference to the best explanation. This view of explanation has been tacitly adopted in many fields of AI for some time now, especially in expert system and planning technology. Only recently it has been formulated as a precise model (Walton, 2004, 2004a). This new dialectical model of explanation presented in chapter 6 analyzes the structure of an explanation as based on an inference or chain of reasoning typically composed of several inferences connected together. Different kinds of inference can be involved, deductive or inductive, but in many cases they are defeasible inferences based on generalizations of the kind studied in chapter 2 that are neither universal nor inductive. The chain of reasoning makes up an account, a connected network of inferences visualized by the diagramming software tool *Araucaria*. As well as being inferential, or reasoning-based, in this sense, the new dialectical model is also pragmatic, in that it portrays the chain of reasoning on which an explanation is based as having a direction and aim. Each agent can possess something, or fail to possess something, called understanding. The aim of an explanation is for one agent to verbally transfer understanding to another, fulfilling the so-called clarifying function of discourse. Thus explanation is seen on the new theory as speech act in a dialogue. The questioner asks a question that indicates he can't make sense of something and the respondent gives an account of it that answers the question, thus helping him to make sense of it by filling in the right gaps in a chain of reasoning.

The problems cited in chapter 5 are in reach of being solved with further work, but in chapter 7 a very interesting and challenging problem is posed that represents work far in the future. This is the problem of constructing a device to aid in the invention of new arguments to prove or argue for a conclusion. Invention has long been a tool wished for in the field of rhetoric, and it would certainly be an extremely useful tool for trial lawyers. It would be a wonderful tool to have, but we are still quite a long way from getting it. Still, the methods applied in the previous chapter do show quite well, in outline, how such a tool could be constructed by building on the other methods. The problem is whether automated systems for argument diagramming applied to legal argumentation, fitting with Wigmore-style diagrams as devices helpful for marshaling evidence, can also be applied to the task of inventing new arguments. It is argued that legal argumentation is a good venue for investigating the question and that the notion of relevance is the key to finding a method of invention useful for legal argumentation.

Even though discussing how to build such a tool remains speculative at present, the idea of having it is so compelling and motivating that it is worth discussion as the final chapter of the book. An automated tool for inventing new arguments is something worth thinking about, even if the project of building it is only a goal that can be reached once the other methods of the previous chapters have been further refined and tested.

Thus an answer to the skeptical customs officer's question of whether there is such a thing as legal logic is provided by this book, or at least a new and promising avenue for getting an answer is opened up. The answer is that legal logic is an informal logic of a kind that models defeasible reasoning, seeing it not as imperfect or fallacious deductive or inductive reasoning, but as a distinctive third type of reasoning. Even though it is fallible, and can be fallacious in some instances, in other instances, it can be used to support a conclusion in such a way that it provides legal evidence for it, even though there may be other legal evidence against it as well. How should such evidence be evaluated? This book does not provide final answers of a kind that, at one shot, makes further investigation into the subject of legal logic unnecessary. Still, by providing tools that can be applied to this problem, and many other central problems of legal reasoning, it offers a new approach that those who wish to study reasoning can take to pursue the objective of developing a working legal logic that deals effectively with legal reasoning.

Acknowledgements

I would like to thank Craig Callen for organizing and chairing the conference 'Visions of Rationality in Evidence Law', held at the Michigan State University College of Law, April 3-6, 2003. Craig was very helpful in giving me advice on looking for material on relevance in evidence law, and it turned out that the conference helped me a great deal to get a better knowledge of current issues and principles of rational argument in evidence law. The book has also benefited a good deal from discussions with other participants in the conference, both during the conference and afterwards by e-mail. I would like to thank Richard Friedman, Erica Beecher-Monas, Mike Redmayne, Greg Mitchell, Michael Risinger, Michael Saks, Roger Park, Ron Allen, Myrna Raeder, Eleanor Swift and Bruce Burns.

I would like to thank John Zelznikow, Director of the Joseph Bell Center for Forensic Statistics and Legal Reasoning in 2003, for inviting me to present an invited address to the Second Joseph Bell Center Workshop on the Evaluation of Evidence on July 1 of that year. I would like to thank John, as well as Gary Davis, Philip Dawid, Jeroen Keppens, Sacha Iskovic, Moshe Koppel, Uri Schild, and Burkhard Shafer for discussions at the workshop that turned out to be particularly helpful. Later discussions with Arno Lodder also helped.

I would like to thank Terry Anderson and William Twining for discussions on argument diagramming and evidence during a visit to the University of Miami in December, 2003. I had the great pleasure of not only discussing these matters with them, but also of sitting in on some of their classes on evidence and seeing Wigmore charts actually being used as tools to teaching law students skills of legal reasoning. These meetings not only fuelled my enthusiasm for the study of argumentation theory as applied to legal reasoning, but supplied me with many points of direction on how it could be potentially useful as a tool for the analysis of evidence in law.

I would like to thank the program committee of the Seventeenth Annual Conference on Legal Knowledge and Information Systems (JURIX 2004) held in Berlin, December 8-10, 2004 for inviting me as keynote speaker. For helpful discussions during and after my talk on argumentation schemes at the meeting I would particularly like to thank Trevor Bench-Capon, Floris Bex, Wolfgang Bibel, Alison Chorley, Tom Gordon, Henry Prakken, Bram Roth, Burkhard Shafer, Bart Verheij, and Radbound Winkels.

The original version of chapter 1 was a keynote speech, 'Methods of Informal Logic and legal Argumentation' given at the conference 'Informal Logic and Legal Argumentation' held in the Institute for Logic and Cognition at Sun Yat-sen university in Guangzhou, China, October 17-19, 2004. I would like to thank Professor Liang Qing-yin for planning the conference, and for comments on my paper I would like to thank Xiong Minghui, Zhang Nan-ning, Tang Ling-yun and Xiong Mai zhi. A Chinese translation of the original paper can be found on the web site of the Institute of Logic and Cognition of Sun Yat-sen University.

The research in this book derives from recent collaborative research on AI and law with Henry Prakken and Chris Reed. However, the arguments put forward here represent my own views, and Henry and Chris may not agree with all of them. Nor should they be held responsible for my failures to solve the problems addressed, or the errors and lapses in my arguments that will undoubtedly be found. I would like to thank the Social Sciences and Humanities Research Council of Canada for two research grants that supported the work on this project, one on argumentation schemes in natural and artificial communication and the other on the dialogue structure of legal argumentation. I would like to thank David Godden for many helpful comments and corrections on an earlier version. For proof-reading I would like to thank Anahid Melikian, for preparation of the text in the Springer format I would like to thank Rita Campbell, and for help with preparation of the diagrams for printing I would like to thank Fabrizio Macagno.

Chapter 1: Informal Logic Methods for Law

In this chapter the basic methods of informal logic are outlined and it is shown how they can be applied to legal argumentation, especially to cases of evidence in a trial. First, the method of argument diagramming is introduced, a method first used in evidence law by the famous evidence theorist John H. Wigmore of Northwestern University.[1] Second, argumentation schemes are introduced. These are common forms of argument in addition to the deductive and inductive forms we are widely familiar with in logic. Matching each scheme is a set of critical questions, and a given argument is evaluated in a dialogue where the scheme, the questions and the answers are all considered together. The third part of the chapter is concerned with the formal structure of dialogues. Six types of dialogue are explained. Finally, some problems concerning the management of commitment in dialogue are examined.

Much work on the dialogue structure of legal argumentation has been accomplished in the new and growing field of computational dialectics (Prakken, 1991; Gordon, 1995; Prakken and Sartor, 1996; Bench-Capon, 1998; Lodder, 1999; Prakken, Reed and Walton, 2003, Verheij, 2005). This work is based on the general approach now most often associated with the term 'argumentation'. It can be contrasted with the traditional approach in logic, where an argument was seen only as a set of propositions with one designated as the conclusion. In the argumentation approach (or, as it is often called, the informal logic approach), an argument is seen not only as a sequence of reasoning containing premises linked to conclusions by logical inferences. It is also seen as being part of a dialogue between (in the simplest case) two parties, called the proponent and the respondent. The methods of argument analysis treated in this chapter presuppose this contextual and social factor of a dialogue setting of an argument. However, to begin with, we will adopt a very simple model of an argument as a set of propositions (premises and a conclusion). Then we will move towards dealing with the complications involved in viewing such an argument as part of an orderly conversational exchange. In this chapter we can only give a brief outline of the basic methods of informal logic and argumentation that will be developed and employed in the work of applying them to legal argumentation and evidence in the following chapters.

---

1 The best source where Wigmore presented his diagramming technique as applied to evidence in law is the second edition of his *Principles* (Wigmore, 1931). A helpful explanation of Wigmore's system of evidence, including the historical and philosophical background of its development is (Twining, 1985).

1. Basics of Argument Diagramming

The technique of argument diagramming is a basic method of informal logic. An argument diagram is made up of two basic components (Freeman, 1991): (1) a set of nodes (points) representing the propositions that are the premises and conclusion in the argument being diagrammed, and (2) a set of arrows joining the points. Each arrow represents an inference. A sequence of points connected by arrows represents a chain of argumentation. In an argument diagram representing a mass of evidence in a legal case, there is always a final conclusion or ultimate *probandum* representing the claim that is to be proved or to have doubt cast on it. This final conclusion is supported by means of a chain of argumentation that usually has an earlier conclusion as one of its premises. For example, in a criminal trial, the ultimate *probandum* for the prosecution is the proposition that the defendant is guilty of the crime he or she was charged with committing. The evidence put forward by the prosecution to try to prove this proposition can be viewed as a chain of argumentation containing premises and conclusions.

A set of premises can go together to support a conclusion in two ways that need to be distinguished. One way is that the argument can have a linked structure. In a linked argument, each premise is dependent on the other(s) to support the conclusion (Freeman, 1991). In a linked argument, if one premise is deleted, the other offers much less evidential support for the conclusion than the two do together. The other way has a structure called a convergent argument. In a convergent argument, each premise provides independent evidential support for the conclusion. Even if one premise is deleted, the other still offers the same evidential support for the conclusion it did before.[2] For example, consider the following pair of contrasting arguments.

Linked Argument

The medical examiner said that the blood found at the crime scene matches the blood sample taken from the suspect.

The medical examiner is an expert.

Therefore, there is evidence that the blood found at the crime scene matches the blood sample taken from the suspect.

This linked argument is diagrammed using *Araucaria* as follows:

[2] This is just one test of the four that have been proposed in the literature (Walton, 1996, 196).

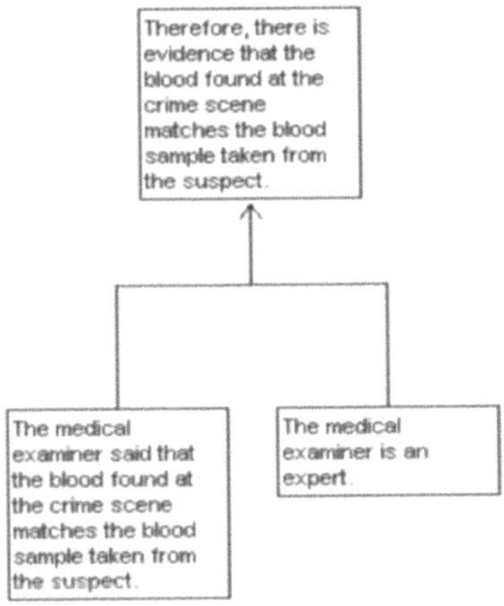

Fig. 1.1. Linked Argument

As the diagram indicates, the two premises in the two bottom boxes are linked together to support the conclusion that appears in the top box. In Araucaria, the conclusion always appears at the top and the premises beneath it, although the diagram can be flipped around so that the conclusion appears at the bottom of the page.

Convergent Argument

Blood found at the crime scene matches the blood sample taken from the suspect.

A witness testified she saw the accused leaving the crime scene.

Therefore, there is evidence that the accused was present at the crime scene.

This convergent argument is diagrammed as indicated below.

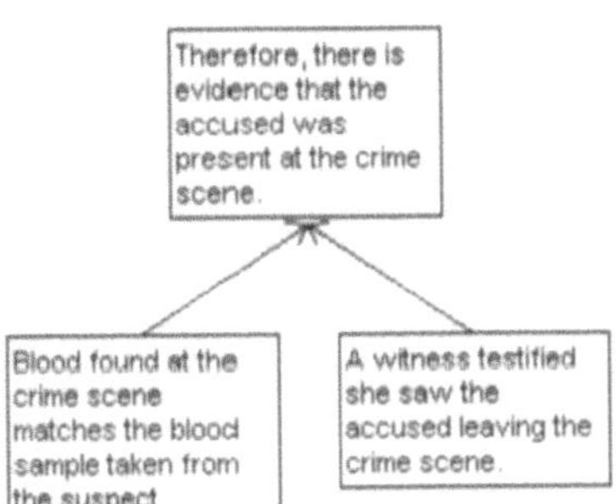

Fig. 1.2. Convergent Argument

In a convergent argument, each premise can be seen as a separate reason to accept the conclusion, based on evidence. In some cases it may be very hard to determine, from the given text of discourse in a case, whether the argument in question is linked or convergent. In such a case, the best policy is to diagram the argument as convergent. However, in many cases, like the one above, it is clear whether the argument is most reasonably taken to be linked or convergent.

Arguments that fit some known pattern or structure warranting the inference are generally linked.[3] For example, consider a typical case of a syllogistic argument that is deductively valid.

All philosophers are wise.

Confucius is a philosopher.

Therefore Confucius is wise.

This argument is clearly linked. To see why, apply the test given above. If the first premise is deleted, the second premise all by itself offers much less evidential support for the conclusion. If the second premise is deleted, the first premise all by itself offers much less evidential support for the conclusion. Thus it should be diagrammed as shown below.

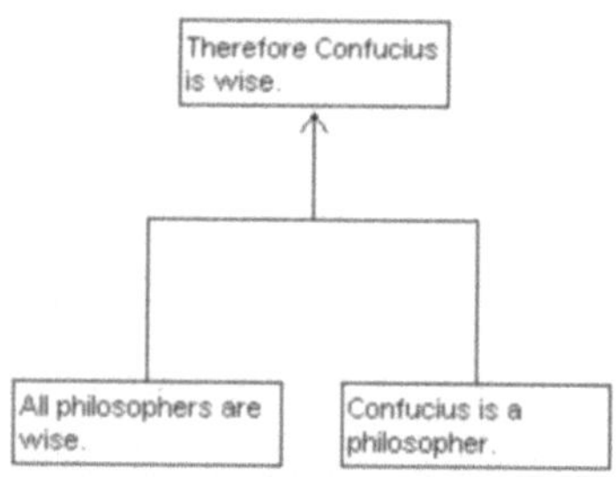

Fig. 1.3. Deductive Lined Argument

In cases of this sort, it is clear that the argument should be classified as linked. In other cases, like the example above, it is clear that the argument should be classified as convergent. In borderline cases, there is additional textual evidence that should be taken into account, like indicator words. For example, if the text of the argument says, "These are my two reasons for believing this", that may be evidence that argument is convergent (Snoeck Henkemans, 1992). Of course, diagramming any argument in a natural language text of discourse depends on how the discourse is interpreted. Context can be very important in some cases. First an analysis of the argument has to be worked out. As part of the analysis the premises

[3] Linked premises are often joined to a conclusion by a known argumentation scheme, as will be shown in the example below.

and conclusion of the argument have to be identified as propositions (statements). The diagram is based on such an analysis.

Another factor to mention is that many legal arguments are based on unstated premises, or even unstated conclusions, that need to be made explicit in order to show how the conclusion was arrived at from the given evidence. Arguments with such unstated premises or conclusions are called enthymemes in traditional logic. An example of how to diagram such an argument is presented in the next section.

2. Araucaria

Araucaria is an automated system of argument diagramming based on an Argumentation Markup Language (Reed and Rowe, 2003). It is available as freeware on the internet.[4] *Araucaria* aids a user to diagram an argument using a simple point-and-click interface. The user inserts the text of discourse containing an argument as a text file into *Araucaria*, and he/she can then use the software to draw in lines representing each of the inferences from the premises to the conclusions in the argumentation. To begin, the argument needs to be pasted into a text document, which is then loaded into *Araucaria*, where it will appear in the box on the left. As the user highlights each statement (premise or conclusion) in the argument, and then moves the cursor to click once in the box on the right, a letter will appear representing that statement. Once all the statements in the argument have been represented by letters, the user then needs to draw in an arrow from each premise, or set of premises, to its conclusion. The argument diagram then appears in the right box. *Araucaria* does not analyze the argumentation. The user has to do that. But *Araucaria* is very helpful in representing the structure of the argumentation in a visual way that displays its premises, conclusions, missing assumptions, and the argument warrants on which the inferences are based. Once an argument has been diagrammed it can be saved in a portable format called *AML, Argument Markup Language*, based on *XML*.

To illustrate to the reader how an argument diagram can be used to represent the structure of reasoning in evidence used in a trial, the following simplified case is presented. This case is a typical sort of murder trial in which there was a victim found dead, and certain items of evidence featured prominently in the trial. Suppose that the victim was stabbed to death and some bits of hair and flesh were found under her fingernails. DNA testing showed that the flesh was that of the accused. The medical examiner, an expert witness, testified in court, at the trial of the accused for murder, that the DNA test showed that the flesh was that of the accused. An eyewitness also testified that she had seen a person leaving the house where the crime was committed, just after the crime had taken place. She identified that person as the accused. These two items of evidence were prominent in the argumentation in the jury trial. One of the tasks of the jury is the so-called

4 The *Araucaria* software can be downloaded at no cost from the following location on the internet: www.computing.dundee.ac.uk/staff/creed/araucaria.

finding of fact. Did the accused in fact kill the victim or not? The two witnesses are examined before the jury in the trial.

To model the structure of reasoning in the evidence presented in this case in the trial, the following propositions are identified and numbered. The final proposition, (F), is the ultimate conclusion, based on the reasoning that leads up to it.

A) Flesh was found under the victim's fingernails at the crime scene.
B) The medical examiner says that the flesh under the victim's fingernails matches that of the accused.
C) Therefore, there is evidence that the flesh found under the victim's fingernails matches that of the accused.
D) A witness says she saw the accused leaving the house just after the crime was committed.
E) Therefore, there is evidence that the accused left the house just after the time the crime was committed.
F) Therefore, the accused committed the crime.

To use *Araucaria* the argument above is inserted into a text document and then cut and pasted into the left box shown in the screen shot below.

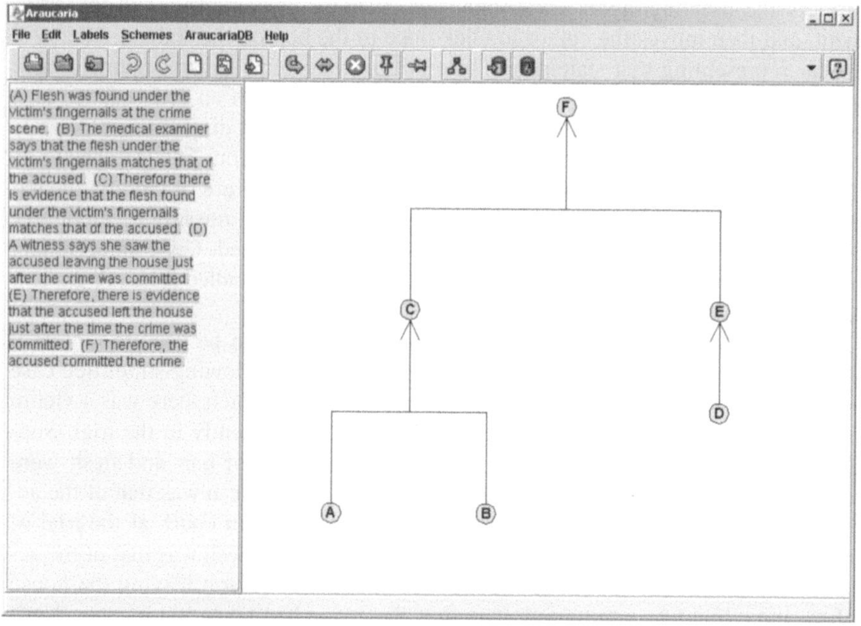

Fig. 1.4. Araucaria Diagram for the Flesh Case

Each statement on the left is highlighted and when the mouse is clicked, the circled letter standing for the proposition appears in the box on the right. Then the user must draw in the arrows representing arguments from premises to conclusions. To make the diagram even easier to read, a full text version (shown below) can be produced.

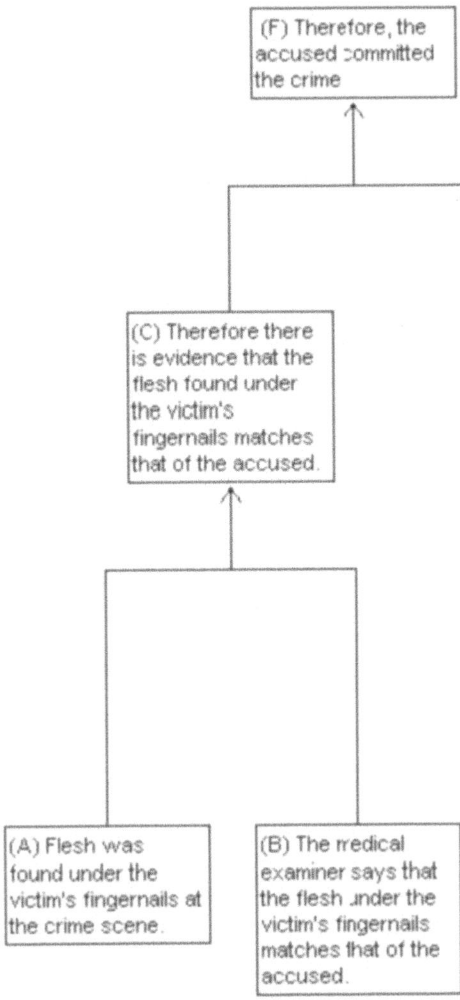

Fig. 1.5. Full Text Diagram for the Flesh Case

In some cases the inference link connecting a set of premises to a conclusion is of a known type. For example, *modus ponens* is a familiar form of deductively valid argument. Such a form of argument, or argumentation scheme as it is called, can also be shown on the diagram, as shown in section 4 below. *Araucaria* contains a set of argumentation schemes, or common forms of argument (Kienpointner, 1992). Some schemes that are neither deductive nor inductive are especially common in legal evidence, including appeal to witness testimony. Many such schemes are described in (Walton, 2004). Some of them will be illustrated in the example in section 4 below.

3. Legal Origins of Argument Diagramming

Argument diagrams have been used to represent legal evidence in a trial. In order to model the evidence in the famous Sacco and Vanzetti case, Schum (1994, p. 77) set up what he called a line of reasoning that linked up the testimony of a witness to the ultimate conclusion of the case. In this case, two Italian Americans, Sacco and Vanzetti, were arrested for the murder of a police officer during a payroll robbery. An important part of the evidence was that Sacco had reached under his coat when arrested, and was found to have a concealed pistol in the coat. Schum used diagrams to represent this piece of evidence in the trial. John H. Wigmore, the famous evidence theorist, had previously used evidence charts to represent evidence on both sides of a case. Wigmore only offered two charts fully representing the mass of evidence in a trial. A small part of one of these, from the Umilian case (Wigmore, 1931) is displayed below.

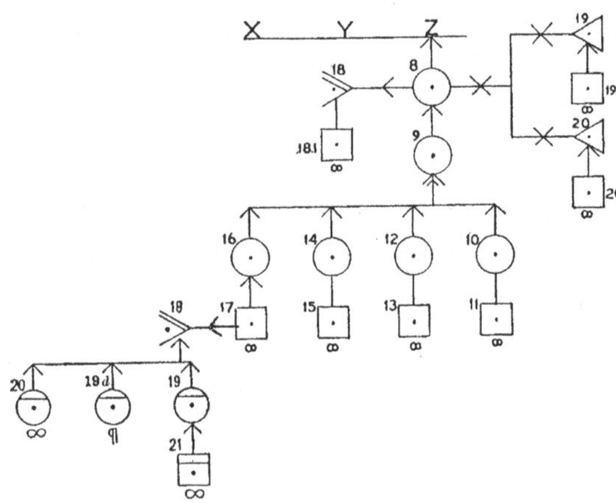

Fig. 1.6. Wigmore Chart for the Umilian Case (Prakken, Reed and Walton, 2003, p. 33)

Each arrow represents an inference. The circles and squares represent testimonial or circumstantial evidential facts. A dot in one of them means, "we now believe it to be a fact" (Wigmore, 1931, 52). The infinity symbol means that the evidence was observed by the tribunal. It is not necessary or useful to go into all the details of Wigmore's elaborate notation for evidence charts here. Twining (1985) and Anderson and Twining (1991) have presented detailed analyses of how evidence charting can be applied to masses of evidence in trials. It is enough here to grasp the general idea of how a Wigmore evidence chart resembles an argument diagram in its main structure. Each square or circle represents some presumed fact that is evidence in a trial, or a conclusion drawn from such a presumed fact. Thus a chart can be used to display the logical reasoning in a typical mass of evidence in a case.

In the diagram below, Wigmore showed the structure of an evidence chart by using P to represent the proposition to be proved (*factum probandum*). T represents a "testimonial assertion", and C represents a "circumstance".

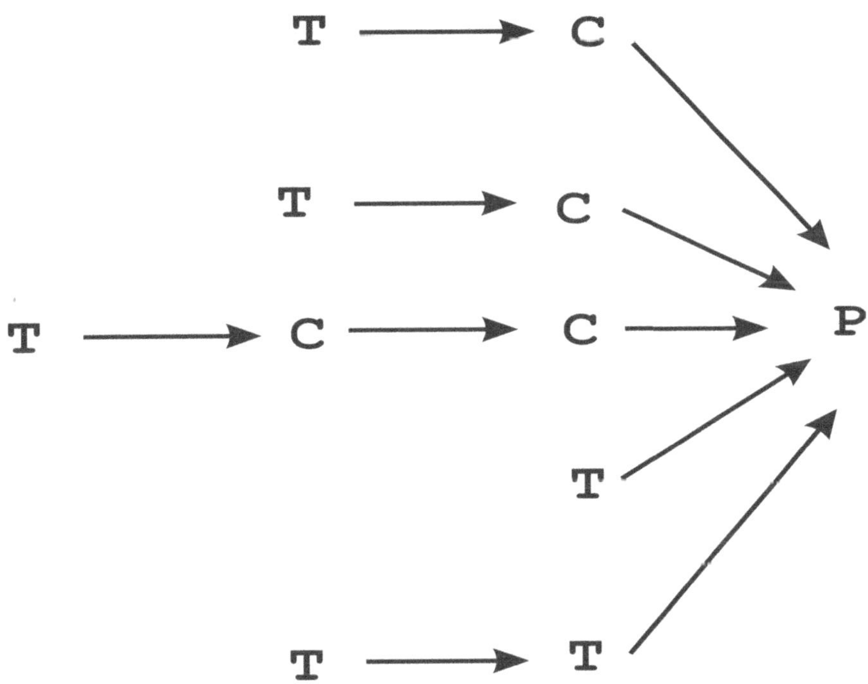

Fig. 1.7. Wigmore's Diagram Representing A Typical Mass of Evidence (Wigmore, 1983, p. 956)

A Wigmore chart representing all the evidence on one side in a trial tends to be quite large and complex. The sketch above gives an overview of the general structure of such a chart as an argument diagram.

One such evidence chart represents the evidence on the prosecution side in a trial while another represents the evidence on the defense side. The essential structure of a Wigmore evidence chart is that of an argument diagram of the kind used in informal logic. Thus Wigmore was an important precursor of the modern informal logic movement. It is highly significant that evidence law, not informal logic, was a main origin of the use and development of the argument diagramming technique.[5]

4. Argumentation Schemes

As noted in section 2 above, the form of an argument can be shown on the diagram. Certain common forms of argument have been formalized as argumentation schemes (Hastings, 1963; van Eemeren and Grootendorst, 1992; Kienpointner, 1992; Walton, 1996). Especially interesting are the defeasible schemes, where the premises do not imply the conclusion either by deductive or inductive inference.

A Current Listing of Typical Defeasible Argumentation Schemes

1. Argument from Popular Opinion: arguing that a statement is generally accepted, and that therefore it can be accepted tentatively as plausible.
2. Argument from Example: arguing that something is true based on an example.
3. Argument from Verbal Classification: arguing that something has a certain property because it can be classified verbally in a certain way.
4. Argument from Sign: arguing that something is present based on a sign or indicator.
5. Abductive Argument: arguing from the existence of a data set in a given case to the best explanation of the data set.
6. Practical Reasoning: arguing from a goal to an action required to realize the goal.
7. Argument from Positive or Negative Consequences: arguing that a course of action is recommended (or not) because it has good (bad) consequences.
8. Argument from Sunk Costs: arguing for continuing a course of action on the grounds that considerable costs have already been sunk into it, which would otherwise be lost.
9. Argument from Ignorance: arguing that a statement is true on the grounds that it is not known to be false.

---

[5] Was Wigmore the inventor of the method of argument diagramming? Richard Whately, the English logician and Archbishop of Dublin, in Appendix III of his textbook *Elements of Logic* (1836, pp. 420-430), entitled 'Praxis of Logical Analysis', described a method of argument analysis (pp. 421-423) by which you can arrive at premises that represent the grounding of an argument. In a footnote on the same page, Whately drew up a diagram to represent such an argument analysis, suggesting students will find it a convenient mode of "exhibiting the logical analysis of a course of argument, to draw it out in the form of a Tree". In the footnote Whatley presented a schematic example that looks very much like a modern argument diagram.

10. Argument from Cause to Effect: arguing that an event will come about because its cause is present in the data.
11. Argument from Correlation to Cause: arguing that one event causes another on the grounds that there is a positive correlation between the two.
12. Argument from Evidence to a Hypothesis: arguing from evidence found and verified empirically to a tentative hypothesis that accounts for it, normally by a theory.
13. Argument from Threat: arguing that a course of action should be carried because if not, the proponent will see to it that bad consequences happen to the respondent.
14. Argument from Fear Appeal: arguing that you shouldn't do something because consequences that are fearful to you will occur.
15. Argument from Commitment: arguing from a respondent's prior commitment to some statement or course of action.
16. Argument from Inconsistent Commitment: arguing that an opponent has committed himself to both a statement and its opposite (negation).
17. Ethotic Ad Hominem Argument: arguing against another party's argument by claiming he is a bad person (has some negative quality of character or ethos).
18. Circumstantial Ad Hominem: attacking another party's argument by claiming his argument is inconsistent with his own practices or commitments, and that this shows bad quality of character (like being a hypocrite).
19. The Situationally Disqualifying Ad Hominem Argument: arguing that an opponent has no right to speak on an issue because he is not in a situation to credibly do so.
20. Argument from Bias: arguing that one should not pay too much serious attention to a person's argument, or should discount it, because he is biased.
21. Argument from Analogy: arguing that something holds in a particular case because it holds in a similar case.
22. Argument from an Established Rule: arguing that the respondent should take a certain action on the basis that it conforms to an accepted rule.
23. Argument from Exception to a Rule: Arguing that a particular case is an exception to the rule, and therefore does not fall under the rule.
24. Argument from Precedent: a form of argument from analogy in which the arguer cites a prior accepted case as providing a guideline for acceptance in a given case at dispute.
25. Argument from Gradualism: gradually proceeding by small steps from premises an arguer accepts through a chain of argumentation to something he doesn't accept.
26. Slippery Slope Argument: a negative species of argument from gradualism in which the arguer claims that if one step is taken, it will lead by a chain of argumentation past a point of no return (that cannot be sharply defined) to a disastrous ultimate outcome.

Properties of defeasible argumentation schemes are elucidated in this study through an important example of a type of argumentation related to fallacies. Take, for example, the appeal to expert opinion, like we have in the murder trial discussed just above. This form of argument is often reasonable, but has been traditionally studied in logic under the heading of the *argumentum ad verecundiam* fallacy.

The scheme representing argument from expert opinion as a form of argument was formulated in (Walton, 1997, p. 210) as follows.

Scheme for Argument from Expert Opinion

Major Premise: Source *E* is an expert in subject domain *S* containing proposition *A*.

Minor Premise: *E* asserts that proposition *A* (in domain *S*) is true (false).

Conclusion: *A* may plausibly be taken to be true (false).

The six basic critical questions matching the appeal to expert opinion, as indicated in (Walton, 1997, p. 223), are listed below.

Critical Questions for Argument from Expert Opinion

CQ1: *Expertise Question*: How credible is *E* as an expert source?

CQ2: *Field Question*: Is *E* an expert in the field that *A* is in?

CQ3: *Opinion Question*: What did *E* assert that implies *A*?

CQ4: *Trustworthiness Question*: Is *E* personally reliable as a source?

CQ5: *Consistency Question*: Is *A* consistent with what other experts assert?

CQ6: *Backup Evidence Question*: Is *E*'s assertion based on evidence?

The expertise question is based on the assumption that the expert has knowledge in a field or practical mastery of a skill. The field question relates to the distinction between scientific fields of expertise and cases where the expert has skills that do not fall into the category of scientific knowledge. The trustworthiness question relates to the honesty and objectivity of the expert as a source of advice.

Based on my analysis of its central structure (Walton, 2002), argument from witness opinion can be said to have the following basic form of argument. The variable *W* stands for an agent that is a witness. A witness is an agent that has incoming information about things it can perceive as facts or data, and that can relay that information to another agent. The variable *A* stands for a statement (proposition).

Scheme for Argument from Witness Testimony

Position to Know Premise: Witness *W* is in a position to know whether *A* is true or not.

Truth Telling Premise: Witness *W* is telling the truth (as *W* knows it).

Statement Premise: Witness *W* states that *A* is true (false).

Conclusion: Therefore (defeasibly) *A* is true (false).

The above scheme is not deductively valid. It is a defeasible inference that can be used to transfer a probative weight from the premises to the conclusion but can default.

What kinds of critical questions should be appropriate for evaluating the form of argument called appeal to witness testimony? Of course, one of the premises of the appeal to witness testimony cited above is the assumption that the witness is telling the truth. Witnesses are examined in courts, and make statements under an oath to tell the truth. As indicated by the truth telling premise, there would be a general presumption that the witness is telling the truth. When evaluating an argument from witness testimony, the evaluator has no direct access to the evidence that the witness presumably possesses. Hence the evaluator may need to test the consistency of the account given by the witness, to see if it is consistent with other evidence that is known about the case independently of the testimony. Thus the critical questions are the following.

Critical Questions for Argument from Witness Testimony

CQ1: Is what the witness said internally consistent?

CQ2: Is what the witness said consistent with the known facts of the case (based on evidence apart from what the witness testified to)?

CQ3: Is what the witness said consistent with what other witnesses have (independently) testified to?

The next two critical questions have to do to with the possible bias of the witness.

CQ4: Is there some kind of bias that can be attributed to the account given by the witness?

CQ5: How plausible is the statement *A* asserted by the witness?

If the statement made by the witness is highly implausible, for example, that can detract from the credibility of the witness. But if two independent witnesses made the identical implausible claim, it could suggest that their observations might be careful and accurate.

One can see that the defeasible argumentation schemes described above cannot be evaluated, as used in specific cases, by the methods of deductive and inductive reasoning that are traditionally used in logic. Such cases of defeasible arguments need to be evaluated on a balance of considerations in a case. When you examine a case of an argument used in a given text of discourse, like a statute in law, for example, you need to try first of all to reconstruct the argument and identify its premises and conclusions. This task is by no means always trivial. Parts of the argument may be implicit. Thus even before an argument can be evaluated, considerable analysis of the text may be needed, in order to determine what the premises and conclusion are.

5. Enthymemes

A kind of argument called an enthymeme is an argument containing a premise or conclusion that was not explicitly stated but that is required to make sense of the argument. For example, if I were to argue, 'All philosophers are wise, therefore Confucius is wise', the implicit premise of my argument is the proposition, 'Confucius is a philosopher'. Arguments with such unstated premises or conclusions are called enthymemes in traditional logic, even though the term may be a misnomer[6]. In some cases, it can be very difficult to fairly judge what the implicit assumption of a given argument is supposed to be (Walton and Reed, 2003). Even so, many everyday arguments, as well as legal arguments, can only be analyzed and evaluated accurately and fairly if unstated assumptions in them are identified as premises or conclusions that the argument depends on. For example, there are some unstated premises in the argument diagrammed below that need to be made explicit.

(G) The witness was in a position to know.
(H) The witness is telling the truth.

Araucaria has a device for inserting implicit premises in enthymemes. With these additional premises inserted, the argument diagram is represented below.

---

[6] The term 'enthymeme' originally may have meant something quite different. Burnyeat (1994), noted that Aristotle (*Prior Analytics*, 70a10) claims that an enthymeme is an incomplete (*ateles*) *sullogismos* from plausibilities or signs, but doubted that Aristotle wrote the word *ateles* in the original manuscript. Burnyeat, following several earlier commentators, hypothesized that what Aristotle really meant by 'enthymeme' is a plausibilistic argument of the kind he treated in the *Topics* and *Rhetoric*. This type of argument is based on a warrant that is defeasible, and thus corresponds to what is now called a presumptive argumentation scheme. Thus there is a case to be made that the term 'enthymeme', in the original Aristotelian meaning, refers to presumptive argumentation schemes, not to incomplete arguments.

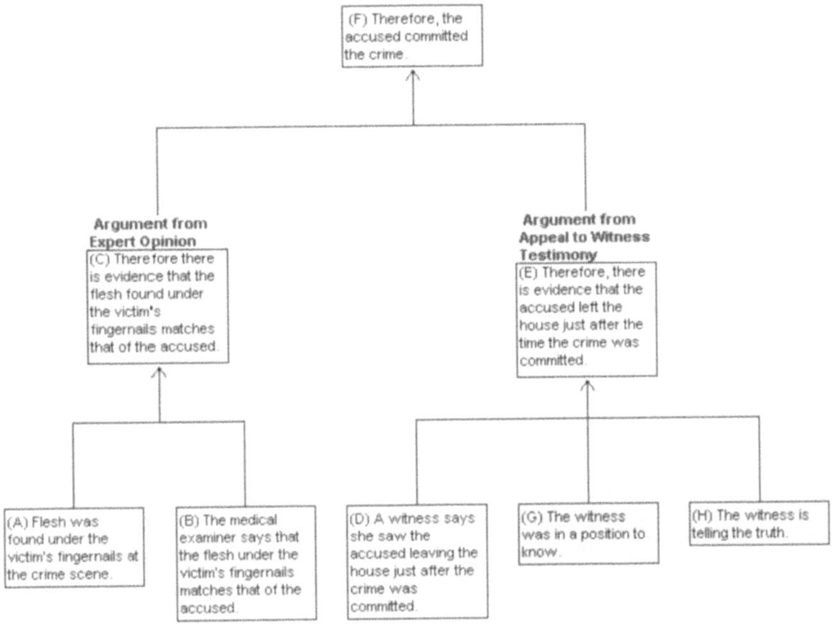

Fig. 1.8. Flesh Case with Schemes

In this diagram, not only are the missing premises made explicit, but the argumentation schemes that warrant the inferences are also displayed. This shows how argumentation schemes can be helpful in finding missing premises in an argument.

The two missing premises added to this argument were drawn from the scheme that gives the basic form of the argument. The argument from expert opinion in the diagram (on the left) also requires the addition of the major premise shown in the scheme for the argument from expert opinion above. To make the diagram even more complete we could have added this additional premise. What these observations show is that schemes can be useful in helping an analyst to identify missing premises in an argument.

There are some other implicit premises that could be added to the argument as well. These premises are generalizations of the conditional form.

(I) If the accused left the house just after the time the crime was committed then it is a hypothesis that the accused was in the house when the crime was committed.

(J) If the accused was in the house when the crime was committed then it is a hypothesis that the accused committed the crime.

To keep things simple, we will not add these premises to the diagram. But if we did, the argumentation scheme for *modus ponens* could also be displayed. In general, to find missing assumptions and use them to build argument diagrams two essential components are needed – argumentation schemes and generalizations. The latter can take various forms (Anderson, 1999). Some are empirical generalizations, while others are common sense generalizations representing common ways of doing things (Twining, 1999).

To identify, analyze and evaluate an argument, the first step is to identify the explicit premises and conclusions. The next step is to draw an argument diagram representing the structure of the argument. The next step is to fill in the argumentation schemes and missing premises. Once this has been done, the critical questions matching each scheme can be used to identify the weak points that may be in the argument and need further proof.

This consideration brings us to burden of proof. Each critical question has to be dealt with individually. Some critical questions demand a reply immediately. The arguer must provide further evidence that meets the requirement of burden of proof, or the argument defaults. In the cases of other critical questions, merely asking the question is not enough to defeat the argument. In some cases, disputes about burden of proof or disproof cannot be resolved in any automatic way. In these cases, it is necessary to move to a meta-dialogue level in which some third party (a judge or referee) must make a ruling on which side has the burden of proof. This brings us to pragmatic matters of context of argument use.

6. Burden of Proof

As Leenes (2001, 109) noted, construction of dialogue games to model legal argumentation has received considerable interest in recent years in AI and law research. Especially important for legal evidence concerns is the allocation of burden of proof. In Lodder's *Dialaw* system (1999), four types of dialogue moves are considered. Making a claim, or making an assertion, as it might also be called as a speech act, is putting forward a statement held to be true or at least acceptable. When you make an assertion in a dialogue, it goes into your commitment set. Thus you are obliged to defend it, if the other party in the dialogue questions your claim. Thus a second speech act is that of acceptance, whereby a party takes on a commitment. A third speech act is that of retraction of a commitment by withdrawing an assertion. A fourth speech act is that of asking a question. But here burden of proof is a little more problematic to deal with in a straightforward rule. If you make an assertion and I question it, does that mean you have to withdraw your claim, or can you ask me for evidence to back up my question? This issue about burden of proof will be a central problem for our paper.

In the general theory of argumentation in dialogue, burden of proof is important at the global level of a dialogue as well as at the local level. At the global level, burden of proof pertains to a participant's goal, sometimes called obligation, in a dialogue. But it does not necessarily apply to all kinds of dialogue in which there is argumentation. For example, in a negotiation, there seems to nothing corresponding to burden of proof, with emphasis on the term 'proof', as such, whereas in other types of dialogue, a participant's goal is to prove (or disprove) something. In legal argumentation, especially of the kind found in a trial, there definitely is a burden of proof that is central, as has long been acknowledged by commentaries on evidence that stress the notions of presumption and burden and proof. But there seems to be a large gap between abstract models of dialogue in the literature on argumentation, in which there are only two parties in a dialogue (a proponent and a respondent), and a trial, in which there may be two sides, but many parties are involved (a judge applies rules of procedure and a trier determines the outcome).

To consider how global burden of proof works in argumentation theory generally, the best kind of dialogue to begin with is the persuasion type. In the persuasion dialogue, there are two participants, called the proponent and the respondent. There are two subcases to be considered. In the dispute, the proponent has proposition A as her designated thesis. Her goal is to prove A, while the respondent's goal is to prove the opposite (negation) of A. Thus each has a burden of proof. In the dissent, the proponent's goal is to prove A, while the goal of the respondent is merely to show that the proponent's attempt is not successful. In the dissent, the respondent's goal is merely one of critical questioning rather proving. However, successful critical questioning can count as a kind of disproving in some instances. Thus in a dissent, the proponent has a burden of proof, but it can be said that the respondent does not, unless you count disproving by critical questioning as a way of discharging a burden of proof. In a dispute, it is clearer that each party has a burden of proof (or disproof). At any rate, each side will have what is called in law an ultimate *probandum*. It is this that will centrally determine burden of proof.

Another factor in global burden of proof is how strong an argument has to be in order for the arguer's burden of proof to be fulfilled. This depends on the nature of the pleading (Gordon, 1995). For example, in a criminal trial, the proponent has to prove beyond a reasonable doubt. This is meant to be a very high requirement of burden of proof. You have to have a very strong argument to fulfill it. In a civil trial, whichever side has the strongest case wins. This is a lower burden. You only need to have an argument stronger than that of the other side in order to win. Farley and Freeman (1995, p. 160) have defined five levels of support: scintilla of evidence, preponderance of the evidence, dialectical validity, beyond a reasonable doubt, and beyond a doubt.

At the local level, burden of proof arises with respect to any kind of move (speech act) that takes place during some point in sequence of dialogue moves. For example, Lodder 1999) uses the following rule for distributing burden of proof at any local level in a dialogue: "whoever advances a standpoint is obliged to defend it if asked to do so". This rule means that if one party in a dialogue makes a move in the form of an assertion of a proposition, then she takes on a burden of a proof with respect to that proposition. If questioned by the other party in the dialogue, she must either prove that proposition (or at least give some evidence supporting it) or give it up, i.e. retract it as a commitment. Here we have burden of proof for the speech act of making an assertion. But is there also a burden of proof attached to asking a question. Or is merely asking a critical question about the other party's assertion enough to invoke a burden of proof requirement that makes that other party have to retract her assertion? These are issues about burden of proof at the local level in a dialogue.

The investigation of burden of proof can only proceed by connecting the local level with the global level. For these issues at the local level that arise about who has to prove what when different kinds of moves are made surely depend on who is supposed to prove what at the global level. If one party has the burden of proof at the global level while the other does not, as is the case in a common law criminal trial for example, surely that will influence what happens with issues of burden of proof that arise at the local level.

Burden of proof can be simple if there is a global rule that applies to the specific argument in question. Sometimes in legal argumentation global rulings clearly indicate which side has the burden of proof. For example, in a contract case, the burden is on the side that claims there is a contract to prove offer and acceptance. Suppose the plaintiff argues that she offered to sell defendant her car and that he accepted. She has to prove offer and acceptance. But suppose that defendant claims he was insane, a claim that would nullify the contract. In any legal system, the burden of proving insanity is on the defendant (Prakken, 1991, p. 89). In such a case, the shift is quite definitely indicated by the global requirements of burden of proof. But what happens at local levels, when the argumentation goes further into details. Suppose, for example (Prakken, 1991) that defendant tries to prove he was insane by citing a court document, but plaintiff questions whether the document is authentic. In Dutch law, the document would be presumed to be valid if it looks authentic, but if the defendant argued that the official court stamp on the document did not look genuine, that would shift the burden to the other side. In legal cases, evidence is often based on defeasible arguments like argument from expert opinion or argument from witness testimony. Often we are dealing with a whole network of argumentation chained together with an ultimate *probandum* (the proponent's thesis) at one end (Prakken, 2001). The problem is that we often deal with some small argument locally in the middle of the chain somewhere, and we may not even know where it will lead, and how it might lead to the ultimate *probandum* or not.

In argumentation in dialogue, global burden of proof has to do with the conditions of winning and losing the dialogue. In a symmetrical dialogue of the type called a dispute, each party has a thesis. To win, a party has to construct an argument with her thesis as conclusion, and it has to be strong enough to prove that conclusion by whatever standard of proof is appropriate, or has been agreed to. One such high standard is "beyond reasonable doubt", while a weaker one is "preponderance of evidence". In an ideal case, these standards are set at the confrontation stage of a dialogue. In an asymmetrical dialogue of the type called a dissent, the one party has such a positive burden while the other, to win, must only find weakness enough in the first party's argument to prevent him from fulfilling his burden of proof. In the dissent each party has a different role from other other. One has to prove what she claims while the other is merely a questioner.

In light of these global conditions, let's reconsider what happens with the critical questions in a given case where an argument from ignorance has been put forward.

CQ1: How far along has the search for evidence progressed?

CQ2: Which side has the burden of proof in the dialogue as a whole? In other words, what is the ultimate *probandum* and who is supposed to prove it?

CQ3: How strong does the proof need to be in order for this party to be successful in fulfilling the burden?

CQ1 represents the depth-of-search factor. If the investigation (dialogue) has been completed and epistemic closure is met, the argument from ignorance is deductively valid or invalid. If the search for evidence is at an earlier stage, the argument from ignorance is stronger the more the search has progressed, or weaker to the extent that the search is less far along. CQ2 raises the question of whether the dialogue is a dispute or a dissent. The question of strength of proof in evaluating an argument from ignorance is CQ3.

This general solution does not apply to the kinds of cases cited by Prakken (1991) where the burden has shifted at a local level. For example, consider once again where the plaintiff has to prove offer and acceptance but the defendant argues he was insane when he signed the contract. The burden now shifts to his side to prove insanity. This problem is a more difficult one. Insanity of one party is a defeater of a claim of contract, but if invoked, the side claiming insanity has to prove it to nullify the contract. Solving this problem takes us to a consideration of speech acts, like making an assertion, at a local level.

When each party puts forward a speech act in a dialogue, the rules may require how that party must respond to the next move made by the other party. The speech act of assertion is the simplest case in point. If I assert a proposition, like 'Snow is white', then I am obliged to prove it (or give an argument supporting that proposition) if the other party challenges it. This is burden of proof at the local level. If I assert a proposition, and you question it, then is I fail to respond to the questioning, I have to give that proposition up as a commitment of mine. But why is this so? What is the rationale of such a rule in a dialogue? It can vary with the type of dialogue, but let's take persuasion dialogue. As above, to win such a dialogue the proponent of a thesis has to find a valid argument with that thesis as conclusion. The argument must have only premises that the respondent is committed to. So if I assert a proposition to you, what I am trying to do is to get you to accept it (as a commitment). For example, if I say to you, 'Snow is white', I am trying to get you to accept this proposition, presumably because I can use it as a premise in my chain of argumentation that will have my thesis as the ultimate conclusion.

We need to have rules telling us what happens to your commitment store, depending on how you respond. If you reply 'yes', there is no problem. The proposition 'Snow is white' goes into your commitment store. But what happens if you don't reply at all, and move on to some other issue. Does that mean you are committed to 'Snow is white' or not? Here there are various options and we need some rule. Does silence imply assent or not? Another problem is what happens if you question the proposition 'Snow is white'. The normal way of doing this is for you to say, 'I don't accept that snow is white. Prove it!' The rule for local burden of proof needs to specify what happens in such an instance. The normal rule is that the respondent doesn't have to accept any statement as a commitment without proof. Thus clearly the rule needs to say that 'Snow is white' is not inserted into the respondent's commitment store in such an instance. The proponent has to make some more moves to try to get the respondent to accept it. But what happens with regard to the proponent's commitment set? Does she need to retract 'Snow is white' from her commitment set once the respondent has challenged it in this way? The answer is that it doesn't really matter all that much in a persuasion dialogue. The proponent's goal, set by her global burden of proof, is to use rational argumentation to get the respondent to become committed to he thesis. What she accepts doesn't really matter for this purpose. It only matters when it is the respondent's turn to argue.

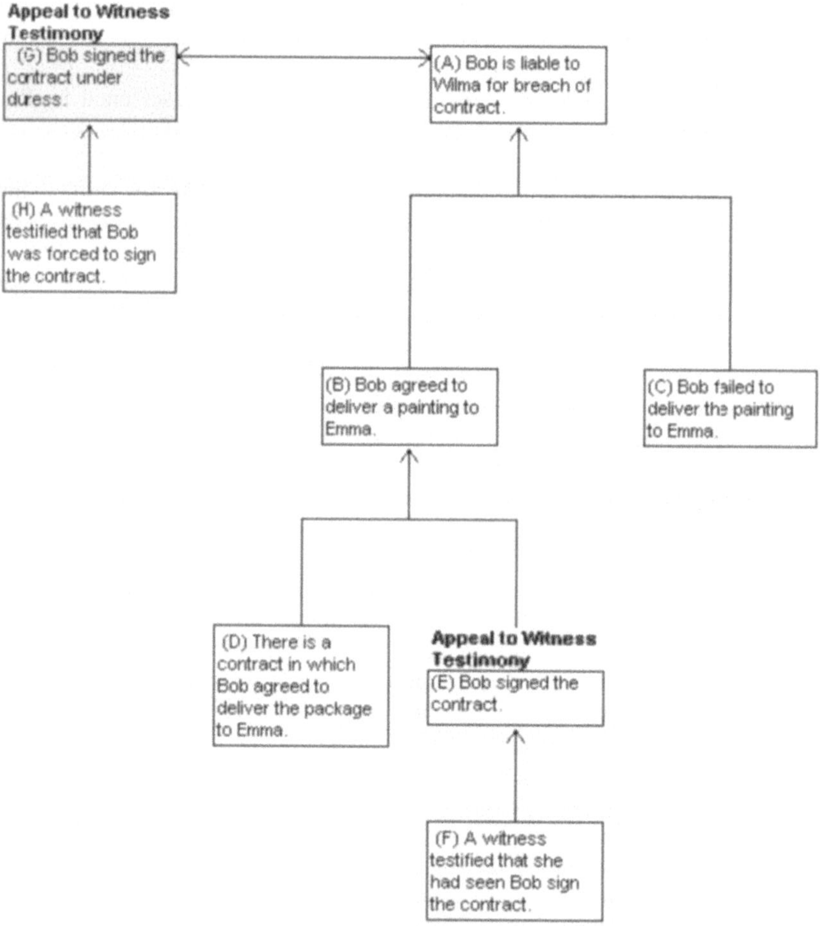

burden is on the claimant once the defense of insanity is brought forward. The relationship of the local to the global burden of proof is displayed in the following

Araucaria diagram. This kind of diagrammatic representation can often be useful in analyzing the structure of a sequence of legal argumentation in a case (Branting, 2000).

The statement F is presented in a shaded box in the diagram, indication it is a refutation of C. The premises G and H are parts of a linked argument supporting F. Which part has the burden of persuasion for each proposition is indicated by "ownership" (Reed and Rowe, 2002) on the diagram.

The problem posed by more difficult cases, ones that we do not attempt to treat here, is that is no simple way of allocating burden of proof. In some cases, the critic has to back up a critical question with further evidence in order for it to make the original argument default. In other cases, merely asking the critical question calls for a reply, and if the arguer does not give it, her argument is immediately defeated. This can lead to an infinite regress, as in the following sort of dialogue.

The Infinite Regress Dialogue

White: You prove it!
Black: You disprove it!

This kind of stalemate can block further progress of a dialogue. Such cases are real. In parliamentary debates, the two sides can dispute about which should conduct an inquiry to find the facts of a disputed issue. In court, the judge often has to rule on disputes between the two sides on which one has the burden of proof. But the problem for AI and law is to build a formal model of dialogue that can provide a rational framework in which argumentation of the kind represented in the infinite regress dialogue can be analyzed and evaluated. Before such a problem can be tackled, the notion of a dialogue has to be formally defined and its key properties must be specified.

7. Types of Dialogue

A dialogue, in the paradigm or basic model, has two participants, often called the proponent and the respondent, who take turns making moves. These moves take the form of speech acts (Jacobs, 1989; Singh, 2000). For example, asking a question, asserting a statement, or putting forward an argument are typical moves in the most common dialogues. A dialogue can be defined formally as a set of participants who take turns making moves according to various rules. There is a set of rules defining permitted types of moves, and a set of rules for determining when a move is appropriate in light of prior moves that have been made. There is also a set of rules determining when a completed sequence of moves fulfills the goal of the dialogue (so-called "win-loss" rules). In the formal theory of Hamblin (1971, p. 130) a dialogue is defined as a triple $\langle n, p, l \rangle$. n is the length of the dialogue, defined as the number of moves made. p is a participant. And l is a locution (speech act). For example, a dialogue with only three moves has the following form.

$$\langle 0, P_0, L_4\rangle, \langle 1, P_{1,} L_{3,}\rangle, \langle 2, P_0, L_2\rangle$$

At move zero, P_0 begins the dialogue by making a move of type 4. At move 1, the other participant, P_1, replies by making a move of type 3. In Hamblin's theory the dialogue contains a sequence of argumentation made up of small connected steps of single arguments and questions. He realized that there could be different kinds of dialogues with different goals and rules.

Such a dialogue can also be represented as a profile of dialogue (Krabbe, 1999), a short sequence of moves where the proponent's moves are paired with those of the respondent. The small profile of dialogue below is an example.

Small Profile of Dialogue

Proponent	Respondent
1. Why should I accept *A*?	Because *B*.
2. Why should I accept *B*?	Because *C*.
3. I do not accept *C*.	Do you accept 'If *B* then *C*?'
4. Yes.	Do you accept *B*?
5. Yes.	Well then you must accept *C*.

In this example, the proponent begins by asking a why-question. The respondent replies by putting forward an argument to give a reason why the proponent should commit to the statement *A*. As the dialogue proceeds, the respondent continues to use arguments including a *modus ponens* argument at moves 3-5. His goal is to get her to commit to *B*, and ultimately to *A*.

Six basic types of dialogue have been recognized that are centrally important in argumentation and the study of fallacies. Table 1 below, citing the six types identified and explained in (Walton, 1998, p. 31), presents a classification of these basic types of dialogue along with the main characteristics of each type. The classification in table 1 is similar to the typology presented in (Walton and Krabbe, 1995, pp. 66), except that certain mixed types of dialogue are also cited in the Walton and Krabbe classification.

Table 1. Types of Dialogue (Walton, 1998, p. 31)

TYPE OF DIALOGUE	INITIAL SITUATION	PARTICIPANT'S GOAL	GOAL OF DIALOGUE
Persuasion	Conflict of Opinions	Persuade Other Party	Resolve or Clarify Issue
Inquiry	Need to Have Proof	Find and Verify Evidence	Prove (Disprove) Hypothesis
Negotiation	Conflict of Interests	Get What You Most Want	Reasonable Settlement that Both Can Live With
Information-Seeking	Need Information	Acquire or Give Information	Exchange Information
Deliberation	Dilemma or Practical Choice	Co-ordinate Goals and Actions	Decide Best Available Course of Action
Eristic	Personal Conflict	Verbally Hit Out at Opponent	Reveal Deeper Basis of Conflict

The central characteristic of persuasion dialogue is that each party is trying to persuade the other to accept a thesis by using rational arguments of a kind that both accept as means of rational persuasion. There are two fundamental kinds of cases. In one, the proponent has a thesis (a designated proposition) to be proved, and the respondent has a thesis to be proved that is the opposite (negation) of the proponent's thesis. In the other type of case, the proponent has a thesis to be proved, while the respondent only needs to cast doubt on the proponent's attempts to prove his thesis in order to be successful in the dialogue. But how does persuasion come into it, and what exactly does persuasion mean?

The simple formula sketched above can help the reader to grasp the nature of persuasion dialogue and see how it works, but it is an oversimplification, especially in one key respect. The reality of persuasion dialogue is that you can seldom persuade a respondent in a simple one-step argument. You usually need a chain of reasoning in which several one-step arguments are linked together. Thus what is required is a slightly more complex account of the components of persuasion like that previously set out in (Walton, 1998, p. 43). According to this account, the following four normative requirements apply to any argument used correctly in a persuasion dialogue.

(*R1*) The respondent accepts the premises as commitments.
(*R2*) Each inference in the chain of argumentation is structurally correct.

(*R3*) The chain of argumentation must have the proponent's thesis as its (ultimate) conclusion.

(*R4*) Arguments meeting (*R1*), (*R2*) and (*R3*) are the only means that count as fulfilling the proponent's goal in the dialogue.

These four requirements represent the fundamental characteristics of successful persuasion as a speech act. They indicate what a proponent needs to do in order to successfully persuade a respondent to become committed to his (the proponent's) thesis. He needs to present an argument, or chain of argumentation, and the argument needs to meet all four requirements (R1)-(R4). Thus, as will be shown in chapter 4, these requirements also define relevance in a persuasion dialogue. An argument is relevant if it can be chained forward to the ultimate conclusion to be proved in a dialogue. But as so far described, the notion of a persuasion dialogue may seem rather abstract to the reader. By introducing the critical discussion as a type of dialogue, and showing how it is a species of persuasion dialogue, the reader can get a more concrete idea of what a persuasion dialogue is.

The critical discussion model of van Eemeren and Grootendorst (1984; 1992) is a normative model of dialogue that has gained central recognition in the literature. The goal of a critical discussion is to resolve the initial conflict of opinions. There are four stages – a confrontation stage, an opening stage, an argumentation stage and a closing stage. At the confrontation stage, the participants identify a conflict of opinions that needs to be resolved. At the opening stage, they both agree to resolve the conflict by rational argumentation. At the argumentation stage, they take turns putting forward their arguments and responding to the questions and arguments of the other party. Ten rules for making these moves (speech acts) during the argumentation stage have been stated by van Eemeren and Grootendorst (1987, pp. 184-293). The gist of these ten rules can be summarized as follows: (1) Parties must not prevent each other from advancing arguments. (2) An arguer must defend her argument if asked to do so. (3) An attack on an arguer's position must relate to that position (and not some other position). (4) A claim can only be defended by giving relevant arguments for it. (5) An arguer can be held to his implicit premises. (6) and (7) An argument must be regarded as conclusively defended if its conclusion has been inferred by a structurally correct form of inference from premises that have been accepted by both parties at the outset of the discussion. (8) Arguments must be valid, or be capable of being made valid, by the addition of implicit premises. (9) Once the respondent has shown that the proponent's argument has failed, the proponent must withdraw it and recognize that it has failed. (10) Formulations must not be unduly vague or ambiguous.

It has been argued in (Walton, 1998) that the critical discussion is a species of persuasion dialogue. Evidence for this claim can be seen in the ten rules. Rule 4, for example, states that an attack on a point of view must be directed to the point of view really advocated by the protagonist. Rule 3 is based on the same idea. Violations of Rule 3 cited are "imputing a fictitious standpoint to someone" and "distorting someone's standpoint" (p. 286). These violations of Rule 3 correspond to the *straw man fallacy,* the fallacy of setting up a distorted version of an opponent's thesis (standpoint), and then demolishing this distorted version, thereby claiming to have refuted the opponent's argument. Both rules conform to the general idea of a persuasion dialogue as defined above. The argumentation of each party must be based only on premises that are commitments of the other party. Similarly, if you look at the other rules of the criticial discussion, they either conform to requirements (R1)-(R4) of the persuasion type of dialogue, or they represent special characteristics that mark off the critical discussion as a special type of persuasion dialogue. Nothing in the ten rules is antithetical to the concept of the persuasion dialogue as defined above.

At any rate, having given the reader some idea of what a persuasion dialogue is, some brief idea of the other types of dialogue can be given. For more detailed descriptions the reader is referred to the analyses given in (Walton and Krabbe, 1995) or (Walton, 1998). A question left open here is the relationship between Aristotelian dialectic and persuasion dialogue. The only remark we will make is that using persuasion dialogue as a model of the argumentation in a Socratic dialogue of the kind written by Plato would be an interesting, and possibly very fruitful exploration. It has to be emphasized that it is a basic assumption behind argumentation theory of the kind presented in this book that the term 'persuasion' has an objective meaning. In this meaning it is taken to refer to rational persuasion in a structured setting with dialogue rules that normatively determine whether an argument move (speech act) is correct (appropriate) or not. Of course, many readers who are not familiar with recent developments in dialogue theory, or who simply do not accept dialogue theory as an objective framework, will simply reject the whole idea as "subjective". Scriven (2002, p. 5) put the point succinctly when he wrote that to the neo-positivist, the term 'persuasion' "has a nasty squishy sound about it", indicating the "evil" of "subjectivism". Thus the neo-positivist will simply reject the whole package at the outset as "subjective". But for the rest of us, there is a distinction to be made between two kinds of persuasion. On the one hand, there is irrational persuasion, of the kind represented by fallacies and clever sophistical tactics of the kind we are routinely subjected to in advertising, propaganda, and public relations. On the other hand, there is rational persuasion of the kind in which a proponent uses rational arguments, with premises already accepted by a respondent, in order to try to get the respondent to accept a conclusion he has expressed doubts about.

This normative ideal would be inappropriately strong for persuasion dialogue. In persuasion dialogue, there is a need for retraction fairly often as the dialogue proceeds. In fact, it is a characteristic of the persuasion dialogue that participants need to be open to changing their opinions once they have been convinced by a good argument or by doubts raised by the other side. A real example of this normative model of inquiry would be an official government investigation into the cause of an air disaster. But of course the inquiry as a type of dialogue is a normative model or theoretical construct. Any real case will depart to a greater or lesser degree from the requirements of the model. But one can see the point by using this example. In an air crash investigation, there is a very careful attempt to collect and test all the data that can be found. At the closing stage, a cause of the crash may be announced, and if so, the evidence must be highly conclusive. Otherwise the inquiry will conclude that the cause of the crash cannot be proved from the data.

Negotiation is a type of dialogue in which there are some goods or resources that are in short supply, and both of the two parties want to possess all of them. At any rate, what one wants, the other wants as well. Thus there is a conflict of interests that is the basis of the need for dialogue. The participants engage in argumentation in order to reach some agreement on how to share the disputed resources. This form of dialogue is feasible if one side wants some part of the disputed goods more than the other does, while the other side has different priorities regarding which parts s/he wants most. Here there may be room for negotiation, so to speak. The two can "make a deal". But notice that argumentation in negotiation dialogue is quite different from argumentation in persuasion dialogue. In persuasion dialogue, each participant is trying to persuade the other to come to accept a proposition as true or false. Truth, or what is taken to be true, matters a lot. In negotiation, matters of truth and falsity of propositions don't matter as much, or so centrally. What matters is the interests of each side. Often interests can be measured in financial terms, but not always. Prestige or esteem is also a subject of negotiation in some cases. At any rate, the goals and techniques of argumentation are different in negotiation dialogue than they are in persuasion dialogue. In negotiation each side makes offers and concessions in a process of bargaining.

In the information-seeking type of dialogue one party lacks information and the other tries to provide it. The questioner who seeks the information assumes that the hearer is in a position to provide it. For example, if I am a tourist in a foreign city, I may approach a person who looks like a local inhabitant and ask him, "Can you tell me how to get to the Central Station?" If he then gives me directions, I will normally assume this information is correct and act on it by heading in the direction indicated. If I forget what the person told me, or if the information begins to seem incorrect, I can always ask somebody else. In contrast to the inquiry type of dialogue, the cost of being wrong is normally not all that high. I am not trying to prove something, but just trying to find out something.

Deliberation is a type of dialogue in which a group of agents tries, through looking at a set of alternatives, to make a decision about which course of action among the possible alternatives to take. Deliberation centrally uses practical reasoning. It is a method of means-end decision-making. The participants are assumed to have common goals, or at least to agree on some common goals. Their collective goal in the deliberation dialogue is to implement these goals in relation to a specific situation where choice is required in order to move ahead. Deliberation can be solitary, where one agent tries imaginatively to look at all the pros and cons on both sides of a choice. Even though such deliberation is undertaken by a single agent, it has a dialogue format because the agent needs to identify and evaluate the strongest possible arguments on both sides of the issue. Deliberation can also involve large groups of agents - for example, in a town hall meeting on whether to install a new sewer system or not. But once again, the argumentation reduces to two sides, the pro and the contra. Thus in the ideal model of deliberation as representing a format of rational argumentation, there are always two sides. At the closing stage of a successful deliberation dialogue, a conclusion is reached on which course of action, among those proposed, is the best one to take. Hitchcock, McBurney and Parsons (p. 7) postulate that a deliberation dialogue goes through the following eight stages. These stages do not necessarily represent the temporal order of the argumentation in a given case. They represent an ideal order of argumentation in the normative model of a deliberation dialogue.

1. Opening of the deliberation dialogue, and the raising of a governing question about what is to be done.
2. Discussion of: (a) the governing question; (b) desirable goals; (c) any constraints on the possible actions which may be considered; (d) perspectives by which proposals may be evaluated; and (e) any premises (facts) relevant to this evaluation.
3. Suggesting of possible action-options appropriate to the governing question.
4. Commenting on proposals from various perspectives.
5. Revising of: (a) the governing question, (b) goals, (c) constraints, (d) perspectives, and/or (c) action options in the light of the comments presented; and the undertaking of any information-gathering or fact-checking required for resolution. (Note that other types of dialogues, such as information seeking or persuasion, may be embedded in the deliberation dialogue at this stage.)
6. Recommending an option for action, and acceptance or non-acceptance of this recommendation by each participant.
7. Confirming acceptance of a recommended option by each participant. We have assumed that all participants must confirm their acceptance of a recommended option for normal termination.
8. Closing of the deliberation dialogue.

This formal model of deliberation dialogue is meant to be useful as a method to help us to evaluate the argumentation in any given case where a group of agents is supposed to be deliberating on what to do.

Eristic dialogue is a quarrelsome type of dialogue in which two parties "hit out" at each other. The goal of each party is to present arguments attacking the other party. The usual method is to allege that the opponent has done something ethically wrong and is therefore a bad person. As one can easily imagine, one of the most common forms of argument here is the *ad hominem* or personal attack argument of the following form: "My opponent's argument must be wrong because he is a bad person who is dishonest and untrustworthy and therefore lacks credibility." But *ad hominem* arguments are not always fallacious, and eristic dialogue is not always entirely bad or unproductive. In a quarrel, the goal of each participant is to articulate some hidden or unarticulated grudge or grievance being harbored against the other party. By bringing such a grievance to light, a quarrel can sometimes lead to "making up" of a relationship. That can be a good outcome. However, in the majority of cases, the quarrel generates more heat than light. Thus eristic dialogue is rightly associated with a degeneration of argumentation into a deadlock, and with fallacies and other underhanded tactics used to try unfairly to get the better of a speech partner.[7]

[7] The ancients were well aware of eristic dialogue and its importance in logic and the study of fallacies. Aristotle wrote in *On Sophistical Refutations* (165b8-165b10) that

The critical discussion is a type of persuasion dialogue in which retraction of commitments is reasonably but not completely permitted (Walton and Krabbe, 1995). In contrast, inquiry dialogue is cumulative, meaning that once a participant commits to a statement it cannot be retracted. In negotiation dialogue the goal is to reach an agreement both parties can live with. The goal of deliberation is to decide on a course of action in a situation requiring a choice (Hitchcock, McBurney and Parsons, 2001). Carberry (1990) has presented an analysis of the structure of information-seeking dialogue in collecting data in computing. There are various mixed dialogues that combine features of the six basic types (Walton and Krabbe, 1995).

Modeling legal argumentation by any formal model of dialogue argumentation is an unsolved problem (Frank, 1963; Walton, 2002), but the notion of a fair trial seems to centrally involve the model of the critical discussion (Feteris, 1999). Of course, a trial is much more complex because more than two parties are involved. In addition to the two sides, there is a judge or jury deciding the outcome.

8. Commitment Operations in Dialogues

Traditional views of reasoning in philosophy have been based on a BDI (belief-desire-intention) model. The problem with the BDI model is that pinning down an arguer's actual mental states can be quite a hard task. Because it is often possible to cite textual evidence to indicate what statements an arguer has committed himself to, the commitment model is a useful alternative. In a dialogue, a participant becomes committed to a statement by asserting it, and it is inserted into his commitments in a commitment store. As a dialogue proceeds, statements can be added to a participant's commitment store or deleted from it, according to the moves made and the rules governing them. If a participant retracts a commitment it is de-

contentious arguments (*eristikoi*) are "those which reason or seem to reason from opinions which appear to be, but are not really, generally accepted". Eristic arguments were seen by Aristotle as quarrelsome arguments in which the sole aim of the arguer is to win, or to appear to win, the argument by defeating, or even humiliating the other side. Aristotle even compared eristic argumentation to unfair fighting, or cheating in an athletic contest (*On Sophistical Refutations* 171b22-171b26). Contentious argumentation was also, of course, identified with sophistry and fallacies. In Plato especially it was identified with the Sophists, who took persuasion of the audience as the goal of argumentation, regardless of the logical worth of the argument used. Dialectic is represented as a positive form of argumentation that can lead to the truth of a matter, or at least to the reasons behind a view being revealed and evaluated. Eristic argumentation is seen as mainly negative. It can be deceptive. In *On Sophistical Refutations* (171b8-171b10) Aristotle wrote, "the man who views general principles in light of the particular case is a dialectician, while he who only apparently does this is a sophist." Thus eristic argumentation can be highly persuasive, because it can be made to resemble dialectical argumentation. Yet such argumentation may have little to do with the real truth of the matter being discussed. It is susceptible to the various fallacies that are common in argumentation.

leted from her commitment store (Krabbe, 2001). In this model (Hamblin, 1970, p. 257), commitment is different from belief. By making a certain type of move in a dialogue, an agent is committed to other statements implied by the move.

Not all problems of commitment management have been solved yet. For example, in the appeal to expert opinion scheme, what happens when the respondent has asked all six critical questions? Does he then finally have to commit to the conclusion unreservedly, or can he still go on asking other critical questions? This question expresses the completeness problem for dialogue argumentation. As shown in (Walton, 1997), there can be subquestions for each critical question matching the appeal to expert opinion. Thus argument closure, ending critical questioning, is only achieved at the closing stage of a dialogue. This completeness problem remains to be solved.

A question that has recently been investigated (Prakken, Reed and Walton, 2003) is how asking a critical questions matching argumentation scheme makes the argument default. Should merely asking the critical question defeat the argument, or does asking the critical question have to be backed up by some evidence in order to make it defeat the argument? In the case of argument from expert opinion, for example, you assume that the expert is an expert in the field of the claim made, and you assume that the expert's assertion was based on some evidence within the field of his/her expertise. The argument doesn't hold up as a well-founded appeal to expert opinion without these assumptions. Merely asking either of these questions makes the argument from expert opinion default if the arguer cannot respond with evidence to back up the assumption. Critical questions 4 and 5 are different in this respect from the other questions. Suppose the question of the expert's trustworthiness is raised. It would normally be assumed that an expert whose opinion has been cited is personally reliable as a source. If the questioner wants to argue that the argument is questionable because the expert is biased, or otherwise unreliable, evidence needs to be produced to back up such a claim. Now consider question 5. Merely asking whether the opinion is consistent with those of other experts, by itself, has little effect. If the expert's offered opinion can definitely be rebutted, by citing contrary opinions of other experts, that is an argument against the claim that demands a response. Critical questions 4 and 5 have a positive burden of proof attached, but the remaining four critical questions do not have this same positive burden of proof attached to them. With these all a critic needs to do is to ask the critical question, and the original argument defaults.

The problem posed is that there is no simple way of allocating burden of proof in such cases, and this can lead to an infinite regress, as in the following sort of dialogue.

White: You prove it!
Black: You disprove it!

This kind of stalemate can block further progress of a dialogue. In court, the judge often has to rule on disputes between the two sides on which one has the burden of proof. The solution is to recognize that there is no automatic incurring of burden of proof to have to reply to any critical questioning of argument in any case by backing up the argument to fulfill burden of proof. In some cases, such disputes about burden of proof or disproof cannot be resolved in an automatic way. It is necessary to move to a meta-dialogue level in which some third party (a judge or referee) must make a ruling on which side has the burden of proof.

9. Legal and Everyday Argumentation

The methods outlined in this chapter were first developed to teach university students, centrally in philosophy courses, how to think more critically and analyze argumentation from a critical point of view. They have also proved to be of interest to those teaching courses in speech communication where, especially in rhetoric, the study of argumentation is centrally important. The idea of applying these methods to legal argumentation is much more recent, and has not advanced very far at this point. There are special problems with trying to apply them to legal argumentation. First, there are many different kinds of legal argumentation, ranging from negotiation to the kind of argumentation lawyers engage in when presenting a case in court. No single type of dialogue or argumentation scheme will fit all such cases. Indeed, as will be shown, legal argumentation often involves a shift or transition from one type of dialogue to another. Still, one paradigm is the model of argumentation to which any method must be directed. That is the kind of argumentation in which evidence is presented in a trial and evaluated by the judge or jury. That type of argumentation is the central focus of this book. This focus does not mean that presenting evidence in court is the only type of legal argumentation that needs to be studied. It only means that this is the logical place to begin.

Another factor that needs to be clearly appreciated is that legal argument is different from everyday conversational argumentation in several important respects. When evidence is presented in a trial, there are procedural rules governing the admissibility of that evidence, how it should be presented, how it can be questioned, and how the proceeding should go generally. These trial rules vary from one jurisdiction to another. Also, there are different types of trials. For example, procedure in a civil case can be different from rules of evidence applied in a criminal case. Such rules of procedure can also vary greatly depending on the system of law adopted. For example, Anglo-American law has trial procedures that are very different from those governed by Continental law.

Such differences suggest that it cannot be taken for granted that legal argumentation should be evaluated in exactly the same way as everyday conversational argumentation. To do so would be a fundamental error. The special contextual feature of legal arguments needs to be taken into account. That said, however, it will be the contention of this book that there are many similarities and common features. Many of the most central cases initially addressed for study are arguments used in a trial where a jury, in the Anglo-American system, decides the outcome based not on special training or expertise, but on its capability for using commonsense, everyday reasoning to understand and judge the arguments presented and questioned in the trial. It is apparent from even the most cursory examination of such cases that, despite the differences of the legal context, the same kinds of arguments are being used and criticized that the members of the jury have used and criticized all their lives in their daily activities.

This much said then, the question is how we can move ahead and apply these argumentation methods to the special context of legal argumentation. The basic way of proceeding has already been illustrated above. We need to take actual cases of legal argumentation, from trials for example, and try to identify the types of argument deployed. We need to carry out tasks of argument analysis, like identifying missing premises, that are already familiar from use of informal logic as applied to everyday arguments. But we need to keep in mind that legal argumentation is different, and that special contexts of use have to be clearly identified. Thinking of an argument from the viewpoint of the dialogue model, as not just a sequence of reasoning, but also as something put forward by a proponent addressing a respondent or other parties, comes very naturally to legal professionals like judges and lawyers. That is, indeed, the framework they are used to. Adopting the dialogue model takes very little convincing in law. But given the very special and often complex institutional frameworks of the law, pinning down the details of the context of dialogue can be much more of a job.

Still, the way forward is to try to apply existing methods of informal logic to cases of legal argumentation not in a dogmatic way, but to explore what is unique and different about legal argumentation, as well as to identify familiar features. This is the way to progress in this new field, and to open up a new method of analyzing legal reasoning that shows promise of some of the problems with law as a framework for rational argument and logical analysis and evaluation of evidence. Law and logic are more and more coming to be typically thought of by the public as fields far apart. It's time to broaden what we take to be logic, and take a step that Wigmore would have approved of, by extending new methods that have proved their worth in analyzing everyday reasoning to cases of legal argumentation.

10. The Level of Difficulty of the Problems

Araucaria is just one method of visualizing the structure of an argument, or sequence of reasoning. There are many other comparable methods, including Wigmore diagrams, diagrammatic tools for visualizing argumentation like *Reasonable*, and generally the use of graph structures like those developed by Pearl (1991) and Schum (1994). All use a tree structure to represent a set of premises and conclusions as nodes in a directed graph, and a set of inferences joining nodes to other nodes. The problem for the analysis of legal argumentation and evidence is not just to apply such a diagram to a case by setting out a key list of the propositions, representing the inferences drawn from premises to conclusions, and filling in the implicit premises (or conclusions). The key problem is that the diagram resulting from such an analysis is only a beginning. It is so because typical legal arguments, in evidence cases for example, carry some evidential weight but are open, both to further evidence as a case proceeds, and even to potential failure (default) as new evidence is collected and evaluated. The reason is that a tentative conclusion drawn under conditions of uncertainty and lack of knowledge on the basis of such evidence. The conclusion is drawn on the rationale that the knowledge base is closed off for practical purposes, because in any legal case, even though there may be a lot of relevant evidence in a case, if more were collected, the new evidence might alter or even reverse the old conclusion. But it is costly to collect new evidence, and it may take a lot of time, but the more delay there is in coming to trial, the more the evidence fades into the past and become harder to collect. Enter the notion of burden of proof.

What the law does to solve this practical problem of when to close off a database to further searching for evidence is to invoke the notion of burden of proof. A burden of proof is set as binding on the argumentation in a given case to determine (a) how much evidence (how strong an argument) is required to for each side to prove its claim (what Gordon, 1995, calls its pleading), and (b) which side has this burden, or how the burden is to be distributed between the two parties. This is all very well, you might say. That is how the law solves the problem of closing off the knowledge base, ruling that the data collected to this point provides all the evidence used to draw a conclusion from what is known. But how can this notion of burden of proof be modeled in AI, so that an artificial agent, for example, could use it to calculate what is the right conclusion to draw from the evidence in a given case, based on the argument diagram that represents the evidence collected and analyzed in the argumentation in the case? This proves to be a much harder problem. The problem is to take an open-ended and inconclusive argument, of the kind so often providing evidence in law, and draw a reasonable conclusion from it, by using some standard to close it off, but at the same time leaving it open to the collection of new evidence. The task almost seems paradoxical, and in a way it is.

The general solution that is advocated in this book is to take the initial tree diagram provided by the analysis of the evidence in a case so far, and to embed it into a pragmatic structure. This pragmatic structure has three components. The first is the asking of an initial question. The second is a search through a knowledge base to try to find the data asked for in the question. The third is a setting of burden of proof that determines when the question has been answered so that further searching can be discontinued, even though it might be opened again later if the answer given is found inadequate for some practical purpose. However, the solution advocated in this book does not answer all the questions or solve all the problems currently confronting research in AI and law. The reason can be briefly explained here. These three components of a pragmatic structure are contextual. They vary from one context of argument use to another. Thus the very same argument, with the same argument diagram may need to be evaluated as correct (reasonable) or not, depending on where it was used in law. The same argument used before a trial, while evidence is being collected, may need to be evaluated quite differently during the course of the trial. For example, during the trial, rules of admissibility and relevance will apply. Or one the trial in over, and an appeal is being made, one again the very same argument may have to be evaluated quite differently.

To accommodate this pragmatic dimension of legal argumentation, in this book the notion of a formal dialogue, as defined above is applied to each problem. So defined, a dialogue is a structure in which there are two parties (on the simplest case) jointly conducting an investigation. The one party is the asker of the initial question. She makes the first move in the dialogue. The other party has a knowledge base, and tries to answer the question by searching for data contained in this knowledge base. The reason it is called a dialogue – admittedly a subjective-sounding notion – is that two parties are involved, and one is asking a question that sets the chain of argumentation into motion, providing its goal and its criteria for a successful search. One can see that it is this dialogue framework that varies from case to case in law. This framework sets the burden of proof appropriate for that case, determining when the search procedure can be stopped, and what ultimate conclusion can be drawn from the evidence collected by that search in the case. Thus in any given case, evaluating the argumentation used in the case requires two components. First, there is the argument diagram, representing all the given data as a set of propositions and a set of inferences from some propositions to others. Second, there is the context of dialogue, representing pragmatic factors of how the argument was used for some specific purpose, to prove something or establish a claim that was in doubt or open to questioning.

The main underlying problem confronted by the book is that there can many be different kinds of dialogue in different cases of legal argumentation. Each different type of dialogue will vary with respect to the three components cited above. A different question can be asked, a different knowledge base can be involved, and a different burden of proof may need to be set that determines when searching for an answer may be concluded. Thus the research conducted in the book consists in taking cases through two steps. The first is that of applying an argument diagram to the case in order to identify and analyze the argumentation given in the case. The second step is that of trying to evaluate the argument as weak or strong in relation to the context of dialogue appropriate for the case. This task seems so hard, and in many cases so unsatisfying, because it leads to a fundamental, underlying problem that has long appeared to be unsolvable, from the point of view of traditional logic. This is the problem of mapping the argument diagram of a given case onto a formal dialogue structure that represents the context of argument use in that case. Carrying out such a task is often difficult because legal argumentation is typically open-ended. The arguments are based on inferences that may hold or fail as a case expands and new evidence needs to be taken into account.

There are two special reasons why this problem appears to be unsolvable. The first is that when we try to represent dialogue factors on the diagram, like asking a critical question or setting a burden of proof on the search procedure furnishing a correct answer, the diagram becomes cluttered and hard to use. For many purpose of legal application, like explaining evidence to a trier, or summing up the *ratio decidendi* of a mass of evidence in a case, we need a relatively simple diagram of the main argument. The second reason is that in many cases of evaluating legal argumentation, the argument may be put forward at an early stage of an investigation. To judge its worth we have to base the judgment on where the argument is supposedly going in the future. Again here burden of proof comes in. To judge whether the argument is relevant, we have to make a predictive judgment of where it seems to going, in light of the ultimate *probandum* in the case. Such a judgment varies, for example according to the stage a trial is in. One of the most exciting problems is that of argument invention. Could we use the argument diagram to help in case preparation for a trial by trying to get a plan based on which ways the line of argumentation in the trial is likely to take? But is such a tool possible in advance of a trial, be cause of the very difficult problem of knowing in advance what strategy the opposition might adopt? Hence the underlying problem posed in this book certainly seems quite difficult, but the progress we will make toward solving it will be highly encouraging. Many other fundamental problems for applying AI to law are posed by moving to the new dialectical framework.

Chapter 2: Generalizations in Legal Reasoning

The subject of generalizations, especially defeasible ones, the kind subject to exceptions, is very important in legal reasoning, and most obviously in evidence law (Anderson and Twining, 1991; Schum, 1994). Gaining a precise understanding of how defeasible generalizations work as premises that are fundamental to the drawing of inferences in legal argumentation remains a key unsolved problem. We still seem to know little, and aside from the pioneering work of Anderson and Twining the problem has not even really been addressed, or seen as important. It is only recently that defeasible reasoning has been taken up as a serious subject of study by computer scientists, especially in artificial intelligence (Reiter, 1987; Prakken and Sartor, 1996, 1997; Verheij, 2000). But recently argumentation theorists have also developed new tools that are also applicable to the study of generalizations, including presumptive argumentation schemes that are neither deductive nor inductive (Kienpointner, 1992; Walton, 1996). Collaborative research between both groups has now led to the development of software systems for argument diagramming that can be applied to the analysis of argumentation as shown in chapter 1 (Reed and Rowe, 2002). In chapter 2 it is shown how these tools are applicable to defeasible generalizations of the kind so common in reasoning in evidence law.

As will be shown, a taxonomy of the different types of generalizations has been constructed (Anderson and Twining, 1991; Anderson, 1999). An interesting classification has even been proposed showing the common ways such generalizations can be faulty and can go wrong in legal argumentation (Twining, 1999). In logic, the traditional fallacy called hasty generalization, also known by names like "accident" and *secundum quid* (overlooking exceptions to a general rule), has traditionally been included for treatment in the textbooks (Hamblin, 1970, pp. 26-31). And knowledge of it is clearly important for avoiding errors in legal reasoning (Saunders, 1993, pp. 367-369). As will be shown through case studies of arguments based on generalizations used in cases of legal evidence, notably some key examples cited by Wigmore (1931), such argumentation is not well treated using models of inference of the deductive or inductive sort exclusively. The present investigation offers an alternative theory of how generalizations function in legal reasoning by combining and applying methods recently developed in argumentation theory and AI.

1. The Necessity and Danger of Generalizations

Schum (1994, p. 81) showed the importance of generalizations in legal reasoning about evidence, using the Sacco and Vanzetti case to illustrate his point. In this case, Sacco and Vanzetti were found guilty of having shot Berardelli on April 15, 1920, based on the testimony of the arresting officer, Connolly. Connolly testified that when arrested, Sacco attempted to put his hand inside his coat, where he carried a revolver. In court, Connolly's testimony about the incident was put forward as evidence of Sacco's consciousness of guilt for having committed this crime (Schum, 1994, p. 77). The chain of reasoning on which the evidence was based in this case depended on generalizations. One is that witnesses generally report an event the way the witness thought it happened. Schum (p. 82) put this generalization in the form of a conditional: "if a person says that an event happened, then it often did happen". Another is that anyone putting his hand under his coat when being arrested for murder, and when there is a weapon there, is showing consciousness of guilt of having committed the crime. Both these generalizations played significant parts in the evidence used to convict Sacco and Vanzetti at their trial.

We need to notice several things about these generalizations. First, they are not absolute generalizations. They do not even seem to be probabilistic generalizations, based on induction or statistics. They seem to be presumptive or plausible generalizations of a kind that are defeasible. Witnesses are known to lie in some cases. Indeed, there was evidence in the Sacco and Vanzetti case that Connolly and others fabricated the story of Sacco's reaching under his coat (Schum, 1994, p. 77). And even if Sacco did reach under his coat, there could have been all kinds of other explanations for this action. Maybe he was trying to hand something over to the officers (Schum, 1994, p. 77). Thus these kinds of generalizations that play such an important part in legal reasoning about evidence are fallible. Negative comments about their reliability as warrants for logical inferences could be extended even further. They can sometimes be misleading and even the key ingredient making a chain of reasoning fallacious. In fact, the Sacco and Vanzetti case is a classic case of wrongful conviction. As it turned out, they were later shown to be not guilty of the murder of Berardelli. What is shown by such cases is that while generalizations are the logical basis of typical legal reasoning about evidence, they are also tricky, and in many instances not all that reliable.

Anderson and Twining (1991, p. 43) made a classification of four types of general propositions. The first type of the generalizations they cite is called the scientific truth. The example they give is the law of gravity. The second type is the common sense generalization. The example they give is that running away indicates a sense of guilt. The third type is the commonly held belief. As examples they cite national or ethnic stereotypes including prejudices, that suggest that a person of such origins has certain characteristics. The fourth type is the generalization that presents general background information bearing on the present case. The example they cite is a generalization about a person's habits or character. This fourth type of generalizations is clearly meant by them to be domain dependent, that is, specific to a case.

Based on this earlier classification of types of general propositions, Anderson and Twining (pp. 368-369) also devised a provisional taxonomy of five types of generalizations.

1. Case-specific generalizations are those that are or may be established in a particular case. They offer the following example: "in most matters concerning their relationship, Edith dominated Freddie". This type of generalization seems to correspond to what they called the general background information type of proposition in their classification of general propositions, above.
2. Scientific generalizations are said to "vary in terms of their certainty" (p. 368). They are based on laws of science, like the law of gravity, or well-established principles, like the technique of fingerprint identification. They obviously correspond to the "scientific truth" type of proposition cited above.
3. The third type is the general knowledge generalization. As an example they cite the following statement: "Palm trees, rain, and high humidity are common in Miami, Florida" (pp. 368-369). Another example they cite is the following statement: "Transactions in securities traded on the New York Stock Exchange are accurately summarized in the Wall Street Journal". They state that these kinds of generalizations are so widely known in a particular community that they tend not to be explicitly stated.
4. The fourth type they call the experience-based generalization (p. 369). They offer the following example: "Someone who has been unfairly treated by the police may, rightly or wrongly, conclude that police officers are not to be trusted" (p. 369).
5. The fifth type is called the belief generalization. It is described as a generalization that has been accepted on a basis of information rather than direct experience (p. 369). They first cite a more general example: "Most Poles are devoted Catholics". Then they cite a case-specific example: "Members of a certain family (the Hatfields) are untrustworthy". As these examples suggest, and as Anderson and Twining state (p. 369), belief generalizations are often based on superficial impressions, prejudices, or speculation, and they may be a irrational as well as rational.

Anderson (1999, p. 459) expressed the variability and limitations of generalizations of the kind used in legal reasoning very well.

> Generalizations can be classified on a spectrum of reliability ranging from well-tested and generally accepted propositions, such as those associated with the law of gravity, to largely untested and sometimes untestable intuitions, such as the generalizations upon which the view that flight from the scene of a crime is evidence of guilt is based, to unfounded biases based upon prejudice, or false stereotypes, such as the generalization that women cannot be effective lawyers that was widely accepted in prior generations.

Generalizations are a source of logical ambivalence in legal reasoning, as in everyday argumentation. They can be very bad or very good. They are necessary for drawing the right conclusion in many instances, but they can also be sources of some of the worst logical faults of prejudice and rigid thinking. Twining (1999, p. 357) expressed this ambivalence nicely by conceding that generalizations are necessary in legal argumentation, but also dangerous, because they "tend to provide invalid, illegitimate, or false reasons for accepting conclusions based on inference". Twining emphasized that they are especially dangerous when implicit or unexpressed, and classified five specific dangers of them, as quoted below (pp. 357-358).

1. The warranting generalization may be indeterminate with respect to frequency or universality (all/most/some), level of abstraction, defeasibility (exceptions, qualifications), precision or "fuzziness", empirical base/confidence (accepted by scientific community; part of everyday firsthand or vicarious experience; speculative etc.).
2. It may be unclear as to identity (which generalization – there may be rival generalizations available to each side in a dialogue) or source (whose generalization – male/female experience in a domestic violence case).
3. There may not in fact be a "cognitive consensus" on the matter, especially in a plural society.
4. Value judgments (including prejudices, racist or gender stereotypes) may be masquerading as empirical propositions.
5. When articulated, a generalization may be expressed in value laden language or in loaded categories.

Many of these dangers can in fact be identified with fallacies or other sources of worry about faulty logical argumentation recognized in logic textbooks and work on informal logic. 1 and 2 are often associated with, or even identified with the fallacy of hasty generalization. 3 is related to the *argumentum ad populum*, a form of argument that invokes a presumption of common knowledge (Freeman, 1995). 4 raises the problem of distinguishing between facts and values in argumentation, and the identification of bias and prejudice. 5 raises concerns and problems arising from use of emotive language in argumentation, including persuasive definitions (Stevenson, 1944) and question-begging uses of terms (Walton, 1999, pp. 132-144). Thus the study of how generalizations work in legal argumentation leads to the branch of logic concerned with informal fallacies. Fallacies are common kinds of arguments that can be erroneous and deceptive in some instances.[1] They can even be used as deceptive tactics to get the best of a speech partner with whom one is engaged in argumentation.

[1] See (Hamblin, 1970).

2. The Fallacy of Hasty Generalization

Logic textbooks that treat fallacies typically include hasty generalization as a main fallacy. But their terminology is not consistent. They may treat the same example or type of argument under varied terms for the fallacy like over-generalization, glittering generality, accident, converse accident, or *secundum quid* (neglect of qualifications).[2] Typically, however, two types of fallacies are emphasized. One is an inductive fallacy that occurs in statistical reasoning from a selected sample to a wider population. The other has to do with overlooking qualifications to a defeasible generalization.

One leading textbook (Hurley, 1991; 2000) treats hasty generalization as an inductive fallacy committed when the sample chosen is too small or is unrepresentative of the population a generalization is about. Quoted below are his first two examples of the fallacy of hasty generalization.

The Car Example

After only one year the alternator went out in Mr. O'Grady's new Chevrolet. Mrs. Dodson's Oldsmobile developed a transmission problem after six months. The obvious conclusion is that cars made by General Motors are just a pile of junk these days (2000, p. 142).

The Prejudice Example

Two weeks ago the Ajax Pharmacy was robbed and the suspect is a black man. Yesterday a black teenager snatched an old lady's purse while she was waiting at the corner bus stop. Clearly, blacks are nothing but a pack of criminals (1991, p. 130).

Hurley's diagnosis of the fallacy committed in these cases is that a conclusion about a whole group is drawn from a premise that mentions only two instances. In both cases, such a small and atypical sample cannot support the general conclusion. The fallacy, according to Hurley's analysis, is one that might appropriately be warned against in any introductory statistics textbook or handbook of statistical fallacies that treats examples of drawing inferences from a selected sample to a wider population (Campbell, 1974). It seems fair to classify this fallacy as relating to inductive generalizations. The prejudice example also suggest how such inferences are related to the kind of thinking that gives rise to stereotypes and bias of a sort that represent common errors of reasoning.

Another leading textbook (Copi and Cohen, 1994, pp. 125-126) treats the fallacy of hasty generalization under the terms 'accident' and 'converse accident'. These antiquated and not very appropriate terms derive from the Aristotelian distinction between essential and accidental properties of a thing being defined. Copi and Cohen defined the two fallacies as follows (p. 125). The fallacy of accident is

2 The variations in the textbook classifications are described in detail in (Walton, 1990).

committed when "we apply a generalization to individual cases it does not properly govern". The fallacy of converse accident is committed when "we apply a principle that is true of a particular case to the great run of cases". What is described in the first definition is definitely a fallacy of some sort, because of the expression 'does not properly govern'. However it is unclear whether the second definition refers to a kind of argumentation that is always fallacious, as opposed to a normal kind of generalization that might be reasonable in some instances but not in others. Anyhow, what Copi and Cohen have in mind is brought out better in their examples, some of which are quoted below (p. 125).

The Hearsay Example

The rule that hearsay testimony may not be accepted as evidence in court is not applicable when the party whose oral communications are reported is dead, or when the party reporting the hearsay does so in conflict with his own best interests.

The Euthydemus Example

In a dialogue with the young Euthydemus, who planned to become a statesman, Socrates drew from Euthydemus a commitment to many of the conventionally accepted moral truths: that it is wrong to deceive, unjust to steal, and so on. Then Socrates (as recounted by Xenophon in his report of the dialogue) presented a series of hypothetical cases in which Euthydemus reluctantly agreed that it would appear right to deceive (to rescue our compatriots) and just to steal (to save a friend's life), and so on.

In both of these cases, the fallacy is not an inductive one, of the kind defined by Hurley. It is one that arises from failure to properly take qualifications of a generalization into account. It has to do with overlooking exceptions to a general rule of the defeasible sort. Copi and Cohen's quote (p. 125) from H. W. B. Joseph defines this sort of fallacy quite well: "there is no fallacy more insidious than that of treating a statement which in many connections is not misleading as if it were true always and without qualification". The fallacy described here is one of mixing up two kinds of generalizations. One is the absolute universal generalization that holds without exceptions and that defaults when one counter-example is presented. The other is the defeasible or qualified generalization that holds subject to exceptions and that can still hold generally even when a counter-example is presented, showing that it fails to hold in the particular case to which the exception applies. The fallacy described by Copi and Cohen is that of treating a defeasible generalization as if it were an absolute universal generalization. This fallacy may be associated with rigid thinking, prejudices and stereotypes.

The two types of hasty generalization fallacy most often recognized by the logic textbooks are distinct, because each involves a different kind of generalization, and a different way of fallaciously drawing an inference to that generalization. Yet both fallacies are about ways of improperly generalizing. This binary approach to the fallacy of hasty generalization, like so much in the current treatment of fallacies, comes to us from Aristotle. He recognized two fallacies comparable to the two cited above from modern logic textbooks. Chakrabarti (1995, p.68) cited the *Prior Analytics* (II.27.70a33) as one text where Aristotle warns against a fallacy that would now come under the heading of hasty generalization. In this passage, Aristotle warns of drawing the following inference: if Pittacus is good, it does not necessarily follow that all other wise men are good. This example is comparable to Hurley's way of presenting the fallacy of hasty generalization as an inductive fallacy if we add as an additional premise the unstated assumption that Pittacus is a wise man. So reconstructed, it can be taken to be an inference from a premise about a property of one wise man to a conclusion attributing the same property to all wise men. One has to add a qualification here, because what Aristotle meant by induction is something quite different from the accepted modern use of the term to refer to statistical reasoning.[3] Nevertheless, there is a point of comparison. Both kinds of inferences go from a sample, or single instance, to a population or wider group of individuals being generalized about. The other fallacy often described as hasty generalization is the second in Aristotle's list of fallacies "not dependent on language" listed in *On Sophistical Refutations*. In this small book on fallacies (166b38- 167a21), Aristotle wrote that the fallacy of *secundum quid* arises from two ways a statement can be meant or taken: absolutely, or in a certain respect. The example cited is the statement 'The Ethiopian is black'. It could be meant or taken absolutely to mean that the Ethiopian is black in all respects. Or it could be meant or taken to mean that the Ethiopian is black in one respect (skin color), but not black in another (color of teeth). Thus from the premise that he is black (meaning black in a certain respect), the conclusion that he is black in every respect does not follow. For example, it would be a fallacious inference to draw the conclusion that he has black teeth. It is this fallacy, properly called *secundum quid*, that fits the examples that Copi and Cohen cited as instances of converse accident, and that many textbook accounts would classify as hasty generalization.

What has been shown so far is that generalizations of the kind that are necessary and vitally important in evidence law are dangerous, tricky, and somewhat unreliable. They are associated with fallacies long recognized in logic, especially the fallacy of hasty generalization. This is perhaps understandable, because the generalizations of the kind so central to evidence law are subject to exceptions, subject to defeat as more evidence is collected in a case, and so are fallible. These features are perhaps understandable, however, because the forms of argument based on them tend to be the ones we use under conditions of uncertainty and lack of knowledge. In the past these characteristics have led to a mistrust of reasoning based on this kind of generalization. Recent research in argumentation theory and AI, while acknowledging the fallible nature of common generalizations, has begun to explore the conditions under which they can support reasoning that can be ac-

[3] According to Chakrabarti (1995, p.66), induction (*epagoge*), as defined by Aristotle, is a process of ampliative reasoning which (usually) reasons from sentences describing particular instances to a general conclusion. Aristotle contrasted induction in this sense with deduction.

ceptable in some cases as meeting a standard of rationality. This standard is often called bounded rationality, meaning that it enables the drawing of a conclusion subject to limitations of various kinds.

3. Generalizations in Evidence Law

To define what a generalization is, for the purpose of analysis of argumentation in evidence law, is not easy. There are two identifying characteristics. One is that a generalization is a species of general proposition, where propositions can be placed at some point, in any given instance, in a ladder of increasing levels of abstraction. The propositions at the top are more general (abstract) while those progressively lower down are more and more specific (concrete), and hence less general. But abstraction is not the only identifying characteristic of generalization. A generalization is a general proposition, in this sense, that figures as a premise in a typical kind of inference in legal argumentation that links a rule (or more general proposition) to a case or instance (referring to a more specific proposition). This linking of the concept of a generalization to different types of arguments or inferences, although it may at first seem question-begging, is a necessary step in providing an adequate definition and analysis of this concept. Anderson and Twining (1991, p. 446) defined a generalization as "a general proposition claimed to be true which is used implicitly or explicitly to argue that a conclusion has been established". This definition at first seems to be question-begging because it defines the notion of a generalization in terms of the notion of an argument as a set of premises used to establish that a conclusion is true. We are then cast back to the question, 'What is an argument?' But it can be argued that the definition is not question-begging, because it is necessary to define generalization within some framework of rational argumentation that offers a prior theory of what an argument is, and what are the different types and forms of arguments. Anderson and Twining's definition, it can be argued, is a good one, and indeed a necessary one, that leads in the right direction towards making sense of generalizations by exhibiting their structure and function in legal argumentation.

A third characteristic is that generalizations can be classified as belonging to one of three types, where each type corresponds to a type of argument: deductive, inductive and presumptive. A main problem that needs to be overcome is the dominant tendency in the past to ignore the third category, and to see generalizations as only associated with deductive and inductive reasoning. Once liberated from this restrictive approach of the past, the analysis of generalizations becomes incredibly powerful as a tool for evidence law, where so many of the generalizations, and the arguments based on them, are of the presumptive and defeasible kind. One of the special features of argumentation that is being studied recently is the role of argumentation schemes in legal argumentation and evidence (Walton, 2002). These are stereotypical forms of argument that can be deductive or inductive, but, especially in legal argumentation, are mainly of a third kind. Current research is interested in how such argumentation schemes can be represented in a format other than that of deductive and inductive reasoning exclusively. The analysis above has indicated that argumentation schemes representing the most common forms of argument in law, like appeal to witness testimony, are generally not deductive or inductive in nature. Attempts to reduce them to some kind of deductive or inductive format distorts the original argument and has a tendency to render them into forms less useful for representing legal argumentation.

The problem now faced is how to integrate the study of generalizations with the emerging study of presumptive argumentation schemes like appeal to expert opinion, appeal to witness testimony, and so forth. Anderson and Twining's provisional taxonomy of five types of generalizations (1991, p. 368) is an excellent starting point for moving further ahead. Case-specific generalizations could also be called empirical generalizations, usually at a low level of abstraction, that sum up data in a given case. Scientific generalizations, when they are put forward as evidence in legal argumentation, are based on the argumentation scheme for appeal to expert opinion. Thus context of use matters when analyzing and evaluating the evidential worth of such generalizations. In a discussion among a group of scientists in a domain of expertise, scientific generalizations play one kind of role in the argumentation. But in a court of law, when evidence is being presented, the judge, jury, or other participants, are presumably not scientific experts in the field of the testimony being presented by the expert witness.[4] In this context, scientific generalizations need to be seen and evaluated as a different species of argumentation.

The third category in the typology of Anderson and Twining is that of the "general knowledge generalization". In the literature on argumentation this form of generalization has often been associated with the form of argument called appeal to popularity and presumption by common knowledge (Freeman, 1995). Often thought to be fallacious in the past, this form of argument has now been recognized as an argumentation scheme that can be presumptively reasonable when the right conditions for its successful use are met. Arguments based on common knowledge tend to be weak when flatly stated, but they are often supported or "bolstered up" by allied forms of argument, like appeal to expert opinion. For example, if financial experts commonly treat the *Wall Street Journal* as a reliable source for accurate transaction summaries, that bolsters up the commonly accepted generalization that the summaries in the *Wall Street Journal* are accurate. This generalization then holds as a presumption in argumentation in which something printed in the *Wall Street Journal* is taken as evidence about some security transaction at issue in a case. The presumption may be rebutted by contrary evidence, but in absence of such knowledge, it is taken to be true.

The remaining two types of generalizations cited by Anderson and Twining (1991), experience-based generalizations and belief generalizations, have played

[4] The common law trial, inherited from the English common law tradition, is the "theoretical centerpiece" of the adversarial justice system in the U.S. Less than ten percent of court filings ever end up in trial, but the trial pervades law and culture because participants in other forms of dispute resolution use the trial as a model (Park, Leonard and Goldberg, 1998, pp. 1-2).

less of a role in recent argumentation theory. It is evident from their comments (p. 369) that these types are more susceptible to prejudice, speculation and fallacy. As they put it, "they may be rational or irrational". They tend to be localized to a specific group and they may be about specific groups. Some examples from Wigmore they cite (p. 369) are the two propositions "All sailors carry knives" and "Most Poles are Catholic". One can see how these generalizations can be important when a witness is examined in court, because the witness may be basing a conclusion on one of them. But logic, or argumentation schemes, are of little help in identifying such unstated premises of this kind. They vary with time and place, with how specific groups tend to see other groups, and so forth. They are empirical, like case-specific generalizations, but they are often unstated and hard to dig out. They can also be highly idiosyncratic to an individual or group. And their role in argumentation is often very strongly tied to the particular commitments and beliefs of a party to an argument. These two types of generalizations would appear, therefore, to be the least susceptible to analysis on the basis of argumentation schemes that represent structures of reasoning common to all rational arguers.

The suggestion of Anderson and Twining was that the analysis of generalizations can be explored by studying the role they play in reasoning in cases of the kind found in evidence law. Following this suggestion, argumentation schemes have great potential as tools for the analysis of legal argumentation, because the scheme, as applied to a given case, often brings out the implicit generalization on which the reasoning is based. That will be our next step. From there, we will go on to study how schemes can be utilized in a technique of argument diagramming of evidence in which case-specific generalizations also play an important role.

4. Argumentation Schemes

Argumentation schemes represent patterns of typical human reasoning of a kind found in arguments in everyday speech as well as in arguments used in legal contexts. As shown in chapter 1, section 4, many of them are presumptive in nature and are based on a kind of fallible reasoning that is subject to defeat as more evidence comes in to a case.[5] As briefly indicated in chapter 1, such schemes need to be evaluated not semantically, as forms of argument abstracted from a conversational context, but as presumptive arguments that need to be judged on a balance of considerations by asking critical questions in a dialogue. The example used to illustrate how this process works in chapter 1 was the argumentation scheme for appeal to expert opinion.

[5] (Walton, 1996).

Argumentation Scheme for Argument from Expert Opinion

Major Premise: *E* is an expert in subject domain *S* containing statement *A*.

Minor Premise: *E* asserts that *A* (in domain *S*) is true (false).

Conclusion: *A* may plausibly be taken to be true (false).

One might try to "deductivize" this scheme by taking the major premise as a rule stating categorically that if an expert says *A* is true, and *A* is the subject domain *S*, then *A* has to be true, without doubt. But this approach would be highly unrealistic as applied to cases of expert testimony in the courts, where typically there are experts on both sides, one testifying to an opinion that is the opposite of the other's. A better approach (Walton, 1997) is to treat appeal to expert opinion as a defeasible form of argument that has some probative weight but that can and should be questioned before resting too much weight on it. On this approach, an argument from expert opinion should be evaluated on a balance of considerations in a dialogue between two parties, called the proponent and the respondent. When the proponent puts forward the argument, the respondent is entitled to ask any one of the following six basic critical questions cited in chapter 1, section 4 (Walton, 1997, p. 223). Once the argument has been put forward, assuming the premises have some support, the respondent is obliged to accept it or ask a critical question. If the premise lacks support, the proponent who originally put the argument forward is obliged to support it by offering evidence. If questioned, she is obliged to provide an adequate answer to the question the respondent chose to ask, or her argument defaults. If she does provide such an answer, however, the argument tentatively stands until the respondent asks another critical question, or otherwise presents suitable reasons for doubting the argument.

The same kind of analysis of the structure of the form of argument called appeal to witness opinion was presented in chapter 1, section 4. When evaluating an appeal to witness testimony, the evaluator has no direct access to the evidence that the witness presumably possesses. For example, in a trial, the trier (judge or jury) is a neutral participant who has no direct access to the facts or involvement in what happened. Direct verification, by observation of the facts, is not possible. Hence the best the evaluator can do is to test the consistency of the account given by the witness, to see if it hangs together, and is consistent with other evidence that is known about the case independently of the testimony. Probing into the consistency of the witness's account is achieved by asking the critical questions cited in chapter 1. The three critical questions that concern consistency are the following.

CQ1: Is what the witness said internally consistent?

CQ2: Is what the witness said consistent with the known facts of the case (based on evidence apart from what the witness testified to)?

CQ3: Is what the witness said consistent with what other witnesses have (independently) testified to?

All three of these kinds of critical questions have been discussed extensively in legal literature on examination of witnesses, and many interesting cases could be considered here. There are many fine points to be clarified. What is most important here, however, is to see how sequences of dialogue in legal cases can involve complex argumentation in which such questions can, in turn, increase or decrease the probative weight of an appeal to witness argument as evidence. A complex sequence of argumentation that can occur in a case of this sort has been studied by Wagenaar, van Koppen and Crombag (1993, p. 38). If one witness has a reason for lying, additional evidence, in the form of testimony of another witness could still support the claim of the first witness.

The fourth critical question to be considered has to do with the bias of the witness.

CQ4: Is there some kind of bias that can be attributed to the account given by the witness?

If evidence can be found by questioning that shows that the account given by the witness is biased, that finding will detract from the probative weight of the appeal to witness testimony as an argument. There are many indicators of bias. One of the most important ones is finding that the witness has something to gain by testifying in a certain way. Another is the language used by the witness. For example, the language may have strong emotive connotations that are accusatory. Another indicator is the selectivity of the witness's account. The account may stress details on one side, but overlook details that should be on the other side. If a witness is biased, it doesn't necessarily follow that the witness is lying. The bias could be unintentional.

The fifth critical question has to do with the plausibility of the claim.

CQ5: How plausible is the statement *A* asserted by the witness?

This plausibility factor can react on the evaluation of the appeal to witness testimony in various ways. If the statement made by the witness is highly implausible, it can backfire on the credibility of the witness. However, in some cases, the implausibility of the statement made can actually be a basis for conjecturing that what the witness claimed is really true. For example, if two independent witnesses have made the same implausible claim, their agreement could suggest that their observations are careful and accurate.

Argument from expert opinion and appeal to witness testimony are cited once again here because they are such common forms of argument in evidence law. But many other schemes on the list given in chapter 1, section 4, could be cited as well, including argument from sign, argument from example, argument from commitment, argument from position to know, argument from expert opinion, argument from analogy, argument from precedent, argument from gradualism, and the slippery slope argument. Each such scheme is based on a generalization that is used as a warrant to draw the inference that leads from the premises to the conclusion of the argument. The warrant (Toulmin, 1958) is a general rule that supports the inference from the premises to the conclusion. In the presumptive argumentation schemes, the warrant is not an absolute, universal generalization. It is a rule, or conditional, as it is called in logic, that is subject to defeat in special cases and holds only tentatively. For example, the following rule can be formulated as the warrant on which appeal to testimony is based.

Warrant for Appeal to Testimony: If witness *W* is in a position to know whether *A* is true or not, and *W* is telling the truth (as *W* knows it), and *W* states that *A* is true (false), then *A* is true (false).

The first three premises are joined together as a conjunction that appears as the antecedent of the conditional expressed in the warrant. The warrant functions as an additional premise. Thus the structure of appeal to witness opinion as a form of argument can be recast as a *modus ponens* inference.

Appeal to Witness Testimony in *Modus Ponens* Form

If witness *W* is in a position to know whether *A* is true or not, and *W* is telling the truth (as *W* knows it), and *W* states that any proposition is true, then *A* is true.

Witness *W* is telling the truth (as *W* knows it).

Witness *W* states that *A* is true.

Therefore *A* is true.

Since this inference has the *modus ponens* form, many might think that it is deductively valid. In traditional logic, it is the conventional wisdom that all inferences having the form of *modus ponens* must be deductively valid. But the above inference is not deductively valid, according to the unconventional account presented here. It is a defeasible inference, because the first premise (warrant) is defeasible. Although it is a structurally correct form of inference that can be used to transfer a probative weight from the premises to the conclusion, it is not deductively valid.

Many cases could be cited to show the importance of generalizations in legal argumentation. What is easily shown is that arguments based on different generalizations of the same kind can be used by the other side in a trial. One can have a plausible argument, based on a generalization that supports a conclusion, and then have a plausible argument, based on a different generalization that supports an opposed conclusion. The two conclusions are opposed. The one argument, as it is said, defeats or refutes the other, making it appear implausible to someone who accepts the first one. In the next section, a case of exactly this sort will be analyzed.

5. Analysis of the Cranberry Cask Case

To follow up Anderson and Twining's suggestion that generalizations can be studied by seeing how they fit into the chain of reasoning used in cases of legal evidence, and at the same time to illustrate some of the problems that arise in analyzing even the simplest cases, it is useful to examine a standard kind of case. The case below is from a student's textbook of evidence law written by John H. Wigmore, presented as an illustrative case of evidence that is partly circumstantial and partly testimonial. It is quoted below directly from (Wigmore, 1935, pp. 42-43).

The Cranberry Cask Case

A respectable farmer in England was charged with larceny of several articles, including a cask marked "P.C. 84." A cask found in his possession, marked "P.C. 84," was positively identified by several witnesses as the one stolen. But the farmer produced numerous witnesses who testified that he had bought regularly his cranberries from a merchant in another town, all of whose casks were marked "P.C. 84." If this *testimony* were believed, the *circumstances* showed that the farmer was innocent, and that the prosecution's testimony was erroneous.

This is a case of stolen goods being identified in the possession of the party accused of stealing them. The argument seems to be that having in your possession a cranberry cask marked P.C. 84 would be unusual. Thus if you were charged with stealing several articles, including such a cask, and it was found in your possession, then that would be evidence you may have stolen the articles. It's a little hard to say what the form of this argument is, but it is a common kind of inference to the best explanation found in police work and evidence law (Josephson and Josephson, 1994; Walton, 2004). It runs something like this. If you have the stolen article, or something that looks like it is the stolen article, then unless you can explain where you got it, the presumption is that you got it by taking it from the party accusing you of theft. The argument could be expressed in the form of a set of premises and a conclusion as follows.

Fact: The theft suspect possessed a cranberry cask marked P.C. 84.

Fact: Cranberry casks marked P.C. 84 are (one might assume) unusual.

Fact: The stolen items included a cranberry cask marked P.C. 84.

Fact: The item found in possession of the suspect appears to be the same as the item he is accused of having stolen.

Generalization: If an item found in the possession of a theft suspect appears to be the same as an item that the suspect is accused of having stolen, that is evidence that the suspect stole the item, especially if it is unusual.

Conclusion: Therefore it is a plausible assumption that the cask found in the possession of the suspect is the same cask as the one stolen.

Therefore it is plausible that the suspect came into possession of the cask by stealing it.

This argument puts a burden of proof on the farmer's side to offer an alternative explanation of where the cask came from. To rebut the argument above, he needs to prove that he got it somewhere else, that is, by some means other than taking it from the plaintiff.

In this case, the farmer contended that he got the cranberry cask marked P.C. 84 from a merchant in another town. To prove this contention he argued from two premises alleged as facts.

Fact: He regularly bought his cranberries from this merchant.

Fact: All the casks of this merchant were marked P.C.84.

If these two statements were true, it would plausibly follow that the cask marked P.C. 84 found in the farmer's possession came from this merchant in another town. That would explain where the cask came from, or at least it would provide a plausible alternative to the explanation that he stole it, as alleged. This adds up to a highly plausible argument that the cask at issue came from a source other than the plaintiff.

In this case, part of the chain of reasoning in the rebuttal is a deductive argument.

Premise: All of the casks of this merchant were marked P.C.84.

Premise: Suppose the cask in the possession of the accused was obtained from this merchant.

Conclusion: The cask in the possession of the accused would be marked P.C.84.

The generalization on which the first argument rested could be formulated in a more general or neutral way, so that it applies to a broader range of cases.

The Missing Property Generalization

If there is property missing from some source, and what appears to be the missing property, or some part of it, is found in a person's possession, then unless he can explain how he obtained that property from another source, it may be assumed that he obtained it from that source.

Thus in a given case, suppose a person is found in possession of missing property. This fact, taken with the missing property generalization, leads to the conclusion that he got it from the source claiming it is missing.[6] Of course, such an argument is defeasible. As the cranberry cask case shows, the argument would be undercut or defeated if it could be shown that the object came from somewhere else. And of course that it exactly what happened in the cranberry cask case.

The method of argument diagramming can be used to identify some important features in the sequence of argumentation in the cranberry cask case. To represent the sequence of argumentation in the cranberry cask case, the first step is to identify the set of statements that function as premises or conclusions in the argument. These are displayed in the key list below.

Key List for the Cranberry Cask Case

(A) The theft suspect possessed a cranberry cask marked P.C. 84.
(B) Cranberry casks marked P.C. 84 are (one might assume) unusual.
(C) The stolen items included a cranberry cask marked P.C. 84.
(D) The item found in possession of the suspect appears to be the same as the item he is accused of having stolen.
(E) If an item found in the possession of a theft suspect appears to be the same as an item that the suspect is accused of having stolen, that is evidence that the suspect stole the item, especially if it is unusual.
(F) It is a plausible assumption that the cask found in the possession of the suspect is the same cask as the one stolen.
(G) It is plausible that the suspect came into possession of the cask by stealing it.
(H) He regularly bought his cranberries from this merchant.
(I) A witness testified that he regularly bought his cranberries from this merchant.
(J) The witness was in a position to know about the suspect's cranberry buying practices.
(K) All the casks of this merchant were marked P.C.84.
(L) Suppose the cask in the possession of the accused was obtained from this merchant.
(M) The cask in the possession of the accused would be marked P.C.84.
(N) It is plausible that the suspect came into possession of the cask by buying cranberries from this merchant.

6 Callen (2003) has analyzed how the missing property generalization functions as evidence in the Huddleston case, a much-discussed case involving suspected stolen property.

The next step is to load this set of statements into *Araucaria* as a text file, where it will appear as text in the frame on the left of the display you see on the screen. The next step is to highlight each statement, using the cursor. As each is highlighted in turn, it will be assigned a letter, and a corresponding circled letter will appear in the frame on the right. Then the user must draw a line from each circled letter to each other circled number that is a conclusion drawn by inference from the first one. Once all the circled letters have been connected by lines, the result is an argument diagram. The argument diagram for the cranberry cask case is displayed in figure 2.1 below.

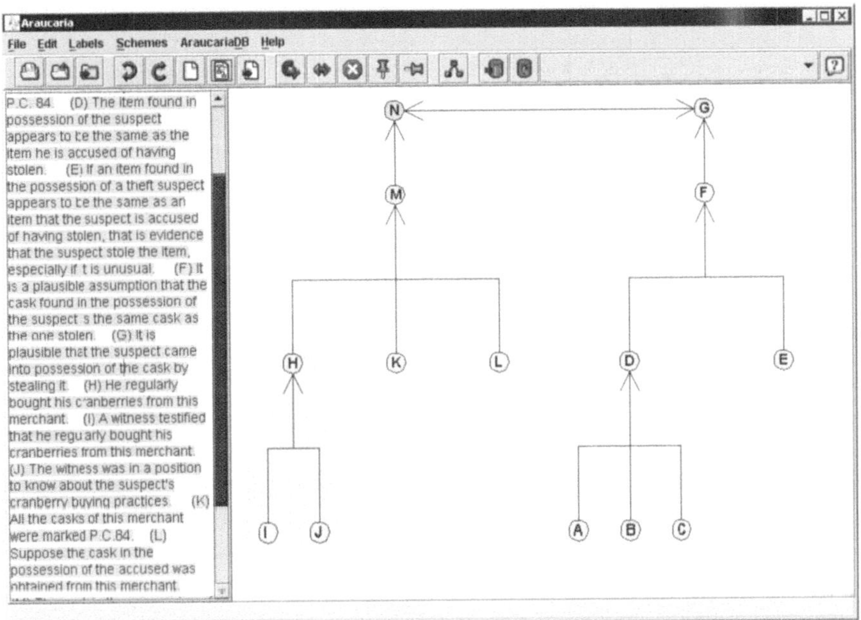

Fig. 2.1. Araucaria Diagram for the Cranberry Cask Case with Text Highlighted

Although the original cranberry cask case was very short, only a few lines in Wigmore's presentation of it, the key list above is quite a bit longer. What has happened is that, in order to trace out the sequence of reasoning, we have had to insert a number of implicit assumptions, missing statements needed to make the sequence of argumentation more explicit. *Araucaria* doesn't do this automatically. It's something the user has to do, although *Araucaria* can help in some instances by deploying argumentation schemes as inferential links. In any event, figure 2.1

gives the reader an idea how *Araucaria* works, by displaying what the user actually sees on the screen after analyzing an argument. But in figure 2.1, only the items (D) to (K) are shown in the pane on the left. To see the rest you would have to scroll either up or down the pane further.

Another way of displaying the argument diagram can be automatically produced by clicking on FULL TEXT in the menu under the FILE icon on the toolbar. The full text diagram for the cranberry cask case is displayed in figure 2.2.

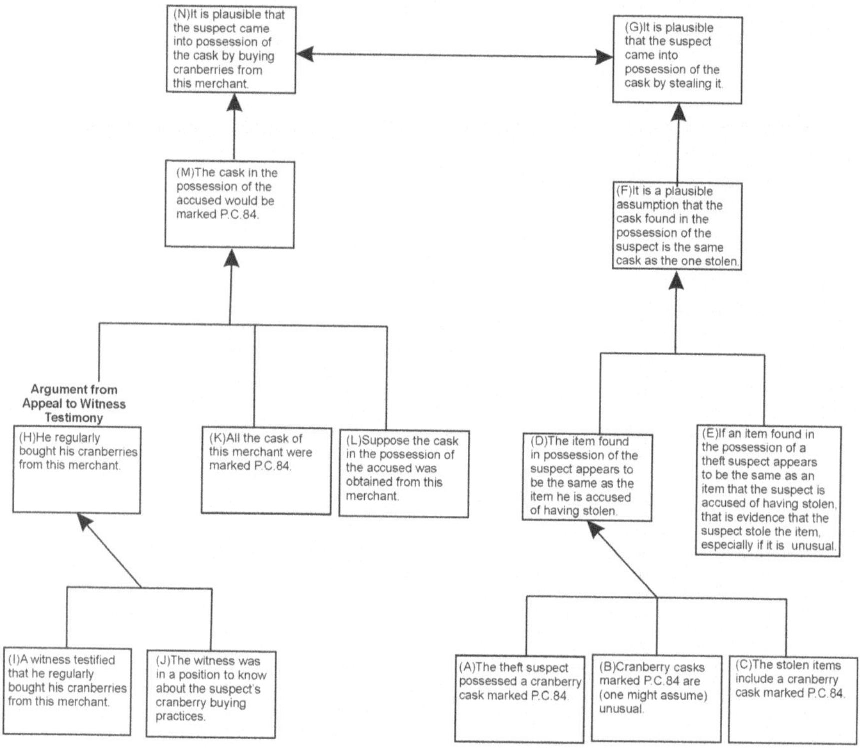

Fig. 2.2. Full Text Araucaria Diagram for the Cranberry Cask Case

Looking at figure 2.2, several features of the diagram can be explained. The original sequence of argumentation is displayed in the tree on the right. Statement (G) is the ultimate conclusion, and statements (A) through (F) function as premises or intermediate conclusions that support (G). Note however that (N) is displayed in a contrasting color, indicating it is a *refutation*, a counter-argument that is aimed at defeating (G). The chain of argumentation on the right all leads into (N), supporting it. Thus what the diagram represents is the evidence for a given statement on one side, and the contrary evidence opposing that statement on the other. *Araucaria* can thus represent refutation or rebuttal, a notion that will turn out to be important below.

Notice that several generalizations feature in the reasoning displayed in the diagram. One is (E), which appears to be a defeasible generalization, but one very important in evidence in criminal cases where stolen goods are involved. There are some other parts of the evidence in this case that depend on a generalization as well. The fact cited above, that the farmer regularly bought his cranberries from this merchant, was supported by further evidence. Numerous witnesses testified to the truth of this fact. The argument thus appears to depend on the generalization that witnesses generally tend to tell the truth. This generalization seems shaky, however, because we know that witnesses are often mistaken, sometimes lie, and generally tend to present an account that fits their own views and interests. Even so, argument from witness testimony does seem to be a common species of argumentation in law that is based on some kind of supporting generalization that is common to all the many cases where the evidence is based on any kind of witness testimony. On the computer screen, the argument from premises (I) and (J) to conclusion (H) is outlined in red, and marked "Appeal to Witness Testimony". This case illustrates how argumentation schemes can be applied to arguments to elicit the generalization used as a warrant to back the argument whereby a conclusion is supported by a premise or set of premises. The user can elicit the set of argumentation schemes from (Walton, 1996), and then click on to a scheme from the list and apply it to an argument in the *Araucaria* diagram. The user can also add new schemes to the list. The result is an argument diagram that displays not only all the premises and conclusions, and how they are joined to each other as arguments, but also argumentation schemes for each argument. In some cases, no known argumentation scheme fits an argument on the diagram. In such cases, the inference may be based on a generalization that can be stated, but does not correspond to a warrant in any known argumentation scheme.

The reconstruction of the argumentation in such a case does not represent the person's actual thinking, or chain of reasoning. But it does enable one to offer a normative model of how that reasoning should be reconstructed, based on the assumption that the arguer is a collaborative participant in some type of dialogue, discussion or investigation. In the case of an argument used as evidence in court, the framework of the dialogue will of course be that of the common law trial. There will be an ultimate *probandum*, and the network of argumentation as a whole will lead into that statement as its end point, as illustrated by the use of the diagram technique by Wigmore and Schum. This form of analysis can reveal a lot about the logical structure of generalizations and the arguments based on them. When conjoined with the known empirical facts of a given case, it is a tool than can help with the identification of generalizations in a case, with their analysis, and ultimately with their evaluation as strong or weak, reasonably justified by the facts or prejudicial and fallacious. As argumentation schemes and argument diagramming systems like *Araucaria* are applied to more and more cases of argumentation in trials, more and more common kinds of generalizations important for evidence law will be identified and analyzed.

6. Deductive and Inductive Generalizations

As a starting point for a theoretical discussion of generalizations, it is best to begin by considering what could be called the conventional or "official" view of them found in logic textbooks. For example, Hurley (2000, p. 38) distinguished between two types of statements as follows: "A particular statement is one that makes a claim about one or more particular members of a class, while a general statement makes a claim about all the members of a class". One might think that the expression 'general statement' can be taken to mean the same as the term 'generalization'. This does not turn out to be true however. A *generalization* is something that is produced by placing a quantifier (universal or existential) immediately prior to a statement and replacing one or more occurrences of a certain instantial letter that appears in the statement with the same variable that appears in the quantifier (Hurley, 2000, p. 433). In classical deductive logic the statements are expressed in a subject-predicate format. For example, where a is an individual and F is a predicate, the statement Fa asserts that a has property F. The universal generalization in classical logic is also a conditional. The universally quantified statement $(\forall x)(Fx \supset Gx)$ says that every individual x that has property F also has property G. It can be classified as an absolute universal generalization in the following sense: a finding of even one individual that has F, but fails to have G, refutes the generalization. An absolute generalization defaults permanently in the face of a single counter-example.

What should be said about existential generalizations? For example, suppose that Sp represents the statement 'Placido Domingo is a singer'. Then $(\exists x)(Sx)$ is an existential generalization representing the statement 'There is at least one singer'. On the official view of classical deductive logic, existentially quantified statements are taken to be generalizations. This view is divergent from common speech. In classical logic, 'some', in the sense represented by the existential quantifier, means literally 'at least one'. On this account, an existential generalization comes out true if only one individual has the property in question. Such an existentially quantified statement does not really seem like a generalization, according to the common meaning of the word. So what should we say here? Are statements prefaced by the existential quantifier generalizations or not? Maybe not, in the common meaning of the term, if 'some' is taken to mean 'at least one'.

Moving around the issue of existential generalizations, let's look at a conventional classification of generalizations presented in (Walton, 1999) that sees generalizations as more of the universal sort. According to this classification, there are three types of generalizations: (1) the universal (absolute) generalization, (2) the inductive (statistical) generalization, and (3) the presumptive generalization. The universal generalization is absolute, meaning that it refers to absolutely all the individuals in the domain of individuals in the subject statement without exception. For example, if we take the generalization 'All men are mortal' as an absolute one, it refers to all men without exception. Thus it is falsified by a single counter-example. To refute the generalization, all you need to do is to find a single case of a man who is not mortal. Let's say we let the predicate letter F stand for the property of being a man, and the predicate letter G stand for the property of being mortal. The universal generalization 'All men are mortal' may then be represented in classical deductive logic by a universal quantifier that governs a conditional. So construed, such a universal generalization has the following form:

$$(\forall x)(Fx \supset Gx)$$

Taking this universal generalization as one premise, and adding the premise that Socrates is a man, where a represents the individual Socrates, we get a deductively valid inference of the following form.

Deductively Valid Inference Based on a Universal Generalization (DVU)

$$\begin{array}{l} (\forall x)(Fx \supset Gx) \\ Fa \\ \hline Ga \end{array}$$

This familiar kind of inference is deductively valid, meaning that if the premises are true, then it can be inferred by logical necessity that the conclusion is too.

Inductive generalizations are not absolute in the way that universal generalizations of the kind associated with all-statements are taken to be. Typical examples of what are taken to be inductive generalizations are statements like 'Most emeralds found so far are green', or '98 per cent of emeralds found so far are green'. Inductive inferences typically have premises of this sort, used to set up inferences comparable to DVU. In this type of inductively strong inference, it is logically possible for both premises to be true even while the conclusion is false. But it is improbable to a greater or lesser degree, calculated by assigning numbers between zero and one to each of the statements, and using them to calculate the strength of the inference based on axioms of the probability calculus. But it should also be noted that absolute universal generalizations can function in some cases as premises in inductive arguments as well. For example, consider the following argument, "All emeralds previously found have been green; therefore the next emerald to be found will be green" (Hurley, 2000, p. 39). Hurley (2000, p. 39) classified this argument as inductive even though the premise is an absolute universal generalization of the kind defined above. Thus it would seem that deductive and inductive types of argument are distinguished not by the types of generalizations they contain as premises or conclusion, but by the nature of the inferential link between the premises and the conclusion.

In the past, absolute universal generalizations and inductive generalizations have commonly been considered in logic to be the only kind worth studying in the curriculum. The study of presumptive, defeasible generalizations that warrant plausible reasoning has been largely ignored by logic in the past, or treated in a purely negative fashion under the heading of fallacies. But in recent times this trend has begun to reverse itself, as defeasible reasoning has become a central concern for AI (Prakken, 2001). A prominent approach to defeasible reasoning in AI is called autoepistemic logic, meaning that it is a model of an ideal rational agent's reasoning about its own beliefs (Moore, 1985). There has also been a more positive approach in evidence law, following Schum's lead, to study how defeasible generalizations support legal argumentation (Anderson, 1999). But there was a precursor to these recent trends in logic towards a more realistic and practical approach to the study of generalizations, Alfred Sidgwick, an early critic of the narrowness of the longstanding preoccupation of logicians with deductive and inductive forms of reasoning. Sidgwick (1893, p. 23) observed that traditionally, logic has only been satisfied with a perfectly universal generalization as a proper basis for an inference. According to this way of thinking, if a rule is admitted to have even one exception, its value to support an inference is lost. Sidgwick argued against this deductivist view by suggesting that the kinds of generalizations we rely upon in argumentation tend to be more of the defeasible kind than of the absolutely universal kind (p. 23).

It is comparatively seldom in actual argument - never, perhaps, where a really disputed or difficult question is raised - that we are able to rest our case on a single faultless generalization, like "All men are mortal" or "Where there is smoke there is fire."

Legal argumentation is full of defeasible generalizations, like those cited by Schum in his analysis of the Sacco and Vanzetti case, that are neither deductive nor inductive. While sometimes weak, faulty, and even wrong in a way that makes them highly misleading, it is these more fallible kinds of generalizations that seem to be the most common.

7. The Third Type of Generalization

Wigmore (1931, p. 17) assumed that there are only two types of inference, deductive and inductive, basing this distinction on Sidgwick (1883) and other logical authorities of the period. Although Wigmore freely used the language of inference to the best explanation when discussing cases, he assumed that the reasoning used in such cases had to be reducible to deductive or inductive forms of argument. For example, Wigmore (1931, p. 20) considered several arguments of a kind commonly found in law.

Last week the witness *A* had a quarrel with the defendant *B*, therefore *A* is probably biased against *B*.

A was found with a bloody knife in *B*'s house, therefore *A* is probably the murderer of *B*.

These inferences are neither deductive nor inductive. They are classic examples of a third kind of argumentation that can best be analyzed by a presumptive argumentation scheme with an accompanying set of critical questions. A biased witness may be telling the truth, but if the argument above can be used in cross-examination to show the bias, it would cast doubt on the appeal to witness testimony as a plausible argument. Similar remarks can be made about the other inference. The finding of *A* with the bloody knife is evidence that supports the conclusion indicated, but only in a chain of argumentation based on generalizations that are defeasible presumptions. There could be other explanations of *A*'s having been found in the house with a bloody knife at the time. That fact may be best explained by the hypothesis of *A* murdering *B*, but it is only a hypothesis that can be supported or refuted by other evidence in the case. Thus the argument is best seen as an abductive or presumptive one. However, on the basis of studying these and other examples, Wigmore adopted the hypothesis that all logical inferences are either deductive or inductive. He concluded that the offering of evidence in court always conforms to the form of inference called inductive (p. 19), although he did recognize (p. 21) that the deductive form may occasionally be used. In his opinion, cases where deductive reasoning is used are (a) an inference involving a supposed general truth of natural science, and (b) testimonial evidence based on an inference involving a supposed general truth of testimonial psychology. This restriction to deductive and inductive reasoning was a weakness of Wigmore's approach, despite its over-all strength. Twining (1985, p. 179) wrote that a strength of Wigmore's approach is its close connection with the discourse and methods of argumentation actually used by lawyers and courts. On the other hand, Twining wrote (p. 179) that weaknesses of his approach are that it was tied to a view of rationality restricted to deduction and induction, and that it drew so heavily on what the writers on logic held about these forms of reasoning at the time.

Wigmore's chart method of diagramming evidence in a case, as can be seen by examining his case of Commonwealth v. Umilian and other cases charted in the *Principles*, makes plenty of use of forms of argumentation, like appeal to witness testimony and argument from sign, that are neither deductive nor inductive.[7] To make any argument diagramming method work, as applied to legal argumentation and evidence, one of the most important things that needs to be added in is the notion of the presumptive argumentation scheme. One aspect of the Wigmore method that is very important, as emphasized by Goodwin (2000, p. 235), is that charting is not an attempt to express reasons for belief, but to express reasons for doubt: "it is (thus) only by careful dissection of the implicit steps of inference that we can lay bare and locate the possibilities of doubt" (Wigmore, 1931, p. 14). Wigmore gave the example of mistakenly inferring that because a coat was found at the scene of a crime, the owner of the coat was the perpetrator. There are various grounds for doubt – the coat may not have been worn by the accused at the time of the assault, for example. Or although the accused may have been the wearer, he may not have been the assailant, but a bystander coming to the assistance of the victim. Wigmore (1931, p. 13) explicitly linked fallible inferences of the kind that are open to doubt with fallacies of the kind studied by Sidgwick (1883). Thus it is important to recognize that the basic purpose of the Wigmore

7 This case has been analyzed in *Araucaria* by Prakken, Reed and Walton (2003).

chart method is more negative than positive. It is to lay bare the possibilities of doubt by making the weak points in a chain of argumentation explicit. This fact is important in relating the Wigmore chart to recent developments in argumentation theory. Argumentation schemes represent typical presumptive forms of reasoning that need to be analyzed and evaluated in specific cases by using matching sets of critical questions. The critical questions function as a device to help make doubts explicit.

It is clear then why Wigmore, in his approach to rationality, failed to (at least explicitly) recognize the third type of argument, which nowadays might be called the abductive, presumptive or plausible argument (Walton, 2001). There remains much uncertainty, however, about what these terms exactly mean and what the differences between them are. Abductive inference is widely taken to be the same as inference to the best explanation (Josephson and Josephson, 1994). Presumptive reasoning is used to move an investigation or dialogue forward tentatively in the face of uncertainty and lack of knowledge. It is based on what is called a presumption, something that can be accepted by agreement temporarily as things go forward in the investigation, unless at some future point new evidence comes in showing it to be unacceptable. Both inductive and presumptive reasoning are nonmonotonic, meaning that when new premises are added to the inference, it can be defeated. Plausible reasoning is based on the notion of plausibility, meaning that a statement seems to be true, based on initial appearances in a case, consistency with other supposed facts in the case, and on testing. A plausible inference is one that can be drawn from given apparent facts, leading to a conclusion that seems to be true, based on those facts as given. It is disputable what the difference is between inductive and plausible reasoning, but one difference is that the negation rule for the axioms of the probability calculus does not apply to plausible reasoning. In other words, one statement can be plausible on a given body of evidence, even though its negation is also plausible, on another given body of evidence in the same case. This situation is typical of a case at trial where each side has a plausible argument, relative to its account of the facts. What this possibility can be taken to show is that plausibility is relative to a given body of evidence or database in the case (Rescher, 1976). At any rate, whatever you want to call it, there is some third kind of reasoning over and above deductive and inductive reasoning, and this third kind of reasoning seems to be extremely common in legal argumentation.

Probably the reason the third kind of generalization has been less widely recognized in logic until recently is that it is less reliable because it is subject to default and fallacies, as indicated above. It could be called presumptive generalization, but there is even less agreement on how to define, label or quantify it, than is the case with universal or inductive generalizations. This type of generalization is associated with a generic statement like 'Birds fly'. Such a statement asserts only that birds generally fly, in the limited sense that birds can generally be expected to fly, unless there is information to the contrary in a given case. This kind of generalization is subject to exceptions, as in cases where Tweety the bird is an ostrich, a penguin, or a bird with a broken wing. Acceptance of this kind of generalization is tentative, meaning that it is open to new evidence that might come in at some later stage of an investigation or argument and might defeat the generalization, as applied to that case. Thus this third class of generalizations is said to be defeasible, meaning those falling into it can default, or fail to continue to hold, as new evidence comes into a case.

Presumptive generalizations, like inductive generalizations, but unlike deductive ones, can still hold (generally) even when there is a known counter-example in a specific case. Deductive inference has the property called monotonicity, meaning that if you add a new premise to a valid deductive inference, it will always remain valid. It is not open to new information, so to speak. Both inductive inference and the third type of inference, which we might call presumptive, as shown below, are nonmonotonic. If defeasibility is taken to be equivalent to nonmonotonicity, both inductive and presumptive inferences are defeasible. A monotonic argument is one that stays correct, to the same standard, no matter how many new premises are added. For example, deductive arguments are monotonic. They stay valid if new premises are added. A defeasible argument, in contrast, can default if a new premise is added. Prakken (2001, p. 191) proposed that defeasibility can be taken to be equivalent to nonmonotonicity, when both properties are applied to arguments.

To see how defeasibility works in a presumptive type of inference, it helps to look once again at the "canonical example" cited by Reiter (1987, p. 149) and many other sources in AI.

The Tweety Inference

Generally, birds fly.

Tweety is a bird.

Tweety flies.

This type of inference preserves a property that could be called plausibility (Rescher, 1976). The statements in the premises and conclusion can be judged to be more or less plausible according to a weak ordering of a larger set of statements representing the data in a given case. Then the strength of the inference can be judged by considering whether the plausibility value of the premises, once the statements in the premises and conclusion are all considered as a group, increase the plausibility value of the conclusion or not. The rule for making such an adjustment is called the *least plausible premise rule* or Theophrastus' Rule (Renon, 1998, p. 112). It is used by Rescher's (1976) system of plausible reasoning as follows: if the inference is structurally correct, once the plausibility value of each premise has been determined, then the conclusion is judged to be at least as plausible as the least plausible premise. There are other rules, called "confidence factors", that have been used in AI to evaluate plausible reasoning. But the least plausible premise rule is one of the most common.

As Reiter (1987, p. 149) and other analysts of defeasible reasoning in computing have often indicated, inferences like the canonical example are judged in relation to an assumption of "absence of information to the contrary". They are lack-of-evidence inferences of a kind associated in logic with argument from ignorance, traditionally called the *argumentum ad ignorantiam*. As shown in chapter 1, section 7, this form of argumentation was traditionally called a fallacy, but more recent research has shown that it is often a reasonable form of argumentation based on a shifting burden of proof. In the absence of any known evidence that refutes a defeasible presumption in a given case, however, drawing an inference based on it can be justified as tentatively acceptable on a balance of considerations. Should new information come in yielding evidence that defeats the claim, the proponent of the original inference must retract that claim. Thus a presumptive generalization is best seen as only shifting a burden of proof to one side or the other in a dialogue format. The proponent first puts forward the defeasible argument as plausible, based on a presumptive generalization as applied to the data collected so far in the case. As long as the respondent finds and reports no counter-example to the generalization, the plausible inference can be used to justify the claim. For example, if there is no evidence in the data collected so far in the case that Tweety is a non-flier, both proponent and respondent can judge the conclusion that Tweety flies as acceptable, on a balance of considerations in relation to what is known now. The proponent has to prove that the premises of the inference are plausible, but if she can do that, the respondent is obliged to accept the conclusion as also relatively plausible. However, suppose the respondent can present a counter-example to the generalization on which the inference was based. Then the burden of proof is reversed. The inference is defeated and the proponent must present a different argument if she wants to maintain the claim made in the conclusion. This reversal of the burden of proof is what is most deeply characteristic of presumptive reasoning from a defeasible generalization, as opposed to the deductive and inductive kinds of inference based on universal generalizations and inductive generalizations.

Presumptive reasoning is based on generalizations representing what is taken to be the normal or expected flow of events in a case that all parties to the argumentation are familiar with. Once a counter-example to the generalization is presented, showing that the case is exceptional in a certain relevant respect, the inference defaults. However, it may not be inductively predictable by statistical methods when an exception will turn up in a case. What matters is whether the case is typical, in relation to the generalization that is the premise of the plausible inference put forward by a proponent. The generalization holds only subject to qualifications. Sometimes the types of qualifications can be listed in advance, thus channeling the lines of rebuttal open to the respondent along certain routes (Keppens and Zeleznikow, 2002). But sometimes the defaults cannot be anticipated systematically. For example, the fact that Tweety has a broken wing means that, although normally he could fly, his flying capability is temporarily atypical in this particular case. That is why one needs to be open-minded about presumptive generalizations and the inferences drawn from them. Such inferences are often associated with prejudices, stereotypical reasoning, rigid thinking and fallacies. They are valuable logical tools in drawing tentative conclusions under conditions of uncertainty and lack of knowledge, but working with them demands care and caution. They can be weak arguments, they can default as an investigation proceeds, and they can be misleading if too much weight is put onto them.

The theory of plausible generalizations requires three components. The first is a database *D* containing a set of statements. These statements can all be expressed in a subject-predicate format, like those in classical deductive logic. For example, if *A* is the statement 'Tweety is a bird', it can be expressed as *Bt*, where *t* stands for the individual Tweety and *B* stands for the property of being a bird. The second is an investigation, *I*, in which new statements are being added to the database. The investigation is a dynamic process, with a beginning point and an end point. If the investigation is cumulative, once a statement has been inserted into the database, it can never be removed. But some investigations are non-cumulative, meaning that retraction is allowed. The third component is the defeasible conditional of the form $A \Rightarrow B$ which means 'generally, but subject to exceptions, if *A* is in the data base, then *B* can be inserted into it'. This type of conditional has an open structure with gaps in it. Consider the example 'Generally, if anything is a bird then it flies'. This conditional could hold as a generalization, but fail to warrant an inference based on it if the investigation turns up a counter-example, like a case of a bird that does not fly. There are also the issues of exactly how the defeasible conditional should be defined, and whether it should be prefaced by a defeasible quantifier, the "generally but subject to exceptions" quantifier. These issues have not been solved so far, but as indicated in the example discussed below, both need to be defined in relation to a dynamic model of argumentation used in search procedures in an investigation that may be incomplete.

Characteristic of the reasoning based on a defeasible conditional are arguments having the form of defeasible *modus ponens* (DMP). Verheij (2000, p. 5) called this form of argument *modus non excipiens*, and contrasted it with deductive *modus ponens*. Such an argument can be reasonable in an investigation, but as long as the investigation is still open, it is subject to default. Consider the Tweety inference once again. This inference could be quite reasonable in an investigation, and the conclusion could hold as a presumption, based on the premises holding at some earlier point in the investigation. But suppose the investigation discovers the fact that Tweety is a penguin, and another generalization, 'Penguins do not fly', is already in the database. This generalization could be absolute or defeasible. In either case, it, and the statement that Tweety is a penguin, are enough, when put together in the data base, to make the Tweety inference default.

What this reveals is that plausible reasoning needs to be evaluated relative to the evidence in a database. A statement that is plausible in relation to a set of other statements in a database may be, taken by itself, quite implausible. How plausible reasoning should be judged to be in a given case depends on how far an investigation has gone along, and how much data has been collected at that point.

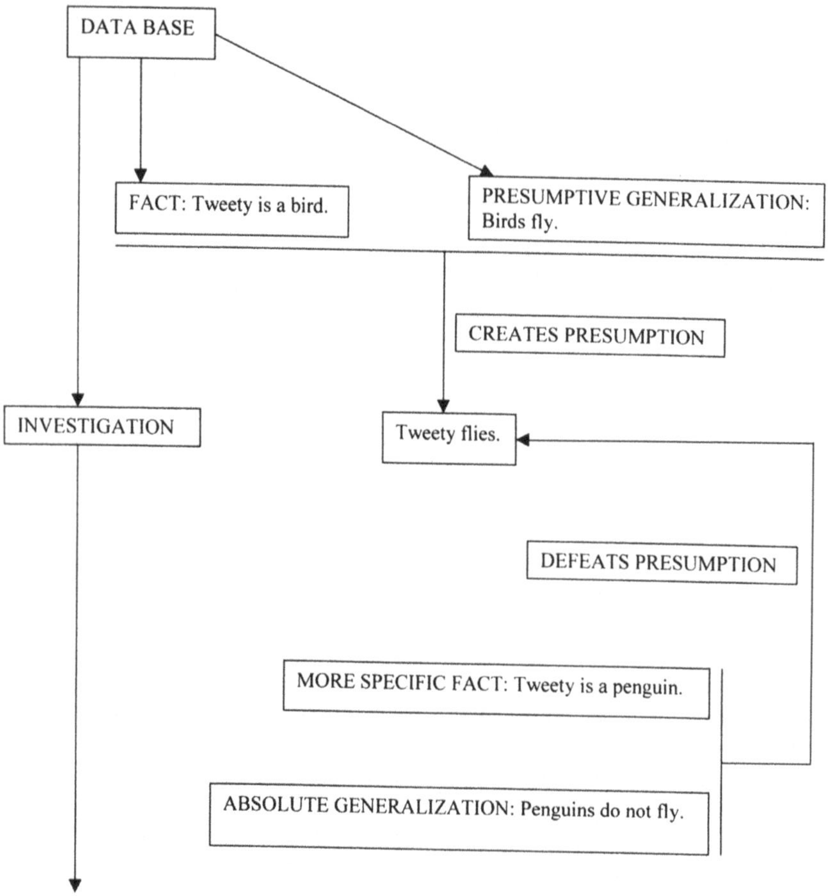

Fig. 2.3. How a Presumptive Inference Defaults in an Investigation

Let's examine figure 2.3 to see how the standard sequence of argumentation from premises in a database leads to the default of a presumptive argument as an investigation proceeds. The first step is finding two statements by the search procedure of the investigation, 'Tweety is a bird' and 'Birds fly'. Let's call the first type of statement a fact. It is a particular statement found in the database, a kind of statement that attributes a property to an individual. When the latter statement also turns up in the database, it combines with the fact in a linked argument, presumptively generating the conclusion 'Tweety flies'. So far, the inference is presumptively reasonable. But then suppose that a new development occurs. As the investigation proceeds, the search procedure finds a new fact, 'Tweety is a penguin', and links it with an absolute generalization found in the database, 'Penguins do not fly'. Let's say this is taken to be an absolute generalization, stating that no penguins fly (none at all). The linked argument produced by combining these two premises is deductively valid. Thus it is stronger than the original argument to the same conclusion, "Tweety flies', and defeats that argument. If it were only a presumptive type of argument, based on the presumptive generalization 'Penguins generally (but subject to exceptions) do not fly', the outcome could be a deadlock. Or it could depend on which of the two arguments is stronger (more plausible). Below, an analysis of the difference between the universal quantifier of deductive logic and a new defeasible quantifier will be shown to determine how such cases should be judged.

Much remains unknown about the third type of generalization, and the kind of plausible reasoning it warrants. The standard approach to autoepistemic logic has been based on a modal logic structure in which an agent reasons about its own set of beliefs. The approach taken above has been different from the traditional one in several respects. In this new approach, an investigation is underway in which statements are inserted into a database (or removed from it) as the investigation proceeds. Rather than being based on a framework of knowledge and belief, the structure is based on statements being inserted into or deleted from a database, where the database represents a commitment store. This does not necessarily imply that such statements are known by an agent or believed by an agent. By showing how generalizations function in a sequence of argumentation in this framework in the canonical example, some insight into its importance and its leading characteristics has been gained.

8. Defeasible Generalizations and Arguments from Ignorance

Defeasible arguments often move ahead under conditions of uncertainty and lack of knowledge by making presumptions. One mode of making such presumptions is the form of argumentation associated with the argument from ignorance: if statement A is not known to be true (false), it is presumed to be false (true). This type of argument has typically been taken to be a fallacy in the logic textbooks (Krabbe, 1995). But in many cases of legal argumentation, it can be shown to be quite reasonable. The presumption of death in law is an example. If there has been no evidence for the past five years that an individual is alive, then for purposes of dividing his estate, he may be presumed to be dead. This form of reasoning is based on reversal of the burden of proof, a highly useful device in legal argumentation (Prakken, 1991). Normally if a claim is made that some person is dead, the burden of proof is on the proponent to support the claim by giving reasons if challenged to do so. The legal presumption above reverses this burden: anyone who claims that the individual is alive is obliged to support that claim. The reason that law invokes such a burden-reversing form of argumentation is practical. It is a useful device for dealing with problems posed by estates and wills of persons who have disappeared.

Another example will help to amplify some aspects of this form of reasoning and show how it relates to generalizations.

The Speed Limit Example

Alice and Bruce are driving along, and she asks him, "What is the speed limit on this street?" He replies, "Wherever no sign is posted, the speed limit is 50k per hour".

Bruce's reply can be taken as a general rule of a kind that warrants an inference in a sequence of reasoning shown in figure 2.4.

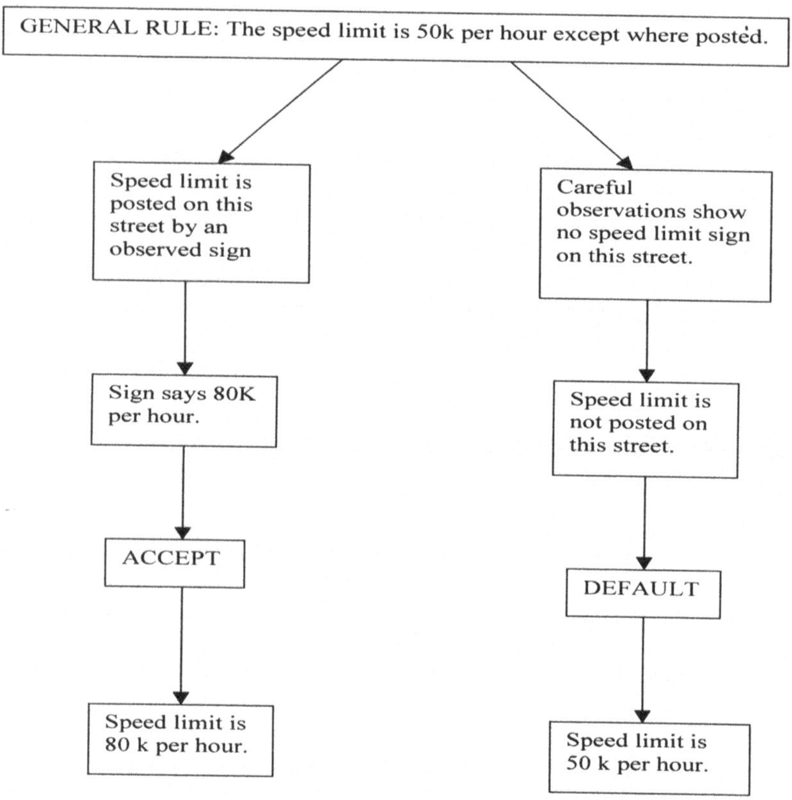

Fig. 2.4. Drawing of an Inference in the Speed Limit Case

There are two possibilities: either the speed limit is posted by a sign or not. If it is posted, then the speed limit is whatever is indicated on the sign. If it is not posted, then the speed limit is 50k per hour. Alice can then make observations as she drives along the street. If she sees no sign, then that is evidence there is no sign. That evidence, or lack of evidence, leads to a chain of reasoning prompting an argument from ignorance. If she doesn't see a sign, or any evidence of one marking the speed limit on this street, after driving along some ways, that can be taken as a reason to infer that the speed limit here is 50k per hour. Of course, that is just a presumption. But as Alice drives along, the more that observation indicates the lack of any such sign, the stronger is the inference to the conclusion that there is no such sign.

The speed limit example shows how negation, or argument from ignorance, can be used to move defeasible reasoning forward in a situation of uncertainty and lack of knowledge. Alice may know that the normal speed limit inside the city is 50k per hour, and she may know that there are exceptions to this general rule. But she is unsure about this street they are driving on. It looks like people are driving pretty fast, suggesting that the speed limit may be higher than 50k per hour, but she knows she should be cautious while driving on a city street. Thus she is in a quandary. She knows there is a general rule that the speed limit is normally 50k per hour in the city, and she knows that there are exceptions. But given the lack of visible signs posting any speed limit, she doesn't know whether this street falls under one of the exceptions or not. Bruce solves the problem using argument from ignorance, which reverses the burden of proof. Alice can infer that since there is no speed limit posted on this street, she must assume that it is not an exception to the rule. In other words, she must draw the conclusion that the speed limit on this street is 50k per hour. The argument from ignorance, as the evidence builds up through observations and searching, warrants a presumptive epistemic closure that seals off the existence of exceptions to the general rule. However, an inference of this sort can still be defeated. If there was no sign, but a 'Speed limit 80k per hour' suddenly became visible, the argument from ignorance would default. It holds only as long as there is no evidence of a sign posting a specific speed limit.

Arguments from ignorance are common in legal argumentation (Saunders, 1993). It has often been remarked upon, in textbook commentaries on *argumentum ad ignorantiam*, that although this form of argument is generally fallacious, there is one setting where it is not. That setting is the criminal trial, where all the defense has to prove to win the trial is that the prosecution has not proved that the defendant committed the crime s/he is charged with. In other words, if it has not been shown that the defendant is guilty, it has been shown that s/he is not guilty. As is often remarked in logic textbooks, the argument from ignorance in such cases is based on the initial distribution of burden of proof in the trial (Hamblin, 1970). The prosecution must prove the charge beyond reasonable doubt, whereas the defense need only show that the prosecution's argument is open to doubt, in order to win. This much said, how burdens and presumptions work in trials is a complex subject. The term 'burden of proof' is ambiguous. It can refer to burden of persuasion or burden of production (Park, Leonard and Goldberg, 1998, p. 88). The former represents the degree to which the factfinder must be persuaded for the claim or defense to be proved (p. 89). The latter "pinpoints, at key moments in the trial, whether a particular party is subject to a peremptory motion if that party does not produce further evidence to support its claim or defense" (p. 93). Thus argument from ignorance appears at a global level, concerning proof of the ultimate *probandum* in a trial. But it also appears at a local level, concerning arguments "at key moments" in a trial.

Argument from ignorance is also a common kind of reasoning in computer science. A typical example begins with a search through a data base (a set of statements), and ends in a finding that the statement searched for is not in it. The conclusion drawn, by default, is that the statement is false. A good example offered by Reiter (1987) is that of the person at Vancouver Airport who scans all the airport monitor listings to see if there is a direct flight between Vancouver and Tokyo. She sees no such flight listed. She is assured that all flights that day going out of Vancouver are listed on the monitors. She draws the conclusion that there is no such direct flight. She could always confirm it by asking at the desk. In such a case, the person is using an *argumentum ad ignorantiam.* The argument could be a reasonable one, on the assumption that all flights going out of Vancouver are indeed listed on the monitors. Reiter calls this the *closed world assumption,* meaning that one is assuming that the data base contains all the relevant information. The data base could be said to be "complete" in this sense.

The argumentation scheme for the argument from ignorance can be put in the following simplified form (to be compared with the more elaborate version given in (Walton, 1996, p. 124). *A* is a statement.

Lack of Knowledge Premise: *A* is not known to be true.

Completeness Premise: If *A* were true, *A* would be known to be true.

Conclusion: *A* is false.

In many cases of argument from ignorance, an investigation or search is underway for information, or to prove or disprove a hypothesis. The completeness premise, in such a case, amounts to the assumption that the search has been so thorough, or so complete, that it would have turned up the statement sought, if that statement were really there to be found. Another common kind of case of argument from ignorance is an appeal to expert opinion, where it is assumed that the expert knows so much about a given subject that if some important statement in the subject were known to be true, this expert would know it. When the expert says she does not have a statement in her knowledge base, the inference can be drawn that it must therefore be false.

A controversy about argument from ignorance is whether the argumentation scheme above, by itself, is sufficient to judge cases where this argument occurs, or whether more needs to be known about the progress of an investigation, the stage it is in, the standard of proof required for completeness, and other matters that could be described as contextual. One of these important contextual matters is burden of proof. These matters will be treated in chapter 3 under the heading of lack of evidence, but one observation that will be important later could be ventured. It can be remarked that argument from ignorance can depend on how a term in an investigation or discussion is defined. The following example will show this.

The Drug/Herb Example

If something is classified as a drug, the burden of proof is on the manufacturer to prove it is safe by conducting clinical trials of a kind required by law before the drug can be marketed. If something is classified as a herb, it can be marketed without any kind of proof of safety. However, if people taking the herbal remedy have significant health problems indicating it may be dangerous, the herb may then be taken off the market.

This example shows how the burden of proof can be reversed, depending on how a substance is classified. It also shows how the argument from ignorance is dependent on burden of proof which, in turn, may be dependent on a verbal classification. This example is especially significant because it suggests that evaluating cases of argument from ignorance may depend on contextual matters that are outside of the factors considered purely by the argumentation scheme. This thesis will turn out to be significant below, when we come to discuss how defeasibility depends on classification.

9. Abstraction and the Defeasible Quantifier

In one of the most famous cases in English law (Donoghue v. Stevenson, 1932, A.C. 562, House of Lords), a woman drank a bottle of ginger beer containing the decomposed remains of a snail, afterwards suffering shock and severe gastroenteritis. Because of the dark tint of the bottle, the snail remains were not detected until most of the contents were drunk. She sued the Scottish manufacturer of the ginger beer, on the basis that he owed a duty to her as a consumer to take care that there should be no harmful contents in the product she bought from him. This general rule that is the basis of her argument can be formulated at different levels of generality. Three of them are quoted below from the analysis of the case by Twining and Miers (1976, p. 179), and I have added a fourth.

Level 1: Scottish manufacturers of ginger beer in opaque bottles owe a duty of care not to allow dead snails to get into the product.

Level 2: Manufacturers of ginger beer owe a duty of care not to allow any snails to get into the product.

Level 3: Manufacturers of articles of food and drink owe a duty of care not to allow any noxious physical foreign body to get into the product.

Level 4: Manufacturers of any product owe a duty of care that the product is not made in such a way that it causes harm to the consumer.

Twining and Miers (1976, p. 179) suggested that in building his argument in court, the advocate for the prosecution would probably be wise to choose level 3. The reason, they indicated, is that the court would likely hold that level 1 and level 2 were "too narrow". By the same reasoning, level 4 might be too broad. But the choice between 3 and 4 might vary with different arguments used at different points in the presentation of the case, and with the level of generality with which the existing rules of law were stated.

At any rate, the analysis of this case by Twining and Miers shows very clearly how generalizations of the kind on which legal argumentation is based can be expressed at different levels of abstraction. The levels of abstraction are determined by inclusion relationships of genus and species, forming a ladder of abstraction.[8] For example, the following ladder has the most inclusive term at the top, and goes downwards to greater specificity, with the least inclusive term of the set at the bottom.

Ladder of Abstraction

Any Manufactured Product

Manufactured Food and Drink

Manufactured Ginger Beer

Ginger Beer Manufactured in Bottles

Ginger Beer Manufactured in Opaque Bottles

Ginger Beer Manufactured in Opaque Bottles in Scotland

Ginger Beer Manufactured in Opaque Bottles in Scotland Containing Decomposed Snail Remains

The levels of generality in the ladder of abstraction are the reverse of the list of four levels of generality presented above.

These observations raise many questions about how generalizations support legal argumentation and how to define the notion of a generalization. One is whether abstraction and generalization are the same thing, or different things that depend on each other in some intimate way. There is quite a literature on abstraction in artificial intelligence, and one can easily see why. In goal-directed reasoning of the kind typical of planning in AI, a sequence of actions can be broken down into subgoals and subactions that link together in a chain tying an abstract goal at one end to a highly specific set of actions or bodily movements at the other end (Russell and Norvig, 1995, pp. 335-364). Action sequences of this sort have

[8] The tree of abstraction is familiar in the AI literature (Gelfond and Przymusinska, 1990). A ladder of abstraction is a linear way representing levels of abstraction. A tree structure can be used to display the inclusion relationships.

long been studied in the field of philosophy called theory of action (Goldman, 1970). One thing that makes such a chain of reasoning hang together, and make sense as a connected sequence of rational thinking, is that the same action is re-expressed at different levels of abstraction at different points in the chain. If studies of actions in this literature help us to understand what abstraction is, and how it works in reasoning, what does that tell us about generalizations, and how they work in legal argumentation?

Another question is whether a generalization is simply a matter of the quantifier, like 'all', 'many' or 'some', that appears in the sentence expressing the generalization. It looks to be so from the way generalizations are treated in the logic textbooks, as indicated above. Or is a generalization at least partly defined by the level of abstraction of the terms used in the sentence? The analysis of the role of generalizations in the Donoghue case above suggests that abstraction plays an important role in defining what we consider to be a generalization, and how general we consider it to be. It also suggests that generalization is a relative notion, meaning that some generalizations are more general than others. It seems that ladders of abstraction are what help us to judge degrees of generality of a related set of statements about the same action or case. This notion of a ladder of abstraction will be one of the tools used in the analysis of presumptive generalizations that follows. The other tool is a new kind of quantifier.

Corresponding to the absolutely universal quantifier $(\forall x)Fx$, meaning "For all x, without exception, x is an F". An example is the statement 'All cows are mammals'. There is also a generally universal quantifier $(\#x)Fx$, meaning "For xs generally, subject to exceptions, x is an F". Let's call this the defeasible quantifier for short. An example is the generalization expressed in the statement 'Birds fly', meaning that they generally fly, subject to exceptions. In classical quantifier logic, the following inference is deductively valid, meaning that if the premise is true, then necessarily, the conclusion is true too.

$(\forall x)\ Fx$

Therefore Fa

An example would be the inference, 'All individuals are, without exception, entities; therefore this individual is an entity'. Corresponding to this deductively valid form of inference there is the presumptively plausible form of inference below.

$(\#x)\ Fx$

Therefore Fa

An example would be the inference, 'Individuals generally, but subject to exceptions, are stable entities; therefore this individual is a stable entity'.

To see how the logic of generally universal quantifiers is different from the logic of absolutely universal quantifiers, it is necessary to see generality as a relative notion. Some statements, in other words, are more general than others. One important criterion of relative generality is the notion of genus-species inclusion. For example, the class of penguins is a subspecies of the class of birds. Therefore, the statement 'Birds have beaks' is more general than the statement 'Penguins have beaks'. Thus in deductive logic, the following syllogism is valid.

All birds have beaks.

All penguins are birds.

Therefore all penguins have beaks.

The form of this inference is that of the *AAA1* syllogism, called Barbara. Now let's compare this inference with the reasoning pictured in figure 1 above. This chain of reasoning started with the Tweety inference.

Generally, birds fly

Tweety is a bird.

Tweety flies.

This linked argument was reasonable as a presumptive inference, and both premises were in the database. Thus the argument supported the conclusion that Tweety flies. But it defaulted, once the new data was discovered that Tweety is a penguin. Now we get to the problem posed above. Does this new finding defeat the original Tweety inference, showing its conclusion to be no longer acceptable? Or is there merely a deadlock between the two opposed claims 'Tweety flies' and 'Tweety does not fly'? There are two cases to be considered, in evaluating this kind of situation.

One case is that where 'Penguins do not fly' is taken as an absolute generalization. In this case, the original Tweety inference is defeated. The new conclusion 'Tweety does not fly' replaces it at the lower part of the chain of argumentation. The other case is that where 'Penguins do not fly' is taken as a defeasible generalization. Let's suppose that 'Penguins do not fly' is taken as being a merely a defeasible generalization, as opposed to an absolute one. For example, let's suppose for the sake of argument that it has been discovered that there are penguins who have learned to fly over short distances between ice floes by running, then flapping their stubby wings. Let's say that this action is taken to count as "flying", and that, therefore, it is conceded as factual that in some unusual cases, penguins fly. Thus the defeasible generalization 'Penguins do not fly', on this supposition, could be contrasted with the absolute generalization, 'Ostriches do not fly', assuming we take it as factual that no ostriches fly. Then how should the chain of reasoning represented above be evaluated? The answer is based on the fact that the category of penguins is less general than the category of birds. It is based on the ladder of abstraction for birds and penguins. Thus, using the criterion of greater specificity provided by the ladder of abstraction, the original Tweety inference is defeated, once the statement 'Tweety is a penguin' has been found in, or inserted into, the original database.

10. Evaluating Argumentation Based on Generalizations

Based on this analysis of how defeasible reasoning should be evaluated in an investigation that keeps turning up new facts and generalizations, a new approach to generalizations based on five methodological tools can be offered. The first tool we need is the argument diagram. *Araucaria* is an especially useful system for analyzing legal evidence, as shown in the cranberry cask case above, because it can display argumentation schemes. A second tool we need is an analysis of the notion of one argument attacking another that distinguishes between two ways of attacking an argument. One is for the attacking argument to attack the conclusion of the original argument. One argument attacks another, in this strong sense, if the conclusion of the one is the opposite (negation) of the conclusion of the other. Thus it follows as a theorem that if a first argument attacks a second, the second also attacks the first. This notion of attack is represented by the *refutation* (double arrow) on an *Araucaria* diagram. But there is also another notion of attack. One argument can attack another by attacking the inferential link between the premises and conclusion of the original argument. A third way is by attacking the premises of the original argument, but we shall not be concerned with this possibility here. Matching the notion of attack, we also need a notion of defeat.

Defeasibility is an important characteristic of arguments based on presumptive generalizations, and so we need a definition of the notion of one argument defeating another. Pollock (1985) drew a distinction between two kinds of arguments that can defeat another argument: rebutting defeaters and undercutting defeaters. A rebutting defeater gives a reason for denying a claim (Pollock, 1995, 40). Thus a rebutting defeater attacks the claim, or conclusion of the argument it is aimed at. An undercutting defeater, in contrast, attacks the connection between the claim and the reason rather than attacking the claim directly (p. 41). Pollock's example (p. 41) illustrates how an undercutting defeater attacks an argument. First, let's consider the original argument in Pollock's example, as paraphrased below.

Fact: This object looks red to me.

Generalization: When an object looks red, then (normally, but subject to exceptions) it is red.

Conclusion: This object is red.

Now consider another argument that undercuts the one above.

Fact: This object is illuminated by a red light.

Generalization: when an object is illuminated by a red light this can make it look red even though it is not.

Conclusion: This object is not red.

According to Pollock (p. 41) this argument is an undercutting defeater but not a rebutting defeater, because of yet another generalization: red objects look red in red light too. Thus the object may still be red, despite the counter-argument above. The counter-argument, however, does undercut the original argument, because it attacks the connection between the claim and the reason. A legal example is the following argument (Prakken, 2002).

Fact: This object looks like an affidavit.

Generalization: If something looks like an affidavit, then it is an affidavit.

Conclusion: This object is an affidavit.

This argument, although obviously defeasible, surely represents a common form of legal reasoning. It is based on a presumption that guides an investigation or action forward, unless a defeater appears. For example, on a more detailed reading of the document, evidence might be found indicating it is not a real affidavit.

The third tool is the distinction between absolute and defeasible generalizations. The defeasible generalization that is the basis of Pollock's example above can be expressed at an even higher level of generality as follows: whenever something looks like an x then it is an x, where x is a variable for any kind of object that can be observed. But, as noted above, this generalization is defeasible, because it is subject to exceptions. Thus arguments based on it are open to attack and defeat.

The fourth tool is the ladder of abstraction. In the data base represented as part of an investigation in figure 1, there needs to be a set of ladders of abstraction representing the genus-species relations, and thus the levels of abstraction of each of the key terms used in any generalization that plays a role in the chain of reasoning in the argumentation. In current AI methodology, such ladders of abstraction are represented by tree structures. Each term in the database is placed at a node, and the branches (lines connecting the nodes) represent genus-species inclusions. Thus in any given case, there is a way of deciding which term is more abstract, i.e. more general, than any other term it is related to as a species or genus.

Sidgwick (1893, p. 8) observed that we never draw an inference from an observed fact to an unobserved conclusion without basing the inference on a generalization. Thus he was led to the following generalization: "inference, we find, always involves generalization" (p. 8). From this generalization he was led to draw an inference linking generalizations to the criticism of inferences (p.9).

Since, then, our inferences from fact to fact depend upon our belief in *general rules* of connection between fact and fact, generalizations about the way things happen in nature, the work of criticizing inferences resolves itself into that of criticizing generalizations.

Drawing this inference was an important insight in its time, because it linked the two subjects of asking critical questions and criticizing generalizations. The fifth tool is the set of critical questions matching the argumentation scheme for the type of argument put forward.

These five tools, when used together, offer a method for handling argumentation based on presumptive and other kinds of generalizations. In this approach, in general, but subject to exceptions, an argument based on an absolute generalization defeats an argument based only on a comparable defeasible generalization. Such a defeat can, in some cases, fail to occur because the absolute generalization is less plausible than the opposing defeasible generalization, meaning it is less well supported by the evidence collected from the data base and employed in the chain of argumentation at the given point where the evaluation is made. When there is a deadlock between two arguments that were each based on a chain of reasoning containing a generalization as a key premise, the argument based on the more specific generalization is judged to be the stronger (more plausible). The rationale behind this evaluation rule is explained by the analysis of the argumentation in the modified Tweety case presented above.

However, using the more specific generalization as a basis for one's argument is not always the best method. Twining and Mier's analysis of the Donoghue case showed that in arguing a case at trial, basing your reasoning on the more abstract generalization may offer the argument that is most convincing to the court. Noting this discrepancy, it is wise to resist the temptation to think that arguments based on generalizations should always be evaluated only on the basis of how general or how specific the generalization is. Generalizations need to be evaluated differently in different arguments depending on how the argument fits into an investigation, and on the stage of the investigation the argument is used in. It is this dynamic factor of argument use that is most important in evaluating argumentation based on generalizations. The tool of the critical questions is highly useful in this regard. As an investigation proceeds, critical questions can be asked that undercut a given presumptive argument at that point in the investigation unless the questions can be adequately answered. Asking the right question at the right point in the investigation can make an argument default until the question is answered.

As shown above, presumptive generalizations have qualifier gaps in them. They are subject to exceptions. As an investigation proceeds, new evidence can come in informing of an exception that fits into a qualifier gap. Once such new evidence fits the qualifier gap in a generalization, the inference based on it defaults. Thus the epistemic attitude best suited to arguing with presumptive generalizations at a midpoint of an investigation, before epistemic closure has been reached, is one of openness to new evidence. The kind of rationality involved is a willingness to give up a claim in the face of evidence that defeats or undercuts it. In scientific argumentation, this kind of evidential situation is the requirement associated with falsification of a hypothesis. If a counter-example to a universal generalization is found, for example, the generalization must be given up. To argue otherwise represents a kind of irrational or fallacious reasoning.

As shown in the car and prejudice examples cited above, the fallacy of hasty generalization can, in some instances, take the form of faulty inductive reasoning from a sample that is too small or unrepresentative to a general conclusion. The hearsay and Euthydemus examples involve arguments based on a presumptive generalization of a kind that is inherently open to exceptions. These arguments are not inductive but plausibilistic in nature. Contrasting with both types is the deductive argument based on an absolute universal generalization of the kind represented by the universal quantifier in classical first-order logic. These generalizations can be ranked in order of strictness. The absolute universal generalization is the strictest, admitting of no exceptions. The inductive generalization is based on probability, generating arguments that are not so strict. The least strict is the presumptive generalization, which is inherently subject to qualifications, and which can easily default in a way that is not possible to predict, as new evidence enters an investigation. Such presumptive generalizations are the warrants on which argumentation schemes, like appeal to witness testimony, for example, are based. One potential fallacy arises from confusion or uncertainty about which of these three categories a generalization in a given case fits. To treat a generalization as more strict than is appropriate is a failure of openness to new evidence. Thus to treat an appeal to witness testimony as a kind of argumentation that warrants its conclusion absolutely, and that could not possibly be open to critical questioning, is a form of this fallacy.

Also interesting from a fallacy perspective is the recognition that generalizations in legal evidence are so often put forward as parts of arguments from ignorance. The argument from ignorance functions as a device to provisionally close off lack of knowledge and move to a presumptive conclusion. But such an argument holds only relative to the lack of knowledge turned up by an investigation that has proceeded so far. Once again, it is a defeasible form of argument. The same attitude of openness to new evidence and critical questioning is a requirement of its non-fallacious use.

Chapter 3: Defeasible Reasoning in Dialogue Systems

The purpose of this chapter is to throw some new light on defeasible arguments using new tools and concepts recently developed in argumentation theory and artificial intelligence (AI). A defeasible argument, to review the definition, is one in which the premises, relative to the given information, support the conclusion, even though new information may defeat the argument. Among the most important tools for studying defeasible arguments are argumentation schemes, especially ones already introduced like those for argument from witness testimony, argument from ignorance, abductive reasoning, and argument from expert opinion. Such forms of argument were often traditionally classified as fallacies, but they clearly are not fallacious in law[1], and often represent reasonable kinds of arguments. Legal evidence, in the most common kind in the most typical cases, is based on defeasible reasoning, but the problem of how to analyze such reasoning has not been solved, even though many solutions have been put forward in AI (Prakken and Sartor, 2003). A very common kind of example of a defeasible argument used in legal evidence, as already indicated, is argument from witness testimony. If a witness testifies that a statement *A* is true, then *A* is accepted as true, or at least the statement that *A* is true is given some probative weight as evidence. However, suppose it is found in a given case that the witness has lied, or that the witness could not possibly have seen the event he claims to know about. Such a finding defeats the original argument from witness testimony. However, in the absence of such defeating considerations, witness testimony can be accepted as legal evidence.

The central contention of the chapter is that defeasible reasoning is best analyzed and evaluated using a dialogue model originally developed in logic to study fallacies and other problematic aspects of argumentation (Perelman and Olbrechts-Tyteca, 1971; Hamblin, 1970; Walton, 1984; Krabbe, 1999). Special features of the dialogue model have been applied to legal argumentation in the new field of computational dialectics (Gordon, 1995; Prakken and Sartor, 1996; Bench-Capon, 1997; Verheij, 1998; Lodder, 2000; Hage, 2000). In such a dialogue model, an argument is to be evaluated in an orderly framework in which one participant makes a move, in the form of a speech act, and then another participant replies appropriately to that move (Lodder, 1999). For example, a proponent puts forward a claim

1 The claim made here is that they are generally not fallacious in legal argumentation, although they certainly are in some instances. Abductive reasoning is different from the other three forms of argument because it has not generally been identified with fallacies.

and then backs it up with an argument that is supposed to represent evidence that will offer a reason for the respondent to accept the claim. At the next move in the dialogue, the respondent expresses doubt about the claim either by raising critical questions about the argument used to support it or by putting forward an opposed argument (a rebuttal or refutation) that supposedly shows that the claim is false. It is the contention of this chapter that defeasibility can only be properly evaluated in this sort of dialectical[2] or dialogue-based framework of argumentation.

1. Common Argumentation Schemes in Legal Evidence

To indicate how important defeasibility is as a characteristic in legal evidence, we might once again cite argument from expert opinion as a case in point. Given the increasing role of technology and highly specialized fields of knowledge in matters to be decided by the courts, judges and juries have become increasingly dependent on experts called upon to testify. Quite often, the courts are dependent on experts in their attempts to reach informed, scientifically sound verdicts. But how reliable is expert opinion? Experts can be mistaken. And in trials, each side pays its own experts to offer testimony. This can often lead to conflicts between expert opinions. To attempt to deal with such problems, a criterion known as the 'general acceptance test' came to be accepted in Anglo-American law (*Frye* at 1014).

Just when a scientific principle or discovery crosses the line between the experimental and demonstrable stages is difficult to define. Somewhere in this twilight zone the evidential force of the principle must be recognized, and while courts will go a long way in admitting expert testimony deduced from a well-recognized scientific principle or discovery, the thing from which the deduction is made must be sufficiently established to have gained general acceptance in the particular field to which it belongs.

There have proved to be some problems with the Frye criterion. The foremost of these is that science changes as any field evolves and new hypotheses come to be accepted while old ones are superseded. Under the Frye criterion, a relevant fact based on expert opinion that is right and up-to-date could be excluded merely because it is not generally accepted yet. Another problem is what to do when there are several generally accepted theories that yield opposing claims, each based on expert opinion. To address these problems the United States Congress adopted the Federal Rules of Evidence in 1975, including a new standard of admissibility for expert testimony stated in FRE 702 as follows:

If scientific, technical, or other specialized knowledge will assist the trier of fact to understand the evidence or to determine a fact at issue, a witness qualified as expert by knowledge, skill, experience, training or education, may testify thereto in the form of an opinion or otherwise.

---

2 The term 'dialectical' historically refers to the use of dialogue structures by Greek philosophers, especially Aristotle, to study fallacies and other aspects of arguments (Hamblin, 1970).

This new rule not only abandoned the standard of general acceptance but broadened the criterion of acceptance to include any knowledge that will be helpful to the trier of facts in a case. The two general standards of admissibility of expert opinion evidence now become those of relevance and reliability. The problem with the FRE rule is that it did not make any reference to the *Frye* criterion, and so looked as though it did not consider the general acceptance criterion as a factor to be considered. This apparent lack of direction led to the famous, often-cited case of *Daubert v. Merrell Dow Pharmaceuticals*, which concerned the admissibility of scientific evidence indicating a causal relationship between *Bendectin* (a prescription drug for morning sickness) and birth defects in children. Such evidence had previously been held inadmissible by the court because it had not been published, and was therefore held not to meet the general acceptance criterion. In this case, the U.S. Supreme Court determined that the Federal Rules of Evidence, using the standards of relevance and reliability, superseded the *Frye* test. This change was seen as ascribing a "gatekeeper" role to judges, making them have to examine and evaluate the soundness of a scientific theory on which a given item of expert opinion testimony was supposedly based. This function, as one might expect, is one that many judges, not being experts or even scientists, could fulfill only with great difficulty. But it at least acknowledged that expert opinion testimony sometimes needed to be examined carefully as evidence and subjected to critical questioning, even before the decision on its admissibility in a trial is made.

It was argued in (Walton, 1997) that argument from expert opinion should, in most typical cases, and this would especially apply to expert testimony used as evidence in law, be seen as a defeasible form of argument. You can treat it as a deductively valid argument or as an inductively strong argument in some instances, but in the vast majority of cases, this way of treating it would lead to serious problems. Generally, it is not a good policy when examining expert witness testimony to assume that the expert is omniscient. Indeed, such a policy would be highly counterproductive when evaluating this kind of evidence in a common law trial. However, there is a natural tendency in everyday reasoning to respect expert opinions and even to defer to them, or hesitate to question them. Questioning the opinion of an expert can seem impolite, unless done in a circumspect way. However, as a matter of fact, experts are often wrong, or what they say can lead to the drawing of a conclusion that is wrong or not supported by the evidence. As a practical matter, one often needs to be prepared to critically question the opinion of an expert by asking the right questions. This approach is especially important in the examination of expert opinion testimony in court, where there can even be conflicting expert opinions on both sides. This approach suggests that argument from expert opinion is usually best seen as a form of argument that is defeasible and is subject to critical questioning.

This brief and incomplete history of how expert opinion evidence, especially of the scientific kind, is treated in law, illustrates how the courts have grappled with the inadequacy of the old Frye Rule. The problem posed by expert opinion evidence is still far from being solved, and we certainly cannot solve it here. But let's merely consider a very simple example of an argument from expert opinion to illustrate some of the dimensions of the problem, and to show the importance of seeing this form of argument as defeasible and subject to critical questioning.

Example of Argument from Expert Opinion

My doctor recommends taking vitamin B for stress.

She is an expert.

Therefore, it is a good idea to take vitamin B for stress.

This argument is a good enough one to bear some weight in discussing the issue, all else being equal, but it is hardly a decisive one that proves its conclusion beyond doubt and closes off the issue by providing scientific proof. For example, Ramon might argue, against Priscilla's argument, that his doctor is against taking vitamin B for stress. Or he might argue that Priscilla's doctor has been influenced by a drug company and is biased. Then we could get into a "battle of the experts", a phenomenon familiar enough in legal argumentation. Appeal to expert opinion is best seen as a form of argument that should carry some weight in securing acceptance of a conclusion if the premises are acceptable. But it is also best seen as a form of argument that is not beyond challenge or questioning. It can default, if the right sort of new evidence comes in. Like the other presumptive argumentation schemes, it represents a defeasible form of argument that carries some probative weight if not critically questioned or refuted by counter-arguments, but that is generally open to defeat in the future as the dialogue proceeds.

2. Defeasible Arguments

Arguments from expert opinion and witness testimony are defeasible because they are open to critical questioning when used in a given case. Even when all the questions have been answered successfully, the argument could still be defeated if new evidence comes in to the case that provides a rebuttal to the original argument. Such defeasible arguments are the woof and warp of legal evidence, meaning that they are very common, and even typical of the arguments used as legal evidence in trials. There tends to be a mass of evidence on each side, composed of a connected network of arguments making up an argument diagram. The Wigmore evidence chart displayed in (Wigmore, 1931) shows very well how the mass of evidence on each side at the end of a trial forms a diagram made up of defeasible arguments that, individually, only provide a small probative weight supporting a conclusion. But a mass of connected defeasible arguments can make a strong case.

Here let us re-examine the canonical example of a defeasible argument, the Tweety argument (Reiter, 1980), cited in chapter 2, section 7, and much discussed over the past twenty years or so in computer science.[3]

The Tweety Argument

Birds fly.

Tweety is a bird.

Therefore Tweety flies.

The Tweety argument is defeasible, as shown in chapter 2. For example, suppose new information comes in telling us that Tweety is a penguin. A penguin is a bird, but it does not fly. Thus the Tweety argument is defeated, at least in this particular case. Both premises are generally acceptable, and true, as far as we know. The argument is structurally correct (more about this below). But then we found that Tweety is a penguin. This new information caused the argument to default. After the new information came in, the conclusion was no longer acceptable. Thus the Tweety argument is a good example of the defeasible type of argument. It was acceptable, but new evidence defeated it.

The first premise of the Tweety argument is a generalization of a kind sometimes called a generic statement. It is not a universal generalization of the absolute kind that can be represented by the universal quantifier of deductive logic. It is not really an inductive generalization either. What it says is that birds normally fly, or that one can normally expect a bird to fly, subject to exceptions. Thus a generalization of this kind fails or defaults when applied to a case that is not a normal or standard one. This premise can be paraphrased as a qualified generalization. It says, 'Generally birds fly, subject to exceptions'. Qualified generalizations contain qualifier clauses. In some cases the qualifier states the envisaged kind of exception explicitly, using a term like 'except'. In other cases, like the Tweety argument, the kind of exception is not stated explicitly. In such cases, the types of defeating evidence may be impossible to categorize or predict. Tweety may be a special type of bird, like a penguin or an ostrich. But then again, he may be just an ordinary run-of-the-mill bird with a broken wing.

As noted above, in some cases there can be a third standard of structural correctness of an argument based on forms of argument (argumentation schemes) that are not deductive or inductive. They are not based on logical necessity. It can also be argued that they are not inductive, although the evidence on this question is much less clear. Sometimes they can be evaluated using Bayesian methods, but in many of the most significant instances, they cannot. In these cases, they are best

3 The Tweety argument is attributed to Marvin Minsky. In the version of it previously discussed, we added the term 'generally' to the first premise to highlight the defeasible nature of the argument.

evaluated using the method called "confidence factors" in AI. If they are neither deductive nor inductive, they represent a third category of argument. Traditional logic has long failed to acknowledge the existence of such forms of argument, or has appeared to do so. They find little place of importance in modern logic textbooks. They are often subsumed under the heading of abductive inference in AI (Josephson and Josephson, 1994). It is mainly recent advances in computing, especially in AI, that have gained for forms of argument falling into this third category at least some recognition as objects of investigation worthy of study. However, it can be argued that these forms of argumentation were recognized as important both in the ancient world and in medieval logic. Unfortunately, their existence was ignored, and even suppressed, as deductive logic became the central branch of logical investigations after Aristotle invented syllogistic logic, and later, after modern systems of deductive logic were established.

There can be found in Aristotle's *Topics*, *On Sophistical Refutations*, and in his *Rhetoric* as well, many forms of argument that are defeasible and imperfect, but represent common forms of argument that are often reasonable. Burnyeat (1994) characterized these as arguments based on premises that are true "only for the most part". That is, when they are tenable, it is because they are acceptable as far as anyone knows at the present stage of a discussion or investigation, subject to new evidence, or exceptions to a rule that might arise in the future. The warrants for these kinds of imperfect inferences have traditionally been called "topics" or *topoi* (places). For lack of any apparent exact structure underlying them, the topics literature languished after Aristotle. There could be many reasons. Possibly deductive logic needed to be established before such imperfect, tricky and unreliable forms of inference could be made sense of in logical terms. Another reason, carefully analyzed by Burnyeat (1994), is that the Greek term covering such forms of argumentation, enthymeme (*enthymema*), was taken to refer to an argument with a "missing" or unstated premise, as indicated above.

An example of an argument called an enthymeme by Aristotle (2.19.24, 1393a6-7), was analyzed by Burnyeat (1994, p. 26) in his examination of the Aristotelian enthymeme "If the sky is clouded over, it is likely to rain". This "argument" really appears to be a weak or defeasible conditional, where the link between antecedent and consequent is qualified by the hedging term "likely". By altering Burnyeat's wording slightly (Burnyeat (1994, p. 29), the conditional can be used as part of a common argument.

For the most part, cloudy days turn out to be rainy days.

This day is a cloudy day.

Therefore this day is likely to turn out rainy.

As Burnyeat pointed out (p. 28), the major premise of the argument could be countered by an opposing argument based on a different defeasible conditional.

For the most part, if the barometer is high, the day is not likely to turn out rainy.

This day the barometer is high.

Therefore this day is not likely to turn out rainy.

Burnyeat (1994, p. 28) pointed out that in this kind of case, the two conclusions of the opposed arguments "contradict each other". Such arguments are typical of the kinds one finds in legal argumentation in a trial. One argument supports the claim of one side, while an opposed argument supports the claim of the other. Citing other examples from Aristotle's writings, Burnyeat argued that what Aristotle referred to by the term 'enthymeme' was not an argument with a missing premise. What he referred to, according to Burnyeat, was a defeasible argument of a common type based on a warrant (usually a non-absolute conditional or quantifier) that is only held to be true for the most part and is subject to exceptions.

In computer science, both absolute and non-absolute conditionals of this sort are typically called "rules". This usage can be compared to Toulmin's terminology, in which non-absolute conditionals are recognized, and based on what Toulmin called a "warrant" (Toulmin, 1958). Whatever terminology is used, two rules of inference are of central importance. The first of the pair is deductively valid, and may thus be classified as an absolute rule.

Strict *Modus Ponens* (SMP)

As a universal rule not subject to exceptions, if *A* then *B*.

A is true.

Conclusion: *B* is true.

The second of this pair of rules is not so familiar in logic. It is similar to strict *modus ponens*, but is non-absolute.

Defeasible *Modus Ponens* (DMP)

As a rule subject to exceptions, if *A* then *B*

A holds as true.

It is not the case so far that there is a known exception to the rule that if *A* then *B*

Conclusion: *B* holds tentatively, but subject to withdrawal should an exception arise.

Although the conclusion is really the same in both forms of argument, the qualifier "tentatively, but subject to withdrawal should an exception arise" is stated in the conclusion of DMP, indicating that the inferential relation between the premises and the conclusion is different from that of SMP. The reason for this feature has to do with recognizing each type of argument in a natural language text of discourse based on textual evidence like "indicator words"(Snoeck Henkeman, 1992).

Basing an AI system on defeasible reasoning fits very well with how rule-based systems work in law. For example, the following kind of inference is used in the ArguMed system of Verheij (1999).

The Tort Argument

If Peter has violated a property right, then Peter has committed a tort.

Peter has violated a property right.

Therefore Peter has committed a tort.

This argument looks initially like an instance of DMP, and if both premises are true, then that is a reason for accepting the conclusion as true. But it is possible for the premises to be true and the conclusion false. These are the cases that defeat (or "undercut", in Verheij's terms) the inference. In this respect, the argument is better classified as having the form DMP. How the ArguMed system models this argument can be shown by an example of defeasible reasoning presented by Verheij (1999, p. 45).

> Peter has violated a property right. As a result, at first sight, he has committed a tort. However, there is a ground of justification for Peter's act. As a result, on second thoughts, Peter's violation of a property right does not justify that he has committed a tort.

In the ArguMed System, rules, and of the kinds of inferences commonly based on them, are sometimes defeasible. As a general rule of law, if Peter has violated a property right, then he has committed a tort. But in this particular case, there is a ground of justification for Peter's act. In this case, therefore, there is an exception to the rule, and the inference defaults (is defeated). Accordingly, Verheij (2000, p. 5), adopted the following policy for applying the two rules DMP and SMP. In a case where both strict rules and rules not admitting of exceptions might possibly come into play, DMP must always be used. In a case in which only strict rules are involved, SMP suffices as the appropriate rule of inference.

Talking about DMP is very confusing at first to those trained in formal deductive logic, for the logic textbooks routinely classify arguments like the tort argument as being deductively valid arguments of the form SMP. For example, according to Copi and Cohen (1998, p. 363), the following argument is deductively valid because it has the SMP form.

The Lawyer Argument

If he has a good lawyer then he will be acquitted.

He has a good lawyer.

Therefore he will be acquitted.

But it would seem better justified to classify the lawyer argument as having the form DMP, based on the natural language text. The first premise may be taken only to mean that if he has a good lawyer then, on balance, but subject to other considerations, he will be acquitted. Given this interpretation of the premise, does it follow that the conclusion has to be true? Not necessarily, unless the structure of the inference has to be that of DMP. But realistically speaking, we all know that even though you might have a good lawyer, that is no guarantee you will win the case. The other side could have an even better one. Of course, one can argue about the meaning of the first premise in natural language, but it is evident that in many typical cases of legal argumentation of the kind we need to analyze and understand, the form of reasoning is really that of DMP.

Indeed, I propose the thesis here that the vast preponderance of the argumentation schemes that are so important to understanding evidence in law have the DMP form. One only needs to look over the examples of these schemes given in chapter 1, and elsewhere in this book, to see that they are all based on the DMP form of argument. Of course, one can always reconfigure them into a DMP form by adding implicit premises, but in the end this device fails. The reason concerns the underlying nature of defeasibility as a feature of argumentation, as explained in chapter 1. Simply using the device of adding implicit premises fails to do justice to how critical questions work in relation to argumentation schemes for defeasible argumentation. The ultimate reason is that such arguments can only be evaluated by bringing in the dialogue notion of burden of proof.

3. Arguments Based on Case Comparison

The argument about DMP in the previous section can be reinforced by a brief consideration of how many of the most common forms of reasoning work, not only in law, but in any case involving an institutional, organized bureaucratic structure in which rules need to be laid down as a basis for decision-making. Once an established rule is laid down, and then applied to a particular case, a precedent is set that is binding on any next case that might be considered. The following argumentation scheme (Walton, 1995, p. 148) represents this defeasible form of argument, where a is an individual and F and G are predicates.

Argument from Precedent

Major Premise: Generally, according to the established rule, if x has property F, then x also has property G.

Minor Premise: In this legitimate case, a has F but does not have G.

Conclusion: Therefore an exception to the rule must be recognized, and the rule appropriately modified or qualified.

The following example is given in this dialogue from (Walton, 1995, p. 94).

Student: I don't think I will able to get my essay in on Tuesday. Would it be OK if I handed it in next week?

Professor: We all agreed at the beginning of the year that Tuesday is the deadline. That is the rule.

Student: Yes, but you said to Ms. Reasoner that she could hand her essay in a week late because she has another assignment due this week. I have another assignment due too. So I should be able to hand mine in a week late too.

The argumentation represented in this dialogue is defeasible, because further questions need to be asked before it can judged whether the argument holds or not.

Critical Questions for Argument from Precedent

CQ1: Does the established rule really apply to this case?

CQ2: Is the case cited legitimate, or can it be explained as only an apparent violation of the rule?

CQ3: Can the case cited be dealt with under an already recognized category of exception that does not require a change in the rule?

But there are other considerations involved in such a case as well, for it is clear that such argument from precedent depends crucially on how similar the student's case is to that of Ms. Reasoner, the case she cited. Thus the argument in all such cases depends on the application of a prior scheme called argument from analogy (Walton, 1995, p. 148).

Argument from Analogy

Major Premise: Generally, case C1 is similar to case C2

Minor Premise: Proposition *A* is true (false) in case C1

Conclusion: Proposition *A* is true (false) in case C2

Critical Questions for Argument from Analogy

CQ1: Is *A* true (false) in C1?

CQ2: Are C1 and C2 similar, in the respects cited?

CQ3: Are there important differences (dissimilarities) between C1 and C2 ?

CQ4: Is there some other case C3 that is also similar to C1 except that *A* is false (true) in C3?

A simple example of argument from analogy can be taken from (Walton, 1989, p. 258):

I infer that a new pair of shoes will wear well on the grounds that I got good wear from other shoes previously purchased from the same store.

These examples are quite simple ones, but they suggest that since so much legal argumentation is based on precedent and analogy, getting a grasp of how legal argumentation works must take account of these two schemes.

There is also a third scheme that is of fundamental importance.

Argument for an Exceptional Case

Major Premise: If the case of *x* is an exception, then the established rule can be waived in the case of *x*.

Minor Premise: The case of *a* is an exception.

Conclusion: Therefore the established rule can be waived in the case of *a*.

The following example dialogue (Walton 1995, p.93) will suffice to illustrate this type of argumentation.

Student: I don't think I will able to get my essay in on Tuesday. Would it be OK if I handed it in next week?

Professor: We all agreed at the beginning of the year that Tuesday is the deadline. That is the rule.

Student: But I had a bad case of the flu last week, and I have a note from my physician to prove it.

Matching this scheme are the following critical questions (Walton, 1996, p. 93).

Critical Questions for Argument from an Exceptional Case

CQ1: Is it the case of a recognized type of exception?

CQ2: If it is not a recognized case, can evidence why the established rule does not apply to it be given?

CQ3: If it is a borderline case, can comparable cases be cited?

The successive application of these three schemes to the data in a given case is highly typical of legal argumentation of the most common and fundamental kind. Thus argument from analogy of one case to another is the glue that holds much legal argumentation together. Of course, the scheme for argument from analogy presented above is very simple. The problem of what roles these schemes play in the technologies for case-based reasoning that have been developed (Roth, 2003) now arises. Later on, this problem will be discussed.

4. Theories of Defeasible Reasoning

In default logics of the kind used in AI, first-order logic is extended with domain specific rules called defaults (Reiter, 1980). A default rule has the following form, where P is a set of statements that act as given premises and D is another statement that could be called a defeater in the sense of (Pollock, 1995).

Form of Default Rule

$$\frac{P : D}{C}$$

A rule of this form tells you that if you know *A*, and you have no evidence that *D* obtains, then you may infer *C*. Another way to formulate a default rule is as a knowledge-based conditional.

KBC: if you know that *P* is true, and you have no evidence that *D* applies, then you may infer *C*.

In the case of the Tweety argument, *A* is 'Tweety is a bird', *D* is 'Tweety is not an exceptional bird' and *C* is 'Tweety flies'. As long as the defeater applies, then the default rule works and the defeasible argument can be treated like any other deductively valid argument. Essentially then, on this theory, a defeasible argument is analyzed as a default inference in which the warrant is a default rule. In terms of traditional logic, the form of the argument is that of the *argumentum ad ignorantiam*, or argument from ignorance, as it is called in the logic textbooks. This form of argument is often called a lack of evidence argument in the social sciences or an *ex silentio* argument in history. In both fields it is commonly regarded as a reasonable but inconclusive form of argument. For example, there is no evidence that Roman soldiers received posthumous decorations, or medals for distinguished service, as we would call them. We only have evidence of living soldiers receiving such awards. From this lack of evidence, it has been considered reasonable by historians to put forward the hypothesis that Roman soldiers did not receive posthumous decorations. Of course, such a conjecture is not based on positive evidence, but only on a failure to find evidence that would refute it. Such arguments from ignorance are common in many fields, not least in law, as will be shown below.

The problem with formal default logics is how you know in a given case whether the default blocker applies. We may not know, for example, that Tweety is an exceptional bird, but then later we may find out that he is. It is in the nature of many defeasible arguments, including arguments from ignorance, that we don't know what lies in the future as new knowledge comes in. Indeed, according to the theory expressed by default logics, all defeasible arguments are arguments from ignorance. Thus in evaluating any given instance of such an argument, it depends on how far along an investigation has gone. If there is no evidence that *D* applies, an arguer can put forward a default argument and the respondent of the argument has to accept the conclusion, at least provisionally. But matters of burden of proof complicate such cases. We may think that Tweety is not an exceptional bird, for example, but if we are very worried that he might be, we might draw a different conclusion. Suppose Tweety has to carry an important message to military forces that depend on the information in the message. In such a case we might have doubts about how much weight we can put on the assumption that Tweety is not an exceptional bird, and look to also using other methods of sending the message. Such matters of burden of proof are very important for evaluating defeasible argumentation in law (Verheij, 2000). Prakken and Sartor (1996, p. 194) have modeled defeasible legal argumentation by using the notion of reversal of burden of proof. The conclusion of a legal argument can be provisionally acceptable even if the proponent has failed to show that there is any positive evidence in favor of it, as long as the case is not closed and the respondent has not found evidence that defeats it. Defeasible arguments in law often have to do with presumptions, like arguments concluding to a presumption of death in the case of a missing person. Such arguments seem to involve a reversal of the normal burden of proof.

Thus there are various distinctive aspects of defeasible arguments that suggest they are more complex than they seem. The default rule does indicate how they work, but is limited in certain respects in explaining how they should be evaluated. The same default argument may be evaluated quite differently at a different stage in the procedure whereby new information is collected and arguments evaluated. At different stages of the process, defeasible arguments may vary in how they should be evaluated. It seems that a burden of proof shifts back and forth, depending on how far along an argument has proceeded. The formal semantical model of the defeat rule can't do a good job of modeling these dialectical aspects of defeasible argumentation. There are advantages of also considering a formal dialogue system for modeling a sequence of argumentation as it proceeds through various stages.

Pearl (1991, p. 177) has classified Pollock's approach to defeasible reasoning on the grounds that the conditions for acceptability of a defeasible claim include the requirement that the additional evidence in a case does not provide an argument against the claim. Such an argument, whether a defeater or undercutter, is presumably brought in as additional evidence at some point in the future in relation to the point in time where the argument is now being considered. It is evidence that goes against the claim, suggesting opposition. Thus Pollock's theory certainly has a dialectical air about it, and would seem to be easily cast in a dialectical framework.

However, Pollock's theory stops somewhere short of being explicitly dialectical. Like Pearl, he models argument as inference graphs with assigned probability values to nodes. The theory of rationality in which these graphs are embedded has two models. One is a belief and knowledge model representing epistemic reasoning. The other is a practical reasoning model representing goal-directed planning and actions. This duality suggests an entry point to a dialectical approach in which arguments can be evaluated by different standards in different frameworks of use, or so-called types of dialogue. But Pollock has stopped just short of adopting a dialectical model for defeasible reasoning.

Some other approaches to defeasible reasoning in AI, like Pollock's, use inference graphs that chain forward, but tacitly recognize a dialectical aspect by using the notions of arguments that attack or defeat a claim represented at one point in the graph. Explicitly dialectical theories of defeasible argumentation have also been put forward in AI. Dung (1995) used such a defeat graph as the basic model, but added that the dialectical status of each argument in the graph can be determined by an argument game between the proponent and an opponent. They take turns making moves in a dialogue game, and the player who runs out of moves wins the game. This game has been extended by Prakken and Sartor (1997) by allowing for what are called priority arguments in the dialogues. These are arguments based on the relative strength of other arguments. The details of these formal games of dialogue are not so important here as the recognition that research is already underway in AI using dialectical game structures to model defeasible argumentation.

5. Computational Dialectics for Legal Argumentation

Prakken and Sartor (2003, p. 11) offered the following example of a legal dispute about contract formation to illustrate how computational dialectics can be applied to legal disputation in a way that helps to reveal several key aspects of the structure of the argumentation used in such a case. Let us call this dialogue the contract dispute. It is quoted from Prakken and Sartor with some minor typographical changes below.

The Contract Dispute

Plaintiff: I claim that defendant owes me 500 euro.
Defendant: I dispute plaintiff's claim.
Judge: Plaintiff, prove your claim.
Plaintiff: Defendant owes me 500 euro since we concluded a valid sales contract, and I delivered but defendant did not pay.
Defendant: I concede that plaintiff delivered and I did not pay, but I dispute that we have a valid contract.
Judge: Plaintiff, prove your claim that you have a valid contract.
Plaintiff: The document is an affidavit, signed by us.
Defendant: I dispute that the document is an affidavit.
Judge: Since the document looks like an affidavit, prove that it is not.
Defendant: This lab report shows that the notary's signature was forged.
Plaintiff: That evidence is inadmissible, since I received it too late.
Judge: I agree: the evidence is inadmissible.

The contract dispute involves several arguments of interest, but two defeasible arguments in it are especially interesting to comment on here. One is the argument by the defendant that the document is not a genuine affidavit because the notary's signature was forged, as shown by a lab report cited. This argument appears to be based on an appeal to expert opinion, assuming the lab report was written by scientists, or experts of some sort, like handwriting experts. The other is the argument that the document in question is an affidavit because it looks like an affidavit. This argument looks to be a defeasible one, and one that would carry probative weight in law.

Pollock (1995, p. 41) offered the following example of a defeasible argument. An object looks red to me, and so I conclude that the object is red. But there is another consideration. An object can look red when it is not, for example when it is illuminated by a red light. If I found out that this object was illuminated by a red light, that new finding would defeat the argument that the object is red because it looks red. But it does not completely defeat the argument, because red objects look red in red light too. In Pollock's terminology this consideration is classified as an undercutting defeater as opposed to a rebutting defeater. It does not show that the conclusion that the object is red is false. But it does give a reason that weakens the link between the premises and the conclusion of the original argument. The original argument still gives a reason to support the conclusion that the object is red. But the argument is defeasible, meaning that it holds tentatively, but is subject to defeat, or at least to weakening, should new evidence of a certain kind come in, and be shown to apply to the case.

Prakken (2003) showed that the argument in this example has a characteristic argumentation scheme. It could be called argument from appearance, to give it a name.

Argumentation Scheme for Argument from Appearance

If something looks like an x then it is an x.

This object looks like an x.

Therefore this object is an x.

Prakken (2003) cited another example of argument from appearance. It is a legal argument, and provided the theme of his paper.

The Affidavit Argument

This object looks like an affidavit.

Therefore this object is an affidavit.

The affidavit argument is defeasible, and is similar to Pollock's red light argument in that both are arguments from appearance. But the affidavit argument suggests convincingly how common and important defeasible arguments are in legal evidence, and by the way, how important argumentation schemes are as well.

As an argumentation scheme, argument from appearance needs to be evaluated in a dialogue format through the asking of critical questions. Each critical question is a potential defeater of the argument. Three critical questions matching the argument from appearance are the following.

CQ1: Is there some reason why this object might look like an x but not really be one?

CQ2: Can the hypothesis that the object is an x be tested by collecting more data?

CQ3: Are there counterbalancing reasons for accepting the hypothesis that the object is something else, as opposed to being an x?

The first critical question can be illustrated by Pollock's example. If an object looks red to me, I might quite reasonably conclude that it is red, at least as a hypothesis. But then I might find out that the object was illuminated by a red light at the time, making it appear red. This finding defeats the argument, because a red light will make any object look red to a normal human observer. Such a finding is a reason of the kind mentioned in CQ1, because the object might look red, but not really be red.

The other two questions can be illustrated by the ancient example of the rope cited as a classic case of the argument from appearance in (Walton, 2002), and originally from the ancient philosopher Sextus Empiricus (*Against the Logicians*, 188). A man sees what looks to him in a dimly lit room like a coil of rope. Adopting the hypothesis that it is a snake, he takes the precaution to jump over it. But then afterwards, he turns back and sees that the object has not moved. He then revises his hypothesis, now drawing the new one that the object he saw is not a snake. Still, he is not sure, and it is wise to be careful if something could be a snake. To test his new hypothesis he prods the object with a stick. The new finding is that the object does not move. The man's previous argument that the object is a snake is even more conclusively defeated than before. The best explanation of all the data having been received at that point in the investigation is that the object is a rope rather than a snake. In effect, the second critical question has been answered by testing the hypothesis once more data has been collected. The third critical question has to do with setting burden of proof for one side more highly where safety is concerned. If something is potentially dangerous, that is reason for taking care to be fairly sure it is not present in a given situation by too easily assuming the situation is safe. In this case, on balance, it is better to assume the object is a snake, not a rope, until more evidence comes in one way or the other.

The contract dispute case shows not only how defeasible arguments are based on argumentation schemes that are common in legal argumentation. It also suggests how such defeasible argument can be analyzed and evaluated in a dialogue format using computational dialectics. If this document looks like an affidavit, and there is no evidence to think it is not, then it should be provisionally accepted that it is an affidavit. The argument holds at this point in an ongoing dialogue or collection and discussion of facts. But then suppose new evidence comes in. Suppose it has been shown by experts that the notary's signature is forged. That new finding defeats the hypothesis that the document is a genuine affidavit. In other words, the proposal is that defeasible arguments need to be analyzed and evaluated using two tools. One is the argumentation scheme for argument from expert opinion and accompanying set of critical questions matching the scheme. The other is the longer sequence of dialogue in which the given argument, with its scheme and critical questions, are embedded.

According to this proposal, defeasible arguments are arguments the evaluation of which should proceed in two stages. First, if the argument is structurally correct according to some accepted standard (like an argumentation scheme), then if the premises are accepted, the conclusion should also be rationally acceptable as a tentative hypothesis. Second, new relevant evidence may come in at a later stage that defeats the argument, meaning that the conclusion should at that new evidential point fail to be rationally acceptable (Pollock, 1987; Verheij, 1996).[4] This second stage of evaluation suggests, following the viewpoint of computational dialectics, that defeasible arguments can best be evaluated as dialectical. To say they are dialectical means that they need to be evaluated in a context of dialogue in which two parties, called the proponent and the respondent (opponent, antagonist) are arguing with each other (Hamblin, 1970, 1971; Mackenzie, 1981, 1990; Walton and Krabbe, 1995; Prakken and Sartor, 1996). According to this dialectical theory, a defeasible argument, when it meets the requirements of correctness in a dialogue, shifts a burden of proof from the proponent's side to the respondent's side. But what, in general, is a formal dialogue system? And what tools can the theory of such systems provide us with that could be applicable to legal evidence?

6. Formal Dialogue Systems

As shown in chapter 1, section 6, a dialogue, in the technical meaning of the term used in argumentation studies, has two participants, called the proponent and the respondent. Let us briefly review the characteristics of this notion of a dialogue before seeing how it applies to legal argumentation. The two participants in a dialogue take turns making moves. The moves are essentially speech acts of various kinds. For example, asking a question is a kind of move. Making an assertion is a kind of move. Putting forward an argument is another common kind of move. A type of dialogue is defined formally as a set of participants, a set of rules defining permitted or required moves, a set of rules for determining how one participant must reply to the prior move of the other participant, and a set for determining when a completed sequence of moves fulfills the goal of the dialogue (so-called "win-loss" rules). The general idea is that a dialogue is a sequence of moves in which two participants take turns, starting at a first move and ending at a last move. In the dialogue theory of Hamblin (1970; 1971), the proponent makes the first move, the respondent makes the next move, and then they take turns, producing an orderly sequence of moves. As shown in chapter 1, each member in the sequence is defined by Hamblin (1971, p. 130) as a triple, $\langle n, p, l \rangle$; n represents the length of the dialogue (the number of moves so far); p is a participant; and l is what Hamblin calls a locution, or what we now call a speech act. Such systems of dialogue have been proposed by Mackenzie (1981, 1990) and Walton and Krabbe (1995). Recently dialogue systems have been used to model argumentation in

4 Actually, Pollock defines defeasibility of reasons rather than arguments. According to Pollock (1987, p. 484), there are two kinds of reasons, defeasible and nondefeasible. A nondefeasible reason entails its conclusion. In contrast, in the cases of a defeasible reason, "additional information may destroy the reason connection".

communications between rational agents in multi-agent systems (McBurney and Parsons, 2002).

As shown in the classification table in chapter 1, there are six basic types of dialogue. In a persuasion dialogue, the goal is to resolve or throw light on some conflict of opinions or unsettled issue. The proponent of an argument tries to get the respondent to commit to the conclusion by using the premises as reasons. The proponent uses the commitments of the other party as these premises. If she puts forward a structurally correct argument that has premises that are all commitments of the respondent, then the respondent is rationally obliged to accept the conclusion. That is the process called rational persuasion. But there are other types of dialogue as well (Walton and Krabbe, 1995). Some dialogues take the form of an investigation that collects facts and then tries to prove or disprove some statement using these supposed facts as premises. Dialogues have four stages (van Eemeren and Grootendorst, 1992). First, there is a confrontation stage in which the issue is formulated. Then there is an opening stage in which both parties agree to follow the rules in order to try to settle the issue by rational argumentation. Then there is an argumentation stage in which the arguments for both sides are brought forward and discussed. Finally there is a closing stage in which it is judged how or whether the issue has been settled. How does this dialogue framework apply to law? The best place to begin is the trial, regarded as the paradigm of argumentation in Anglo-American law.

On the persuasion dialogue model, the purpose of the fair trial is to resolve a conflict of opinions by rational argumentation, and the two opposed sides are supposed to present the strongest possible argument supporting its opinion (Feteris, 1999). This model, it can be argued (Walton, 2002), fits the advocacy system often held up to represent the framework of argumentation in the Anglo-American common law trial (Frank, 1963). At best, however, the persuasion dialogue model is a simplified version of what happens in such a trial. The trial has three participants, including a neutral trier, a judge or a jury, who decides the outcome, and applies rules of evidence and other procedural rules that apply to the argumentation in a trial. Hence even if the logical core of the argumentation in a common law trial can be viewed as a persuasion dialogue, there is an institutional setting surrounding it, with other participants and trial rules that are specific to a court. Wigmore (1931) distinguished between what he called the science of proof, or principles of logical argumentation generally, and the trial rules used to judge argumentation in a judicial tribunal. Twining (1985, p. 156) explained the distinction by writing that although the trial rules are broadly founded on the science of proof, "the practical conditions of trials bring into play certain limiting considerations not found in the laboratory pursuit of the Science". Hence "the Rules do not and cannot always coincide with the principles of the Science". To put it a different way, the normative model of rational argumentation in a persuasion dialogue is abstract and general, while the trial rules exist independently as part of an institution.

The trial is a multi-staged process of dispute resolution and evidence collection. According to Park, Leonard and Goldberg (1998, pp. 4-8), it has nine stages. The first stage is the pre-trial litigation stage, including discovery, motions, and hearings. The second stage is that of jury selection. The third stage is the presentation of opening statements to the assembled court by the attorneys for both sides. The fourth stage is the calling of the witnesses and their examination by both sides. The fifth stage is the opportunity for rebuttal. The sixth stage is the point where either side can make a motion for judgment. The seventh stage is the putting forward of closing arguments by both sides. The eighth stage is that of jury instruction by the judge. The ninth stage is the period in which the jury makes its deliberations and reaches a verdict. No one model of dialogue can represent the argumentation that takes place during all these different stages. Even so, in a broad overview, it can be extremely useful to view the argumentation put forward by both sides, not only supporting its own opinion but also criticizing and attempting to rebut the arguments of the other side, as taking the form of a persuasion dialogue. This view, at any rate, has been maintained in (Bench-Capon, 2002) and (Walton, 2002). Much more work needs to be done showing how other types of dialogue fit into this central persuasion dialogue framework. For example, witness testimony and examination may turn out to be best analyzed using a model of information-seeking dialogue in which the reliability of the information is tested by critical examination.

Using the whole apparatus of a formal dialogue structure with all its stages and rules may not be necessary to help analyze a text of argumentation. Often the most useful tool is the profile of dialogue, a relatively short table of moves of the kind illustrated in chapter 1, section 6. In that example the respondent replied to the question by giving a reason why the proponent should accept statement *A*. As the dialogue proceeded, the respondent kept trying to persuade the proponent to accept *A*, using a *modus ponens* form of argument at moves 3-5 to try to get the proponent to accept *C*. The idea of using such dialogue structures as frameworks of argument use goes back to Aristotle, as shown by Hamblin (1970). But it languished for two millennia, despite some interest in the subject in the middle ages. The Lorenzen School in Germany took up a dialogue approach to logic that predated Hamblin's work. They developed a formal semantic model of deductive reasoning based on a dialogue structure. Hamblin was unaware of this development, or at any rate did not mention it in his work. These historical matters of how the field began to develop in the twentieth century are outlined in (Walton and Krabbe, 1995). Hamblin's main motivation was practical. He wanted to use formal dialogue structures as a method of analyzing logical fallacies. He clearly expected that there would be different kinds of formal dialogues. But understandably, his remarks were hazy on what the exact goal of a dialogue should be, or what should count as "winning" or "losing" (to put the issue in competitive terms). The idea was broadly that the two participants were trying to engage in argumentation with each other by using step-by-step sequences of reasoning - for example, of the kind familiar in deductive logic. In the more recent literature, it has been shown that there is not just one type of dialogue, and that there should be collective goals for each distinctive type. Defeasible arguments in all these types of dialogue will, of course, share certain fundamental characteristics. But how a defeasible argument should be evaluated in a given case may depend on the context of dialogue in which the argument was used in that case. For example, how burden of proof is judged can vary in different types of dialogue.

Chapter 1, section 7 described briefly, in an introductory fashion, how commitment operations work in dialogue. Now we can introduce a little more general theory of commitment in dialogue. The proponent and the respondent each have what are called commitment sets (Hamblin, 1970, 1971). A commitment set, in the simplest case, is just a set of statements. They could be written on a blackboard for example, so that both commitment sets are visible to both participants. Various rules in a dialogue govern what kinds of moves can be made, how the other party must respond to a given move at the next move, and what happens to this commitment set at each move. Commitment rules determine what statements go into or are taken out of each commitment set at each move. For example, if the proponent asserts statement *A* at some move, then *A* is added to her commitment set. If a participant retracts commitment to statement *B* at some point in a dialogue, and he or she was committed to *B* previously, then *B* is now removed from his or her commitment set. Among the most difficult problems is the formulation of rules of retraction of commitments for various types of dialogue (Krabbe, 2001).

'Persuasion' in formal dialogue theory, as indicated above, refers not to psychological persuasion but to rational persuasion. A proponent persuades a respondent to commit to a statement *A* in this sense by presenting a structurally correct argument with *A* as conclusion containing only premises that are already commitments of the respondent. The speech act of persuasion has been accomplished in such a case because the respondent was not committed to this particular statement, but now he is. Several different formal models of persuasion dialogue have been constructed in (Walton and Krabbe, 1995). Some, called rigorous persuasion dialogues or RPDs, have rules that do not allow the participants much flexibility, but the advantage of an RPD is that it is fairly simple while at the same time being formally rigorous. But RPDs model argumentation only in a simplistic way that does not express many of the important features of empirical cases of natural language argumentation. Another kind, called PPD or permissive persuasion dialogue, is more flexible and is closer to empirical argumentation.

No matter what type of dialogue is concerned, and no matter which rules are selected, and there can be many variations, arguments are always evaluated in light of three factors. These are how the argument was put forward in a dialogue, how that move affects the commitment sets of both parties, and in some cases how the respondent replied to the argument. The device of commitment is useful, and does not get into all the problems that have been encountered with the BDI (belief-desire-intention) model of argumentation as rational belief revision.[5] A belief is an internal entity, and using the BDI model can involve an argument evaluator in the mysterious metaphysics of iterated beliefs. Commitment is a less opaque concept. You are committed only to statements you have gone on record as accepting in a dialogue. The idea is that a public record is kept of a participant's set, as each move is made, so that if an arguer claims that he never said something, the other party can go back over what he said or didn't say, and use this as evidence in de-

[5] The BDI model was introduced in chapter 1 section 7.

termining commitment. Thus commitment represents acceptance of a specific statement, judged by the evidence available from the prior text of dialogue in a given case.

7. Lack of Knowledge Inferences

One example of such a defeasible type of argument is the *argumentum ad ignorantiam* of the logic textbooks introduced in chapter 1 and further analyzed in chapter 2. To review, this argument has the following general form: statement *A* is not known to be true (false), therefore *A* is false (true). It is also sometimes called a lack of evidence argument or *ex silentio* argument, when it is presumed not to be fallacious. As shown in (Walton, 1996, chapter 5), argument from ignorance needs to be seen as an inherently dialectical form of argumentation. The context most often helpful to grasping the structure of this form of argumentation is that of an ongoing investigation in which facts are being collected and inserted into a knowledge base. In such a context, the argument from ignorance can be represented using argumentation schemes comparable to those given in (Walton, 1996, p. 147).

Argument from ignorance, or the lack of knowledge inference, represents a form of reasoning that is fundamentally important in both computing and law. To cite an example in computing, suppose an expert system on coffee production in South America is asked whether Guyana is a major coffee producer and replies that 'Guyana is a major coffee producer' is not in its knowledge base. The questioner can infer, using argument from ignorance, that Guyana is not a major coffee producer. To cite an example in law, consider the burden of proof in the criminal law. If the allegation that the defendant is guilty is not proved in the trial, the conclusion should be drawn that the defendant is not guilty. Neither of these arguments seems to be deductively valid unless the evidence is complete. In many cases of argument from ignorance of the most common sort, the evidence is incomplete. The facts are not all in yet. We do not have what is called epistemic closure (Reiter, 1987), meaning that the knowledge base can be assumed to be complete. In such cases, participants will dispute on who has the burden of proof, and we have dialogues like the infinite regress dialogue cited in chapter 1, where one party says of a claim, "You prove it!" and the other replies, "You disprove it!"

In principle, the argument from ignorance is a reasonable kind of default argument that can rightly be used to shift a weight of presumption in a balance of considerations argument, based on burden of proof, but it depends on a premise indicating depth of search. For example, if no evidence has been found that Ed is a spy, one could reasonably conclude by *argumentum ad ignorantiam* that he is not a spy, but only on the assumption that a thorough security search into Ed's activities has been carried out. Similarly, if a large number of rats have been given a certain drug, and did not experience any harmful effects of a kind that were anticipated, this negative outcome may have some worth as evidence for the conclusion that ingestion of this drug does not produce this outcome. Negative evidence is generally regarded as less significant than positive evidence in scientific research. However, some researchers see this priority given to positive over negative evidence as a kind of bias inherent in current methods of scientific research (Sterling, Rosenbaum and Weinkam, 1995). It has been recognized as a bias that affects statistical findings on the outcomes of scientific research, and that ought to be corrected, or brought into less of an imbalance. Now the trend is toward taking negative evidence into account. Argument from ignorance is thus being accepted as nonfallacious.

The argument from ignorance is quite familiar in computer science, where it takes the form of negative reasoning from a knowledge base. Reiter (1987, p. 150) gives the example of an airline flight schedule presenting a list of flight numbers and pairs of cities they connect. He then adds, "We certainly would not want to include in this data base all flights and the city pairs they do *not* connect, which clearly would be an overwhelming amount of information." But by negative reasoning from this knowledge base, a viewer of the flight schedule listed on an airport monitor can infer that, if two cities are not stated as connected in the list given, there is no flight connecting them. This kind of negative reasoning from a given knowledge base is highly familiar in computer science, and is a reasonable species of *argumentum ad ignorantiam*. Such arguments are frequently associated with default inferences and nonmonotonic reasoning, of a kind where lack of knowledge warrants the drawing of a presumptive inference on how best to draw a conclusion on what to do in a situation of uncertainty. More and more, it is being recognized in computer science, that this kind of reasoning is commonplace and useful, and is generally reasonable, as opposed to being fallacious.

A very simple example adapted from (Walton, 1996, p. 251) can be used to show to the reader how common the argument from ignorance is in everyday reasoning, and how it can function as a reasonable kind of argumentation. Suppose Wilma can't find her pen, and she asks Bruce, "Is it in the desk?" Bruce replies, "I don't think so, because I have a pretty good idea what's in the desk", and then Wilma continues, "Yes, but have you looked in the desk?" In this small dialogue is contained the basic idea of how the argument from ignorance works. When Bruce replied that he didn't think the pen was in the desk, he was drawing an inference on the basis of the argument from ignorance. He was indicating that, as far as he knew, the pen was not in the desk, and then from this premise of lack of positive knowledge, he was drawing the conclusion that (probably, or plausibly), the pen was not in the desk. Wilma's reply questioned how thorough Bruce's search was, perhaps suggesting that he should actually go and look through the desk, to make sure the pen was not there. She was questioning the strength of his argument from ignorance by questioning the depth-of-search premise that is always an additional (in this case nonexplicit) premise in the argument from ignorance.

Our particular interest focuses on forms of argument of kinds both common in law and of interest in modeling common kinds of argumentation where burden of proof can be problematic. Such forms of argument were often traditionally considered to be fallacious in logic textbooks, but recent work has indicated that they are often reasonable arguments, under the right conditions, as used in dialogue, particularly in cases where there is incomplete knowledge. The argument from ignorance can be represented as a form of reasoning in three different ways, a dialectical way, an epistemic way and a formal way. In the dialectical format, the argument from ignorance is represented with two premises and a conclusion, as displayed in the form of argumentation scheme below (Walton, 1996, p. 254).

Dialectical Argumentation Scheme for Argument from Ignorance

If *A* were true, *A* would be known (proved, presumed) to be true.

A is not known (proved, presumed) to be true.

Therefore, *A* is (presumably) false.

Along with this positive version of the scheme there is also a negative version.

Dialectical Argumentation Scheme for Negative Argument from Ignorance

If *A* were false, *A* would be known (proved, presumed) to be false.

A is not known (proved, presumed) to be false.

Therefore, *A* is (presumably) true.

In the pen case, the depth-of-search premise equates to the conditional premise above. Wilma was asking Bruce, in effect, whether if the pen were in the desk, he would know that. So generally, we can see how the argument from ignorance is based on a characteristic argumentation scheme that shows its structure as a kind of reasoning that can be correct or reasonable, as used in many cases in everyday reasoning.

If epistemic closure can be established in a case, the argument from ignorance can be treated as a deductively valid form of argument. The reason is that the conditional premise can be taken to be a certainty, relative to the epistemic closure assumption. But in many instances, where lack of knowledge is characteristic of the case, the argument from ignorance is not deductively valid. It is a defeasible form of argument. It holds tentatively in a dialogue, subject to the asking of critical questions by the other side. Three critical questions are vitally important in evaluating such cases.

Critical Questions Matching the Dialectical Scheme for Argument from Ignorance

CQ1: How far along has the search for evidence progressed?

CQ2: Which side has the burden of proof in the dialogue as a whole? In other words, what is the ultimate *probandum* and who is supposed to prove it?

CQ3: How strong does the proof need to be in order for this party to be successful in fulfilling the burden?

CQ2 and CQ3 are about the burden of proof. The latter is about which party has the burden, corresponding to CQ2. The former is about how strong the proof needs to be, corresponding to CQ3.[6] CQ1 is also very important. As the examples above illustrate, the argument from ignorance often arises at a mid-point in a dialogue during the argumentation stage. To evaluate such a case, two steps have to be taken. First, we have to go back to the starting point of the dialogue where the ultimate *probandum* was set. Second we have to look at the collection of evidence in the dialogue so far, in relation to that starting point.

In contrast with the dialectical scheme, there is an epistemic version of the argument from ignorance that has been recognized. In this scheme, *D* is a domain of knowledge and *K* is a knowledge base.

Epistemic Version of the Argument from Ignorance (Walton, 1992, p. 386)

It has not been established that all the true propositions in *D* are contained in *K*.

A is a special type of proposition such that if *A* were true, *A* would normally or usually be expected to be in *K*.

A is in *D*.

A is not in *K*.

For all *A* in *D, A* is either true or false.

Therefore, it is plausible to presume that *A* is false (subject to further investigations in *D*).

Formally speaking, where '*KA*' represents the modality 'proposition *A* is known to be true', the argument from ignorance takes two forms.

[6] According to Park, Leonard and Goldberg (1998, p. 88) there are two meanings of burden of proof. One is the determination of the quantum of evidence (or standard of proof) required to establish an ultimate fact. The other is "the allocation of risk that the factfinder will not be persuaded to that prescribed degree of certainty".

Logical Form 1 of Argument from Ignorance

~K*A*

If *A* then K*A*

Therefore ~*A*

Logical Form 2 of Argument from Ignorance

~K~*A*

If ~*A* then K~*A*

Therefore *A*

Forms 1 and 2 are species of *modus tollens* (MT) arguments. But they are only deductive MT if the database is assumed to be complete (epistemic closure). Thus what we are normally dealing with is a species of MT argument that is not deductively valid.

The question is then raised: if the argument from ignorance can be correct in some instances as represented by the forms above, what kind of correct reasoning does it represent? It seems to be a knowledge-based form of reasoning based on assumptions about what is and what is not known in a case.

The fallacious kind of *argumentum ad ignorantiam* arises where one party in a dialogue tries to use this kind of argumentation as a tactic to force the burden of proof or disproof around the other way. By such a tactic, the respondent's ability to prove anything, or even to raise appropriate critical questions in the dialogue, is blocked or impeded. Such cases may occur even in cases where the burden of proof has been clearly set on the proponent's side. At the opening stage of the dialogue, the proponent may try to avoid fulfilling the burden by trying to shift it to the other side, making it appear as though the other side must prove its claim (which may not even be possible), or lose the debate. The most visible kind of case of this sort is the "kangaroo court" or so-called "witch hunt" type of tribunal, which has the trappings of a fair criminal trial, but where the defendant is presumed to be guilty. The classic cases cited here are the witchcraft trials, especially the Salem witchcraft trials of 1692, and the McCarthy tribunals of the 1950's. The Salem witchcraft trials were actually legal proceedings, but the so-called "spectral evidence" claimed by witnesses to prove that someone was a witch (in league with the devil), was difficult to disprove, because it was supposedly only visible to the person testifying. The McCarthy tribunals were televised proceedings that were made to look to viewers a lot like trials, but they were not legal trials. McCarthy posed as having evidence that the defendant was a "communist sympathizer", but the allegations were more often based on innuendo. In one case, cited by (Copi, 1982, p. 112), McCarthy stated, "I do not have much information on this except the general statement of the agency that there is nothing in the files to disprove his Communist connections." One problem here for the person accused of being a Communist sympathizer was that it was extremely difficult to prove such a negative thesis - that he is not a Communist sympathizer - because of the vagueness of the charge, and the smear on his trustworthiness created merely by the accusation itself. But the main problem was the reversal of the burden of proof. The accused was put in the position of having to try to fulfill this heavy, or even impossible, burden of proof.

How is the fallacy in such a case a misuse of argument from ignorance? It seems that the fallacy is an epistemic failure in which lack of knowledge is improperly treated as evidence of a kind that should be based on knowledge and not mere speculation or supposition. The problem is that the accused party cannot refute the accusation. If he tries to deny it, he would be discredited as a Communist who cannot be trusted to tell the truth, etc. The fallacy is one of failure of due process in which there has been an illicit shift in the burden of proof. The defendant must prove he is innocent, but this is impossible for him to conclusively prove. Yet it is the only standard of evidence the tribunal will accept. Prima facie arguments, such as "I've never given them money, gone to a meeting, or distributed literature for them," are just not acceptable as sufficient.

An example that can be used to illustrate how the nonfallacious *ad ignorantiam* works as an argument is the foreign spy case, cited in (Walton, 1989, p. 45).

The Foreign Spy Case

Mr. *X* has never been found guilty of breaches of security, or of any connection with agents of the foreign country he is supposedly spying for, even though the Security Service has checked his record. Therefore, Mr. *X* is not a foreign spy.

This argument from ignorance is defeasible, because it is not possible to be absolutely certain that Mr. *X* is not a foreign spy. Mr. *X* could have avoided detection through many security searches, as Kim Philby did. Hence arguments from ignorance tend to be defeasible arguments, even though they can be conclusive in some cases. The argument from ignorance can be seen to be a very common kind of defeasible argumentation, once you learn to recognize it.

There is a very common principle often appealed to in knowledge-based systems in AI called the closed world assumption. Essentially, the closed world assumption means that all the information that there is to know or find is listed in the collection of information one already has. But there are different ways of representing information. According to Reiter (1980, p. 69), the closed world assumption is met if all the positive information in a data base is listed, and therefore negative information is represented by default. Reiter (1980, p. 69) offers the airport example below to illustrate how the closed world assumption is linked to default.

The Airport Example

Consider a data base representing an airline flight schedule and the query "Does Air Canada flight 113 connect Vancouver with New York?" A deductive question-answering system will typically treat the data base together with some general knowledge about the flight domains as a set of premises from which it will attempt to prove CONNECT (AC113, VAN, NY). If this proof succeeds, then the system responds "yes".

If the system searches for a flight of the designated type and does not find one in the data base, it will reply "no". Reiter (1980, p. 69) described the form of argument used in this sequence of knowledge-based reasoning as: "Failure to find a proof has sanctioned an inference." As noted above, this kind of inference by default from lack-of-knowledge has traditionally been called the *argumentum ad ignorantiam* in logic. A traveller is scanning the flight monitor at the airport. If he assumes all flights are listed (closed world assumption), he infers by argument from ignorance that any flight not listed is not offered. This may be just an assumption, but if he has reason to think that the monitor lists all flights, the closed world assumption can be invoked. Once the data base is closed off, the argument from ignorance is conclusive. But in a typical case, such an inference may be neither deductively valid nor inductively strong. It may be merely a defeasible inference that leads to a provisional commitment to a course of action, but should be seen as open to new evidence that might come into an investigation and needs to be added to the knowledge base.

In legal argumentation, argument from ignorance is closely associated with distribution of burden of proof in a trial. In a criminal trial, the prosecution has to prove its claim beyond a reasonable doubt, while the defense, to win, needs only to show that the prosecution's argument is too weak to prove its claim according to that standard of proof. This asymmetry involves an argument from ignorance. If the defense can show that there is a lack of evidence to support the prosecution's claim (ultimate thesis to be proved in the trial), then the defense has shown that this claim does not hold up and must be rejected. This form of argumentation meets the requirements for the argumentation scheme of the argument from ignorance. Thus argument from ignorance is fundamental to the argumentation structure of the trial in the adversary system.

Argument from ignorance is also common in more special forms in legal argumentation. For example, as shown by Park, Leonard and Goldberg (1998, p. 103), there is a presumption that writing has been accurately dated: "unless the presumption is rebutted, the writing in question will be deemed accurately dated". Another example (p. 153) concerns character evidence. Suppose a first person was in a position to hear derogatory statements about a second person if any were made. And suppose the first person testifies that he heard no such comments. This testimony counts as evidence of the first person's good character. The form of argument in such a case is that of argument from ignorance. If no evidence of bad character was found or reported by the witness, this lack of such a finding may be taken as evidence of good character.

Arguments from ignorance having the form of the argumentation scheme set out above are best analyzed as defeasible arguments at some stage of a dialogue or investigation in which evidence is being collected and assessed. All of the examples described above have a typical pattern of reversal of burden of proof characteristic of the *argumentum ad ignorantiam*. This shift can be illustrated by the following dialogue sequence discussed by Krabbe (1995, p. 256).

The *Ad Ignorantiam* Shift Sequence

Proponent: Why *A*?

Respondent: Why not-*A*?

This pattern of shifting back and forth of the burden of proof in dialogue is characteristic of the argument from ignorance as cited in the infinite regress dialogue in chapter 1. However, the argument from ignorance is not always a defeasible argument. As noted above, in a case where a knowledge base is closed, the argument from ignorance can be conclusive. Thus, generally speaking, arguments from ignorance need to be analyzed and evaluated using two tools. One is the argumentation scheme. The other is the placement of that scheme in a context of dialogue.

8. Other Argumentation Schemes in Evidence Law

There are two other argumentation schemes that are so fundamentally important in evidence law, and that underlie the structure of many other argumentation schemes in such a fundamental way, that they need to be discussed in any attempt to model defeasible legal reasoning in evidence law. One is the scheme for abductive reasoning. As indicated above, Keppens and Zeleznikow (2002) showed how the reasoning in a typical crime investigation proceeds on a basis of best explanation of the facts as new evidence comes in. When a dead body is found by the police, if there is no evidence of foul play, the hypothesis of natural death may be the best explanation. But if a subsequent forensic investigation in the lab shows evidence of a known poison, for example, the earlier hypothesis may be given up. In the light of the new evidence, a better explanation of the facts at that point may come to be selected by the police as the most plausible conclusion. Much legal evidence is of this sort. As the facts are collected, a best explanation stands out from the competing explanations that could be offered. By abduction, the investigators tentatively accept the conclusion that the best explanation is a working hypothesis to be adopted as a way to move the investigation forward. Of course, such an argument is defeasible, if the investigation is incomplete. And even if the police investigation is closed and the case goes to trial, the argument will be tested once again in that forum.

There is a connection between abduction and various argumentation schemes. For one thing, abductive argumentation is itself an argumentation scheme (Walton, 2001). But several other argumentation schemes also appear to be abductive in nature, and are thus closely related to abduction. Argument from appearance, as defined above, is one of these. If I see an object and it looks red, the best explanation may be that it actually is red. This argument proceeds from a premise that reports a visual appearance, some data or fact, in other words. It then draws by inference a conclusion that provides the best explanation of the given fact. Of course, it is not the only explanation that might be offered. Another would be the statement that the object is being illuminated by a red light. But in the absence of definite knowledge that this is so, it would be reasonable to infer that it looks red because in fact it is red. Thus abductive argumentation, as illustrated by this example, is inherently defeasible. The best explanation is not the only one that might be offered. And if new facts come in showing that one of these other explanations is better, the original explanation may have to be given up.

Peirce (1965, p. 375) noted that abduction is often based on visual observations, and offered an example that showed he was well aware of its common use as a form of evidence in scientific fields like paleontology.

The Fossils Example

Fossils are found; say, remains like those of fishes, but far in the interior of the country. To explain the phenomenon, we suppose the sea once washed over this land. This is another hypothesis.

In his discussion of the fossils example (p. 375), Peirce used the word 'explain', showing that he saw abductions as inference to the best explanation. The kind of reasoning used in the fossils example can also be shown to be defeasible. As a general rule, it can be stated that fish require water to survive. But such a rule is subject to some exceptions under special or unusual circumstances. Some fish can survive on land for some time. However, in the absence of any knowledge of such special circumstances, it is reasonable that this fish skeleton found far into the interior where there is now no water is evidence that there was water there at one time. That is the best explanation, unless a better one can be given by bringing in new information showing that the situation was special or unusual in some way. It is shown by such cases that abductive reasoning, in science as well as in law, is often based on a defeasible argument from appearance.

Argument from appearance is defeasible during the earlier stages of an investigation, but may become stronger or weaker as the investigation proceeds, and more facts are collected. Close inspection of data at an archeological site, a crime scene, or in a medical examination of a patient, typically leads to a hypothesis that is one among several being considered. As more data comes in, the hypothesis can be tested, and then supported or defeated. Either way, the investigation can move along. Keppens and Zeleznikow (2002) gave an example of forensic evidence by describing the typical problem facing police officials encountering a dead body.

There are four standard hypotheses that are automatically considered as alternatives: homicide, suicide, accident, or natural causes. The officials arrive at a best explanation in a given case by finding factual evidence that tends to support one hypothesis as the most plausible and eliminates others as less plausible candidates as the investigation proceeds. It is well known that once prosecutors have selected a hypothesis, they may concentrate exclusively on looking for evidence that supports it, and ignore relevant evidence that supports alternative hypotheses. Thus defeasible arguments have an important function for guiding an investigation, but they can also be associated with bias and fallacies when too much weight is put on them. It would seem that abduction is a reasonable form of argumentation when considered in the context of an ongoing framework of dialogue or investigation in which evidence is being collected and assessed. But it can also be a form of argument that can go wrong, or be deficient in various ways. To evaluate cases, an argumentation scheme is needed.

The argumentation scheme for abductive argument presented in (Walton, 2001) is based on two variables. The variable *F* stands for the given set of facts in a case. A given set of facts is a set of statements that are presumed to be the facts in a given case. They are not "facts" in the sense that they are true, and cannot turn out to be false if new information comes in. They are said to be facts meaning that their truth is not in question for the present purposes, even though it could come into question later in an investigation. In other words, the concept of a fact is a dialectical notion rather than a notion that implies truth. The variable *E* stands for an explanation in a sense that is also dialectical. A set of statements *E* is judged to be a satisfactory explanation of a set of facts *F* if and only if *E* is a set of statements put forward by an explainer in a dialogue that gives the explainee in the dialogue a better understanding of *F*. An explanation, according to this dialectical definition, is a response offered to a particular type of question in a dialogue. The satisfactoriness of an explanation, in such a dialectical view, depends on the type of dialogue the two parties are engaged in, on how far the dialogue has progressed, on what has been said in the dialogue before the explanation was attempted, and on the collective goal the dialogue is supposed to fulfill. Given this dialectical account of what the facts of a case are, and what a satisfactory explanation is, the argumentation scheme for abduction can be formulated as follows.

Abductive Argumentation Scheme

F is a finding or given set of facts.

E is a satisfactory explanation of *F*.

No alternative explanation *E'* given so far is as satisfactory as *E*.

Therefore, *E* is plausible as a hypothesis.

The term 'hypothesis' in the conclusion indicates that an argument of this form is defeasible. The conclusion is only a tentative assumption, relative to the progress of the dialogue to a given point. It is not proved beyond doubt by the premises, but only set in place as an assumption that both parties to the dialogue should accept for the time being, so that the dialogue can progess further. As the dialogue proceeds, the abductive conclusion may stay in place, but new information may defeat it. Thus an abductive argument carries a certain "weight" as a dialogue moves forward. But that weight can be lightened, or even removed (undercut or rebutted) through the asking of appropriate critical questions by the other party in the dialogue. The following critical questions (Walton, 2001) provide a basis for evaluations that center on many of these same factors, or comparable ones.

CQ1: How satisfactory is *E* itself as an explanation of *F*, apart from the alternative explanations available so far in the dialogue?

CQ2: How much better an explanation is *E* than the alternative explanations available so far in the dialogue?

CQ3: How far has the dialogue progressed? If the dialogue is an inquiry, how thorough has the search been in the investigation of the case?

CQ4: Would it be better to continue the dialogue further, instead of drawing a conclusion at this point?

The evaluation procedure outlined above explicitly analyzes abductive argumentation as dialectical. Each inference to the best explanation put forward in a given case has some weight in a dialogue, making its conclusion an assumption that should be reasonably accepted for the present on a balance of considerations. But each single abductive argument needs to be evaluated in a dialogue containing other competing explanations of the same set of facts.

It takes little convincing to get those interested in evidence law to accept the view that many of the most fundamental kinds of arguments used in law are abductive. Much more controversial is whether abductive inference represents a third type of argument to be distinguished from deductive and inductive arguments.[7] Perhaps the most important point to be made is that many of the most common arguments used in evidence law, and especially those that are abductive, have an underlying general form based on a major premise, or warrant, to use Toulmin's term,[8] that is a qualified generalization. Such generalizations are sub-

[7] The reader is referred to the discussion of this controversy in the analysis of abductive reasoning set forth in (Walton, 2004).

[8] Toulmin (1964, pp. 103-107). Toulmin clearly saw warrants as defeasible in his model of argument. He expressed the conclusion using the wording "so, presumably", basing it on an inference containing an "unless" qualifier. Meeting the qualifier by showing that there is an exception to the warrant defeats the inference to the conclusion in Toulmin's model (p. 105). There has been much uncertainty and controversy on the subject of exactly what Toulim meant by 'warrant', as shown by Hitchcock (2004).

ject to exceptions, and the arguments based on them are defeasible. They typically take the form of argument called defeasible *modus ponens*.

Argumentation Scheme for Defeasible *Modus Ponens*

Generally, but subject to exceptions, if something has property F, you can also expect it to have property G.

Object a has property F.

Therefore object a has property G.

This form of argument is called defeasible *modus ponens* (DMP), as opposed to the deductively valid form of *modus ponens* that is so familiar in deductive logic: if A then B; A; therefore B. DMP is a special subtype of *modus ponens* arguments that applies to defeasible arguments.[9] Of course, this claim is highly controversial. Many would claim that DMP is not really a form of *modus ponens* argument at all, and that any argument that is an instance of *modus ponens* is deductively valid. But whatever you call it, DMP is a common form of argumentation.

Since DMP is not deductively valid or inductively strong, the problem arises of how to evaluate arguments having this form. The formal system of dialogue proves to be a nice model for this purpose. A dialogue is a sequence of moves, M_1, M_2, ..., M_n. Suppose the proponent puts forward an argument of the form DMP at any given move M_1, and the respondent is committed to the premises of this argument, what are the options for the respondent at the next move? He must either commit to the conclusion, or he must challenge the argument in some way. One way would be to cite an exception to the rule in relation to the specific case under discussion. Another might be to mount some sort of counter-argument. Another might be to ask an appropriate critical question of some sort that applies to this form of argument and casts doubt on its acceptability. But if the respondent doesn't make any of these kinds of moves right away, he must commit to the conclusion tentatively, subject to possible later retraction. Thus an argument of the DMP form has rational bite in argumentation. It does shift a burden of proof onto the conclusion in a dialogue, even if that burden can later be removed.

9 Verheij (2000) recognized DMP as a form of argument widely used in legal argumentation.

9. Dialogue Conditions for Defeasible Arguments

It is somewhat easier to devise dialogue rules for deductive arguments than for defeasible arguments, because defeasible arguments are more complex to evaluate. Defeasible arguments are open-ended. They are not conclusive in the way deductive arguments are. To illustrate how this open-endedness works, consider the canonical example of the Tweety argument as it might typically be put forward in a dialogue.

The Tweety Profile of Dialogue

Proponent	Respondent
1. Tweety flies.	How can you prove that?
2. Tweety is a bird.	So what?
3. Birds fly.	Yes, they generally do.
4. Therefore Tweety flies.	But Tweety is a penguin.
5. Oh, really?	Therefore Tweety does not fly.

In the Tweety profile, the proponent put forward a defeasible argument. At move 3, the respondent conceded the major premise of the argument. At move 4, the proponent drew the conclusion. But then, at his turn in move 4, the respondent defeated the argument by bringing in new information about Tweety. This profile shows how things should go ideally in a dialogue in which one party has brought forward a defeasible argument. She properly used a defeasible generalization as a premise. This premise, along with the other one, formed an argument having the form of DMP. The respondent indicated at move 2 that he accepts the premise that Tweety is a bird. At move 3, he indicates acceptance of the generic premise that birds fly. Thus at the next move, the respondent must commit to the conclusion that Tweety flies, in order to follow the commitment rules of a persuasion dialogue. The big problem is whether the respondent can now retract commitment from one of the premises. At move 4, he doesn't retract directly. Instead he offers a new bit of evidence in the form of the statement 'Tweety is a penguin'.

The Tweety profile of dialogue illustrates a key feature of defeasible argumentation. The proponent conceded that he was wrong, and that his prior argument is now defeated. An important feature of a defeasible argument in a dialogue is the following condition.

Openness to Defeat (OTD) Condition: When the proponent has put forward a defeasible argument in a dialogue, he must be open to giving it up and admitting its defeat at any future move by the respondent that defeats the argument (in the proponent's opinion) at any point before closure of the dialogue.

What sort of move defeats a defeasible argument like the Tweety argument? The defeater has to be an exception to the rule postulated by the generic premise. Such a defeasible rule is subject to exceptions. So the respondent, to defeat the argument, has to come up with information in the given case that presents an exception to the rule. The OTD condition requires that if the respondent comes up with such a case, and the proponent admits that it constitutes an exception to the rule, then the proponent has to give up his argument. Thus the respondent no longer has to accept the conclusion. Indeed, both parties must now retract commitment to the conclusion.

The OTD condition says something about all future moves of a dialogue between the move where the defeasible argument was put forward and the closing move of the dialogue. It says that at all such moves, the proponent must retract the conclusion, if the respondent makes the sort of move that defeats the argument used to prove it. There is no way to predict when a respondent may come up with such a defeater before closure of a dialogue. So defeasible arguments are characteristically open-ended. They have to do not just with the argument as presented, but with the future stretch of dialogue beyond the argument in a dialogue that provides the framework of argument use.

A second key feature of defeasible argumentation illustrated by the Tweety dialogue is the reversal of burden of proof. At move 1, it is shown that the proponent has the burden of proof. The respondent asks, "How can you prove that?", referring to the proponent's claim that Tweety flies. The proponent then fulfills this burden of proof by putting forward a defeasible argument to support it. That should be the end of it, if the argument was not defeasible. But then at move 4, the respondent asserts that Tweety is a penguin. Why should the respondent say this, if the burden of proof was on the proponent? The answer is that the burden has shifted to the respondent's side. It could now be called the burden of disproof. The respondent made an allowable move by bringing forward an exception to the rule posited by the proponent's major premise in his prior argument. This shift of the burden of proof from one side to the other is characteristic of a defeasible argument.

The pattern of argumentation characteristic of defeasible argumentation has the following sequence of dialogue moves.

The Characteristic Dialogue Sequence of Defeasible Argumentation

1. The proponent puts the defeasible argument forward.
2. One premise is a generalization or a conditional warrant (rule) that admits of exceptions.
3. If the respondent is committed to the premises, he must commit to the conclusion.
4. But his commitment to the conclusion is only tentative.
5. The dialogue must remain open to the respondent's finding an exception to the rule.
6. As soon as the respondent cites such an exception, the proponent's argument defaults.
7. The respondent can now retract commitment to the conclusion.

This sequence of argumentation has the reversal of burden of proof characteristic of the typical presumptive argument of the kind often used in law. An assumption is accepted tentatively in a dialogue as a way of moving the dialogue forward, but it can be defeated if new evidence comes into the dialogue.

For example, in law, a person who has disappeared without a trace for a determinate number of years may be presumed dead, for purposes of settling an estate. The basis of the reasoning is an argument from ignorance. If there is no evidence that the person is alive, then the conclusion can be drawn by inference (after the stated period) that he is dead. But if such a person turns up, the presumption that he is dead is defeated.

At stage 7 of the dialogue sequence, retraction to the conclusion of the argument is shown as a key dialectical feature of defeasible argumentation. In a persuasion dialogue, and in some of the other types of dialogue as well, retraction is allowed, although not in all circumstances and not without penalty. Retraction of one statement may require retraction of other statements that it is closely related to by inference. For example, if the proposition that a person is dead is retracted then the proposition that someone else may inherit his estate may also need to be retracted, even though it was accepted previously. However, the problem of retraction has not been solved for persuasion dialogue, even though proposed solutions to it have been put forward (Krabbe, 2001). Thus in the dialectical approach, the problem of defeasiblity is recast as a problem of determining conditions for retraction in the various types of dialogue.

10. The Dialectical Approach to Defeasible Arguments

The general hypothesis that has been put forward in this paper is that defeasible arguments in legal argumentation of a kind highly familiar in evidence law can be evaluated in the dialectical framework set out above. When the proponent puts a defeasible argument forward, if the respondent is committed to all the premises then he has to commit to the conclusion of the argument, but only tentatively. The proponent needs to retract commitment if new evidence of the right sort comes into the dialogue later, and the respondent uses this evidence to defeat the argument. Thus these kinds of arguments are fallible and the kind of commitment they incur is tentative. They can be accepted, but then defeated later in a chain of argumentation that runs through a dialogue. In some cases, they can even be used wrongly or inappropriately in a dialogue, and can be fallacious. Indeed, traditional logic textbooks mainly classify these forms of argumentation under the heading of informal fallacies. But more and more research is supporting the theory that they are not always fallacious (Hansen and Pinto, 1995), and that in many instances, they are reasonable but defeasible arguments.

What is essential to a defeasible argument as a type of argument? The dialectical theory above cites three characteristics: openness to defeat, reversal of burden of proof, and retraction of commitment. These three characteristics can be modeled best in a dialectical theory in which an argument is seen as sequence of moves made by a proponent and a respondent who take turns. The dialogue should be seen as having four characteristic stages.[10] The sequence of argumentation in the argumentation stage should be seen as moving towards the closing stage. Thus there are two ways to view a dialogue in a given case. It can be open or closed. In typical cases, defeasible arguments are viewed as having been put forward, and as not yet being defeated, while assuming that the dialogue is still open. At this stage, commitment to the conclusion of the argument is still tentative and subject to possible retraction as the dialogue proceeds. This tentativeness has often been the basis of a traditional feeling of distrust about defeasible arguments. They have often been seen as unreliable or even fallacious. The argument from ignorance is an excellent case in point. We need to get over this wholesale rejection of defeasible arguments and see them as arguments that can go wrong, but are often quite reasonable. They are typically reasonable in cases of uncertainty and lack of knowledge where some decision for action needs to be made or a presumption adopted. They should give way to deductive or inductive arguments when harder evidence comes in. They are fallible.

Openness to defeat can be viewed as an epistemic characteristic rather than a dialectical one, if one sees epistemic closure, and epistemic openness, its contrasting opposite, as properties of the completeness of a knowledge base. If an argument is open to defeat, presumably on the epistemic model, what that means is that new knowledge can still come into the knowledge base. But the notion of this new knowledge or evidence defeating a claim does seem to have a dialectical aspect, suggesting an opposition between a pro and a contra side. Pollock's distinction between defeaters and undercutters also has a distinctly dialectical flavor. It is harder to try to view burden of proof as an epistemic feature without bringing in any dialectical aspects. Moreover, Pollock's additional distinction between practical and epistemic rationality can very easily be seen as a move towards evaluating the same sequence of reasoning by different standards when used in a different type of dialogue. The dialectical notion of stages of dialogue is also very well adapted to defeasible reasoning.

One of the most important things about defeasible arguments is that they are often used during the argumentation stage of a dialogue, before it has reached the closing stage. One needs to take a stance of being open-minded about such arguments, and be ready to give them up if new evidence comes in. It is perhaps because of the human tendency to be reluctant to admit defeat, and thus to close off argumentation too soon, that the problems with defeasible arguments often arise. These matters have to do with dialectical factors like presumption, default, burden of proof, and openness and closure of argumentation in a dialogue. As the form of default rule above indicates, such arguments depend on a default blocker that makes acceptance of an argument conditional on lack of evidence to support a key assumption. Such an argument is based on a mixture of knowledge and lack of knowledge. It is always an *argumentum ad ignorantiam.*

In an argument from ignorance, it is argued that a statement A is not yet known to be true (false), and argued on this basis that A is false (true). The premise may

[10] Van Eemeren and Grootendorst (1992, pp. 34-37).

be taken to mean that A is not yet known to be true (false) at some point in an investigation or collection of data that is underway. At least, that is what the premise means if the case is a typical sort where epistemic closure has presumably not been reached yet in the sequence of argumentation. But what this means, according to the dialectical analysis of such a case, is that the argumentation is still open to possible defeat in the future as more information is collected. The dialectical model portrays the context as one of an information-seeking and accumulating type of dialogue. The proponent urges the respondent to accept the conclusion that A is false (true) based on the findings up to that point in the dialogue. If the respondent does accept the conclusion of the argument from ignorance it is a tentative commitment that is open to retraction as the dialogue proceeds. Only when the dialogue reaches the closing stage does the argument from ignorance become non-defeasible. The conclusion is then based on the knowledge collected to that point, and it is assumed that the knowledge base is complete, by epistemic closure.

One might criticize the dialectical approach put forward above by saying that it is very general. Although it may give philosophical insight into the notion of defeasibility as a general concept of argumentation, it does not set out any formal system of dialogue with rules for winning or losing an argument. As a reply to this criticism, it should be made clear that a central aspect of the dialectical approach is its pluralism. The thesis is that defeasible arguments need to be evaluated somewhat differently in different types of dialogue. Treating a case of argumentation as a sequence of moves in a zero-sum game may be appropriate if the context is that of a critical discussion or persuasion dialogue where the goal is to resolve a conflict of opinions. Or an eristic dialogue can also be treated as a zero-sum game where one party wins if and only if the other loses. But in another case, where the context is that of deliberation dialogue, for example, treating the argument as a sequence of moves in a zero-sum game may be misleading and inappropriate. The goal of a deliberation dialogue is to decide on a best available course of action by coordinating the goals and actions of a group (see table 1 above) in a collaborative manner. It is also reasonable to assume that treating information-seeking dialogue or inquiry as zero-sum games would not yield a terribly helpful model of defeasible argumentation. Thus striving for dialectical generality, it may be wiser to stop short at the very general characteristics cited above, and then realize that there will be no single system of formal dialogue with rules for winning and losing an argument that will encompass all defeasible arguments. The rules for evaluating defeasible arguments will be different in legal argumentation than in scientific argumentation. The rules for evaluating defeasible arguments may even be different at different stages of a scientific investigation. At the earlier discovery stage, the burden of proof and the way of evaluating hypotheses may be quite different from those at later stages of testing and theory construction. The pluralism of the dialectical approach could be an advantage. What is common to all defeasible argumentation in all types of dialogue is the characteristic dialogue sequence of defeasible argumentation (above).

All that said, the dialectical approach of treating the context of dialogue in certain kinds of cases of argumentation as that of a dispute or zero-sum game, could be highly appropriate in some instances. For example, in the kind of argumentation used in a trial, the prosecution and defense sides can be seen as engaging in a dispute or conflict of opinions characteristic of the persuasion dialogue. Speaking of the argumentation in such a trial in terms of winning and losing is appropriate. Prakken (2001) has presented a formal dialectical system for analyzing and evaluating defeasible arguments in what he calls dynamic disputes. This analysis is nicely applicable to legal argumentation because it evaluates defeasible arguments not only for logical soundness, but also for procedural fairness (p. 189). Prakken (2001, p. 191) in fact acknowledged that disputes of the kind he studied can be embedded in persuasion dialogues. This progress in applying the dialectical approach to defeasible argumentation in special contexts suggests that this approach is no longer purely theoretical or philosophical.

The dialectical approach can provide insight and tools for analysis when applied to common types of defeasible argument associated with informal fallacies.[11] In a typical appeal to expert opinion, it is assumed that the expert source is fallible. The expert can be seen as representing a knowledge base that is incomplete. Of course, the expert can be said to be omniscient, but this form of appeal to expert opinion is comparatively rare. Generally, it is best to see appeals to expert opinion as defeasible. Such an appeal can be defeated by attacking a premise, or it can be undercut by asking a critical question. Thus the dialectical structure required to evaluate it is the same as that of the argument from ignorance. Both are best seen as defeasible arguments that typically occur in the middle of a dialogue that is open to future moves by both participants and possibly also to the collection of new data that both parties will accept as evidence. If it is assumed that the dialogue has reached the closing stage, then epistemic closure can be invoked, and the argument can be treated as non-defeasible. In either case, the framework required to properly evaluate the argument is one of a dialogue that is open at its argumentation stage but then later reaches a closing stage. To evaluate such an argument, one needs to situate it at a point in a dialogue.

Much insight can be gained from this dialectical analysis on how to judge individual cases of such arguments where allegations have been made that a fallacy has been committed. Fallacies are typically argumentation tactics used to obstruct the proper progress of a dialogue, often by trying to shut down another arguer's capability to carry on with the dialogue that has been started. For example, a common problem with appeals to expert opinion is that the proponent tries to treat the expert as an infallible source that cannot be questioned. The proponent tells the respondent that he is not an expert, and that therefore he is not entitled to say anything further on the subject. In effect, the strategy is to invoke epistemic closure on the dialogue by trying to rule out the respondent's capability to ask critical questions or to make other relevant future moves in the dialogue. The same dialectical analysis can be applied to arguments from ignorance. Epistemic closure may be invoked to try to shut down the respondent's right to bring forward relevant evidence in the future that could defeat the defeasible argument from ignorance.

But in many of the most common cases of defeasible argumentation, the dialogue is assumed to be incomplete. Thus we need to see such arguments as poten-

11 The dialectical analysis can be applied to formal fallacies as well (Krabbe, 1996).

tially open to defeat, yet as having a tentative standing in support of a conclusion on a balance of considerations in an ongoing dialogue.

Chapter 4: Relevance Determinations of Legal Evidence

In this chapter, *Araucaria* is applied to some cases of legal argumentation to help make judgments of relevance of evidence. A method called argument extrapolation was constructed in (Walton, 2004) for the purpose of determining relevance in argumentation. The method used in the paper combines *Araucaria* with argument extrapolation. It could apply to all kinds of cases of legal argumentation, but the main application of this chapter is to Anglo-American evidence law. It was shown in (Prakken, Reed and Walton, 2003) how *Araucaria* can be used to represent the evidence in a case used by Wigmore (1931) to illustrate his diagrammatic method of evidence charting. A next step is to see how *Araucaria* could be used to model legal relevance. Doing so is not straightforward in some cases, because much of the evidence that could potentially be used to argue for the ultimate conclusion to be proved in the case may not have been presented yet in a trial. In this chapter, no lengthy and complex case of evidence held to be relevant in a trial is studied, but several short and relatively simple examples are presented, analyzed, and diagrammed using *Araucaria* and argument extrapolation.[1] One of these cases concerns the highly controversial notion of conditional relevance. Through studying these cases, a general method of determining relevance of evidence in a trial is constructed.

In section 6, the method of determining relevance in a case is summarized as a sequence of ten steps that have to be applied to the data in the case. Although this method is helpful for assisting a user to analyze a given argument and then use the analysis to make a determination of relevance of the argument, it also has several limitations. These limitations are discussed in section 7. The method arose from attempts to help students improve skills of critical thinking in logic courses not specifically designed to deal with legal argumentation. Historically, logic was mainly concerned with the identification of fallacies of relevance. However, applying such notions to law is problematic, because a central concern in law is to design trial rules for admissibility of evidence based on some underlying notion of relevance, and there is no one-to-one correspondence between relevance as defined in the trial rules and relevance as defined in logic. This apparent mismatch has led to several problems that are posed and partly solved in chapter 4.

---

1 More complex cases involving relevance of character evidence will be studied in chapter 5.

1. Logical Relevance

The notion of relevance in argumentation has ancient roots, both in the classical *stasis* theory of Greek rhetoric (Hohmann, 1989), and in the Aristotelian theory of fallacies (Hamblin, 1970). The problem in the past has been that these notions have been highly unclear. Hamblin (1970, p. 31) showed that relevance has traditionally been used in logic textbooks as a "rag-bag" category in which to throw defective or fallacious arguments that cannot be diagnosed by any clearer criteria as failed arguments. But now new work in argumentation studies has presented a sharper analysis of the notion, by defining it conversationally. According to the theory of relevance in argumentation presented in chapter 4, there are two parties in any dialogue, called the proponent and the respondent. In the type of dialogue called the critical discussion, classified as a type of persuasion dialogue, there is a conflict of opinions between the two parties. The proponent has a designated thesis (a proposition). To win, she must prove it using rational argumentation based on premises accepted by the respondent. Thus the proponent has a pro viewpoint, meaning she has a positive attitude toward her thesis. The respondent has a contra viewpoint. Either he has an opposite thesis (the negation of the proponent's thesis), or he has expressed doubt about the acceptability of the proponent's thesis.[2] Given this conflict of opinions, each side uses chains of argumentation to try to prove his or her thesis from premises accepted by the other side. Whoever achieves such a proof first, wins the dialogue. This was the basic framework of dialectical relevance from chapter 4.

In this framework, and in types of dialogue other than the critical discussion as well (Walton, 2004), it is fairly easy to give a general characterization of relevance. The thesis of each side provides an aiming point or target for the argumentation used to prove that thesis by a chain of argumentation. In a dialogue, the proponent has the task of constructing a chain of rational argumentation that is rationally binding on the respondent and that leads to her conclusion. This analysis of relevance in argumentation is not new. Arguably, it fits the ancient model of *stasis* theory very well, at least insofar as persuasion dialogue is concerned. It can also be extended to other types of dialogue. Persuasion dialogue represents an attempt to get at the truth of the matter by revealing the strongest arguments that can be used to support a viewpoint as well as the strongest criticisms that can be made against it. Negotiation, in contrast, is not truth-oriented. The goal is to divide some contested resources by reaching an agreement that both parties can live with, or "make a deal". Thus the same argument might be relevant in a negotiation dialogue, but irrelevant in a persuasion dialogue. The classic example, the reader will recall, is that of the *argumentum ad baculum*. For example, a threat to go on strike or to cut wages could be a relevant argument when used in negotiation. But the same threat could be outstandingly irrelevant when used as an argument in a persuasion dialogue, like a critical discussion in a philosophy seminar. Used in that context it could properly be judged a fallacious *argumentum ad baculum*.

[2] In describing dialogues, the general convention is adopted that the proponent is female and the respondent male.

The main practical interest in relevance in logic has been the concern about fallacies of relevance. Several of the leading informal fallacies, *argumentum ad baculum*, appeal to pity, appeal to popular opinion and *ad hominem* arguments, have been classified as fallacies of relevance. It is not too hard to see why, because these types of arguments can easily function as powerful emotional distractions from a relevant line of argumentation. However, there is also a more pure fallacy of irrelevance called the *ignoratio elenchi*, usually translated as misconception of refutation. According to Aristotle's account (*Topica* 162a13 - 162a16), an argument commits this fallacy when it proves something other than the conclusion it is supposed to lead to. An example of this fallacy offered in a leading logic textbook (Copi, 1982, p. 110), can be used to illustrate it.

The Horrible Crime of Murder Example

In a law court, in attempting to prove that the accused is guilty of murder, the prosecution may argue at length that murder is a horrible crime. He may even succeed in proving that conclusion. But when he infers from his remarks about the horribleness of murder that the defendant is guilty of it, he is committing the fallacy of *ignoratio elenchi.*

Aristotle's account of the fallacy tells us that there are two main requirements for the committing of it. The first is a positive requirement, while the second is a negative one that may derive at least partly from the first. The positive requirement is that the argumentation in a given case is supposed to lead to (or at least toward) proving some specific proposition as ultimate conclusion, often called the ultimate *probandum* in law. The other requirement is that the argumentation is not supposed to lead away from proving that designated conclusion. In Aristotle's terminology, if it is a line of argumentation that leads to some conclusion other than the one to be proved, it is irrelevant. Irrelevance in this sense is regarded as a defect of rational argumentation, a failure of proof.

2. Legal Relevance

It is not hard to appreciate how a failure of relevance can be a serious defect in legal argumentation in a trial. The prosecution in a criminal trial has a burden of proof, to prove or at least make a case that the defendant is guilty of the crime he is charged with having committed. Going on at length about the horribleness of murder might do nothing logically to prove the defendant is guilty of having committed this crime, but it might psychologically prejudice the jury to think so. Such a tactic could work as an "irrational means of persuasion" (Twining, 1999, p. 359) that could influence a jury by evoking powerfully suggestive emotions. Prejudicing a jury by using arguments that are logically irrelevant but psychologically persuasive could subvert the goal of making the outcome of the trial a decision based on deliberating on the evidence.

It is significant that the logic textbooks chose this legal case to illustrate the *ignoratio elenchi* fallacy. Legal relevance is a procedural requirement of admissibility of evidence in a trial ruled on by the presiding judge. According to rules of evidence, even if evidence has some slight probative value, a judge may rightly exclude it as irrelevant. Thus legal relevance refers to "evidence whose probative value is great enough to justify the delay, expense, prejudice or confusion that is involved in considering it" (Park, Leonard and Goldberg, 1998, p. 125). A distinction has to be drawn between legal relevance and logical relevance. The same proposition could be logically relevant as a premise that could be used to support a conclusion by giving evidence in favor of it, but legally irrelevant, as determined by a judge in a trial. This distinction introduces a complication into using the horrible crime of murder example to illustrate the fallacy of *ignoratio elenchi* in a logic textbook for readers other than law students. Still, legal relevance, however it might be judged in trials, should surely be based on some underlying notion of logical relevance, or relevance as applied to argumentation outside of special contexts like that of a trial governed by explicit rules of evidence and due process.

According to Wigmore (1931) there is a science of proof (logic) in which logical relevance can be defined, but there are also trial rules that judges use to make determinations of relevance in judicial tribunals. According to an influential passage in Wigmore's *Principles*, quoted by Twining, (1985, p. 156), the trial rules are, broadly speaking, founded on the science, but do not always coincide with them.

> The principles of the Science as a whole, cannot be expected to replace the Trial Rules; the Rules having their own right to exist independently (but) for the same reason, the principles of the Science may at certain points confirm the wisdom of the Trial Rules, and may at other points demonstrate the unwisdom of the Rules.

The trial rules have their own right to exist independently because they are meant to serve the institution of the fair trial. Legal relevance is a procedural notion meant to be applied by a judge in a trial to determine what evidence should be considered admissible at that time and place. Logical relevance, according to the example above, is determined by using the argument diagram representing the chain of reasoning in a case, to see if the chain connects up with its ultimate conclusion. Park, Leonard and Goldberg (1998, p. 125), define logical relevance as follows: "the term *logically relevant* has sometimes been used to refer to evidence that has any tendency in logic to establish a proposition". The distinction between logical and legal relevance is clearly fundamental to grasping argumentation in evidence law. But the history of the subject, chronicled in volume 1A of Wigmore's treatise, *Evidence in Trials at Common Law*, 1983, pp. 1004-1095, shows how difficult it has been to get the right balance between these two notions.[3] Ball (1980) moved from deductive logic to define relevance in terms of probability. There have been many attempts to define relevance using statistical probability of

[3] The various theories have been summarized in a set of footnotes written by the editor, Peter Tillers, in the 1983 edition of Evidence in Trials at Common Law.

one sort or another. Tillers (Wigmore, 1983, p. 1013) concluded after his discussion of all the various theories, however, that abstract theories of relevance have had little direct influence on proof-taking processes in courtrooms.

The history of evidence law tends to support the view that legal relevance should be based on some underlying notion of logical relevance. The 1983 edition of volume 1A of Wigmore's treatise, *Evidence in Trials at Common Law*, pp. 1004-1095, contains a useful series of footnotes written by the editor, Peter Tillers, that summarize Wigmore's views on relevance and show how they developed from views of other leading relevance theorists of the time. Michael and Adler (1934, Part I, p. 1279) theorized that an evidential proposition can be directly relevant to a conclusion if it is probative of it in a single step of proof, or indirectly relevant to it by a transitive inferential relation from one step to another. Using this criterion, Michael and Adler (1934, Part I, p. 1279) hypothesized that relevance is "entirely a matter of logic". Wigmore held that although the rules of evidence are based on "rational grounds of everyday logic", or the science of proof as he called it, they are also based on trial rules.

As noted in chapter 1, Wigmore was a pioneer in the use of argument diagramming to map out the structure of argumentation used as evidence in a case at trial in relation to an ultimate proposition to be proved in a case. According to his account, the job is partly logical, because there is a science of proof, meaning an underlying structure of logical reasoning. But in a trial, the question of whether evidence is to be judged relevant or not is a procedural matter. Thus in making judgments of relevance in a trial, there is always a relationship between the science of proof and the trial rules that apply in a judicial tribunal (Twining, 1985, p. 156). Hence the notion of relevance as defined and implemented in any given set of trial rules will never coincide exactly with the underlying notion of logical relevance they are based on conceived in the abstract. Still, there is a complex relationship between the two, and the trial rules cannot be understood without basing them on the underlying notion of logical relevance.

Wigmore held that the science of proof gives evidence of what he calls its "probative value", its capability to offer evidence to support or raise doubts about the rational acceptability of a conclusion. Wigmore's theory of evidence was built around the central notion of a chaining of inferences representing the mass evidence in a case leading to the ultimate *probandum*. The notion of relevance of evidence in a trial can be visualized, following Wigmore's theory, by looking back at Wigmore's diagram representing a typical mass of evidence in chapter 1, section 3. The ultimate *probandum* in the trial is represented by proposition P, the root of the tree. The other nodes in the tree represent testimonial assertions (T) and circumstances (C) entered into the trial as evidence. To define relevance in very simple terms, in relation to this diagram, we could say that an item of evidence is relevant in a case if it fits in somewhere in the diagram for the case as a node in the tree leading to the ultimate *probandum*. Of course, such a definition of relevant evidence is simplistic, because each T or C on the Wigmore diagram really represents an argument, for example an argument from witness testimony. The problem is to generalize Wigmore's basic notion of relevant evidence to see how it could be represented in a modern argument system like *Araucaria*.

3. Examples of Relevance Determinations

Argument diagramming is a technique that has been used in law for analyzing the structure of argumentation in evidence in trials (Wigmore, 1931; Friedman, 1986; Schum, 1994; Gordon, 1995; Verheij, 1996; Prakken, 1997; Lodder, 1999). Most encouraging is the application of Wigmore charting methods to the analysis of evidence in legal cases carried out by Anderson and Twining (1991). But Wigmore charts are highly complex, and appear quite formidable to the potential user. To work up to them, a good research policy could be to begin with simple and basic structures of argument analysis, with the ultimate aim of building up a formal method that could, once further developed, perform an evidence diagramming function comparable to that of a full Wigmore chart. It is best to begin with basic features of an argument. In *Araucaria*, as shown in chapter 1, section 1, an argument can be diagrammed as linked or convergent. Let us briefly review some of the basics of this distinction. In a linked argument, each premise is dependent on the other(s) to support the conclusion (Freeman, 1991). In a convergent argument, each premise provides independent evidential support for the conclusion. In a convergent argument, each premise can be seen as a separate argument for the conclusion, an argument that can stand on its own. Sometimes indicator words in the given text of discourse present evidence to show that the argument is linked or convergent. Sometimes the structure of an argument (its argumentation scheme) indicates that the argument is linked, and is therefore best analyzed as linked rather than convergent.[4] There is also a deletion test concerning probative weight that can be performed. In a linked argument, if one premise is deleted, the other by itself offers much less evidential support for the conclusion than the two do together. By contrast, in a convergent argument, even if one premise is deleted, the other still offers the same evidential support for the conclusion it did before. In other words, the test can be performed as follows. Delete one premise, and see if the probative weight thrown on the conclusion by the other is significantly reduced. If so, the argument is linked. Otherwise it is convergent. The indicator words, the argument structure and the deletion test are not sufficient in all cases to judge whether a given argument is linked or convergent. If doubt remains, the best policy is to diagram the argument as convergent.

In law, relevance is determined both by a *probandum* and by conventions regarding how that *probandum* is to be proved.

---

[4] Many arguments used in law as evidence are based on defeasible generalizations (Prakken, 2002; Verheij, 2002) that are presumptive in nature (Keppens and Zelznikow, 2002). Such arguments are not deductive or inductive, but are based on presumptive argumentation schemes of the kind studied in (Walton, 1996).

The Painting Example

For example, suppose that the *probandum* in a case is that Bob is liable to Emma for breach of contract. Emma claimed that Bob agreed to deliver a painting to her and that he failed to do so. She brought forward several arguments to support her claim. She claimed that Bob signed a contract in which Bob agreed to deliver the painting to Emma. A witness testified that she had seen Bob sign the contract. Bob did not dispute any of Emma's arguments, but he claimed that he signed the contract under duress and that he could prove it. A witness testified that Bob was forced to sign the contract.

To prove breach of contract it is required to prove two subsidiary propositions. One is that there was a contract between the parties. The other is that one party failed to carry out what he had agreed to do as part of the contract. Anything that is relevant to these subsidiary propositions will also be relevant to the ultimate *probandum*. It follows that any argumentation not relevant to the subsidiary propositions will fail to be relevant to the ultimate *probandum*.

To represent the argumentation in the painting example, it is helpful to draw up a key list of the propositions explicitly stated as part of the case.

Key List for the Painting Example

(A) Bob is liable to Emma for breach of contract.
(B) Bob agreed to deliver a painting to Emma.
(C) Bob failed to deliver the painting to Emma.
(D) There is a contract in which Bob agreed to deliver the painting to Emma.
(E) Bob signed the contract.
(F) A witness testified she had seen Bob sign the contract.
(G) Bob signed the contract under duress.
(H) A witness testified that Bob was forced to sign the contract.

The problem is to show how we know or can prove that H is relevant as evidence in the case. To prove it, some line of argumentation between H and the ultimate *probandum* A has to be shown. The crucial part of the argumentation is that H can be used to support G, and G, in turn, can be used to refute A. At least, G, if true, would be evidence that counts against A. To show how we know that, other implicit premises have to be inserted. These premises would be based on the legal rule that a contract signed under duress would be nullified. But even without analyzing the argument this deeply, a diagram can be drawn showing the line of argumentation that indicates how H is relevant.

Figure 4.1 below shows the *Araucaria* diagram that has been drawn to represent the argumentation in the painting example.

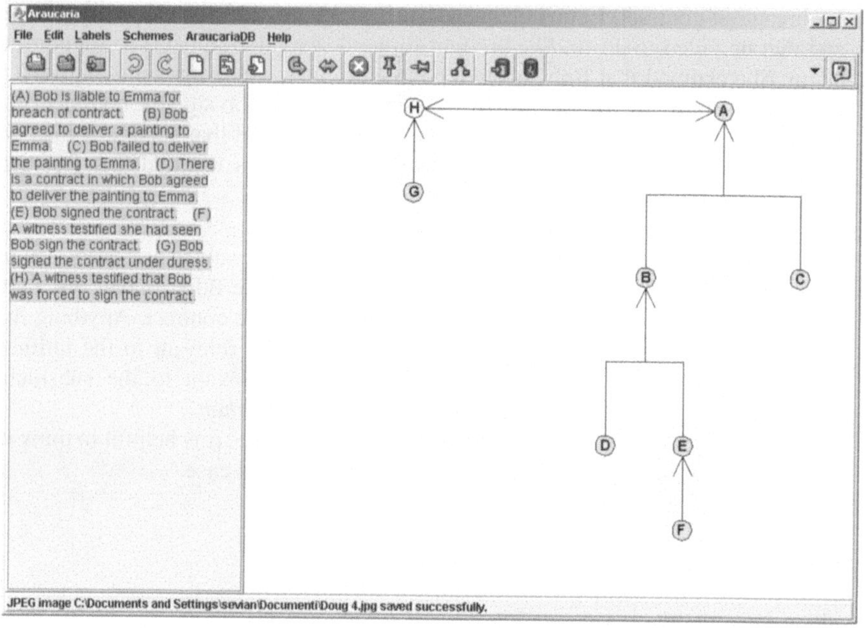

Fig. 4.1. *Araucaria* Diagram of the Painting Example

To draw the diagram, the key list was pasted in a text document, which was inserted into the box on the left side of the *Araucaria* display. As each statement is highlighted in turn, a circled letter representing it is displayed in the box on the right side. To construct the diagram on the right side, an arrow is drawn from each set of premises to the conclusion inferred from them. The statement *G* is drawn as a refutation of statement *A* by clicking on the icon on the toolbar designated "refutation". A refutation is always drawn as a double arrow on the same level as the statement refuted by it. Refutation represents the notion of evidence against a claim. It can be viewed as being like opposition or negation.

The shaded areas around two of the arguments mark argumentation schemes. In both instances the argumentation scheme used as a warrant of the inference is appeal to testimony.[5] By clicking "Full Text" under "File" on the toolbar, the following diagram is produced in which each of the statements appears in a text box.

---

[5] It might be mentioned here that the argumentation scheme for appeal to witness testimony can be used to make two additional premises explicit in both of the arguments marked by the shaded areas. Thus these arguments can be analyzed as enthymemes. See

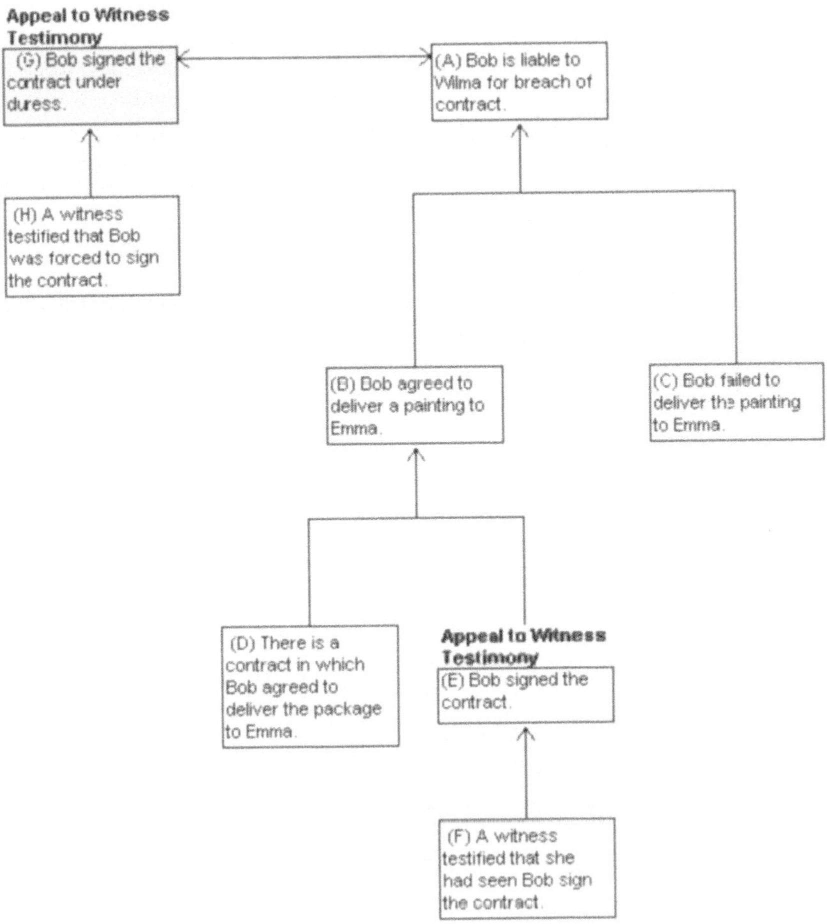

Fig. 4.2. Full Text Diagram of the Painting Example

In the full text diagram, marking of argumentation schemes is made explicit.

Another case that is a good illustration in determining relevance is the following example based on a case in (Wigmore, 1935, p. 8).

(Walton and Reed, 2003) on how to apply argumentation schemes in argument diagramming using *Araucaria*.

The Unpaid Suit Example

Pickard was accused of theft. It was alleged that he picked Suitman's pocket, taking Suitman's credit card and using it to make some purchases. Pickard presented a witness, Taylor, to prove that the suit of clothes worn by Suitman was made for him by Taylor but is still unpaid for. The court excludes this, because Suitman's failure to pay for his clothes is no excuse for theft under the criminal law, and therefore not relevant.

In this case, Pickard might have been justifiably upset because he knew that Suitman had failed to pay for the suit Taylor made for him, and that provided Pickard with a motive for picking Suitman's pocket. Still, in law, Suitman's failure to pay for the suit is not regarded as an excuse for Pickard's committing theft. Thus as evidence, it is not held to be relevant in the trial of Pickard for theft.

The explicit statements in the unpaid suit example are represented in the key list below.

Key List for the Unpaid Suit Example

(A) Pickard is guilty of theft.
(B) Pickard picked the pocket of Suitman.
(C) Pickard took Suitman's credit card.
(D) Pickard used Suitman's credit card to make some purchases.
(E) Pickard presented a witness, Taylor, who testified that he made Suitman's suit, and that Suitman never paid for it.

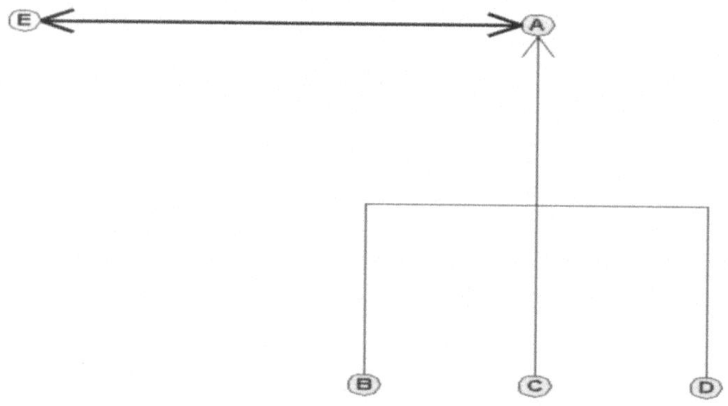

Fig. 4.3. *Araucaria* Diagram of the Unpaid Suit Example

The *probandum* is statement *A*. To begin to draw the argument diagram, a linked argument can be drawn from *B*, *C* and *D* to *A*. *E* is meant by its proponent to function as a refutation of *A*. However, as Wigmore pointed out, failure to pay for the suit is not regarded in law as an argument that would defeat or excuse the charge of theft. Thus any line of argument from *E* to *A* would fail, and would not be relevant. The *Araucaria* diagram displays *E* as well as the relevant parts of the argument.

As we look at the diagram, the relevant evidence supporting the *probandum A* is displayed on the right. The double-headed arrow displays *E* as a refutation. But this part of the diagram is incorrect. *E* does not provide evidence that refutes *A*. This is not because *A* is false. *A* may well be true. The reason is that the argument from *E* to *A* is not accepted in law as a reason for mitigating or defeating the charge of theft.

So far *Araucaria* has only been used to diagram manageable arguments of the kind found in relatively modest texts of discourse. How to fill out an explicitly given argument by adding in missing premises and conclusions in enthymemes has been studied (Walton and Reed, 2004). But once again, the cases studied are relatively modest, not taking a lot of contextual information into account. The question is whether *Araucaria* could be used to assist with judging relevance in a given argument. One capability needed for this purpose is a method of argument extrapolation that could extrapolate a given argument diagram forward towards the end point provided by the ultimate *probandum*. Another capability needed is the textual and contextual evidence in the given case as material to start from, called the evidential base. The evidential base is a set of propositions and a set of argumentation schemes that represent the evidence already accepted as having probative weight by all parties to the argumentation. It can be seen as comparable to a knowledge base in computing, made up of a set of propositions called facts and a set of rules, or general propositions, that warrant the drawing of derived facts by inference from the explicitly given facts. All the premises and the conclusion of the given argument, along with all the other propositions in the evidence base, are the start points of the argument extrapolation. The ultimate *probandum* is the end point.

4. Determination of Relevance by Argument Extrapolation

The theory of relevance in argumentation offered in (Walton, 2004) is basically dialectical, meaning that in the case of a particular argument to be evaluated for relevance, the argument needs to be seen as part of a dialogue. Let us review the fundamentals of this dialectical approach outlined in chapter 1. There are six basic types of dialogue: persuasion, negotiation, inquiry, deliberation, information-seeking, and eristic dialogue. There are two parties in any basic type of dialogue called the proponent and the respondent. The proponent has a thesis to be proved, or to be argued for, and she has a pro attitude toward that thesis. The respondent has a contra attitude. Either he has an opposite thesis, or he has doubt about the truth or acceptability of the proponent's thesis. Each uses a chain of argumentation to try to prove his or her thesis. For example, the proponent's thesis provides an aiming point for her argumentation. In persuasion dialogue, the proponent has the goal of creating a sequence of rational argumentation where the conclusion is her thesis, and all the premises are commitments of the other party. Rational persuasion by a proponent in a dialogue is defined as using an argument where all the premises are accepted by the respondent and where the argument is rationally binding by some standard of structural correctness of the argument from the premises to the conclusion. Persuasion dialogue is different from negotiation dialogue. The former represents an attempt to get at the truth of the matter discussed, while the goal of the latter is not truth-oriented, but only to divide up resources or "make a deal".

These notions were introduced in chapter 1, but reviewed above to show their implications for defining relevance in the dialectical framework. When relevance is defined in this kind of framework it should be called dialectical relevance, meaning that the relevance of an argument (or other speech act) needs to be determined in light of the use of that argument in a context of dialogue. The first implication of adopting such a dialectical approach to relevance is very striking. The same argument could be relevant in one type of dialogue but not in another. For example, the same argument could be relevant in a negotiation dialogue but not relevant in a persuasion dialogue. It is widely accepted that a threat to impose a sanction could be a relevant argument in the context of a negotiation. But that same argument could be irrelevant in a persuasion dialogue. In that context it could rightly be classified as an instance of the *ad baculum* fallacy.

According to the analysis of rational argumentation in a persuasion dialogue offered in (Walton, 1999, p. 121), there are four basic requirements for an argument to be accepted as dialectically relevant in this type of dialogue. These four conditions were previously mentioned in chapter 1, section 6, as general requirements for rational persuasion.

(R1) The respondent accepts the premises as commitments.
(R2) Each inference in the chain of argument is structurally correct.
(R3) The chain of argumentation must have the proponent's thesis as its (ultimate) conclusion.
(R4) Arguments meeting (R1), (R2) and (R3) are the only means that count as fulfilling the proponent's goal in the dialogue.

These four conditions, it can be argued, apply to relevance not just in the persuasion type of dialogue, but to other types of dialogue as well. Relevance always needs to be judged in relation to three factors. The given argument in a case represents a start point of judging relevance in the case. A chain of argumentation moves forward from the start point. That chain of argumentation aims toward an end point, some ultimate conclusion to be argued for in the case. The argumentation in the case is relevant if it goes from the start point to the end point. Otherwise it is not relevant.

In this framework relevance was defined in terms of a chain of argumentation with a starting point and an end point. The starting point is a given argument as represented in the text of discourse of an individual case, and the chain of argumentation is represented by an argument diagram. The diagram provides an analysis of all the premises and conclusion, both explicit and implicit, of the argument, and the steps of inference joining each set of premises to each conclusion drawn from them. As the existing chain of argumentation moves forward from this start point, it aims toward an end point, some ultimate conclusion to be argued for, called the ultimate *probandum* in law. It is assumed that this proposition is known, or can be identified. In a trial, it will be clearly identified at the outset. In everyday conversational argumentation, it may be explicitly identified or it may not be. In any event, the argumentation used in any particular case can be judged relevant or irrelevant only if it proceeds from a starting point that can be clearly mapped out, say by an argument diagram, to a clearly identified end point.

This criterion is clear enough, but problematic when applied to some cases. It will often happen, for example, in legal argumentation in a trial, that the argument to be evaluated occurs at the early stage of the presentation of evidence. The judge cannot determine where the lawyer's argument is going yet, and thus there is not enough data yet to reach a firm decision on whether her argument is relevant or not. Some discussion may take place at this point, and the judge may give the lawyer some time to show why her argument will be shown to be relevant. These observations show that relevance is not only a matter of what type of dialogue an argument is part of, but also depends on what stage the dialogue is in, and how far the argumentation has gone at the point relevance is being judged. For these reasons a more sophisticated method for determining relevance was constructed in (Walton, 2004).

The method used to determine relevance in a given text of discourse in a case in (Walton, 2004) is called *argument extrapolation*. To determine relevance of an argument, the argument as given in a text of discourse is extrapolated forward to see whether it leads to the ultimate *probandum* in the case. The method is contextual, in that it requires information other than the given premises and conclusion of the argument being considered. It requires that the ultimate *probandum* be known. And it may require information about what can be accepted as having been proved already in prior arguments relating to the given one. The general procedure is visualized in figure 4.4.

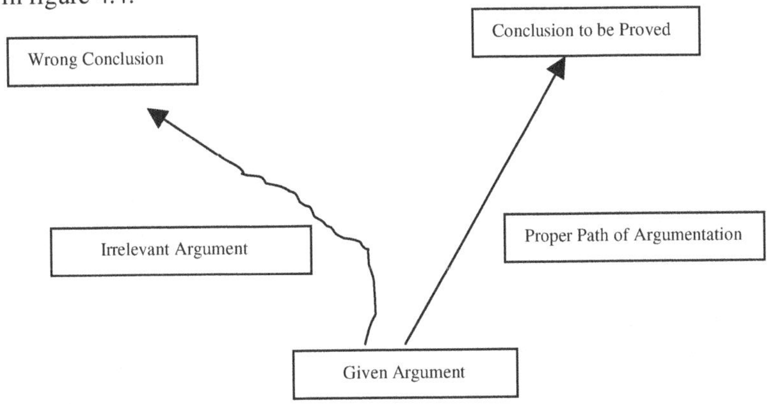

Fig. 4.4. Argument Extrapolation to Determine Irrelevance

We start with a given argument in a text of discourse in a case, at the bottom of figure 4.4. From this data base we apply argumentation schemes to this data over and over, extrapolating forward to try to get a chain of argumentation reaching from the data base to the conclusion to be proved (ultimate *probandum* in the case). If the attempt succeeds the argument is relevant. This chain of argumentation is shown as the proper path of argumentation on the right in figure 4.4. But suppose that the chain of argumentation goes off in a different direction, as shown by the path on the left, representing an irrelevant argument. Evidence of such a path, shown by the argument extrapolation from the data, indicates a judgment that the argument is irrelevant.

In typical examples of the fallacy of *ignoratio elenchi* offered in logic textbooks, very little context is given. In the horrible crime of murder example, we know that the ultimate *probandum* is the proposition that the defendant is guilty of the charge of murder made by the prosecution. But we are not told what stage the trial is in, and what evidence has been brought forward so far. The best one can do in such a case is to attempt a provisional evaluation, based on where the argumentation seems to be leading, given the evidence that has been brought in so far. Thus as will be shown in section 7 below, in many real cases there may not be enough data to prove that the given argument is relevant, or that it is irrelevant, and questions have to be asked. Still, in such cases, it can be very useful to put forward a provisional criticism alleging that the argument, so far, appears to be irrelevant. The critic can ask the arguer to show how her argument is relevant. Thus in a trial, the advocate for the opposing side may object, saying "irrelevant", and the judge may then ask the arguer to show how her argument is relevant or rule it inadmissible. Thus the method should not always be expected to apply automatically to every case and give a definite verdict of 'relevant' or 'irrelevant'.

How does the method of extrapolation determine the relevance of a given argument based on the start points and the end point? It begins by filling in the missing premises using argumentation schemes, but something else is needed as well. For example, in the horrible crime of murder example, it is possible to construct a line of argumentation from the start statement, 'Murder is a horrible crime', to the end statement, 'The defendant is guilty of murder'. It is plausible that murder is a horrible crime, and it may even be plausible that the defendant looks like a horrible person, is suspicious in appearance, or has a bad character, as shown by previous convictions, for example. Therefore it might be plausible to draw the conclusion that the defendant is the kind of person who might commit a murder. But how plausible is it that he must have committed the murder he is accused of, because he is a horrible-appearing person, or because he has committed other horrible crimes? There is a chain of argumentation that can be filled in by argument extrapolation that leads from the start points to the end point using this kind of evidence base. This is the kind of argumentation that would be considered irrelevant by evidence rules in law because, although it has some slight probative weight, it might tend to prejudice a jury. Arguing at length that murder is a horrible crime might have some slight logical relevance, but it is a rhetorical tactic that might also prejudice the jury by evoking powerful emotions. Just because a person has a suspicious appearance, or has committed other crimes, it does not logically follow with much probative weight that he has committed this particular crime he is charged with in this case.

But here a theoretical problem concerning fallacies of relevance is posed. Looking at the horrible crime of murder example, there are two possible diagnoses of the fallacy that was supposedly committed. One diagnosis is that the prosecutor was wandering off the line of argument and trying to distract the jury emotionally by going on at length about how horrible the crime of murder was. He was not arguing to any specific conclusion, but merely distracting the jury. The other diagnosis is that he was arguing to another specific conclusion, namely the claim that the defendant is a bad person. On this interpretation he was attacking the character of the defendant. Thus, looking at figure 4.4 again, he was trying to prove what is called the wrong conclusion. These two failures of relevance could be seen as representing two different fallacies of relevance, and we return to this possibility in section 7. Still, in either case, a failure of relevance is the root of the problem. Thus an argument tool like *Araucaria* can be used to diagnose the problem.

Araucaria could be applied to the horrible crime of murder example in much the same way it was applied to the painting example and the unpaid suit example. In order to apply it, however, we would have to know what the lawyer said exactly in his speech about murder being a horrible crime. We could then insert this discourse set into a text document and use *Araucaria* to identify the premises and conclusions in it and produce an argument diagram. As done in the other two examples above, we could then make a determination of whether these premises and conclusions form an argument diagram that has the ultimate *probandum* as conclusion. Any evidence that the argument veers off in a different direction when extrapolated forward supports the hypothesis that the argument is irrelevant and offers grounds for questioning its relevance.

It is not within the space requirements of this chapter to attempt to deal with any lengthy mass of argumentation that would be characteristic of a real case of relevance determination in a trial. The best that can be done is to consider one highly controversial and problematic type of case, and use *Araucaria* to offer a way of addressing the problem. This type of case is classified under the term conditional relevance. Before tackling it, we need to deal with two concepts that are essential to the project. One is the notion of probative weight. The other is the notion of an enthymeme.

5. Probative Weight and Enthymemes

Any attempt to define relevance of a kind that could be useful for legal argumentation needs to start with the definition of 'relevant evidence' in Rule 401(a) of the *Federal Rules of Evidence*.

Rule 401(a)

"Relevant evidence" means evidence having any tendency to make the existence of any fact that is of consequence to the determination of the action more probable or less probable than it would be without the evidence.

The FRE does not define the terms 'more probable' and 'less probable', but they can be taken to refer to what Wigmore called "probative weight". The "action" is the ultimate *probandum* in the given case. What it means to say that a "fact" (proposition) is of consequence to the determination of the action, is that it leads by a chain of reasoning to the ultimate *probandum*. Through such a chain of reasoning, from a set of premises (facts) the ultimate *probandum* can be shown to have more probative weight or less probative weight. Note, as well, that relevant evidence is only required to have a tendency to boost up or lessen the probative weight of the ultimate *probandum*. It need not actually do so. Rule 401 is therefore permissive in how it defines relevance. An item of evidence can be relevant even if it has only a small effect on altering the probative weight of the ultimate *probandum*. For example, suppose a man had a serious quarrel with his wife one morning, and on his way to work he had an accident with the car. The incident in the morning might have had an effect on his driving. Therefore, testimony about the quarrel could qualify as relevant evidence in the trial concerning a personal injury case under rule 401 (Park, Leonard and Goldberg, 1998, p. 124). This analysis of relevance in a persuasion dialogue, it was argued in (Walton, 2004), fits Wigmore's notion of logical relevance as a chain of argumentation that is supposed to have probative weight as evidence in relation to an ultimate *probandum* in a case.

In *Araucaria* (Reed and Rowe, 2003, p. 15), it is possible to indicate whether an argument is strong or weak by assigning values to the nodes representing the statements in the argument, or to the arrows representing the argument from a set of premises to a conclusion. For example, you could assign probability values between 0 and 1, or you could mark the components of an argument with plus, minus or zero, according to some many-valued logic. This information can be displayed on the diagram, or it can be hidden. The possibility of assigning evaluations of this sort means that one could not only assign probative weight to an argument, but also that the probative weight could be distributed over the diagram using a rule, like the least plausible premise rule. According to this rule, the conclusion of a deductively valid argument must have at least as much plausibility as the least plausible premise. For example, suppose you have an argument that has the form *modus ponens*, and one premise has a value of .8, the other has a value of .6, and the conclusion has the value of .3. By the least plausible premise rule, the value of the conclusion must be upgraded to .6. The least plausible premise rule can also be applied to arguments that are not deductively valid, but where the conclusion follows from the premises by a presumptive argumentation scheme. This can be done by assigning a value to the conditional that functions as the warrant of the argument. For example, suppose once again that one premise has a value of .8 and the other has a value of .6. Furthermore, suppose that the conditional that has these two statements as conjunctive antecedent has a value of

.5, while the conclusion has an initial value of .3. By the least plausible premise rule, the value of the conclusion has to be upgraded to .5. In effect, the argumentation scheme that enables the conclusion to be derived from the premises functions as an additional premise that can be assigned a plausibility value in the case.

Without making things too complex, it might be added here that the least plausible premise rule applies only to evaluating linked arguments in a diagram. In a convergent argument, the conclusion needs to be revised upward to the value of the most plausible premise. In a convergent argument, each premise is in effect an independent argument for the conclusion. Thus the complete method of evaluation uses a *maxmin rule* that assigns values for linked arguments based on a least plausible premise rule, and values for convergent arguments based on a most plausible premise rule.

The other factor that needs to be dealt with here is that many legal arguments are based on unstated premises, or even unstated conclusions that need to be made explicit in order to show how a conclusion was arrived at from the given evidence. The term 'enthymeme', as indicated in chapter 1, is used to refer to an argument with one or more premises (or a conclusion) that were not explicitly stated. Simply plugging in premises or a conclusion needed to make the argument valid may not represent what the arguer meant to say, however (Burke, 1985; Gough and Tindale, 1985; Hitchcock, 1985). The arguer may have been putting forward an invalid argument, or basing her argument on a false premise, perhaps without realizing it. The kind of controversy surrounding enthymemes can be illustrated by an example. A student was overheard to say, "I should have gotten an A in that course because I worked very hard in it". The missing assumption would seem to be the generalization, 'If you work very hard in a course, you should get an A in it'. This generalization seems dubious, however. If you work very hard but don't do very well on the assignments in the course, you may not deserve an A. It does seem that the student's argument is an enthymeme based on this unstated assumption. But once the student is confronted with the assumption as being a missing premise of his argument, he may back off and claim that he didn't really mean to say or imply that statement at all.

Putting in a premise or conclusion not really meant by the arguer, or that fits with his position, may even commit the straw man fallacy of distorting an argument in order to make it more easily refutable (Scriven, 1976, pp. 85-86). To contend with such problems, Ennis (1982, pp. 63-66) drew a distinction between needed and used assumptions in enthymemes. Used assumptions represent reasons an arguer really meant to build her argument on, while needed assumptions are only missing statements needed to make it valid (or otherwise structurally correct). Another device useful in studying enthymemes is the principle of charity, which holds that one should choose among interpretations by picking the one that makes the best possible sense of an argument (Gough and Tindale, 1985, p. 102; Johnson, 2000, p. 127). Thus analyzing enthymemes can be problematic in some cases (Walton and Reed, 2004). Still, using argument diagramming effectively to represent real cases of argumentation clearly depends on enthymemes, especially in legal argumentation (Prakken, 2002).

6. Conditional Relevance

In ruling on relevance, a kind of problem has been posed that was addressed by the FRE by supplementing rule 401(a) with rule 401(b). The latter says that relevance can be "conditioned on fact", meaning that evidence is admissible if it is relevant only if taken together with additional statements not yet proved.

Rule 401(b)

When the relevancy of evidence depends upon the condition of a fulfillment of fact, the court shall admit it upon, or subject to, the introduction of evidence sufficient to support a finding of the fulfillment of the condition.

Rule 401(b) expresses the notion of conditional relevance. A proposition put forward as evidence in a trial is conditionally relevant, according to 401(b), even though it does not throw probative weight by itself on the ultimate *probandum* as required by rule 401(a), if it does throw such weight once supplemented with another proposition, even though that other proposition has nor been proved yet as factual in the trial.

Ball (1980, p. 437) cited a relatively clear example that can be used to illustrate conditional relevance.[6]

The Letter Example

If a letter purporting to be from Y is relied upon to establish an admission from him, it has no probative value unless Y wrote or authorized it.

The letter relied on to establish the admission from Y is conditionally relevant because even though it has no probative value by itself, once the statement that Y wrote or authorized the letter is added, the two of them taken together make up a conjunctive proposition that does have probative value. As Morgan (1929, p. 167) expressed the criterion, "To say that the relevancy of *A* depends upon the existence of *B* is only to say that it requires a combination of *A* and *B* to produce a relevant factor in a case". Thus a statement *A* is conditionally relevant in a case if it is not relevant by itself, according to Rule 401(a), but becomes relevant in another sense (conditionally relevant) if, taken together with another statement *B*, the pair of them are relevant according to 401(a). This secondary kind of relevance, so defined, is said to be conditional, because relevance is taken to depend on a further statement that needs to be added in but that has not been proved yet.

Rule 401(b) has been controversial, and many commentators have expressed suspicion about it, alleging that it is too vague, and that it could open floodgates by making the notion of relevance too broad. Nance (1995, p. 419) showed that there has been "a substantial body of academic criticism of the traditional doc-

---

[6] A range of leading evidence cases where conditional relevance is a central feature have been analyzed by Callen (2003).

trine" of conditional relevance. Ball (1980, pp. 441-453) pointed out that it is difficult to precisely measure how much more relevance is needed to get the initial statements over the threshold from slightly relevant, or conditionally relevant, to categorically relevant. He concluded that conditional relevance is a "myth". Friedman (1994) argued that conditional relevance is misleading and too formalistic, and that it ought to be replaced by a notion of conditional probative value. Tillers (1994) expressed doubts about Ball's idea of abolishing conditional relevance, but disagreed with Friedman's idea of replacing it with conditional probative value. While there seems to be a need for a rule like 401(b) to deal with problematic cases of conditional relevance, this rule has only been applied to a narrow range of cases, possibly because many feel that the notion of relevance itself has not been defined with enough precision to provide guidance on how rule 401(b) should be applied.

Conditional relevance has certainly proved to be a problematic notion in evidence law, even throwing doubt on the viability of the project of applying logical relevance to legal determinations of relevance. Could this notion be clarified using the tools described above? Let's examine the letter example using these tools. The letter example is sketchy, but let's try to fill it in enough to be of use to reveal something about conditional relevance cases. We aren't told what the ultimate *probandum* in the letter case is. Anyhow, let's call it *D*. The key list for the letter example contains only one explicit statement, as indicated below.

Key List for the Letter Example

(A) A letter purporting to be from Y contains an admission from him.

The problem now is to analyze how *A* can be extrapolated forward so that, through an intervening chain of argumentation, it might throw probative weight onto *D*. The following missing premise needs to be added in.

(B) Y wrote or authorized the letter.

The letter example presumes that *A* has probative weight in the kind of case being considered, but in the absence of *B* carrying probative weight in the case, the argument fails to throw probative weight onto *D*. What is assumed is that there is a linked argument having *A* and *B* as premises. From this linked argument a conclusion can be drawn. We are not told what it is, but let's call it *C*. Next, what is assumed by the example is that there is a chain of argumentation leading from *C* to *D*, and that via this chain, the probative weight thrown onto *C* by *A* and *B* is in turn thrown onto *D*. Thus it follows that the linked argument from *A* and *B* to *C* would be relevant if *B* had probative weight in the case. However, *B* has not been proved yet. At this point in the trial, *B* lacks probative weight. Thus the linked argument from *A* to *C*, depending on the unproven premise *B*, is conditionally relevant.

The *Araucaria* diagram for the letter example, analyzed as above, is presented in figure 4.5 below. The intervening argumentation connecting *C* to *D* is only represented on the diagram by a single arrow.

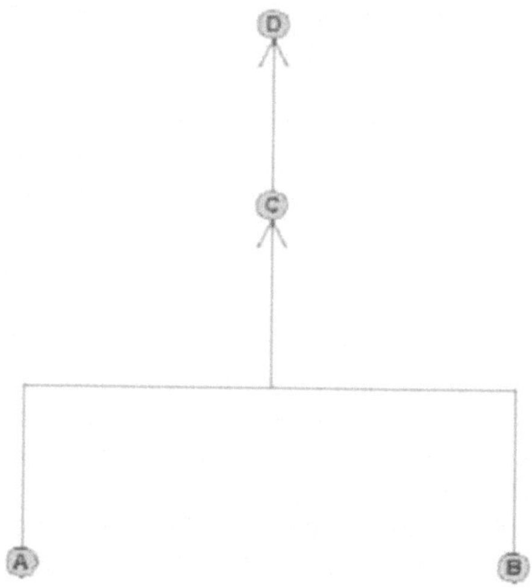

Fig. 4.5. Diagram of the Letter Example

As figure 4.5 shows, there is a linked argument from premises *A* and *B* to conclusion *C*. But *B* is diagrammed as a missing premise. From *C* there is chain of argumentation leading to *D*. This argumentation is not explicitly represented in the diagram. Nor is it in the letter example. It is merely assumed for the purposes of the example that the admission made in the letter provides relevant evidence in the case.

Numbers or other symbols indicating the evaluation of each statement and each inference drawn in the diagram have not yet been inserted. But to grasp how conditional relevance works, you need to take the probative weights of the statements into account. There are several assumptions about such evaluations that need to be considered if the example is to illustrate the typical problem posed by conditional relevance.

Assumption 1: A has a high probative weight in itself. That is, it is assumed that the letter exists and could be presented to the court as evidence.

Assumption 2: It is assumed that there is doubt whether *B* is true or not. In other words, there are two possibilities. *B* could have high probative weight, or it could have little or no probative weight as evidence.

Assumption 3: If *B* did have probative weight, the linked argument from *A* and *B* to *C* would throw that probative weight onto *C*. Thus *C* would now have probative weight.

Assumption 4: If *C* had probative weight, it would throw that probative weight onto *D*, through an intervening chain of argumentation. Thus *D* would now have probative weight (or more than it had before, anyhow).

Assumption 5: If *B* lacked probative weight, the linked argument from *A* and *B* to *C* would fail to throw any increased probative weight onto C.

Assumption 6: If assumption 5 is correct, the argument from *C* to *D* would fail tothrow probative weight onto *P*.

The pattern of argumentation that typically gives rise to the problem of conditional relevance in a case requires a consideration of two possible scenarios. One is represented by the first four assumptions applying to the case. In this scenario, the argument is relevant. The other is represented by assumptions 1, 2, 5 and 6 applying to the case. In this scenario, the argument is (at best) conditionally relevant. These two scenarios are represented respectively by figures 4.6 and 4.7 below. In these diagrams, a value has been attached to each node, representing the initial probative weight of the statement at that node. A value has also been attached to each arrow, representing the probative weight of the inference from the premises to the conclusion.

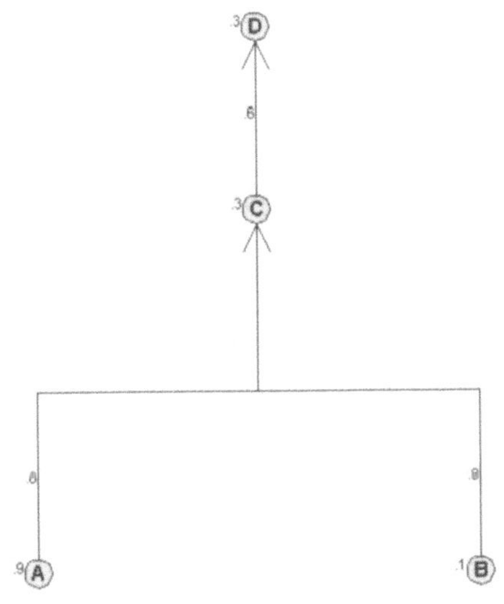

Fig. 4.6. Diagram of the Letter Example with Initial Values

In figure 4.6, *A* has been assigned a very high value (.9), while *B* has been assigned a very low value (.1). The inferential link joining the premises *A* and *B* to the conclusion *C* has also been assigned a high value (.8). For purposes of illustration, let's also assign a low value to *C* (.3), but a fairly high value (.6) to the inference from *C* to *D*. Let's say that the initial value of *D* is .3. In this case, even though there is a chain of argumentation from the premises *A* and *B* to the ultimate conclusion *D*, that argument does not increase the probative weight of *D*.

By way of contrast, look at figure 4.7 below.

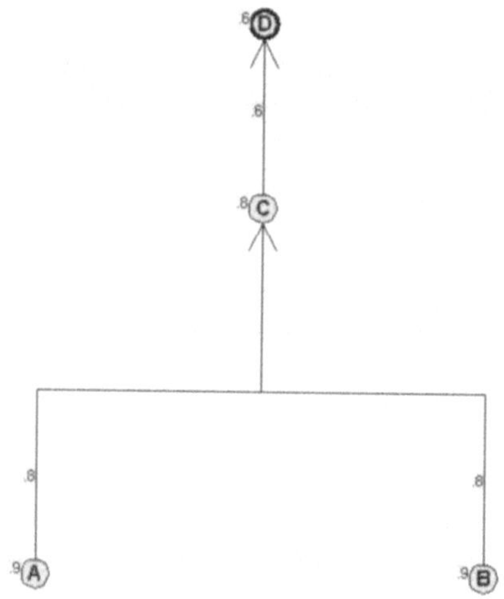

Fig. 4.7. Diagram of the Letter Example with Revised Values

In figure 4.7, premise *B* has the same high value as premise *A* (.9). By the modified least plausible premise rule, the value of *C* now needs to be revised from .3 to a new value of .8. By the same rule, the value of *D* needs to be revised from .3 to .6. In short, the argument from *A* and *B* turned out to be relevant to *D*.

The letter example shows how a case where evidence is held to be conditionally relevant can be analyzed and evaluated using *Araucaria,* provided probative weights can be assigned to each node and arrow in the diagram representing some initial evaluation of how strong each item of evidence is taken to be. Once the argumentation in the mass of evidence has been analyzed using the diagram, a readjustment of these values can take place, using some rule like the least plausible premise rule. This readjustment can then be used to determine whether the argumentation represented on the diagram is relevant or not. Following rule 401(a) such argumentation is to be judged to be relevant as evidence only if it effects a readjustment upward or downward from the base line of the initial probative weight assigned to the ultimate *probandum*.

A small readjustment implies that the evidence is only slightly relevant, whereas a large readjustment would show that the argumentation is strongly relevant evidence. If so, relevance is a matter of degree. But in making judgments of admissibility of evidence in a trial, one should not mistakenly base such judgments only on unduly precise numerical calculations of degrees of increase or decrease of probative weight. The same principle holds in applying the distinction between linked and convergent arguments using the deletion test mentioned in section 2. In a linked argument, if one premise is deleted, the other by itself offers much less support for the conclusion. But there is no magic number saying exactly how much should qualify as "much less" in every case.

7. Summary of the Method

The general method for determining relevance of an argument in a given case follows these ten steps.

(1) Identify the statements that can be taken to be the premises and the conclusion of the given argument. Insert these into an *Araucaria* diagram as nodes.
(2) Identify any argumentation schemes that connect premises to conclusions and mark these on the diagram.
(3) Fill in any unstated premises and conclusions in the given argument, and insert these on the diagram using the *missing premises* icon on the toolbar.
(4) Identify the statement taken to be the ultimate *probandum* in the case.
(5) Search through the database representing the statements accepted so far as evidence in the case and select any statements that could be added to the diagram and used to move the argumentation already on the diagram further toward the ultimate *probandum.*
(6) Add in these statements to the diagram along with additional missing premises that would produce a line of argumentation that shows promise of reaching the ultimate *probandum.*
(7) Keep repeating steps 5 and 6 until either the ultimate *probandum* is reached as a conclusion or it is not possible to go any further because all possible arguments have been constructed using the statements in the evidence base.
(8) In some cases, especially those concerning the issue of conditional relevance, the evaluation capability of *Araucaria* needs to be used to determine the relevance of the argumentation in a case. A value has been attached to each node and each arrow, representing the initial probative weight of the statement at that node or arrow.
(9) Once all the nodes and arrows on the diagram have been inserted, carry out a re-evaluation of the mass of evidence by readjusting the initial values, using a rule like the least plausible premise rule.
(10) If the initial values went significantly up or down once the readjustment has been made, this finding is evidence that the argumentation represented on the diagram is relevant.

In using the method, you have to realize that once you have constructed the diagram representing a mass of evidence in a case, you can pick out any single statement (fact) or any local argument (like a one-step argument) and use the diagram to determine whether that statement or argument is relevant. You can also use the diagram to take one local argument in the case and determine whether it is conditionally relevant. However, the determination of relevance depends on how well you have analyzed the evidence in the case, and on how much evidence there currently is at that point in the case. As shown in Wigmore's use of evidence charts (Wigmore, 1931; Prakken, Reed and Walton, 2003), the mass of evidence in any real case can be quite large, especially once the trial is over and all the evidence is collected together in a mass of evidence on each side.

Using this method it can be shown in easy cases that an argument is relevant, but there are hard cases where it can be disputed whether the argument is relevant or not. The basic method in hard cases is to begin by constructing an argument diagram representing the evidence known in the case, then chain this argumentation forward to see whether it moves toward or even reaches the ultimate *probandum*. Of course, the problem is that in the hard cases, such a chain will only go part way and will depend on unstated premises and conclusions, for example in the form of common sense generalizations. In the letter example, the missing premise is that Y wrote or authorized the letter. The argument based on this premise is in turn based on the generalization that if an agent wrote or authorized a letter containing an admission in the form of a statement asserted, then that agent is committed to that statement. This generalization might arguably fall under the scheme for argument from commitment, but is better classified as a common sense generalization (Anderson, 1999). The method is to analyze the given argument in this fashion by filling in the unstated premises and conclusions to build up a structure represented by an argument diagram. The diagram can then be used to estimate whether the projected chain of argumentation goes toward the ultimate *probandum* or away from the proper line of argumentation needed to prove it. A key tool in the method is the set of argumentation schemes, including deductive and inductive forms of argument as well as presumptive argumentation schemes. The argument extrapolation is performed by applying the schemes to the statements in the knowledge base recursively to generate new arguments that are then represented in the diagram.

8. The Problem of Diagnosing Fallacies of Relevance

Throughout the history of logic, relevance has mainly been studied under the heading of fallacies. But it is clear that relevance is important in law most centrally because it is a procedural tool used to rule on admissibility of evidence in trials. These two fields have much to learn from each other, but at present there is a gulf between them. Not all cases where an argument is dismissed as irrelevant, for example in a trial, could be classified as cases where some fallacy of relevance has been committed. The term 'fallacy' is too strong to gain much hold in most cases where evidence is ruled inadmissible in law on grounds of failure of relevance to be shown. Still, there is much about the notion of relevance to be learned in what Wigmore called the science of proof.

As outlined in section 6, the general method of determining logical relevance or irrelevance of argumentation in a given case is clear, in outline. However, as noted in connection with the discussion of the horrible crime of murder case above, there are many problems posed of how to apply it to actual cases, and arrive at some diagnosis of the precise nature of the failure. The problem taken on in traditional logic was to be able to identify fallacies of relevance, like the fallacy of *ignoratio elenchi* supposedly committed in the horrible crime of murder case. But it is a problem that the logic textbooks have recognized two kinds of fallacies that could be classified under this heading. One is the fallacy of going off in a wrong direction, diverging from the proper line of argumentation required to prove the ultimate *probandum*. This tactic represents a fallacy of attempted distraction, sometimes called the red herring fallacy. The problem with this failure of relevance is that the arguer may not be proving anything at all, but merely going on a filibuster. The other is the fallacy of arguing to the wrong conclusion, as represented in figure 4.4. As mentioned in section 1, just before the introduction of the horrible crime of murder example, according to Aristotle, an argument commits this fallacy when it proves a conclusion other than the one it was supposed to prove. What's really the difference between these two fallacies? An example might help.

In a much-used logic textbook Hurley (2003) offered an example of a failure of relevance classified as an instance of the red herring fallacy (2003, p. 132).

The Parking Example

Professor Conway complains of inadequate parking on our campus. But did you know that last year Conway carried on a torrid love affair with a member of the English department? The two used to meet every day for clandestine sex in the copier room. Apparently they didn't realize how much you can see through that fogged glass window. Even the students got an eyeful. Enough said about Conway.

The arguer's strategy in the parking example is evidently to excite the interest of the audience by presenting a story about Conway that is emotionally stimulating and distracting. Not only doesn't it lead to any particular conclusion about the parking issue, it leads away from the proper line of argumentation needed to prove that parking is adequate or inadequate by interposing a distracting story about clandestine sex. On this analysis of the parking example, the error is not the fallacy of wrong conclusion, but merely that of red herring. The arguer is not so much trying to prove anything, but merely trying to lead the audience off in a different direction, away from the conclusion that is supposed to be proved. But, as indicated in the discussion of the example in section 1, there is another interpretation of the failure of relevance in this case. It could perhaps be classified as an attempt to attack Conway's character, and thus it would be arguing for the conclusion that Conway is a bad person, ethically speaking, and therefore his argument should be dismissed, or given little credibility. So classified, the argument in the case would fall into the *ad hominem* category.

The general problem is that even with cases, like the parking example, that are supposed to be paradigm cases of the red herring fallacy, it is usually possible to find some "wrong conclusion" that is being argued for instead of the real conclusion to be proved. The problem is that every case of what is supposed to be the red herring fallacy collapses into a case of the wrong conclusion fallacy. Despite this problem, it was argued in (Walton, 2004) that the two subtypes should be distinguished as being different failures of relevance. According to the analysis of (Walton, 2004), when an arguer uses a stream of rhetoric that doesn't prove some specific conclusion other than the one to be proved, and merely diverts from the issue, the fallacy of irrelevance should be classified as red herring. This fallacy is committed when the line of argumentation goes off onto some colorful issue meant to get the audience excited and distracted. It is a diversion without any specific target. On this analysis, the argumentation in the parking example should be classified as a red herring because it diverts away from the issue of inadequate parking to the exciting allegation of the sexual incident in the copier room.

In the classification system of (Walton, 2004, p. 243), the wrong conclusion and red herring fallacies are subsumed under a more general category of failure of relevance called misdirected argumentation. This general fault refers to cases in which there is a line of argumentation moving along other than the path of argumentation leading towards the conclusion to be proved. In some such cases the path leads to the wrong conclusion, and in these cases the fallacy of wrong conclusion can be said to have been committed. In other cases the path leads away from the conclusion to be proved, but not to any specific alternative conclusion, as far as we can judge from the data given in the case. Thus the criterion for distinguishing between wrong conclusion and red herring can be formulated as follows. When an argument extrapolation has been carried out, and it has been shown that the path of argumentation has as its end point a specific conclusion that is one other than the conclusion to be proved, the fallacy is that of wrong conclusion. If the argument extrapolation shows that the path of argumentation initially looks like it is moving toward the designated conclusion to be proved, but then it strays in a different direction, the fallacy is that of red herring. But in order for the case to be classified as a red herring, the extrapolation, and the analysis of the case based on it, must show that the path of argumentation does not have some specific conclusion other than the ultimate *probandum* of the case as its end point.

The distinction between red herring and wrong conclusion is important for law for the following reasons. In some cases the FRE rules an argument inadmissible as evidence in a trial simply because there is no evidence, as shown so far in the case yet, that the argument is relevant. This notion of inadmissibility can be said to correspond roughly to the red herring notion in logic. It means that the argument, so far as one can judge from the point it has reached so far, is of little probative worth. But in other cases, an argument might be ruled irrelevant because it might tend to prejudice the jury. In this kind of case, the worry is ostensibly that the argument is going to a wrong conclusion. For example, it might be an *ad hominem* argument in which the character of the defendant is attacked, and this attack is used somehow to suggest that the defendant is guilty. In such a case, the problem is that the argument goes to the wrong conclusion. Thus arguments held to be fallacious, like the *ad hominem* type of argument, are also problematic in law, at least partly on grounds of failure of relevance. This sort of problem is taken up in more detail in chapter 5.

9. Legal Relevance as a Procedural Concept

In easy cases, an argument extrapolation may determine whether the argumentation in the given case is relevant or not. But in hard cases, it may be harder to judge where a pleader is going with a line of argument based on some newly offered evidence that doesn't chain forward to the ultimate *probandum*. The reason, in many hard cases, is that we are still at the beginning of the stage of the case where evidence is being presented. We simply don't know yet where the argument is leading, and by default, it may be analyzed as irrelevant. However, it could still be conditionally relevant, because if the right new evidence is filled in, it might have probative weight for supporting the ultimate *probandum*. Keppens and Zeleznikow (2002) offered a typical kind of example of this sort of case. Police officials encounter a dead body. There are normally four plausible hypotheses that could explain the evidence: "homicide", "suicide", "accident", or "natural causes". Which conclusion should be drawn in a given case? It will depend on whatever other evidence is available. If a suicide note was found, for example, that will point towards suicide. But at an early stage, no hypothesis may stand out yet as the most plausible one, and so whether some finding at the crime scene is relevant may be difficult to judge. In most cases, death by suicide or homicide is rarer than death by natural causes (Keppens and Zeleznikow, p. 2), and so, unless one of these hypotheses is suspected, there is a danger that relevant evidence may be overlooked. At a later stage, however, where a hypothesis has been supported as plausible, more evidence can be collected and then tested. At this later stage it might be much clearer whether a given item of evidence is relevant or not. Thus determinations of relevance can be partly based on the method set out above, but are partly contextual. They depend on the goal of the procedure used to collect and evaluate evidence, the rules for the procedure, and the stage the procedure is in. Determining relevance in a trial depends not only on the trial rules that apply, but also on the experience of the judge. The argument extrapolation will, in effect, be performed intuitively by the judge, based on knowledge of the trial rules and on skill in applying them to a particular case.

To apply the method as a tool to judge relevance in a given case, procedural assumptions have to be made about what type of dialogue the argumentation is supposed to be part of. If the context of dialogue is that of a common law trial, we can adopt the adversarial model of the trial as a dialogue process with burden of proof set by law for each type of trial. The purpose of the trial is to resolve a conflict of opinions by bringing forward relevant arguments on both sides in a critical discussion (Feteris, 1999; Walton, 2003). In a trial, there is always an ultimate *probandum* providing an aiming point of any chain of argument used as an argument in the case.

Wigmore (1935, p. 8) clearly recognized this contextual variability of relevance when he cited the example of two friends dining at a restaurant. They were discussing the subject of how to grow a certain type of rose in a garden when the waiter approached with the menu. One of them then said, "I cannot listen to that testimony now, because the only issue before us is whether we are to consume a lamb chop or a porterhouse steak." This example shows that whether an argument is relevant depends on its place in the type of dialogue the arguers are supposed to be taking part in. In the conversation about what to choose from the menu, once the waiter has arrived, and deliberation is needed to choose something from the menu for dinner, the previous argumentation about the Corona rose is irrelevant to the deliberation. Here there has been a dialectical shift (Walton, 2002, pp. 308-313) from a critical discussion on roses to a deliberation on what to choose for dinner. This kind of example suggests that one can't make a judgment of relevance only by the method of extrapolating forward. It also depends on the framework of dialogue the argument is part of. The same argument could be relevant in a negotiation but irrelevant as part of a critical discussion aimed at finding the truth of the matter being discussed. Thus different heuristics might be needed for different types of dialogue, or might be employed in different ways. The best approach is to begin with the easier cases and work up a method that applies the reasoning structure to them. These methods can be applied to any subject domain. From there, the heuristics that apply to special types of cases commonly found in trials need to be studied. It will be these heuristics that will be useful as applied to the harder cases.

Legal relevance should, in light of these considerations, be seen as a procedural notion used to limit time spent on listening to argumentation that will turn out to be of little or no probative value in reaching an informed and intelligent decision on the issue being tried. An irrelevant argument could be based on true premises and on a form of inference that is valid or logically strong. It might be a good argument in the sense that it carries probative weight warranting acceptance of its conclusion. But it is useless in a trial if it carries no probative weight bearing on the ultimate *probandum* in the trial. The problem with such arguments is how to identify them, and thus to exclude them from a trial as inadmissible, before they waste too much time, or divert the attention of the court onto matters that are of little or no value as evidence. The method of argument extrapolation provides a logical model, a normative structure of how such a task of determining relevance should rationally be carried out. But how a judge who must carry out this task in such a context of dialogue like that of a trial in the common law system, for example, is another matter. There are unsolved problems of computational dialectics concerning the structure of the trial as procedural argumentation structure that remain unsolved, as will be shown in chapter 5. As will be shown in chapter 5, within a trial there can be a dialectical shift from one type of dialogue to another when a witness comes to be examined. Such a shift will affect determinations of relevance.

Chapter 5: Methods Applied to Problems of Evidence

In chapter 5 various key problems of reasoning about evidence in law that show promise of being solved by the new methods, and some others now introduced, are formulated and studied. Although none of these problems can be entirely solved by these methods at their current state of development, two factors stand out. One is the centrality of the problems to law, and in particular the problem of grasping the key concepts of reasoning on which any theory of evidence must be based. The other is the plausibility of the hypothesis that some combination of the methods can be used to throw new light on the problems, and can lead to a new and promising dialectical approach. Thus the intent of chapter 5 is not to solve all the problems posed, but to indicate how the methods brought to bear on them, when put together, provide a direction for research that shows great promise in leading to the developments of a technology that will solve them. The intent is to show that, using these methods, there is a real hope of constructing a unified legal logic that will be useful in revealing the logical structure of legal evidence based on defeasible argumentation. Deductive reasoning will always be at the core of logic (Bibel, 2004), and surely represents the first step for analyzing legal reasoning. But because of defeasibility, deductive logic cannot take us far enough, by itself.

The limited potential of deductive and inductive logics, as applied to evidential reasoning in law, was that these tools couldn't get enough of a grip on typical forms of legal evidence like circumstantial evidence, witness testimony and character evidence. These forms of evidence are based on inferences of a kind that carry some probative weight in deciding an issue, but are far from conclusive, and do not respond all that well to evaluation by assigning probability values to the propositions in them. The argument of chapter 5 is that if they are modeled as defeasible arguments of a kind fitting argumentation schemes, much light can be thrown on how they do represent rational inferences that can be drawn from factual premises as logical reasoning. Chapter 5 takes the next step towards confronting more complex features of legal reasoning by introducing what is called case-based reasoning, with all the new features and complications this step involves. In law, each individual case is unique, to some extent at least, and therefore no technology of representing legal reasoning will be of much practical use unless it can take this contextual variability of cases into account.

1. Case-Based Reasoning

Case-based reasoning (CBR) is a technology used to solve a problem posed in a given case by drawing on similar cases retrieved from a database (library) of past cases. The solution to the problem posed in the given case is achieved by matching the given case against the retrieved cases by a process of analogy. CBR depends on a capability of matching one case to another, as similar, and even the capability of picking out the most similar cases from a library. Some cases will be more similar than others to a given case, depending on the description of the problem posed in the given case. CBR is a broad field of research that is centered in AI, but has also been intensively studied by social scientists, especially in the area of cognitive science. Legal CBR is a prominent area of research in AI and law. Work on CBR done in AI and law has been one of the most important streams of results that contributed to CBR as a general field (Rissland, Ashley and Loui, 2003). Among the most important of the systems that have been developed are the HYPO system, which produces point-counterpoint arguments in trade secrets law, and the CATO system, which teaches law students how to create case-based arguments. HYPO analyzes a given case by retrieving similar cases from its knowledge base, and makes a judgment of which cases are most "on point". It then generates a skeleton of an argument, arguing for one side by making a legal point, and then argues for the other side by responding with a counterpoint (Rissland, 1990, p. 1971). CATO has templates for argument moves, like argument from analogy, and rules for distinguishing, that show how to attack a rule (Ashley and Rissland, 2003, p. 41).

As a form of argumentation, legal CBR is based on a similarity comparison of one case to another, a given or "old" case that has been decided, and a "new" one that has not. The process of reasoning is one of drawing the same kind of conclusion in the new case that was drawn in the old one. How this process of reasoning works as a form of argumentation from one case to another was described in chapter 3, section 3, as resting on argument from analogy. Much legal reasoning, as shown in chapter 3, is used to decide cases based on argument from precedent, a type of argumentation clearly based on argument from analogy. But what makes one case similar to another, as far as argument from precedent of the kind used in law is concerned? It is the *ratio decidendi*, the reason why the precedent case was decided in a certain way, which then re-applied to the given case. Thus *ratio decidendi* is essentially an argument of a certain type, or a combination of such arguments chained together, leading to a conclusion. Thus it is apparent that CBR is based on argumentation schemes, especially argument from analogy and argument from precedent, described in chapter 3, section 3. And it is apparent that it is based on combining such arguments into patterns or structures representing chains of arguments, like those represented by the argument diagrams in chapter 1, for example. The problem posed here is how to analyze the precise relationship that holds between CBR on the one hand, and argumentation schemes and diagrams on the other hand. This problem has not, so far, been studied in argumentation, AI or law, even though it is obvious that the argumentation methods presented in chapter 1 are designed to apply to individual cases of the kind commonly addressed in law.

How case-based reasoning represents a use of argument from analogy in which features of one case are compared to those of another can best be explained by considering an example used by Bench-Capon and Sartor (2003). In this example arguments for and against a problem case are constructed by comparing it to two similar cases that are taken to provide precedents.

The Wild Animals Example (Chorley and Bench-Capon, 2004, p. 94)

In all three cases, the plaintiff (P) was chasing wild animals, and the defendant (D) interrupted the chase, preventing P from capturing those animals. The issue to be decided is whether or not P has a legal remedy (a right to be compensated for the loss of the game) against D. In the fox case, *Pierson v Post*, P was hunting a fox on open land in the traditional manner using horse and hound, when D killed and carried off the fox. In this case P was held to have no right to the fox because he had gained no possession of it. In the ducks case, *Keeble v Hickeringill*, P owned a pond and made his living by luring wild ducks there with decoys, shooting them, and selling them for food. Out of malice, D used guns to scare the ducks away from the pond. Here P won. In the fish case, *Young v Hitchins*, both parties were commercial fishermen. While P was closing his nets, D sped into the gap, spread his own net and caught the fish. In this case D won.

The fish case (*Young*) is taken to be the problem case, while the fox case (*Pierson*) and the ducks case (*Keeble*) are taken to be the base cases that provide theories that can arguably be used for the purpose of deciding the problem case. A theory is a hypothesis from the data given that can be used to construct a line of argumentation from features of the base cases that moves toward resolving the issue in the problem case. A hypothesis is a tentative conclusion formed by matching one case to another by analogy, or by distinguishing between two cases, arguing that one is different from the other in a certain respect. In the system AGATHA the line of arguments for and against a hypothesis is represented as a dialogue between the plaintiff's side and the defendant's in which one argument is opposed to another. This dialogue sequence of pro and contra argumentation is used to create a theory, and then by introducing new arguments, replace it with a better theory. Thus AGATHA uses argument from analogy to generate hypotheses, and then to replace them with better ones, through similarities and differences between one case and another. To represent the line of argumentation as successive hypotheses are formed, and then either defeated or supported, AGATHA uses a dialogue framework.

The wild animals example was analyzed in this dialogue format by Bench-Capon and Sartor (2003) by using two kinds of features of a case they called factors and values. The four factors and three values in the wild animals example, as identified by Bench-Capon and Chorley (2004, p. 94), are the following.

The Four Factors

pNposs: the plaintiff did not have possession of the animal.

pLand: the plaintiff owned the land.

pLiv: the plaintiff was pursuing his livelihood.

dLiv: The defendant was pursuing his livelihood.

The Three Values

LLit: the value of reducing litigation.

MSec: the value to secure enjoyment of property rights.

MProd: the value to promote productive activity.

Using these factors, and value preferences that rank the values, one can reconstruct a chain of argumentation leading to a resolution of the problem case. We won't go into the details, but it is easy to see how the arguments are produced. The defendant forms the first hypothesis by arguing that the fish case (set as the problem case) is similar to the fox case, in which it was held that the plaintiff had no right to the fox. The plaintiff then forms an opposing hypothesis which is constructed by arguing that the ducks case is more similar to the fish case than the fox case is. The plaintiff might support this hypothesis by arguing that the ducks case is similar to the fish case, because in both cases the plaintiff was pursuing his livelihood. And so the argument continues in a sequence in which hypotheses are produced and value preferences applied to them.

Chorley and Bench-Capon (2004, p. 96) displayed a sequence of ten hypotheses as a profile of dialogue in which ten theories are put forward, and the factors and values used to support or attack the theory are attached to each theory. At the final move, the defendant wins. However, the details of the dialogue sequence, or who won, are less important for us here than the general structure of case-based reasoning, and its main features, illustrated by the analysis of the example. Arguments from analogy is used to argue from the similarity of one case to another, and argument from difference is used to counter argument from analogy, producing a pro-contra dialogue. Such argumentation is holistic in nature because it is based on the evident similarity immediately apparent between a pair of cases. But a more fine-grained analysis of such argumentation can be given by eliciting specific factors and values. Once such factors and values are stated precisely, the outcome of the dialogue can be computed so that there is a winner and a loser. But as Chorley and Bench-Capon noted (p. 97), there can be various ways of providing heuristics for evaluating theories, and more tools for more sophisticated kinds of evaluations of case-based reasoning are being developed. Still, the wild animals example provides a very useful explanation of how case-based reasoning works and what its basic components are. The wild animals example illustrates how argument from analogy as used in CBR can be automated by using three components: factors, values, and profiles of dialogue. Other research has shown how argumentation typical in CBR can be modeled by using these three components, along with argument diagrams.

2. Argument Diagramming and Case-Based Reasoning

Recent investigations have shown more fully how argument diagrams can be used to model the argumentation used in case-based reasoning. The diagrams used are very similar to *Araucaria* diagrams except for one feature called entanglement, illustrated in the diagram below. In *Araucaria*, and also in the argument diagramming systems familiar in informal logic, propositions appear as nodes of the diagram, and arrows representing inferences are always drawn from nodes to nodes. Thus an arrow is never drawn from a node to an arrow. But it is precisely this drawing of an arrow from a node to an arrow that defined entanglement. An example is given below. Roth and Verheij (2004, p. 636) used the following argument diagram to represent part of the line of argumentation in a Dutch case of dismissal law.

Diagram 1 for Dismissal Law Case

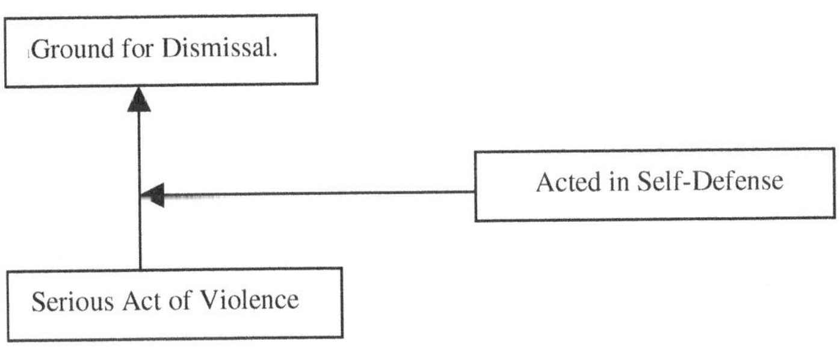

Fig. 5.1. Diagram 1 for Dismissal Law Case

According to the Dutch Civil Code, having committed a serious act of violence is a pressing ground for dismissal from a job. But if the employee acted in self-defense, that would be a ground of justification, according to the Act. Thus in diagram 1 above, an arrow is drawn form the Acted in Self-Defense node to the arrow joining the other two nodes. Thus entanglement, in this case, appears to represent a conjunction of three claims. The first is that, as a general rule, normally a serious act of violence would be a pressing ground for dismissal. The second is that the agent acted in self-defence. That finding in this case would show that the case is an exception to the general rule. The third is that if it can be shown that the agent acted in self-defense, such a finding would defeat the inference from Serious Act of Violence to Pressing Ground for Dismissal.

Representing the notion of entanglement on the argument diagram appears to be quite favorable, because it enables us to extend the normal argument diagram of the kind used previously in this book. And so it enables us to represent an important thesis about refutation of argumentation. It could be called the three ways thesis, the thesis that there are three ways to refute an argument. The first is to mount a counter-argument attacking the conclusion of the original argument. The second is to attack one or more of the premises of the original argument. The third is to attack the inferential link between the premises and the conclusion of the original argument. In standard systems of argument diagramming, like *Araucaria*, the first two ways of attacking a given argument can easily and straightforwardly be represented on the diagram. It is simply represented as another argument that leads to the conclusion of the original argument, or to one of its premises. Or there could be several refutations represented, each one as an argument attacking a premise of the original argument. But as shown in chapter 1, attacking the inferential link between a set of premises and a conclusion of a given argument is problematic in a standard system like *Araucaria.* The reason is that such an attack involves the asking of critical questions matching the argumentation scheme that warrants the inference from the premises to the conclusion. This, in turn, raises serious questions about burden of proof, as shown in chapter 1.

If we turn to diagram 1 for the dismissal law case above, once again, we need to ask what the argument represented by the entanglement arrow represents. This argument appears to refute the original argument for dismissal by acting as what was called an undercutter (Pollock, 1995) in the chapter on defeasible reasoning. In the diagram above, the inference drawn for the undercutter is represented as an arrow leading to the arrow representing the previous inference it undercuts. On this interpretation, there is an inference from the Acted in Self-Defense node that, because it represents an exception to the rule, undercuts the inference from the Serious Act of Violence node to the Pressing Ground for Dismissal node. But does this entanglement arrow represent an undercutter, that merely raises questions about the prior inference, or is it a defeater, a stronger form of refutation that shows that the prior inference does not hold? It seems more like a defeater. If true, it defeats the original argument that the employee should be dismissed for the reason that he committed a serious act of violence.

Verheij and Roth (2004, p. 635) use another diagram to represent another kind of argument that could also be classified as representing refutation of a sort. However, in this instance the structure of the argumentation can be represented by a standard argument diagram without a need to use entanglement.

Diagram 2 for Dismissal Law Case

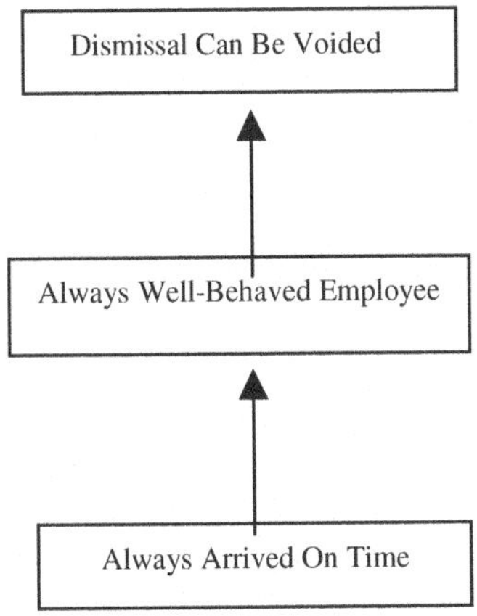

Fig. 5.2. Diagram 2 for Dismissal Law Case

In this diagram, the proposition that dismissal can be voided is supported by the statement that the individual was always a well-behaved employee. This proposition is in turn supported by the proposition that he always arrived on time. If we connect this diagram to the reasoning represented by the previous diagram, we could draw an arrow from the top proposition, that dismissal can be voided, to the conclusion of the previous diagram, the proposition that there is a pressing ground for dismissal. This arrow should be drawn, in *Araucaria* fashion, as a darkened double-headed arrow representing a refutation (defeater). Putting the two diagrams together in this way, a larger argument diagram is produced. The larger diagram represents the total body of evidence in the case, as so far described.

The problem is that it is unclear whether the argument structure in diagram 2 represents an undercutter or defeater. In this case, it looks like the bottom node offers one reason to support the middle node, which in turn offers one reason to support the top node. In other words, the structure is one of a chain argument, called a serial argument in the standard terminology of informal logic. It looks like each node offers some support for the one above it, but also that this support is not a conclusive reason to accept the proposition at that node as true. In other words, it looks like the argumentation represented by the diagram could be better classified, in Pollock's terms, as an undercutter rather than as a defeater, or conclusive refutation.

Thus while it looks like the feature of entanglement is potentially useful for representing legal argumentation, precisely how it should be interpreted is questionable. This feature raises the same problems about the notions of burden of proof, critical questions, and undercutters versus defeaters, that were raised in chapter 1. The underlying problem is how a defeasible argumentation scheme can support an argument from a set of premises to a conclusion, even if the support given to it remains partial or tentative. Such an argument is open to critical questioning, and therefore can be undercut, or even defeated altogether, as a trial or other form of investigation proceeds. As new evidence is collected during the searching process, the old argument that was once accepted as reasonable is refuted, and gives way to a new one that is opposed to it. Thus it is now helpful to turn back to some of the most common defeasible argumentation schemes used in legal argumentation to better understand the conditions for their refutation.

3. Witness Testimony as Evidence

The basic tools for analysis and evaluation of witness testimony as evidence have been presented in chapter 1. The central one is the argumentation scheme for argument from witness testimony, along with its accompanying set of critical questions. The tool is applied to the testimony offered in a given case, and then missing premises in the argument can be located. These can often be a focus for directing critical questions. One of the main problems with this form of argumentation is that it can be taken as conclusive, obviating the need for considering critical questions or countervailing evidence in a case. This characteristic is typical of how many kinds of defeasible arguments can become fallacious instruments of deception. Critical questioning is shut down, thought unnecessary, or even suppressed. The fallible argument that should be seen as open, and subject to possible retraction in dialogue, becomes fixed and rigid. Questioning it is not allowed, or even thought to be necessary.

The fallibility of witness testimony as evidence has been demonstrated dramatically in recent years by social science research (Loftus, 1994) findings that long-term memory can be highly misleading. An old memory of a past event, like seeing a face, may be very fuzzy in a witness's memory, and it can be easy to substitute another face seen later. This hypothesis about the fallibility of human memory has been dramatically confirmed by many recent findings of wrongful conviction shown by DNA evidence. According to a survey of wrongful conviction cases in Canada (Anderson and Anderson, 1998, pp. 8-16) five factors are important in understanding how such errors occurred.

1. Juries are generally inclined to accept the testimony of a witness as fact, and without it, the prosecution would be forced to rely on circumstantial evidence that juries would generally find insufficient for conviction (p. 11).
2. Expert witnesses can "step over the boundaries separating science from advocacy," (p. 15), leading to the well-known problems of "junk science".
3. Judges can be biased toward the side of the prosecution, in trying to maintain public confidence by preserving the reputation of prosecutors or police officers (p. 15).
4. The police, under pressure to get a conviction, especially in murder or rape cases widely reported by the media, can lose, misinterpret, overlook or exaggerate evidence (p. 14).

5. A jailhouse informant "planted" in the cell of the accused to get a "confession", gets "special consideration" by the police, like sentence reduction, but the jury is not informed of the deal, and takes him to be a credible, unbiased witness (p. 14).

Many of the cases of wrongful conviction that have been collected and studied by Anderson and Anderson and others have abundantly confirmed the hypothesis of Loftus (1994) and other social science investigators of testimony that there is a psychological bias factor. In many cases, the witness may be exposed to the suspect many times before the trial begins. As the witness repeatedly views the same suspect, she becomes convinced that he is the person she witnessed committing the crime. The commitment of the witness to this opinion can become so fixed through repeated incidents of this sort that she will persist with it even though overwhelming evidence demonstrates that it cannot be true. Prosecutors are sometimes so dogged and persistent in doing what they see as their job, prosecution, that they can remain convinced of a suspect's guilt even when it is clear to anyone not involved in the case that they have to be wrong.

The problem here is that advocacy for a side, or for a preferred view, becomes fixed, and is no longer subject to critical questioning. On the other hand, testimonial evidence is inherently fallible, and should always be seen as open to critical questioning. Evidence in a case needs to be judged as a whole mass in which a network of inferences is connected one with the others. But there is a natural human tendency to fix on one argument, to ignore or undervalue other relevant arguments, and to stick with that one argument as the central most convincing evidence, denying all counter-arguments and critical questions. This fixation of evidence can be hard for a jury to resist, given a tendency to accept witness testimony generally, and especially expert witness testimony.

Essentially it is for reasons like this that the testimony of a witness is not held to be admissible as evidence in a trial unless the witness can be questioned before the court. The opposing side needs to have an opportunity to ask critical questions, and generally to cross-examine the witness, in order to raise doubts about the testimony that the trier should take into account. Thus in the Anglo-American system, the adversarial trial is the method whereby evidence in the form of witness testimony is evaluated. In science, a hypothesis is always subject to testing on the basis of experiments and continued collection of empirical findings. The format of such testing of legal evidence is the trial. Questions are put to the witness, and if they can't be answered appropriately and convincingly, conclusions are drawn by default. Thus the dialogue format of a trial as a method of testing evidence is based on the embedding of one dialogue within another. The trial starts out as a critical discussion in which two opposed sides each attempts to persuade the trier that its argument is stronger than that of the other side, or meets the burden of proof set for it, thus defeating the other side. This format is one of an adversarial contest in which it is hoped that two able advocates will present the strongest arguments on both sides. Then the trier can decide which side wins. But the trial is not merely a purely adversarial contest between the stronger and the weaker arguments, a kind of debate or rhetorical contest. The arguments on both sides can be probed for weaknesses and tested by various means. They can be tested against other relevant facts. They can be tested for consistency. They can be probed by the asking of critical questions that draw attention to hidden assumptions and other critical weaknesses that open them to doubt. Thus to grasp the trial as a method of finding the truth of a disputed matter, we need to take the examination type of dialogue seriously as a part of the process.

The basic problem in this book all along has been to situate defeasible argumentation schemes into pragmatic frameworks representing dynamic types of procedure in which questions are asked, arguments are put forward, questioned an even refuted, and a given argument chains forward towards some goal or outcome. In chapter 1, we identified six types of dialogue of this sort. But what about legal argumentation? It doesn't fit any of the types of dialogue in any simple way. And indeed if you look at the adversarial trial in common law, although it fits the critical discussion in some respects, it is more like a drama or play in which there are many participants with different roles. Thus we have a very basic problem posed here. How can we get a fit between one or more of these abstract types of dialogue and the kind of legal argumentation that one might observe, for example, in a common law trial when evidence is brought forward to support or attack a claim? This problem is a hard one, that is not yet amenable to any straightforward solution. Still, there is a characteristic shift from one type of dialogue to another that can be observed in every trial when a witness takes the stand. The witness answers questions and offers testimony in answer to these questions. The questioner is said to be conducting an examination of the witness. This process of asking and answering questions is evidently some systematic type of dialogue different from a lot of the other kinds of dialogue that take place in a trial. If so, what are its defining characteristics?

4. Examination

It is helpful to begin with some attention to the commonly accepted meaning of the term 'examination' outside the legal context. This term has several primary senses that are important in education and science. One is the notion of examining something under a microscope. This meaning conveys the idea of looking at some object with care, and perhaps looking at it to study some features of the object one is interested in. A second meaning refers to the kind of examination used to test a student's knowledge of a subject in education. A third, related to the first one, is the examination of a patient by a physician. The physician typically looks at some parts of the patient's anatomy, observing data, especially anything unusual, or anything that might be a symptom, and may follow up the examination by arriving at a diagnosis, and also by sending the patient to the lab for tests. A fourth meaning refers to examination of a witness or party in a legal context. The examiner puts questions to the party being examined and that party is supposed to give to the questions. When the questioner represents the opposing side in a trial, the dialogue is called a cross-examination. What is common to all these examples are three levels of the procedure, each following up on the preceding one. The first level is the collection of data or information. At the second level, the information given at the first is tested to confirm whether it is accurate and a hypothesis may be drawn to try to offer some explanation of the data. At the third level, the hypothesis is tested against other data and against competing hypotheses that may explain the same data. At this third level as well, evidence for or against the competing hypotheses may be weighed on a balance, and a conclusion may be drawn concerning which is the best.

This process of examination is a method of collecting and testing evidence in a trial. Most of the evidence in a typical trial comes to the attention of the judge or jury who weighs the evidence through the process of examination of witnesses. From the testing of the answers given through a sequence of following questions and replies, conclusions are reached in the form of hypotheses. Examination can be seen to have the structure of an orderly goal-directed dialogue. There are two primary participants, the questioner and the respondent. Of course, in a trial, many other participants are also involved. The judge may exclude questions or answers on the grounds that they are irrelevant, or on the grounds that they are leading or complex questions. Such restrictions suggest that examination is a type of dialogue that has a goal of the seeking of truth, or at least relevant evidence, of a kind that enables a rational decision to be reached concerning the outcome of the trial process.

Feteris (1999, p. 174) has shown how the argumentation in a legal process like a trial forms a complex network of argumentation that can be viewed as a critical discussion at its core. For example, in the Dutch civil process, there is a conflict of opinions between the parties. But that is not the end of the story. The critical discussion must be made intelligent by the introduction of information into it through the process of questioning witnesses and other parties to the trial. The central aim is to resolve the conflict of opinions by means of rational argumentation, but this dialogue needs to be supplemented by a process of presentation and examination of witness testimony. This process of examination is a separate type of dialogue in its own right, joined to the critical discussion that is the core of the trial.

The trial is an adversarial process, but one moderated by legal rules of procedure that the judge is obliged to uphold, and if necessary enforce. Even the examination part has an adversarial aspect. By convention, cross-examination is defined as the examination by the other side following the prior examination of the first side. Park, Leonard and Goldberg (1998, p. 31) define cross-examination as the questioning of a witness by a lawyer other than the lawyer who called the witness to testify. Cross-examination often tends to involve careful strategies of asking carefully orchestrated sequences of questions, and can often appear to be hostile. The witness may be confronted with a contradiction in her testimony, or her character may be attacked. Character is generally inadmissible as evidence in criminal cases, meaning that the prosecution should not be able to argue that the defendant is a bad person, and is therefore guilty. Rule 404 of the Federal Rules of Evidence states, "Evidence of a person's character or a trait of character is not admissible for the purpose of proving action in conformity therewith". However, numerous exceptions are allowed. A main one is that character evidence may be used to attack the credibility of a witness.[1] According to Rule 608, the credibility of a witness may be attacked by offering evidence that the witness has shown a bad character for veracity (truthfulness). So attacked, a witness can then attack this charge and argue in defense of her good character.

Because of its complex characteristics, the structure of examination dialogue is a little hard to make sense of at first. But it may help at this point to show how Aristotle, and other argumentation theorists in the ancient world, recognized it as a distinctive and important type of dialogue. In a significant passage in *On Sophistical Refutations* (165a40 - 165b12), Aristotle presented a classification of four types of arguments used in discussions: didactic (pedagogical) arguments, dialectical arguments, examination arguments, and contentious arguments. Didactic, or pedagogical, are those used in teaching a student about some subject. Dialectical arguments are defined as those that start "from generally accepted opinions (*endoxa*)", and "reason to establish a contradiction"(165b4-5). Aristotle's notion of dialectical argument is hard for the modern reader to grasp. The best examples are the early Socratic dialogues written by Plato. Socrates begins the dialogue by getting his interlocutors to agree to some generally accepted opinion. Then, by asking a series of questions, he probes into the reasons behind the opinion. Quite often, he leads the interlocutor by a chain of reasoning to a problematic outcome like a contradiction (Robinson, 1962). But the intent is not to "shoot down" the interlocutor. The goal of the dialogue is to shake up his dogmatic preconceptions and those of the audience. Thus dialectical argumentation, on the Aristotelian model, can be described as a process in which questioning of current views by arguing both sides of the issue, leads to a deepened understanding of the issue by both sides (Evans, 1977, p. 2). In Aristotle's view, dialectical arguments are different from scientific proofs. Scientific proofs start from axioms that are not in dispute. Dialectical arguments, in contrast, are based on *endoxa* that are generally accepted but that are often superficial. A thorough discussion can raise questions that throw the *endoxon* into doubt. Even though the *endoxon* may not be either proved or refuted by the argumentation in the dialogue, light can be thrown on the reasons behind both it and opposed views.

Now that we have at least some grasp of what Aristotle meant by dialectical arguments, we can proceed to inquire into how he defined examination arguments. Examination or peirastic arguments (*perastikoi logoi*) were defined in *On Sophistical Refutations* (165b4-165b6) as those "based on opinions held by the answerer and necessarily known to one who claims knowledge of the subject involved." Such arguments, are "fitted to test someone's alleged knowledge and are based on the views held by the respondent" (Nuchelmans, 1993, p. 37). Aristotle felt that the examination form of dialogue, like the dialectical form, is not based on knowledge of any particular domain or subject by either party to the exchange. He wrote in *On Sophistical Refutations* (172a32) that examination can deal with any subject-matter. It is a universal skill of questioning and reasoning that can be applied in many, or even all, domains of knowledge and understanding. As a practical matter, everyone may need to use examination dialogue at some time or other. Its

[1] This nature of the exception is more fully detailed in rules 607, 608 and 609.

purpose, according to Aristotle (*On Sophistical Refutations* 172a33), is to "attempt to test those who profess knowledge." As noted above, Socrates displayed his skill in examination in the Platonic dialogues. But these examples represent a high level of sophistication in managing a subtle discussion on abstract philosophical issues.

At a more practical level, each of us needs to make use of skills of examination to get the best health care we can when we visit a doctor or dentist. It is hard to put critical questions to an expert, especially when you are dependent on him for medical treatment. But you will do better if you make the effort to ask questions and try your best to grasp the technicalities in the form of specialized information that the doctor or dentist may endeavor to convey to you. This kind of case represents a familiar practice of the skills of peirastic dialogue.

There is also one other point of classification of dialogues that deserves mention. Guthrie (1981, p. 155) drew a distinction between two subtypes of examination dialogue he found described by Aristotle, who called them "peirastic" and "exetastic". Guthrie characterized peirastic argumentation as the "testing or probing" of a view, while he identified exetastic argumentation with examining a view critically (p. 155). But what does this supposed distinction really amount to? It is hard to say, with much precision. Perhaps a useful distinction could be attempted as follows. Exetastic argumentation has a harder edge to it. Peirastic dialogue is testing or probing a view by asking its proponent critical questions that try to clarify and explain it. The aim is for the respondent to come to understand it for practical purposes, even though he is not an expert in the field of special knowledge in which the view falls. The aim here is primarily one of clarification or improved understanding. Exetastic dialogue comes to the fore when the questioner tries to probe more deeply into the reasons supporting the view held by the other party, or the lack thereof. Thus in exetastic argumentation, the questioner may be trying to actually attack the view critically, and may express serious doubts about the truth of the claim.

In the ancient treatise on argumentation called the *Rhetorica Ad Alexandrum* (Anaximines, 1965), exetastic argumentation was described as the kind of argumentation where the one party in a dialogue attacks the other for not practicing what he preaches. This type of argumentation sounds like *argumentum ad hominem* of the circumstantial type recognized in modern logic, where one party attacks the alleged contradiction found in the views expressed by another party. This way of characterizing exetastic argumentation certainly makes it seem to have a harder edge than other instances of peirastic argumentation. It seems to involve an attack designed to expose a contradiction or other logical view in a person's argument. Of the two types of dialogue then, the peirastic type seems more like a subspecies of information-seeking dialogue, while the exetastic dialogue seems more infused with what Aristotle called dialectical argument, or the persuasion type of dialogue, where there is opposition between two contrary viewpoints. It is very hard to tell, however, how Aristotle might have really meant to draw such a classification. Hamblin (1970) was probably right to suggest that Aristotle was uncertain, and that he changed his mind at different points in the development of his views. Even so, the distinction between the peirastic and the exetastic subtypes of examination dialogue, as drawn and emphasized by Guthrie, is useful. It seems to articulate an important distinction to reflect on, whatever Aristotle might have really thought about it.

Having come to this point in the exposition, it has to be admitted that there remains some uncertainty about the precise distinction between dialectical and examination arguments. Hamblin (1970) observed some key ambiguities in how Aristotle appeared to treat examination arguments in different writings. Hamblin (1970, p. 59) was of the opinion that Aristotle was "not quite sure" whether dialectical arguments and examination arguments were supposed to represent two different kinds of argumentation or whether the one was supposed to be a special subtype of the other. He even pointed out (p. 59) that "in different places" Aristotle "makes each a subclass of the other." In one passage, it appears that Aristotle only made a three-fold distinction among types of dialogue, and that he collapsed the dialectical and examination categories into one. To support his observation, Hamblin (1970, p. 59) cited the passage in *Topics* 159a25, where Aristotle wrote, "the contrast between the three kinds of argument – didactic, dialectical or examination, and contentious – is clearly drawn." But you could also cite the remark in *On Sophistical Refutations* (171b7) where Aristotle wrote, "the art of examination is a kind of dialectic". Guthrie (1981, p. 155) interpreted Aristotle as classifying examination dialogue as part of dialectic, even though he acknowledged that it appeared to be a distinctive subtype or component of dialectical argumentation. However, in other passages, like those quoted above from *On Sophistical Refutations*, Aristotle portrayed dialectic and examination arguments as two separate categories. It is understandable for some confusion and uncertainty to remain on this point. Examination arguments have never really been defined precisely and they seem to be mysterious and elusive in certain respects. It does seem right that examination is a type of dialogue that is embedded at key points in a wider type of dialogue format that Aristotle would have called dialectical. But it also appears in many instances that argumentation can occur in a hybrid type of dialogue that combines features of the information-seeking and the persuasion types (the latter being the modern category that would appear to best correspond to what Aristotle calls dialectical argument). On the other hand, examination sometimes appears to be a distinctive type of dialogue in its own right, especially when considering explanations as well as arguments in a text of discourse. Thus one would expect some uncertainty on questions of classification until examination dialogue is better explored. Even so, Aristotle's recognition of examination as a distinctive form of dialogue, and his attempts to classify various species of it, are highly significant.

The recognition of examination as a distinctive type of dialogue is revolutionary in its implications for computational dialectics, especially as applied to the analysis of legal argumentation and evidence. It implies that there is a distinctive pragmatic framework different from that of the critical discussion type of dialogue, that comes into play when a witness is examined in court. In a trial, there is a shift from the main type of critical discussion dialogue in a trial to an examination dialogue during which a witness is examined. This process of examination is more than just a sequence of questioning of the witness. It involves argumentation in which what the witness says is tested, by probing into it critically as an account of some alleged event that is consistent, and that offers a coherent and intelligible explanation of what happened. This notion of the production of an account or so-called script that is probed and critically tested in a trial has already been studied in cognitive science and law, most notably through the theory of anchored narratives (Wagenaar, van Koppen and Crombag, 1993). According to this theory, the process of examination in a trial can produce criminal evidence when a witness is interviewed. The reason is basically that the account given, called a script, is critically tested through the process of questioning it in a trial. Through this process, the questioner finds contradictions and other logical weaknesses in the script, and she asks further questions to try to resolve them. Such a process can result in one of two outcomes. One is that the script may be refuted and found implausible as evidence. The other is that the script may be improved, once tested through the process of examination, and accepted as evidence that is relevant to the ultimate *probandum* in the case.

Another sweeping implication of the recognition of examination as a distinctive type of dialogue in its own right is the importance of inference to the best explanation, or abductive reasoning, in legal argumentation. When a witness offers an account (story or script) in a criminal trial in answer to questions asked by an examiner, what is offered is an explanation of some event that supposedly occurred, some fact. Through the process of examination, a questioner attempts to elicit other competing explanations of the same fact, and to evaluate, or to enable the trier to evaluate, which is the best explanation. We turn to a consideration of the role of abductive reasoning in legal argumentation in section 6 below.

5. Circumstantial Evidence

The distinction between circumstantial and testimonial evidence has no real standing in law as fundamental to classifying different types of evidence in trial rules of procedure for judging the admissibility of evidence. For example, it is not a fundamental distinction in the Federal Rules of Evidence. However, though the distinction is a hard one to draw with precision, and there are different theories about it (Walton, 2002, chapter 3), it can be useful in helping us to understand evidence in law from a philosophical point of view. For example, Wigmore often used the distinction to classify and analyze different kinds of evidence. Circumstantial evidence refers to evidence that is drawn by means of a certain kind of inference from a premise to a conclusion. The premise is a factual proposition describing certain circumstances of a case. The conclusion drawn by inference is that this proposition can be taken to imply another one that is relevant as evidence in the case being considered. For example, a knife found at a murder scene is a circumstance that may have implications concerning the issue of how the crime was committed or who committed it. Circumstantial evidence can be contrasted with testimonial evidence, which always involves a special kind of inference drawn from a premise reporting witness testimony. It is based on the assumptions that the witness was in a position to know about something, and is telling the truth about it. Circumstantial evidence, by definition, is not based on witness testimony, but on the circumstances themselves that were supposedly factual findings in a case.

Circumstantial evidence is taken to represent an inferential process that depends on an interpretation of circumstances that is fallible, and can also be accounted for in other ways, by drawing a different conclusion. It is a form of evidence that can be questioned. It depends on an assumption about how things can normally be expected to go in a kind of situation that all of us are familiar with. According to an early manual on evidence (Gilbert, 1769, p. 5): "Circumstantial evidence is proof of certain facts and circumstances in a certain case, from which the jury may infer other and connected facts, which usually and reasonably follow, according to the common experience of mankind". But sometimes the unexpected happens, because a case is not like the ones we are familiar with in some respect. For example, suppose a man is seen running away from a crime scene. If a witness testified to this fact, the evidence would be testimonial. But the fact itself can be seen as a circumstance that, if true, suggests guilt. Why? The reason is that normally, in our common experience, the perpetrator will try, as speedily as possible, to escape from the crime scene, in order to avoid providing any evidence of his guilt. Given this normal pattern of action, if a man is seen running away from a crime scene, it will be taken to imply that he was "fleeing", suggesting that his intention was to get away and escape detection. This conclusion, in turn, is taken as evidence of guilt. Of course, it is only circumstantial evidence, because there could be many other plausible explanations of his action. He might have just been in the area by coincidence, and was trying to catch the bus.

There are many problems with maintaining this distinction in all cases. You could argue that testimonial evidence, for example, is also a kind of circumstantial evidence. Or you could argue that circumstantial evidence should be contrasted with some kind of evidence other than testimonial evidence. These arguments and many others have been put forward, all suggesting the distinction is a debatable one, and is fuzzy in certain respects (Walton, 2002, chapter 3). Even so, the distinction is a useful one that can be used to classify types of evidence in a rough way that at least represents how different kinds of evidence can be based on certain underlying forms of inference. We can say that circumstantial evidence is rarely if ever conclusive by itself, but is based on a fallible kind of inference from supposedly factual circumstances of a case based on normal expectations about how things would normally be expected to happen in that type of case. For all of us, as human agents, have some grasp of how things normally go in situations we are all familiar with. Testimonial evidence is also based on a fallible form of reasoning from what a witness claims to have seen, or to know about, to a conclusion about the way something happened, or about the way things really are. This form of inference too can go wrong, for as we know from social science research and from unjust conviction cases, as indicated above, witnesses are often wrong. They often, for example wrongly identify a criminal from a lineup, because memory of faces is highly fallible, especially over time.

The expression 'circumstantial evidence' is often taken to suggest that a conjectural inference is used to draw a conclusion by defeasible reasoning from some facts or circumstances of a case. Such a suggestion implies that the conclusion drawn only represents one explanation of what happened, and that other competing explanations may also be possible, or even plausible. In many instances of circumstantial evidence in law, for example, the kinds of cases cited in chapter 1, in which a bloody knife is found at a crime scene, the evidence can be analyzed as a sequence of argumentation using an argument diagram. The argumentation scheme for abductive reasoning is a tool that enables us to reconstruct the logical reasoning in the evidence in such cases much more effectively.

6. Abductive Reasoning

The assumption is that in addition to deductive and inductive reasoning, there is a third kind of reasoning that is defeasible and contextual. Many would say that this third category should be called abductive reasoning. The current conventional way of drawing this three-way distinction can be illustrated by citing a standard example used in a recent paper of Preyer and Mans (1999, p. 12).

Deductive Reasoning: Suppose a bag contains only red marbles, and you take one out. You may infer by deductive reasoning that the marble is red.

Inductive Reasoning: Suppose you do not know the color of the marbles in the bag, and you take one out and it is red. You may infer by inductive reasoning that all the marbles in the bag are red.[2]

Abductive Reasoning: Suppose you find a red marble in the vicinity of a bag of red marbles. You may infer by abductive reasoning that the marble is from the bag.

This canonical example indicates how abductive reasoning is taken to be different from deductive and inductive reasoning. Of course, deductive and inductive reasoning are already quite familiar to us, and they have been extensively analyzed in logic and statistics. But abductive reasoning appears to be mysterious. To some it might appear to be a special kind of inductive reasoning. But as Woods (1999, p. 118) pointed out, Peirce did not think so. Peirce (1992, p. 142) wrote, "There is no probability about it. It is a mere suggestion which we tentatively adopt." Peirce also used the terms 'hypothesis' and 'best explanation' in describing abductive reasoning, as shown below. So what kind of reasoning is this, if it is not inductive?

Abductive reasoning is a kind of guessing by a process of forming a plausible hypothesis that explains a given set of facts or data. As Preyer and Mans (1999, p. 12) point out, in this case the hypothesis, 'The marble is from the bag' could "serve as part of the explanation for the fact that a red marble lies on the floor". This account gives a clue about the nature of abductive reasoning, as being a dis-

---

[2] The Preyer-Mans example is a little misleading in that, according to standard statistical methodology, drawing an inductive inference from one finding would be too small a sample. To make the example more realistic, consider a finding of several red marbles with no other colors of marbles found in the sample.

tinctive kind of reasoning in itself, different from deductive and inductive reasoning. Consider the example, and how the conclusion is derived from the given data. I see the red marble on the floor. I see that it is near the bag. I know that the bag contains red marbles. I then construct the hypothesis, or guess, that the red marble on the floor came from the bag. How? Well, the red marble didn't just appear on the floor. It came from somewhere. There is no other obvious source, let's say. Although there is no hard evidence it came from the bag, that hypothesis appears to be the only plausible explanation that offers itself. No other hypotheses are more plausible. The explanation concerns the source of the marble. It could have gotten where it is by coming out of the bag, and somehow (we do not know how) arriving at its present location on the floor. What is significant in the given case is not only the known facts, but also the boundaries of what is known. There is the bare room, the bag of red marbles, and the single red marble on the floor near the bag. No other relevant facts of the case are known. From this set of data, one explanation of the given location of the marble stands out.

As a species of inference to the best explanation, abductive inference can be defined as having three stages. First, it begins from a set of premises that report observed findings or facts – the known evidence in a given case. Second, it searches among various explanations that can be given for these facts. Third, it selects out the so-called "best" explanation, and draws a conclusion that this explanation is acceptable as a hypothesis. The sequence of reasoning in the red marble case could be represented schematically as follows.

Positive Data: the red marble is on the floor, near the bag of red marbles.

Hypothesis: the red marble came from the bag.

Negative Data: No other relevant facts suggest any other plausible hypothesis that would explain where the red marble came from.

Conclusion: The hypothesis that the red marble came from the bag is the best guess.

The best guess is just an assumption, or presumption. It could be overturned by new information that suggests otherwise. But given what is known and what is not known about the facts of the case, that hypothesis is the best guess, or the most plausible one. There are lots of other possible explanations. Somebody could have put the marble there to make it appear that it came from the bag, for example. But in the absence of any relevant known facts of this sort, the hypothesis that the marble came from the bag is the only explanation that is given any plausibility by the actual facts of the case. Abductive inference is defeasible, meaning that the conclusion is only a hypothesis that is subject to retraction if further investigation of the facts in the case shows that another of the alternative explanations is better.

Abduction is often portrayed as a kind of "backwards' reasoning, because it starts from the known facts and probes backwards into the reasons or explanations for these facts. The etymological derivation of the term is from the Latin *ab* (from) and *duco* (lead). If you have a given knowledge base, then by abduction you are taking one proposition in that knowledge base, and trying to trace its derivation from prior propositions in it. Abductive inference is tied to the known or presumed facts of a case, but can be altered should this set of given data be altered. For this reason, abductive reasoning has also been called "retroductive" (Woods, 1999, p. 118). It is a kind of reasoning that leads backwards from the given set of facts, to hypothesize a basis from which those facts could be inferred. From the positive and negative data above in the red marble case, a conclusion can be drawn by a process of negative reasoning sometimes called *argumentum ad ignorantiam*. Since no other plausible explanation of the red marble being on the floor is suggested by the known facts, from closure of the boundaries of what is known in the case we can infer that the marble came from the bag of red marbles. If these boundaries are altered by new facts of the case, of course, that conclusion may have to be retracted. Negative reasoning from a knowledge base is called *argumentum ad ignorantiam* in logic. But in computer science, it is known as the lack-of-knowledge inference (Collins, Warnock, Aiello and Miller, 1975, p. 398). Abductive reasoning should be seen as not only a kind of knowledge-based reasoning, but also as tied to what is not known in a case.

There are two argumentation schemes representing abductive reasoning (Walton, 2004, 288). One is a defeasible *modus ponens* form of inference. It is forward moving. The other is based on a dialogue model of explanation, and represents a typical abductive inference of the backward type, going from data to a best explanation. Explanation (Walton, 2004, chapter 2) is defined as a speech act in which understanding is transferred from a questioner to a respondent by means of offering an account. An account is a set of particular and general statements that can be colligated together, but some fit the data better than others. A_i is one particular account selected from among a given set of accounts, $A_1, A_2, \ldots, A_n$. Each account given may be successful in explaining the data D, but some are more successful (better) than others.

Backward Argumentation Scheme for Abductive Inference

D is a set of data or supposed facts in a case.

Each one of a set of accounts $A_1, A_2, \ldots, A_n$ is successful in explaining D.

A_i is the account that explains D most successfully.

Therefore A_i is the most plausible hypothesis in the case.

Corresponding to a backward abductive inference there is also a forward abductive inference, represented by an argument diagram made up of a sequence of defeasible *modus ponens* inferences.

Forward Argumentation Scheme for Abductive Inference

D is a set of data or supposed facts in a case.

There is a set of argument diagrams G_1, G_2,...,G_n, and in each argument diagram *D* represents premises of an argument that, supplemented with plausible conditionals and other statements that function as missing parts of enthymemes, leads to a respective conclusion C_1, C_2,...,C_n.

The most plausible (strongest) argument is represented by G_i.

Therefore C_i is the most plausible conclusion in the case.

The backward and forward schemes represent two different uses of abductive inference that can be applied to the same case. The backward scheme represents inference from the observed data, or given facts in a case, to a hypothesis claimed to be the best explanation of those facts. The forward scheme represents abductive inference as having a defeasible *modus ponens* form, and as being an argument from a set of premises, some of which are conditionals, to a plausible conclusion.

Once introduced to the notion of abductive reasoning, some are inclined to think it is so powerful as a tool for the analysis of legal evidence that all defeasible forms of argumentation are abductive. What has been shown here is that not all defeasible argumentation of the kind studied in connection with legal evidence in previous chapters is abductive. Abductive reasoning is a special kind of argumentation in its own right, with an argumentation scheme showing its distinctive characteristics. Nonetheless, the importance of abduction in legal evidence is not hard to appreciate. Let's just briefly consider forensic evidence as a case in point.

7. Forensic Evidence

Many of the examples of forensic evidence studied in previous chapters are based on a kind of defeasible reasoning in which a tentative inference is drawn from a set of data or facts to a conclusion. It often seems to be a kind of disjunctive reasoning that leads to acceptance of a course of action in a deliberation or to acceptance of a hypothesis as an investigation moves forward in which more and more data is being collected and assessed. If a conclusion is accepted, it can later be rejected if contrary data come in during a sequence of argumentation as new facts are collected. Such a conclusion has tentative status in moving the investigation forward, even though later it can be retracted, and then a different hypothesis may be accepted. The best way to represent the part of the sequence is to see it as an instance of abductive reasoning, or inference to the best explanation. First, the forensic scientist observes, collects and tests data in a case. Then she examines the data. Then she arrives at a hypothesis, based on an inference to a best explanation of the data. The next stage is that she testifies as an expert in court. Her testimony is examined in the trial in the form of an examination dialogue in which an argument from expert opinion is critically questioned. Then the trier weighs the argumentation on both sides of the case and makes a judgment on the outcome in light of the requirements of burden of proof set down at the beginning of the trial. Thus the conflict of opinions is resolved, but an appeal can be made if it is or can be shown that there is new evidence that was not properly taken into account.

Forensic evidence as presented in a trial can be based on various schemes, but two are central. One is use of abductive reasoning, while the other is argument from expert opinion. Abductive reasoning is used by the scientist, or expert in a domain of knowledge, to draw an inference from data to what is taken to be the best explanation of the data. This is scientific evidence based on abductive reasoning within the science. When such evidence is presented in court, however, the context of dialogue has changed. It is presented as argumentation from expert opinion to the court, who must then collectively question and examine it as legal evidence. First, this evidence is presented by the expert source, in a dialogue with the lawyer questioning her. Next, the testimony is examined, in a process in which the lawyers on both sides have a chance to participate. Finally, the trier, the judge or jury, weighs this evidence, judging it as strong or weak, and placing it as part of the mass of evidence on one or both sides of the case. If relevant, this piece of evidence will affect the outcome as the judge or jury arrives at a final decision on the ultimate issue put before the court. Thus two different contexts of dialogue are involved, and forensic evidence is based on an embedding of the one dialogue into the other.

This lengthy process is one in which the same argument, for example an abductive argument based on forensic evidence, goes through many stages in which it is examined and critically questioned, reformulated and tested. According to the traditional approach, the process is one of belief revision, based on deductive or inductive reasoning from premises describing observed facts. According to the new dialectical methods of argument evaluation described here, the process is one in which participants in a sequence of connected dialogues take on commitments provisionally and then modify them, sometimes even retracting them, as the process continues. To fully appreciate how abductive argumentation works in such a model, we need to review the notion of commitment first explained in chapter 1, section 7.

In chapter 1, section 7, it was shown how the notion of commitment is an alternative to the notions of belief, desire and intention used to frame the traditional theory of rational thinking in western epistemology. Commitment was adopted as the central notion of rational argumentation by van Emeren and Grootendorst (1984; 1987; 1992). Let's review the notion of commitment in dialogue, as formalized by Walton and Krabbe (1995) in different types of dialogue, but especially in persuasion dialogue. As shown in chapter 1, commitment is taken to be different from belief. Belief, as the term is used in the BDI model, is taken to be an internal psychological state of a person or agent. As noted above, the problem for the BDI model is how one agent judges what the beliefs of another agent really are. In traditional philosophy, this was called the problem of other minds. The problem is that one person can't directly tell what another person really believes. Indeed, it can even be a problem for one person to figure out what she herself really believes about some issue or subject. Commitment, unlike belief, is not private or impossible to access directly. A participant in a dialogue is committed to a proposition (statement) when she has gone "on record" in some public way as supporting it, or saying it is true or acceptable for her. Thus it is possible that she might be committed to a proposition she does not actually believe. In a Hamblin-style game of dialogue, each participant has a commitment set, and the commitment rules determine how additions to or deletions from that set are made. The commitment rules determine when retraction of commitment is allowed. Thus what determines commitment is not something private. It is a public set of moves (speech acts) recorded in a dialogue, and there is a set of rules governing the various kinds of moves, which specify how each type of move affects addition and deletion of commitments. Belief necessarily implies commitment, whereas commitment does not necessarily imply belief. Hence commitment is the weaker of the two notions. Defeasible arguments of the kind considered in this chapter need to be continually updated as new evidence comes in to a case. Traditionally such updating was seen as belief revision based on empirical evidence.

The model of inference to the best explanation suggested as a good approach here is based on commitment, not belief, and is not an empiricist view. In traditional terms, it could be called a pragmatic view, or pragmaticist view, to use Peirce's term. The commitment-based pragmatic view is an alternative to the BDI view that rational arguments are based on true beliefs, or beliefs of any sort. Such arguments are based on commitments that often do, especially at the discovery stage in scientific argumentation, go beyond observable entities and processes. This way of proceeding is especially useful in working with multi-agent systems. In autoepistemic systems, where an agent is reasoning based on its own internal states, the belief model can be most useful and appropriate. However, in cases where one agent is attempting to reason with another agent, or communicate with another agent by asking questions, it is better to adopt the commitment model. The reason is that one agent does not have direct access to the internal mental states of the other, and has to base hypotheses about such internal mental states on what is accessible, namely the commitments of the other agent, as exhibited by the evidence of how the other agent acts and how it communicates in dialogue with the first agent. This will be shown to be important in the evaluation of character evidence in the next section. But it is also important in the evaluation of forensic evidence in the context of a trial where such evidence is based on expert testimony. As shown in previous chapters, this form of evidence is not well analyzed as being a form of deductive or inductive reasoning from factual premises. As shown in chapter 2, it is typically based on a third type of generalization that is neither deductive nor inductive.

Previous theories of abductive reasoning were based on a BDI model, and for the most part they attempt to reduce abductive reasoning to some form of deductive reasoning (Josephson and Josephson, 1994). Basically, these are attempts to model inference to the best explanation as a process with three components arranged in the following structure. The hypothesis *H* that explains the data *D* is conjoined to a background theory *T*, so that there is a deductively valid argument from the premises *D* to the conclusion *H*. The problem with all such theories is that, in typical cases of abductive reasoning, the hypothesis and the theory don't entail the data deductively, unless the theory contains escape clauses that close off the inference to further revisions or possible defeat. Thus to make the deductive model work, the background theory has to be loosened up or made less than universal. It must be such that room is made for exceptions to the rule. One way to do this (Pearl, 1988) is to require only that the explanation make the data sufficiently probable. Another way is to loosen the theory so that the explanation is only required to lead to the data by means of a defeasible inference. The situation here is comparable to the evolution of explanation theories. The first theory, the deductive-nomological or DN theory, tried to model the explanation on the pattern of a deductively valid inference. Then an inductive model was added, in an attempt to make the theory plausible. Finally, other ways were considered, like adding *ceteris paribus* clauses, to make the theory plausibly applicable to realistic cases of explanations. To call the model "deductive" appears in the end to be a kind of misnomer, but because of the strong preference for deductive reasoning, philosophical theorists cling to the view of their model as being essentially deductive. But this model does not fit the kind of reasoning used in forensic evidence, typically based on defeasible generalizations, very well.

Perhaps the most notable attempt to add modifications to make the deductive model applicable to explanations commonly found in law, everyday conversational argumentation, and in the social sciences and history, is the belief-revision theory (Boutilier and Becher, 1995). According to this theory, an explanation *E* is conjoined to an agent's set of existing beliefs, *T*, and these two sets of statements together entail the given data *D*. Thus in a case of medical diagnosis by abductive reasoning, the physician conjoins her existing set of beliefs with the explanation she has arrived at, and these two deductively imply the set of data in the case. The set of beliefs corresponds to the knowledge base of the agent at the time the abductive reasoning was carried out. Various developments of this theory have been concerned with the problem of how to deal with the kind of inconsistency that might appear when the set of statements making up the explanation turns out to be inconsistent with the agent's beliefs. Gardenfors (1988) argued that the least "entrenched" beliefs ought to be given up, leaving the agent with a "contracted" set of them. But Reiter (1987) asked why the more entrenched beliefs should always be preferred over the less entrenched. He argued that in order to make consistency-based abduction useful, another notion has to be added. This is the notion of a system behaving correctly, so that some of the data can be classified as anomalous or abnormal. On this approach, if two statements in a data set conflict with each other, the one that is abnormal can be given up as a belief. An even more complex belief-revision theory was put forward by Doyle (1979; 1992). This theory depends on an operation called dependency-directed backtracking (*DDB*), performed when the system reaches a node in the chain of reasoning that contains a contradiction. The problem is whether that node should be left in place, or whether it ought to be changed, removing the contradiction. What *DDB* does is to chain the reasoning backward, removing not only the contradiction, if that is called for, but also the premises that led to it.

Doyle's belief-revision theory is remarkably similar to the theory of retraction of commitments in permissive persuasion dialogue presented in (Walton and Krabbe, 1995,p. 144-149). This theory uses external stability adjustment and internal stability adjustment as tools for managing retraction of commitments. These tools apply to the kind of case considered by Doyle and Reiter, where an arguer in a dialogue is found to have a set of commitments that is inconsistent. The solution presented in Walton and Krabbe (1995, p. 148) is roughly to the effect that the arguer must chain backward and retract the commitments that function as premises on which the commitment in question is based. The main difference between the theory of dependency-directed backtracking and the method of internal stability adjustment is that the former is expressed in a BDI framework while the latter is expressed in a commitment framework. Thus although one can see a convergence of findings between AI and argumentation theory (formal dialogue theory) here, the analysis of the form of abductive inference presented above can be based on a commitment framework.

In the end it may not matter which term we use, whether it is 'commitment' or 'rational belief'. The main thing is that we have to do justice to the way legal evidence works, and should properly be analyzed and evaluated. We need to see it as a necessary but dangerous form of reasoning that can be fallacious in some instances, but that we can't do without, either in law or in everyday thinking and argumentation. The main thing is that we need to see it as a kind of argumentation to which the methods of chapter 1 can be applied. It needs to be seen as based on defeasible argumentation schemes that require for their evaluation not only an argument diagram displaying the chain of reasoning and the ultimate conclusion to be proved, but also some consideration of the context of dialogue. Such a context must include a tracking of not only the acceptance of a conclusion, or any other proposition accepted during the course of an argument, but also its retraction. But the conditions for retraction are generally more difficult to define, with many sequences of argumentation, than those for acceptance. Thus the problem of how to evaluate forensic evidence points the way to the more general problem of how to update and modify commitments as a dialogue proceeds.

The problem of analyzing forensic evidence using a dialectical model of abduction seems relatively easy once we start to consider other kinds of evidence that are important in legal evidence judgments but tend to be much more fuzzy and prone to fallacy. One of these is character evidence. Character judgments are associated with many tricky and even fallacious forms of argument that can be dangerous indeed. Arguments based on character judgments are often linked to smear tactics, reputation attacks and use of innuendo. They are closely related in logic to *ad hominem* arguments, and in the public sphere to stereotyping and prejudice. But clearly we do reason based on character judgments all the time, in business affairs as well as in law. What is vital is whether we do it badly or well. Once again, dialectical abductive reasoning can help.

8. Character Evidence

According to the Federal Rules of Evidence, the most significant set of rules concerning the use of character evidence in trials, character is not generally admissible as evidence. Character is defined as a habit, trait or disposition, like honesty. However, as the term is used in law, character is more than merely a value-neutral statistical description of an agent's propensity to perform an action. It is an ethical concept based on the assumption a person has ethical qualities, like trustworthiness that can be judged from his or her actions and reputation. However, the logical problems about character judgments and inferences drawn from them is that it is unclear how data or factual evidence should be used to support the truth or accuracy of claims made about a person's character. If a theory could be devised that would show how character evidence should be evaluated in a trial, it would be useful to guide legal professionals who base their judgments on evidence rules, like the Federal Rules, that concern this kind of reasoning.

Character claims are not subject to proof or disproof in a direct way that normal factual evidence about a single action is. The character ban does not prohibit such singular judgments, but is directed to broad generalizations about character, like allegations claiming a person is a liar, a rapist, cruel, or lazy (Park, 1998, pp. 718-719). The ban does not exclude evidence of having carried out single actions like having abused a particular spouse, or having robbed a particular bank (p. 719). This kind of claim could be admissible as evidence in a trial. Also, a claim about an agent's character or past acts could be judged relevant if cited to prove the existence of a motive. However, general claims that an agent is an ethically bad person can be extremely powerful arguments used to influence a jury. To prevent juries from being overwhelmed by such character attack arguments, exclusionary rules were devised, and over the years they have been added, making more and more exclusions. The problem now is that many wonder if such exclusions have gone too far, giving a jury an incomplete picture of the evidence that is needed to properly judge a case. However, the problem goes much deeper than this. The real problem is that no very deep attempt was made to define character in the Federal Rules, probably because how to define it in a useful way is an unsolved problem in ethical philosophy. The problem is that we seem to have lacked the resources to grasp the kind of reasoning used when external evidence about an agent's actions is used to draw an inference to a conclusion about the agent's internal states and properties, like qualities of character. But now there is a new approach that shows promise of solving the problem. It is the hypothesis that abductive reasoning is used to draw such an inference and the conclusion is about the agent's commitments, as opposed to his beliefs or desires. The key is the notion of commitment.

What is needed is a new approach to understanding the process of reasoning that stands behind a character judgment that can reveal how this process, although inherently fallible and conjectural in nature, is based on logical reasoning from a set of given data in a case. It needs to be shown how character judgments can be supported by evidence based on simulative reasoning that is in turn supported or refuted by factual evidence. In simulative reasoning one agent uses its reasoning capability to understand the reasoning of the other agent. The one agent forms a hypothesis about the acts and goals of the other agent, and uses the given factual information of a case to support this hypothesis. The reasoning results in a supposition that is only plausible, but it can be an intelligent hypothesis based on good evidence, in some cases. Such judgments are fallible, however. The plausibility of the judgment is limited by the extent to which a reasoned act of empathy is possible from the shared contexts and the known data in a case. Case studies need to be used to show how this form of evidence takes the form of an inference to the best explanation based in contextual frameworks, called scripts in AI, shared by the two parties (Wagenaar, van Koppen and Crombag, 1994). The second party relies on this shared context to simulate the reasoning of the first party, and to draw conclusions by inference to the best explanation from observations or reported facts about what the first party did, and how he reacted to events. The support for the conclusion drawn is judged within an evidential network of abductive inferences forming a chain of reasoning in which one inference leads to another.

Using a question-answer (dialogue) model is now widely accepted in AI and law, but it appears to be a new, or at least innovative approach as applied to history. But it had been proposed as early as 1946 by the British archaeologist and philosopher R. G. Collingwood. Collingwood used the notion of "reenactment", in his book, *The Idea of History*, as the basis of his famous theory of historical explanation. The problem is that reenactment seems (especially to its positivistic critics) to be a highly subjective process. It has remained hard to determine how judgments based on it could be verifiable on the basis of objective evidence and clear reproducible logical reasoning. This empathetic kind of judgment, in both history and law is typically one of hindsight in which the evaluator does not have complete access to the original situation. Collingwood's theory about evidence used to support or criticize historical explanations of human actions is that it should be based on a process of question and answer. This theory didn't seem very exciting at the time, especially in the climate of logical empiricism that prevailed for so long. But new developments in artificial intelligence, cognitive science, linguistics and argumentation theory, as mentioned above, have now taken us much closer to an objective grasp of how simulative reasoning works. The new findings in pragmatics and argumentation theory have studied different dialectical structures, like information-seeking dialogue and deliberation, that represent different types of goal-directed conversational frameworks. These new approaches to reasoning and argumentation make Collingwood's theory much more attractive and exciting. And of course, especially in law, the approach that bears further investigation is the hypothesis that character evidence is based on abductive reasoning that should be judged in a context of examination dialogue.

Here one problem leads to another. Let's assume that reasoning drawn from assumptions about an agent's character can be analyzed on an abductive model, so that we have some basis for judging when such an argument is weak or strong. We still face the problem of devising criteria for helping us to judge when such character evidence should be considered relevant in a trial. This problem routes us back to the analysis of relevance in chapter 4. The approach suggested by the method recommended in chapter 4 is to collect the data in a given case, draw up an argument diagram representing it, and use this evidence to make a relevance determination. Of course, such a determination also needs to be partly contextual, and needs to take the place of the given argument in the context of dialogue into account. But now we have even better tools for analyzing such cases because we can model character judgments using abductive argumentation schemes. Thus once again the problem is by no mean solved, but the new tools for solving it point the way to a promising method of handling the kind of evidence that has proved to be extremely troublesome in the past.

9. Evaluation of Evidence

The biggest and most basic problem faced by the new approach to evidence in law is how to evaluate evidence as weak or strong by some formula, or method of calculation. After all, inductive reasoning has the Bayesian rules of the probability calculus that are used to evaluate probabilistic reasoning (Schum, 1994). In evaluating plausible reasoning, can we not take the same approach of attaching numbers to the propositions in an argument diagram and to the inferential links drawn as arrows that join the network of propositions together? Such an approach has often proved tempting in law, but has also often been argued against (Nissan, 2001). However, we saw in the chapter on relevance that it is the most helpful approach in making judgments about claims concerning conditional relevance. Basically there are two methods we can use. In a linked argument, the best rule is the least plausible premise rule. It says that the new plausibility value assigned to the conclusion of the argument should be at least as high as that of the value of the least plausible premise, or that of the inferential link joining the premises to the conclusion, if that is greater. In the case of a deductively valid argument, the plausibility value of the inferential link would be 1. Thus the rule would reduce to simply raising the value of the conclusion to that of the least plausible premise. By contrast, in a convergent argument, the value of the conclusion should be raised to that of the most plausible premise. The reason is that in a convergent argument, each premise provides an independent means of support for the conclusion. If one is weaker, it can be disregarded, for what is important is the support given by the stronger premise. But even though this numerical approach of labeling the points of a diagram with numbers is sometimes helpful, it does not seem to represent the main tool that is needed to evaluate the evidence in a legal case. Far more important is the structure of the diagram itself representing a mass of evidence on one side of the case tied together as a package. What is important is not so much any single item of evidence by itself, but how that item fits into the larger package and tilts the outcome to one side or the other on a balance of considerations. An argument based on character evidence, for example, may be very weak by itself, but taken together with other evidence in the case, it may be enough to swing the balance to one side or the other. As we have repeatedly seen, a single item of legal evidence may be weak and defeasible by itself. It is how it fits into the body of evidence in the case that matters more.

The basic problem with this new approach is that it is very hard to adapt to a new philosophy of logical reasoning in which there are now three kinds of arguments – deductive, inductive and abductive. The third type of argument has often been held to be untrustworthy and subjective in the past. Indeed, arguments of this sort have traditionally been classified as fallacious. The problem then is one of how we can define the notion of plausible reasoning in a way that it can be accepted as part of rational thinking of a kind that would support the idea that evidence, of the kind so important in law for example, could be seen as fitting the model of this type of reasoning.

The very best definition of plausibility was given by Carneades, a Greek philosopher who lived well after the time of Plato and Aristotle.[3] His most important legacy to philosophy was his famous theory of plausibility. According to Carneades' theory, something is plausible if it appears to be true, or (which is even more plausible) if it appears to be true and is consistent with other things that appear to be true. And thirdly, it is even more plausible still if it is stable (consistent with other things that appear to be true), and is tested. According to the epistemological theory of Carneades, everything we accept, or should accept, as reasonably based on evidence, is subject to doubt and is plausible only, as opposed to being known (beyond all reasonable doubt) to be true. Some accounts of Carneades' theory of plausiblity are given in the writings of Sextus Empiricus.[4] In *Against The Logicians* (*AL*), Sextus described the theory of plausibility Carneades proposed as a solution to problems he found in earlier skeptical and Stoic views. According to this theory, there are three criteria for plausible acceptance. The first has to do with experiencing a presentation or appearance in a convincing way. When a subject experiences a "presentation" (something that appears to him), it may be "apparently true" or seem convincingly true (*AL*, 168-170). Such a presentation, according to Carneades' theory, represents a proposition that should be accepted as tentatively true. Of course, as a skeptic would point out, one could be mistaken. But the theory rules that if a proposition is based on a presentation that is apparently true, then that proposition should, for practical purposes, be accepted as true, even though it is not known for sure to be true, and might later be shown to be false or dubious. As Sextus put it, sometimes we accept a presentation that appears true, but is really false, so "we are compelled at times to make use of the presentation which is at once both true and false" (*AL* 175). The second criterion is a pres-

---

3 Carneades (c. 213 - 128 B. C.), born in Cyrene, Cyrenaica (now in Libya) was the head of the third Platonic Academy that flourished in the second century B.C.

4 Carneades wrote nothing himself. His lectures were written out by one of his students, but unfortunately, none of these survived either.

entation that is both plausible in the first sense, and is also "irreversible", meaning that it fits in with other presentations that also appear true (AL 176). Sextus offered a medical illustration in which a physician initially concludes from his high temperature that a patient has fever but then supports this inference by other findings like soreness of touch, or thirst (*AL* 179-180). The third criterion involves the tested presentation (*AL* 182-183). Sextus cited the classic Carneadean illustration of the rope (*AL* 188). A man sees a coil of rope in a dimly lit room. It looks like a snake, and he infers the conclusion that it is a snake. Acting on this assumption, he jumps over it. But when he turns back, he sees it did not move. Then he readjusts his inference, inferring the new conclusion that it is not a snake, but a rope. But then again, he reasons, snakes are sometime motionless. So he carries out a test. He prods the object with a stick. If it still fails to move, that finding would indicate that the object is indeed a rope.

This simple example of what we can now recognize as abductive reasoning reveals the link between Greek skeptical philosophy and the modern pragmatic approach to informal logic. It is not a legal case or a case of scientific reasoning in a special domain of knowledge. It's a case of everyday reasoning of the kind all of us are capable of. Under conditions of uncertainty and lack of knowledge a hypothesis is formed as a best explanation, then retracted using argumentation from lack of a positive finding. Through the process of collecting further data as the investigation proceeds, the new hypothesis is then retracted, and commitment to the original one is made. Changing one's opinion in such a situation is not a symptom of being illogical, but one of reasoning defeasibly and rationally in the face of new data. It is this process of conducting an investigation based on asking and answering questions, and moving ahead with an open mind on the basis of the evidence at that point, that is the pragmatic framework of dialogue needed to evaluate legal reasoning as evidence.

Chapter 6: Dialectical Explanation in AI

It was shown in chapter 5 how fundamental abductive reasoning (inference to the best explanation) is for the analysis and evaluation of many kinds of evidence in law. Clearly, however, no understanding of abductive reasoning can be gained until we have a much better idea of what an explanation is. In chapter 6, the new dialogue-based theory of explanation (Walton, 2004; Walton, 2004a) is presented and refined. It is dialectical, meaning it is based on a framework of formal dialogue in which two agents take turns asking and answering questions. Each move in the dialogue is a speech act governed by rules determining what kinds of moves can be made. Explanation is thus modeled essentially as a kind of speech act used in an orderly process of communication. Each participant is viewed as an agent, an entity that can carry out actions based on its internal goals. The part of the theory developed especially in this chapter is the inferential aspect. *Araucaria* is used to model a chain of reasoning in an explanation, in a way comparable to its use in the previous chapters as a method of argument diagramming.

Recent work in AI has given a strong push toward such a dialogue-based approach to explanation. Cawsey's study (1992) of the computer generation of explanatory dialogue used an interactive or dialogue approach. The new theory also received much support from the dialogue-based analysis of explanation for advice-giving in expert systems presented by Moore (1995). In her view (p. 1) explanation is "an inherently incremental and interactive process" that requires a dialogue between an explanation presenter who is trying to explain something and a questioner who has asked for an explanation. At the same time, developments in multi-agent computing (Wooldridge, 2000) have given rise to structured conversational processes in which rational agents communicate by asking questions and putting forward arguments in an internet environment, raising questions about argument and explanation as different kinds of speech acts that are important parts of such structured processes. A parallel development in argumentation theory is that two participants called a proponent and a respondent can conduct rational argumentation with each other in an orderly way by means of what is often called conversation or dialogue (Grice, 1975; Hamblin, 1970, 1971; Hintikka, 1995; Walton and Krabbe, 1995). These developments provide the resources for a new dialectical approach to explanation.

1. Systems for Explanation in Computing

Recently there have been several important developments in computer science that counter the logical empiricist's argument that no agent-based model of explanation can be based on a clear or objective underlying logical structure of reasoning. One such development is the technology of multi-agent systems in distributed computing. What is called an agent is typically a software entity (softbot), but it could also be a robot or a human agent. Generally, a rational agent is an entity that has goals, that takes actions to try to fulfill these goals, and that has the capability of receiving information about what is happening in its immediate environment (Wooldridge, 2000). But as well as these three basic characteristics, an agent also has the capability of *feedback*: once it sees consequences of its actions, it "corrects" its next actions by steering them more towards the goal it is aiming at. The four capabilities are the basic defining characteristics of an agent in multi-agent systems (Wooldridge and Jennings, 1995). Dialectical argumentation is increasingly being used in AI as a model of how an agent reasons in a dialogue structure of argumentation by examining arguments on both sides of an issue, as shown in the previous chapters. The dialectical approach to argumentation and explanation is seen as one that is of great interest for AI research on multi-agent systems. A main problem of multi-agent technology is to develop standard protocols for agent communication so that teams of agents can collaborate with each other on collective tasks (Singh, 1998). The form in which an agent asks or replies to a question in dialogue with another agent is a very important problem to be solved in order to make multi-agent systems that are useful. Thus a dialectical model of explanation could be very useful to help solve this problem. At the same time, the development of multi-agent systems itself helps to provide an orderly conversational structure that throws light on the dialectical structure of explanation.

Another development in computing, especially in AI, is a special kind of reasoning that is distinctive from deductive and inductive models of reasoning that have been so prominent in logic in the past. This kind of reasoning was known to Aristotle as *phronesis* or practical wisdom, and is sometimes called the Aristotelian practical syllogism. In the past, in philosophy, it has also often been called teleological or purposive reasoning. Means-end reasoning, as it is most called in AI, is goal-directed reasoning that culminates in an action, based on the information that an agent has about its situation (Huhns and Singh, 1998, p. 87). As shown in chapter 1, practical (means-end) reasoning can be defined as a process of chaining together inferences of the following form, where the agent is represented by the first-person pronoun 'I': I have a goal, *G*; as far as I can tell, the best means to carry out goal *G* is action *A*; therefore, I should carry out action *A*. The term 'should' in the conclusion expresses the so-called "prudential ought". This basic form of practical inference becomes more complex when applied to cases of practical reasoning. As indicated in chapter 1, other factors may need to be considered, raising critical questions that should be asked. For example, there may be more than one way to carry out goal *G*. One action may be less costly than another, for example. Another complication is that an agent may have multiple goals, or even conflicting goals. Another complication is that carrying out the proposed action may require carrying out other actions that are necessary to carry out the first action. In a complex case, there may be a lengthy chain of actions required, instead of a single action.

Another branch of AI and computing that is relevant to the kind of agent-based practical reasoning used in explanation of actions is that of planning. Planning utilizes practical reasoning based on an agent's goals, and systematizes methods for carrying out sequences of actions that will supposedly lead to the fulfillment of the goal by actions that the agent is capable of in a given situation (Schank and Abelson, 1977). As noted in chapter one, planning also frequently involves coordinating the actions of one agent with the actual or predicted actions of another agent. A plan is an attempt to extrapolate a line of practical reasoning into the future, based on what is known of the past, and what can be expected to plausibly happen in the future (Wilensky, 1983). Plan recognition (Carberry, 1990) is the ability of one agent to recognize the planning of another agent.

It is an interesting project, in light of the considerations shown above, to take further steps towards the development of a pragmatic and dialectical account of the concept of an explanation. The aim of such a project should be to study how explanations are used in everyday conversational exchanges, but including explanations of a technical or scientific sort. The term 'dialectical', as used in the sense outlined above, indicates that the focus is on a relationship between two parties where one explains something to the other. More explicitly, this means that explanation is viewed as a type of verbal exchange between two participants in some conventionalized type of conversation. Or to put the matter in another way, alluding to Collingwood's theory of explanation in history (1946), explanation is viewed as a process of question and answer. To put the matter in still another way, the project is to analyze explanation using the same dialectical framework that has been used to analyze argumentation in studies like (Hamblin, 1970) and (Walton, 1998). In the new dialectic (Walton, 1998), arguments are evaluated differently in different contexts of dialogue. The project is to explore whether explanations can also be evaluated contextually as used in a dialogue.

Within informal logic and argumentation theory, there has been very little work exploring the role of explanation in argumentation. But there has been some very interesting and provocative work in the field of artificial intelligence that suggests how explanation could be treated in a dialectical framework. This work is quite exciting and promising in many ways, suggesting that a revolution in the way philosophers view explanation is coming. Many interesting cases of ordinary explanations have been studied in (Schank, 1986). Schank has identified and classified many different kinds of explanations. His analysis of explanation could be seen as dialectical in nature, broadly speaking. Or at any rate they suggest the value of adopting a pragmatic and dialectical approach to explanation. Schank's work has shown how the cases he studied can only be properly understood as explanations that work, or are successful, when they are being used in relation to a background story or so-called script. Three other books in the field of artificial intelligence (Cawsey, 1992), Josephson and Josephson (1994), and Moore (1995) have also exhibited what appears to be a dialectical viewpoint on explanation.

Cawsey (1992) and Moore both used as their data bases actual cases of dialogues consisting of verbal explanations and other speech acts in which one person tries to explain to another person how something, for example an electronic circuit, works. The speaker cannot give a satisfactory explanation to the hearer in one move. So the hearer has to ask further questions. Such explanatory dialogues are common in recent computer systems, for example in expert systems (Moore (1991, 1995). The work of Cawsey and Moore has many significant implications for argumentation theory. It suggests a more deeply pragmatic way of looking at explanation from the approach that has been characteristic in recent philosophy. It suggests the usefulness of a move from the older logical empiricist approach towards a new pragmatic and dialectical approach.

The recent work on abductive inference in AI (Peng and Reggia, 1990; Josephson and Josephson, 1994) also suggests the importance of taking a new dialectical look at the concept of explanation. Inference to the best explanation is centrally important not only to artificial intelligence, but to logic, law and argumentation theory. The very notion of abduction as inference to the best explanation ties the concepts of argument and explanation so tightly together as to show that we can't understand the one without the other. This observation by itself is enough to show the vital importance of explanation for the analysis of evidence in logic and argumentation. The Josephsons' analysis (1994, p. 28) has shown that the Peircian trichotomy of deductive, inductive and abductive inference may be not the best taxonomy of inference types, and that the implications of the need for a better taxonomy have wide-reaching implications for redefining how inference is related to causality and to explanation. Their remarks on the nature of explanation at the end of their first chapter (p. 29) resonate with philosophical implications. They connect explanation essentially with question-asking and answering, especially in relation to why-questions. They evoke the Collingwoodian notion that all questions have presuppositions (p. 29): "An explanation-seeking why-question rests on a Given, a presupposition upon which the question is based." But what do they mean by 'Given' (as capitalized by them)? As they put the point (p. 29), "This Given is not absolutely firm, even though it is accepted at the outset, for in the end we may be happy to throw it away." The Given represents the famous notion of presupposition (or presumption) in the literature on questioning. At the same time, it represents the notion of "the data" or "set of observations" that is so fundamental as a basis for abductive inference. The KNIGHT system of explanation generation developed by Lester and Porter (1997) bases an explanation on a given question posed as requesting a reply from a given knowledge base (in biology). In general, it should be noted that the importance of the notions of questioning and answering for the analysis of the concept of explanation reveals its underlying dialectical nature.

These logical connections between explanations and question-answering may seem highly abstract and philosophical to some readers. They can easily be put in a practical perspective by examining the most common kinds of cases of explanation dialogues. Suppose a questioner has some water appearing on the floor in part of her basement. She asks an expert, a contractor with many years of experience in the building trade, about the problem. What is wrong? Why is the water there?

Where did it come from? How can it be permanently removed, so the problem will not recur? He responds to these questions initially by asking her a number of specific questions that ask for more detailed information about the situation. What kind of basement is in the house? Are there windows in the basement? Where are the windows? Where is the water in relation to basement windows? What type of floor and walls are in the basement? What kind of ventilation is there in the basement? As she answers these questions, he may ask more questions, and an extended dialogue is produced. When he is satisfied with the answers to these questions, he then offers a tentative diagnosis of the problem, based on what she has told him. He then tells her what steps she needs to take to deal with the problem. The dialogue is asymmetrical in an important sense. He is an expert, and has access to certain facts and information. His goal is to try to explain certain relevant aspects of the situation she has described to him, in non-specialized language that she can understand. When he uses any technical terms that are used in the building trade but are not used in common speech, he takes some effort to explain what they mean very clearly in everyday language.

In the recent AI systems for explanation generation, the logical structure underlying the process of generating an explanation involves a knowledge base and inferences drawn from that knowledge base. The inference engine is based on rules as applied to the so-called facts, or on some other inferential method, like one that uses frames instead of rules. For example, the KNIGHT system (Lester and Porter, 1997) constructs explanations from a biology knowledge base in biological anatomy, physiology and development. To use the system, a question is put in, like "What happens during embryo sac formation?" The system then provides an explanation that answers the question. For example, it might reply, "Embryo sac formation is a kind of female gametophyte formation. During embryo sac formation, the embryo sac is formed from the megaspore mother cell. Embryo sac formation occurs in the ovule." Lester and Porter (1997) developed a method of empirically evaluating explanations produced by the KNIGHT system. The KNIGHT system for generating explanations does not fit the covering law model of explanation. To explain embryo sac formation, it uses different relationships in the biology knowledge base to draw inferences. For example, in the knowledge base, embryo sac formation is classified as a species of female gametophyte formation. The former is related to the latter by a species relation. Embryo sac formation is also related to the megaspore mother cell by a "formed-from" relation (Lester and Porter, 1997, p. 70). Knowledge-based systems of explanation of the kind used in AI resemble DN explanations in that both types of explanation are based on inferences formed into a chain of reasoning. But in the AI systems, the chain of reasoning does not have to derive from laws. In these systems, a question is asked that queries a proposition, and the system answers the question by supplying a chain of reasoning that traces the proposition back to premises it can be derived from in the system's knowledge base. This type of explanation is called a trace explanation

Moulin et al. (2002, pp. 174-176) showed how, in addition to trace explanations, there are two other kinds of explanations used in knowledge-based systems. These are called strategic explanations and deep explanations. Let's begin with trace explanations. In first-generation expert systems, the system produced an explanation in response to a user's how or why questions by producing a so-called execution trace. An execution trace is a sequence of inferences leading from statements in the knowledge base to the statement queried (Scott et al., 1977). As Moulin et al. (2002, p. 174) noted, trace explanations are not all that helpful for users who have limited information about the system's knowledge. However, such a user is often one who is in most need of an explanation. Two other kinds of explanations can be more helpful. Strategic explanations place an action in context by revealing the problem-solving strategy of the system used to perform a task (Chandrasekaran, 1986). This type of explanation is close to the notion of historical explanation as re-enactment of a rational action offered by Collingwood (1946) and developed by Dray (1964). The question asked is about an action, and the explanation cites the goals of the agent, along with an account of how goals are related to actions in a sequence of means and ends. The third type of explanation, deep explanation, is distinctively different from the other two types, and more complex. It is based not only on the knowledge base of the system, but also that of the user. It requires two separate knowledge bases, and not only that, it requires a transfer from the one set to the other. To provide a deep explanation, the system must not only provide knowledge from its knowledge base, but in such a way that it fills in the gaps in the user's knowledge base. Such a deep explanation is called reconstructive by Wick and Thompson (1992), meaning that the system has to reconstruct what the user knows, its point of view, so to speak, in order to fill in the gaps. Presumably, the filling in of these gaps is what is needed for a successful deep explanation of a kind that will help the user make sense of what was queried. Deep explanations go even further beyond the DN model than trace or strategic explanations because the system must try to simulate the point of view of the user. This ability appears to require a capability for empathy of a sort, in which the system must try to figure out what the user is lacking, or fails to understand. This ability, much more explicitly than with trace explanations or strategic explanations, suggests a dialogue framework in which two parties, each with a separate knowledge base or commitment set, must interact verbally with the other.

2. Philosophical Views of Explanation

A twentieth century theory of explanation that was very popular during and after the advent of analytical philosophy is the covering law model of explanation. The covering law model has two variants, one deductive and one inductive. The deductive variant was called the deductive-nomological model (DN model) by its leading exponent Carl G. Hempel (1905-1997). During this period a view called logical empiricism, or logical positivism, was widely advocated, and is still very influential in philosophical thinking about the concept of explanation. Logical empiricism confines the limits of what is meaningful to statements that are empirically verifiable, or that can be proved by logical reasoning from empirical statements. The term 'logical reasoning' was taken in the logical empiricist view to refer to deductive or inductive reasoning. Deductive reasoning refers to the kind of reasoning used in propositional logic and in syllogistic logic (or its modern counterpart, quantifier logic). The term 'inductive reasoning' is not so easy to quickly define, but it is generally taken to refer to the kind of reasoning used in probability and statistics (and particularly in the probability calculus). The schema that was used by Hempel (1965, p. 174) to define an explanation is based on three variables. E is a sentence representing the thing to be explained (explanandum). $L_1, L_2, \ldots, L_r$ are general laws (like those of Newtonian mechanics). $C_1, C_2, \ldots, C_k$ are statements of particular occurrences. An explanation, according to Hempel, may then be schematized as a deductive inference of the following form.

$C_1, C_2, \ldots, C_k$

$L_1, L_2, \ldots, L_r$

E

An example (Achinstein, 1983, p. 8) is the following sequence of three statements.

This metal was heated.

All metals expand when heated.

This metal expanded.

The first two statements can provide an explanation of why the metal expanded, in the given circumstances. The explanation is that the metal was heated, and all metals expand when heated. The latter statement is a general law in Hempel's sense. In this example, the inference from the first two statements to the third is deductively valid. Thus a DN explanation can be treated as a species of argument. Indeed, it is a familiar type of argument, essentially because of the meaning of the term 'all', as interpreted by Hempel (and generally in deductive logic). 'All' is taken, in deductive logic, to admit of no exceptions. A general law based on this exceptionless use of the word 'all' could be called an absolute generalization. The term 'all' in the example above is presumably meant in this absolute sense, represented by the universal quantifier in logic. Hence if the premises are true, in the example argument, then the conclusion must necessarily be true. According to the DN model then, an explanation is a kind of argument. It is a deductively valid kind of argument, based on general laws and particular circumstances.

As noted above, the covering law theory has a variant that admits of explanations based on inductive arguments, called inductive-statistical (I-S) explanations. I-S explanations are inferred inductively from premises that are probabilistic laws as well as other premises that describe particular circumstances. An I-S explanation has the same form as the DN model (as displayed above), except that the set of general laws can contain some inductive generalizations as well as some absolute generalizations. Hempel (1965, p. 301) gave the example of a child who was found to have mumps. This finding could be explained by pointing out that he had recently been playing with a friend who had the mumps. According to Hempel (p. 301), the antecedent factors in this case are Henry's exposure and the fact that he did not have mumps before. But then how do these antecedent factors connect up with general laws to explain Henry's getting the mumps? Hempel wrote, "we cannot adduce a general law to the effect that under the conditions just mentioned, the exposed person invariably contracts the mumps". Thus Hempel suggested that what can be asserted (p. 301) "is that the disease will be transmitted with a high statistical probability." In such a case then, according to the logical empiricist view, a law used in an explanation can have an inductive or statistical form. It is ironic that Hempel should have used this particular example to illustrate the I-S model. Years later medical diagnosis arguments like the one cited by Hempel would be analyzed as abductive inferences in AI models of diagnostic problem-solving (Peng and Reggia, 1990). In these AI models, the antecedent factors and circumstances of a case are all assembled in what is called a knowledge base, a database comprising the relevant facts and some rules of inference. By drawing inferences from these facts, competing explanations are given, in response to a query, and then the best explanation can be selected out from the alternatives. A rule could be a statement like, 'If someone is exposed to the mumps, and she has not had the mumps before, then she could get the mumps.' Such a rule sets up an inference that could be part of an explanation of why or how Henry got the mumps.

The structures on which the three kinds of explanations in knowledge-based systems cited above are based on do not appear to conform to the DN model. It seems that the system's ways of getting the explanation from the knowledge base, selecting a successful explanation, transmitting it to the user, and responding to the user's difficulties, has many essential aspects not captured by the DN model at all. The DN model has not been very useful in providing an analysis of the logical structure of how the process of explanation works in AI explanation generation systems like the KNIGHT system.[1] There have been many criticisms of the logical empiricist view of explanation over the years. The most prominent perhaps have centered on historical explanations of particular events and actions. The notion

[1] According to the present state of conventional opinion in philosophy, there is "widespread abandonment" of the covering law theory, and "currently no consensus on how to understand explanation."(Kitcher, 1998, p. 1). Analytical philosophers tend to try to explain explanation by using an inferential model, seeing an explanation in logical terms as an inference from one set of statements to another (Achinstein, 1993). They tend to see the project of explaining explanation by using a pragmatic model as impossible even before trying it. According to the survey account of explanation given in the *Routledge Encyclopedia of Philosophy* (Kitcher, p. 1), offering a pragmatic theory amounts to believing "that there is no general account of explanation." This remark is revealing. It indicates that there has long been an entrenched resistance in current philosophy to any movement taking us beyond an inferential model of explanation towards a pragmatic model.

that general laws in history are a required part of historical explanations seems highly implausible. Many of the most common kinds of historical explanations use an agent's presumed goals or intentions to explain the agent's actions, without (apparently) being based on general laws of the sort cited in the DN model or its inductive companion, the I-S model (Dray, 1964). These observations have led to a climate of opinion in philosophy that restricts the applicability of these models to explanations in the natural sciences – particularly in physics and chemistry – and allows for some other kind of model of explanation in history and the social sciences.

Aside from its problems about applying to historical explanations, the DN model has been very popular in philosophy for a long time, despite several telling criticisms that have been advanced. The most serious and fundamental criticism was that of Scriven (1962), who argued that quite satisfactory explanations can be given of events in everyday situations without appealing to covering laws. For example, if someone explains why he spilled a bottle of ink, the explanation can be quite successful even if it makes no reference at all to laws of physics about falling objects. What was vital about Scriven's criticism was that it showed the need for a pragmatics of explanation to deal with particular cases. Kitcher (1998) expressed this point very well.

At the heart of Scriven's complaint lay the recognition that the covering-law model had failed to show how the idealized derivations that supposedly highlight how the explanatory work is done are adapted, in specific local situations, to transmit understanding from one person to another. Without a *pragmatics* of explanation, an account of how the ideal arguments that fit particular logical forms relate to what people actually do in giving explanations, it was possible to challenge the claim that the structure exposed by the logical empiricists reveals the crucial features that make the explanation successful.

Scriven's criticism was fundamental, because it showed how the DN model does not even attempt to address the central issue for any theory of explanation. A theory of explanation, as noted in Kitcher's remark, needs to show how understanding is transmitted from one person to another in a particular case. The DN model does not even really attempt to deal with this issue. It simply bypasses it, apparently assuming that such pragmatic matters are of no significance. The logical empiricists would have simply assumed that such matters are "subjective" and that no objective knowledge about them is possible. This claim simply is not plausible when applied to everyday explanations of the kind cited by Scriven. It might seem to be more plausible if applied exclusively to scientific explanations within a domain of scientific knowledge, where both explainer and explainee are presumed to have prior expertise. Perhaps because of these developments in AI, the current view in philosophy is that the DN model is no longer the received view, and philosophers of science are coming around to the view that explanation needs to be understood in "the general context of interpersonal communication" (Faye, 1999, 61).

Advances in explanation generation systems in AI have now shown that clarity in how an explanation is expressed, and the terms used in the explanation, are essential properties of an explanation, in addition to scientific accuracy. The

KNIGHT system is based on a biology knowledge base that includes taxonomy in the form of a large hierarchical structure of biological objects (Lester and Porter, 1997, p. 69). As noted above, the KNIGHT system is based on biological classifications of species, and on knowledge links about the origins and locations about biological entities. Each such link can be used to set up a chain of inferences, in the planning component of the KNIGHT system. The chaining of links is set into a discourse format that responds to the question asked in the explanation query. The explanations generated from this knowledge base are designed to be not only scientifically accurate, but to be expressed in a text of discourse that answers a user's question with an explanation that is understood by the user (p. 71). Among the criteria used to judge the explanations several, like coherence, organization and writing style, had a pragmatic dimension, even though the explanations were meant to be useful mainly to a questioner with some scientific knowledge of biology.

AI systems for problem solving, for example in medical diagnostic systems, typically use search strategies that combine inferences into chains of reasoning. These chains of reasoning can search into a knowledge base to find premises on which to base a conclusion (Russell and Norvig, 1995, pp. 55-85). They can also seek out an explanation in answer to a query. The kind of reasoning used in such knowledge-based systems has pragmatic elements that outrange the kind of single-inference, covering law warranted structures in the DN model. The chain of reasoning has some goal or end point towards which it is aimed. For example, in the case of an explanation, the sequence of reasoning is aimed towards responding to the question asked by the explainee. Also, the laws or generalizations that warrant each of the inferences admit of exceptions in a way that is impossible to predict in advance, in a given case. The explanations given are often tentative in nature. They may be good explanations, even if incomplete, because they state a hypothesis that clarifies something that was problematic or unclear, providing a basis for experimental testing and further questioning. Explanations of this sort do not appear to be deductive proofs.

Josephson and Josephson (1994, p. 17) point out that you can always turn an explanation into a deductive proof by including enough additional propositions in the premises. As they show, however, this capability does not show that explanations have to be deductive proofs. To illustrate the point, they cite an ordinary explanation: he has burns on his hands because he sneezed while cooking pasta and upset the pot (p. 17). The Josephsons (p. 17) contend that it is simply wrong to argue that sneezing and upsetting the pot were logically sufficient for the occurrence of the burns. These observations lead to various modified versions of the DN or I-S models that could be advocated. But these developments have led to further criticisms and problems. Coffa (1974) showed that I-S explanations require an essential reference to the state of knowledge. These and other criticisms of the I-S model (Salmon, 1970) showed that seeing explanation as a form of inductive argument does not work, because it ignores pragmatic facts like relevance that are essential to how explanations actually work in particular cases. Another main criticism of the DN model and the I-S model is that it is not easy to define the concept of a law. Certainly a law is some kind of generalization. The terms 'general law' or 'covering law' indicate that some notion of generality is essential to the concept of a law, as the term was used by Hempel and others who defended his view of explanation. Whether the positivistic view of explanation is right or wrong, the concept of a generalization is quite important for any theory of explanation.

Despite all these plausible criticisms, the covering law model has retained a certain degree of plausibility as an account of explanation, especially for scientific explanations. Why should this be so? The reason is that science, and each field of natural science like physics or chemistry, looks for generalizations or laws under which particular events can be subsumed, and thereby explained. These generalizations, once accepted as part of a scientific theory in a discipline, have special status as commitments in that discipline. They represent what can be called "understanding" in that discipline. Take the example above about metal expanding when heated. The scientific theory of molecular motion can be used to both prove and explain why metal expands when heated. The generalization that metal expands when heated is no longer an accidental fact, as shown by this theory, but is a general law. Once the theory was accepted, then any particular instance can be brought under a generalization that fits the theory. Such a generalization will successfully explain the theory for any respondent who accepts the theory, and especially for those in branches of science, like physics and chemistry, who are committed to that theory. To express the point pragmatically, a case of a DN explanation like the one about heating metal above works because a generalization is used that can be backed up by an accepted scientific theory. The pragmatic lesson is that acceptance, including acceptance of theoretical models in a scientific field, is a key component of what makes an explanation acceptable. Another lesson is that generalization is a key aspect of what makes for an explanation, and generalization can be an important aspect of what is taken to be understandable in a science. So the covering law model has grasped one important aspect of what an explanation is, even though it has interpreted it in an absolutistic way that is too limited to do justice to explaining how explanations really work. There is much more to be learned about the notion of an explanation, whether it is supposed to be a scientific explanation (of the kind typical in the natural sciences) or not.

3. A Review of the Logic of Generalizations

In logic textbooks, it is often assumed that a general statement is a kind of statement preceded by a universal quantifier. In other words, a general statement is a universal generalization, one about all members of a class. For example, as Hurley (2000, p. 38) defined the notion in his leading logic textbook, "A general statement makes a claim about all the members of a class." This view of the matter makes deductive logic the only kind of reasoning that is necessary for dealing with arguments based on general statements. But logic textbooks also allow for inductive generalizations. Hurley (2000, p. 682), for example, allows for inductive generalizations as well as universal generalizations. This view that there are only two kinds of generalizations that are significant for logical reasoning is a kind of positivistic view that has pervaded the teaching of logic for a long time, and still does. It seems to support and tie in with the positivistic view of explanation. But recently in computing studies, a third sort of generalization, and the reasoning based on it, has come to be highly prominent. It was called the defeasible generalization in chapter 2. According to the analysis given in chapter 2, this third type of generalization is classified as presumptive in nature, as contrasted with deductive and inductive types of argument. As shown in chapter 2, there are three kinds of generalizations: (1) the universal (absolute) generalization, (2) the inductive (statistical type) generalization, and (3) the presumptive (defeasible) generalization.

To review the differences among these three kinds of generalizations, and show lowing variant to the classical case can be used. Take one premise to be an ihow they work in explanations as well as arguments, let's use the classic example, used over and over again in writings on AI, the Tweety example from chapter 2, called the "canonical example" (Reiter, 1987, p. 149). To explain how the example can be applied to deductive reasoning, let's begin with the universal generalization, 'All birds fly'. As a universal generalization, of the kind cited in logic above, using this general statement is falsified by a single counter-example. By citing even one case of a bird that does not fly, it can be proved that the universal generalization 'All birds fly' is false. Such a universal generalization is symbolized in logic as follows. Let the variable F stand for the property of being a bird, and the variable G stand for the property of being a flier. Using this symbolization, the universal generalization 'All birds fly' is conventionally analyzed in deductive logic as having the form $(\forall x)(Fx \supset Gx)$. This form of universal generalization can function as a premise to show that the following argument is deductively valid: All birds fly; Tweety is a bird; therefore Tweety flies. This argument is deductively valid, meaning that it is logically impossible for the premises to be true and the conclusion false. It is valid because of its form. The reason is essentially that the premise 'All birds fly' is translated using the universal quantifier.

To illustrate how inductive generalizations can be used in arguments, the folnductive generalization, like 'Most birds fly', or '90 per cent of birds fly'. Take as another premise the statement that Tweety is a bird. These two premises, taken together, can be part of an inductive argument that supports the conclusion that Tweety flies. Such an argument is not deductively valid. But it represents a kind of inference that is inductively strong. If the premises are true, they can function as part of an argument that makes the conclusion probable to some degree.

The defeasible kind of argument based on the third kind of generalization is very familiar in a lot of recent work in computer science (Reiter, 1987). Consider once again the kind of generalization used in the classical case, but let it be expressed by the statement 'Birds fly'. Put in this form, the statement is not about all birds, or even some numerically expressed proportion of birds. What this statement asserts as a generalization is that birds generally fly, even though not all do, in every instance. To put it in the form of a conditional, what it asserts is that if something is a bird, it can normally be expected to fly in a typical case. In other words, if all we know is that Tweety is a bird in a given case, then there is a presumption that Tweety flies that is put into place. But if more information comes into the case, it may turn out that this presumption will be retracted or cancelled. For example, it might turn out that Tweety is an ostrich or a penguin, or a bird with a broken wing. Once this knowledge becomes part of the argument, the argument to the conclusion that Tweey flies will be refuted. What is shown is that the presumptive type of generalization is defeasible in nature, meaning that if new information comes in, the argument can "default". In other words, the presumptive type of generalization is contrasted with the absolute generalization. The absolute generalization is not subject to exceptions. It holds for all cases, with no exceptions. The presumptive generalization, on the other hand, could still hold, even if a counter-example is found.

The defeasible interpretation of the classic example is represented by the following argument: 'Birds fly; Tweety is a bird; therefore Tweety flies'. This argument could be quite reasonable in a given case to suggest provisionally accepting the conclusion that Tweety flies. If there is no definite information in the case to the effect that Tweety is an ostrich or a penguin or has a broken wing, for example, then accepting the hypothesis that Tweety may be presumed to fly could be quite reasonable. Of course, it has to be recognized that such a conclusion should not be accepted in a dogmatic or closed way. The inference should be seen as defeasible.

At present it is controversial whether the defeasible type of inference illustrated by the Tweety argument is based on a special kind of inductive reasoning like "subjective probability", or whether it represents a different kind of reasoning called plausible reasoning. Plausible reasoning, according to a leading theory (Rescher, 1976), is said to be based on what one can expect or presume to be true in a normal type of case. But according to Rescher and to leading exponents of abductive inference like Josephson and Josephson (1994) normality of a case is not a statistical or inductive notion, based on numerical or Bayesian calculations of the kind used in the probability calculus. If it is not, as some contend, then the presumptive argument is a third type of argument, not reducible to deductive or inductive argument. If so, the defeasible generalization is a distinctive and independent type of generalization in its own right. And if this is so, it is extremely important for rethinking the concept of explanation, and the kind of logical inference it is based on. What is suggested is that recent philosophical views of explanation, because they tend to be based so heavily on deductive and inductive models of inference, have tended to overlook the involvement of generalizations (often also called "laws" or "rules" or "general statements") that are defeasible. The Josephsons (1994, p. 30) hypothesized that the reason why traditional mathematical logic has been so " remarkably unsuccessful in accounting for reasoning outside mathematics" is that "the universal quantifier of logic is not the universal quantifier of ordinary life, or even ordinary scientific thought". Sidgwick (1893, p.23) made the same point a century earlier when he remarked that it is "comparatively seldom in actual argument" that we rest our case on a "faultless generalization" that fails if it has even a single exception. As contrasted with the universal generalization of logic, Sidgwick wrote (pp. 22-23), "our ordinary loose generalizations have many exceptions, and in the absence of knowing the contrary any given case may be an exception and not come under the rule." But Sidgwick was out of the mainstream, and the impact of recent work on abductive inference in AI has still not been absorbed into, or in many cases even been recognized by mainstream logic. Thus the inferential basis of explanation has long been taken to rest exclusively on deductive and inductive models, leaving no room for consideration of the pragmatic aspects that are evident in realistic cases of explanations.

4. Logical and Pragmatic Aspects of an Explanation

An assumption on which the dialectical model of explanation rests is that a distinction can be made between argument and reasoning, along the lines proposed in (Walton, 1990). According to this analysis, reasoning is chaining together of inferences, and argument is the use of such a chain for some purpose in a context of conversation. Explanations (like arguments) contain reasoning. The reasoning can be of many different kinds. It can be practical reasoning, or deductive reasoning, as indicated by the DN model, or inductive reasoning, as indicated by the I-S model. Many explanations are based on causal reasoning. Causal reasoning tends to be practical in nature, and context-sensitive, rather than being straightforwardly deductive or inductive. However the study of the inferential structure of causal reasoning is such a huge subject, on which there is so little agreement, that it has to be excluded from the scope of this investigation. It will have to suffice to examine only some short examples of explanations. Many explanations, including legal, historical, and everyday conversational ones, require essential reference to human actions and goals. Some comments on this type of explanation are made below (section 6). Other cases of everyday explanations seem to be about events, or how mechanical systems work, but indirectly involve reference to human actions or goals. A good place to start is to examine an example of this sort. It will be shown how this kind of case utilizes reasoning based on (often implicit) premises that take the form of defeasible generalizations. Such generalizations make essential reference to the ways things are usually done, as practices, or can normally be expected to, in a situation familiar to both the questioner and the explainer.

A relatively simple example from everyday conversational speech can be used to illustrate how the new dialectical theory of explanation works.

The Radiator Dialogue (Walton, 2004a, 189)

Questioner: Why are radiators usually located under windows, when windows are the greatest source of heat loss?

Respondent: The windows are the coldest part of the room and that is why the radiators are placed underneath the windows. The air that comes in contact with the windows is cooled and falls to the floor. This creates a movement of air in which the cold air from the window is heated when it passes the radiator. But if the radiator were placed at an inside wall, then the warmest part, towards the inside, would stay warmer and the coldest part of the room, where the windows are, would stay colder. This placement would not be a comfortable arrangement for habitation of the room. Therefore, the radiators are normally placed beneath the windows in a room.

The question poses a problem or puzzle. It is a why-question that contains a presupposition (presumption, given) that the windows are the greatest source of heat loss in a room. It is a generalization but not an absolute one. It is a kind of defeasible generalization that asserts that normally in a room, the windows are the greatest source of heat loss. It is this presumption that sets up the puzzle that prompts the question. For if the windows are the greatest source of heat loss, then putting the radiators under the windows in a room would seem to be uneconomical. Since building practices generally avoid doing things that are uneconomical, an explanation for the current practice of putting the radiators under the windows seems appropriate. The next aspect to note is that the respondent in his explanation uses a sequence of hypothetical reasoning. He asks what the consequences of putting the radiator on the inside wall (away from the windows) in a room would be? He then uses a chain of reasoning to show that these consequences would be that the room would not be comfortable for the people in it. He then builds up a second sequence of reasoning, showing how placement of the radiator under the window in a room generally leads to a convection current that mixes the warm and cold air, making the room comfortable for the people in it. Another defeasible generalization is that, other things being equal, people prefer a room that is comfortable. In building practices, comfort in a room is an important goal that can be balanced off against cost. Hence by linking goals, actions and generalizations in a sequence of practical reasoning, the explanation can be judged to be successful in answering Alice's question. Radiators are normally located under windows in a room. But the windows are the greatest source of heat loss. The question paints a picture of the hot radiator under the window wasting a lot of heat, if the windows are the greatest source of heat loss. But this doesn't make sense. Heat loss is wasteful. Conservation of energy is an important and often-stressed goal in designing human habitation. Unnecessary heat loss is a bad thing, and so why the normal placement of radiators would lead to such apparently unnecessary heat loss is puzzling. The answer solves the puzzle. But how does it do that?

The answer offers an explanation by a counterfactual strategy of postulating two suppositions and then constructing a chain of reasoning that flows from each supposition along with other premises taken to be true. *Araucaria* can be used to represent this chain of reasoning. The argument diagrams produced in previous chapters represented chains of reasoning in arguments. The normal use *of Araucaria* is to represent arguments. The novelty here is that *Araucaria* is used to represent the chain of reasoning in an explanation, in this instance the chain of reasoning in the radiators case.

The answer given by the respondent in the radiators dialogue contrasts two hypothetical situations. One is the hypothetical situation in which the radiators were to be placed on an inside wall. The other is the actual situation representing current normal practice in which the radiator is placed near the window. The figure below represents the hypothetical situation. All the explicit statements made by the respondent in the radiators dialogue above are labeled by letters. Each of these appears in a box, represented as a node in the diagram. The arrows from nodes to other nodes represent inferences in the chain of reasoning represented by the whole diagram. Some implicit premises have been added, and they appear in the shaded boxes. Statement B is the supposition that the radiator is placed on an inside wall. Statement A is an additional proposition asserted by the respondent as part of the explanation offered. The remaining two statements at the lowest level of the diagram are implicit assumptions.

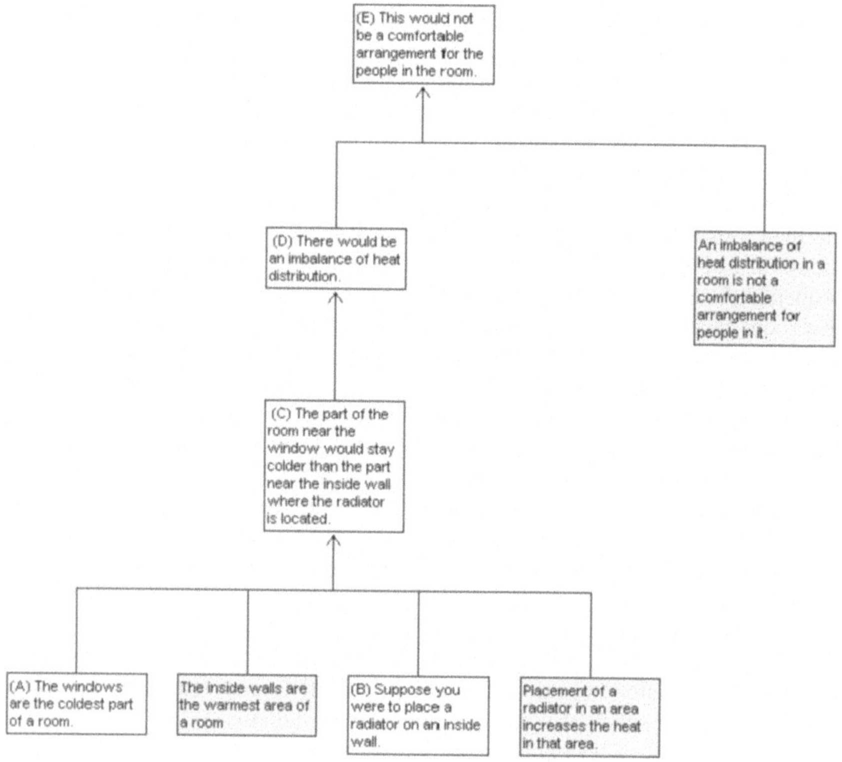

Fig. 6.1. Diagram 1 for Radiators Case

All four statements are then linked together as premises required to draw an inference to conclusion C. But C leads by another step of inference to outcome D, which, taken along with another implicit premise, leads to the final conclusion E. Thus what is shown is that the supposition B, taken together with other assumptions, sets up a chain of inferences that lead to E. This whole structure fills in gaps by connecting up a sequence of reasoning, revealing the structure of one part of the explanation in the dialogue.

Now we can contrast this part with another part of the explanation. The structure of this second part is shown in the figure below.

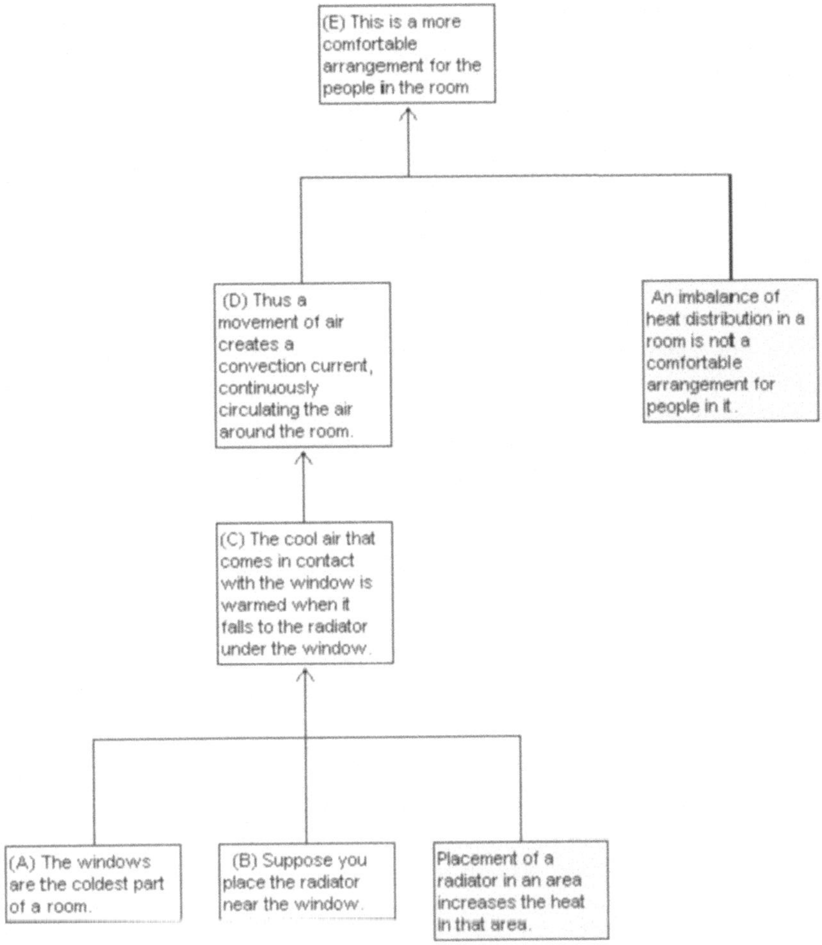

Fig. 6.2. Diagram 2 for Radiators Case

This diagram represents what flows from the supposition that the radiators are placed near the window, representing the normal situation. It explains by filling in gaps. Instead of the heat merely escaping through the window, as supposed in the question, the explanation shows how a convection current is set up by the movement of air. Thus the explanation could be classified as a contrastive one. It contrasts the whole sequence of reasoning surrounding one supposition with that surrounding a contrasting supposition. Then each is evaluated in line with the goal of comfort for the people in a room.

On the surface, this explanation looks like one that could be analyzed by a model, like the DN model, that makes no essential reference to human actions and goals. But this surface analysis starts to fail, once the explanation is analyzed in any depth. As shown above, analyzing how the explanation works involves essential references to human goals and actions, like making a room that is comfortable for habitation, or making a building that is economical. All of us are aware that designing a building with rooms that are uncomfortable, because one part of a room is warm while the other side is cold, would not be practical. People would not buy a house or other building constructed in this way, if given a choice between it and a house or building with comfortable rooms. What is shown then is that the explanation does have a structure. It is based on a sequence of reasoning. The sequence of reasoning also contains implicit premises that take the form of rough and defeasible generalizations about what people generally find acceptable or not, and about common practices.

Notice that the explanation involves matters of the physics of air movement. But Bob expresses the explanation in non-technical language that anyone with normal human experiences can understand. He presumes that Alice would understand quite well why people would not find a room with unequal heat distribution comfortable. Although laws of physics, in the form of laws of heat and particle motions could be given, they are not necessary. If deeper scientific explanations based on such laws were requested by the questioner, it would be appropriate to use them in the chain of reasoning. But the way the case stands, the explanation is more successful because it is expressed in language and in generalizations that the questioner would presumably understand. In other words, there are many implicit assumptions about what one could normally expect the questioner to understand.[2] This aspect is brought out by the use of unexpressed premises in the *Araucaria* reconstruction of the reasoning in the case. In this case, the inferential structure is a chain of reasoning, or more accurately two chains of hypothetical reasoning used as the basis of a contrastive explanation. The two chains show the consequences of radiator placement in one position or another in a room with windows. By contrast, one is shown to be more in line with human goals and practices than the other.

Note that even though there is a chain of reasoning used, the case is one of an explanation and not an argument. The questioner is not expressing doubt that radiators are normally placed under windows. Indeed, this assumption is a given in her question. She is puzzled why placing radiators under windows is the normal practice. His explanation has the goal of getting her to come to understand why it is the normal practice. The respondent is not trying to remove the questioner's doubt by using a chain of argumentation. It is better classified as a chain of reasoning used in an explanation. But what's the difference, anyway? Can one draw a clear distinction between explanation and argument? If not, the radiators dialogue is very puzzling.

---

[2] A text planning method has been devised by Horacek (1997) to adapt explanations to the knowledge of the respondent and also to take the respondent's inferential capabilities into account. For example, certain pieces of information can be left implicit in an explanation designed for the case in which the respondent is an expert, and can be expected to already know and accept some implicit premises of an inference that would have to be made explicit to a less expert respondent.

The fact that *Araucaria*, a method of argument diagramming, has been used to represent the structure of the two accounts presented in the two diagrams above poses a problem. We want to say that argument and explanation are different speech acts, yet clearly something like a chain of argumentation is represented in each diagram. What we need to say is that each diagram represents a chain of reasoning within an account offered as an answer to a question. One point is that we need to draw a distinction between reasoning and argument. Another is that two diagrams are used to contrast two different accounts each representing a chain of reasoning. Thus the explanation is a contrastive one. What is important is the contrastive feature of why-questions of a kind that call for an explanation of something. According to Faye (1999, p. 71) it is this contrastive feature that "endows answers to why-questions with their explanatory force". Thus while an explanation may often look a lot like an argument in that both contain a network of inferences of the kind pictured above, the two speech acts are different for essentially pragmatic reasons. They represent answers to different questions.

These considerations raise the general problem of how to draw the distinction between an argument and an explanation. The subtler problem related to this distinction is that, according to the new dialectical theory, an explanation is a speech that conveys understanding by making sense of some subject queried by filling in gaps in that subject. It does this by connecting a set of propositions together into a unity by connecting them up with logical inferences. The propositions are seen as nodes connected to each other by inferences seen as arrows (arcs) joining the nodes. The whole structure can be visualized as a graph-like diagram representing a chain of reasoning joining the nodes by steps of inference. But, a critic will then say, isn't this just an argument diagram, of the kind we are now familiar with in logic and argumentation study? Indeed, there are even software packages now available, like *Araucaria*, for assisting a user to draw an argument diagram. But this program is designed to visualize argumentation. Isn't it just confusing to imply that such a tool could be applied to represent reasoning used in an explanation? The answer is that an explanation can often be analyzed as based on a chain of reasoning, even though a distinction needs to be drawn between reasoning and argument. On the new dialectical theory, explanation and argument need to be seen as two separate speech acts, both containing reasoning. Of course, it is all very well to say this, but once again it is so general and controversial that it is hard to get general agreement on it.

What will be argued for here is also very controversial, namely that argument diagram systems like *Araucaria* can also be used to display the structure of reasoning used in an explanation to help a questioner understand something. This suggestion points to a new potential use of a tool that is already in use for helping to analyze arguments. But to prove that the tool applies successfully to many kinds of explanations, especially complex ones in science, is a major undertaking. The best that can be done here is to achieve the pioneering objective of showing that this route is possible, and shows some promise. Thus we will take a fairly simple example of an everyday conversational explanation that has already been discussed in the literature on abductive reasoning, and show how *Araucaria* can be applied to it in a way that shows the promise of the new dialectical theory of explanation.

5. Explanation and Argument

How can one determine, in a given case, whether something is an explanation or an argument? This task is not as easy to carry out as you might think. For there are cases where a given text of discourse could be interpreted as expressing either an argument or an explanation. And there are questions on the issue of whether argument and explanation are mutually exclusive. A leading textbook on AI even tells its readers (see below) that, in some cases, a proof, a species of argument, can be a good explanation. Nevertheless, the problem of distinguishing between explanations and arguments is one that must be faced by introductory logic textbooks. The reason is as follows. When you first teach students to use logic to evaluate arguments, they tend to see any bit of discourse they are confronted with as expressing an argument. This tendency is quite natural. However, there is a problem. Suppose the student evaluates a given text of discourse as containing a weak or fallacious argument. The student then criticizes the argument. But suppose that the passage in question is not really an argument at all, but an explanation. In such a case, the student has committed an error by misapplying logic. In order to anticipate and correct such a potential error, logic textbooks need to define what an argument is, and contrast it with the concept of an explanation. The definition of the concept of an explanation does not have to be too precise or theoretically rich. But it does have to be clear enough to enable the student to avoid the kind of error described above.

The currently most popular logic textbook, (Hurley, 2000), provides the following test to enable the reader to distinguish between an argument and an explanation. This test, found in many logic textbooks, could be called *the matter of fact test.*

> To distinguish explanations from arguments, identify the statement that is either the explanandum or the conclusion (usually this is the statement that precedes the word "because"). If this statement describes an accepted matter of fact, and if the remaining statements purport to shed light on this statement, then the passage is an explanation (Hurley, 2000, p. 21).

The reason the matter of fact test works in a useful way is that Hurley has already defined 'argument' and 'explanation' in a particular way. An argument (p. 1), "as it occurs in logic, is a group of statements, one or more of which (the premises) are claimed to provide support for, or reasons to believe, one of the others (the conclusion)." When it comes to recognizing arguments in a given passage or text of discourse, Hurley (p. 14) adds a specific requirement. A passage contains an argument only if it "purports to prove something". And then two requirements are added, as follows.

Two conditions must be fulfilled for a passage to purport to prove something:

(1) At least one of the statements must claim to provide evidence or reasons.
(2) There must be a claim that the alleged evidence or reasons supports or implies something – that is, a claim that something follows from the alleged evidence (Hurley, 2003, p. 13).

By way of contrast, an explanation (p. 20) is defined as "a group of statements that purports to shed light on some event or phenomenon." Given these definitions, the matter of fact test works fairly well, along with other criteria to help the student avoid the error of confusion between explanations and arguments that may use the same indicator-words like 'because' or 'thus'. Consider the following example (p. 20).

The Challenger spacecraft exploded after liftoff because an O-ring failed in one of the booster rockets.

The statement that the O-ring failed is not being used to prove the statement that the spacecraft exploded. That the spacecraft exploded is not in doubt. Most of us graphically remember seeing the exploding spacecraft on TV. The passage quoted above is not trying to prove that statement by providing evidence or reasons that support or imply it. The passage assumes that it is an accepted matter of fact that the spacecraft exploded, and is trying to show why it exploded. So the passage contains an explanation, as opposed to an argument. Of course, the matter of fact test is not the only kind of evidence needed to judge whether something is an argument or an explanation. And in the case of many passages, because of unclarity, or simply lack of information, the passage could be interpreted as either an explanation or an argument. But even so, the matter of fact test is useful to help prevent students from falling into the error of routinely or uncritically treating non-argumentative passages as if the passage expressed an argument.

What is most interesting about the textbook treatment cited above is that what is essentially a pragmatic test is being used to determine, in a given case, whether a passage expresses an argument or an explanation. It is a question of how the discourse is being used in the given case. If it is being used to fulfill a probative function – if it "purports to prove something" – then it is an argument. If it is being used to throw light on something that is not in doubt, and does not need to be proved, then it is an explanation. To make this pragmatic distinction, it is often useful, in addition to applying the matter of fact test , to know what kind of book or article the passage in question came from. Did it come from an editorial in a newspaper, from a college textbook, or from an encyclopedia? In many cases, this information is helpful, and can be used alongside the matter of fact test and the indicator words in the passage.

Where the matter of fact test runs into some trouble is in the area of so-called hypothetical arguments, where there is a chain of reasoning, but the premises are merely hypotheses or assumptions. In such a case, the conclusion is not really a claim, held to be proved by evidence or reasons that support it. The problem with such cases is that they challenge what is meant by the term 'argument', as used in logic. Does an argument need to have a conclusion that is a claim, purported to be proved by the premises, as held by Hurley's definition? Maybe not, if there are such things as hypothetical arguments. But perhaps the term 'argument', in the sense used in logic, should not really apply to such cases. Instead, perhaps they should be classified under the heading of hypothetical reasoning. Following the account of (Walton, 1990) there could be a distinction drawn between reasoning and argument. According to this way of drawing this distinction, reasoning is a chaining of inferences. Reasoning does not necessarily purport to prove the conclusion as a claim, whereas argument requires the existence of a probative function. The conclusion of an argument, by this way of drawing the distinction, is always a claim, with a burden of proof attached. If this sort of distinction between reasoning and argument can be upheld, the matter of fact test can be defended against the criticism that it wrongly excludes hypothetical arguments from being classified as arguments.

As noted at the beginning of this section, a leading AI textbook (Russell and Norvig, 1995, p. 326) tells its readers that a proof can, in some cases, be a good explanation: "A proof is one kind of explanation – if we ask, "Explain why you believe that (proposition) *P* is true," then a proof of *P* is a good explanation. If a proof is a species of argument, then what Russell and Norvig are claiming is that, in some cases, an argument can be an explanation. They go on to offer an example that seems to confirm that what they are claiming is that, in some cases, an argument, even a hypothetical argument, can be an explanation (p. 326).

> If a proof is not possible, then a good explanation is one that involves assumptions. For example, if we ask, "Explain why the car won't start," there may be not enough evidence to prove anything, but a good explanation is, "If we assume that there is gas in the car, and that it is reaching the cylinders, then the observed absence of activity proves that the electrical activity must be at fault."

It appears from their interpretation of this example that Russell and Norvig have adopted a view of explanation and argument in which a hypothetical argument, as well as a proof, can be a good explanation in some cases. On their interpretation, the conditional that is the last sentence in the quotation above is not only a hypothetical argument but is also a good explanation.

But if the distinction between reasoning and argument can be analyzed in the way maintained above, a quite different interpretation of the kind of case posed by Russell and Norvig can be given. The conditional above can be classified as a sequence of hypothetical reasoning. If it is a fact, or given data, that the car won't start in the case presented by Russell and Norvig, then no argument to prove this statement is needed. What is useful is an explanation. And the conditional cited above could function as such an explanation, provided the assumption that there is gas in the car is also a given. As things stand, the conditional cited by Russell and Norvig is only a chain of hypothetical reasoning. It need not be classified as an argument, and would not be useful as an argument, in the case cited.

6. The Pragmatics of Explanation

Now the general purpose of an explanation, as opposed to that of an argument, has been stated, and we have some notion of how the structure of reasoning in an explanation works. What is missing is a pragmatic structure of explanation. In the new dialectic (Walton, 1998) arguments are analyzed and evaluated pragmatically with respect to how the given argument was used for some purpose in a conversational interaction represented in a framework of conventionalized types of dialogue. In the new dialectical theory of explanation (Walton, 2004; Walton, 2004a), an explanation is something that fits the missing pieces in a jigsaw puzzle together, enabling the whole picture that is meant to be represented to be seen. On this theory, the purpose of an explanation is to produce understanding of something that is presently not understood. Understanding is something an agent has when it can put all the parts of something together into a unified whole. But understanding cannot be understood in holistic or absolute terms. To grasp it, you have to compare lack of understanding of something that presents a puzzle or problem, expressed in a question about that thing, and then understanding of it as conveyed by an answer to that question that solves the problem.

The positivist objection, right at the outset, is that understanding is a subjective notion, and that therefore no objective account of it is possible. Of course, the premise that understanding is subjective, in that it is relative to an agent, is true. But the inference to the conclusion that no objective account is possible is a fallacious one. What we mean by 'agent' is not an individual person with mental states like personal desires and beliefs, but a rational agent of the kind familiar in multi-agent systems in computing. Such an agent can be seen as containing a set of statements representing its commitments, and these commitments can be related to each other by logical reasoning. There can be various ways a set of commitments can be related to each other in a logical structure. They could be related by deductive or inductive reasoning, or by argumentation schemes, like practical reasoning. In practical reasoning, some statement represents an agent's goals while other statements represent means that could be used to carry out these goals. Still other statements represent information the agent has or learns about concerning particular circumstances of its present situation. For, example an agent's set of commitments could be inconsistent, meaning that one of them leads by a sequence of logical inferences to the negation of another.

The notion of understanding can be defined in the new dialectical approach in the same way that commitment was defined. When one agent communicates with another, it does not always just present one statement in answer to a question. Sometimes it presents a connected set of statements, as in the explanation offered by the respondent in the radiators dialogue. The other agent can understand such an account if it can join the nodes together by inferences that fit into a structure, like for example a structure of practical reasoning. The dialectical model is meant to be a logical theory of the structure of an explanation, not a psychological theory of the feeling of understanding something an individual has when she thinks she grasps something. A psychological feeling of understanding something can be illusory, because you can think you understand something even when you really don't, or at least don't properly understand it on the logical definition of 'understanding'.

In the new dialectical approach, a given argument is analyzed and evaluated with respect to how it uses a sequence of reasoning that contributes, or not, to the goal of the dialogue. Can such a dialectical framework of analysis and evaluation be applied to cases in which an explanation is part of a conversational exchange? The remarks above suggest how it could be. The Josephsons, as noted, view an explanation as essentially an answer to certain kinds of questions. The usefulness and promise of such a pragmatic view is not only indicated by recent work in AI. Support for it can be found in some analyses of explanation, like those of Bromberger (1966) and van Fraassen (1993), who see the study of explanation as a branch of the logic of question and answer (erotetic logic). As noted above, this approach is based on the Collingwoodian view of explanation. Collingwood, the Josephsons, and the others who have linked the concept of explanation to the asking and answering of questions, can be classified as taking steps towards, or even (in some cases) being early exponents of, the dialectical view of explanation. In recent times, it seems to be the field of computing in which dialectical views of explanation have been most fully endorsed and explored. As noted above, the analysis of explanation presented by Cawsey can be described as deeply dialectical.

The radiators case is one of explanation in an everyday conversational context. Once the explainee understands roughly how convection works to normally distribute heat and cold in a typical room, the explanation is successful. In other contexts, the problem of how to evaluate an explanation could be more complicated. The cases presented by Cawsey (1992) involve sequences of questions and answers in a lengthy conversation between two speakers. One is trying to explain to the other how some piece of computing machinery works. The other keeps replying by asking questions about the explanations given by the first speaker. Could the *Araucaria* model be applied to longer cases of sequential explanations of this sort, involving extended conversations? Without actually working up a case study of such a lengthy example, it can be indicated why the *Araucaria* model is applicable to such cases. The *Araucaria* model presented is not only pragmatic. It could also be classified as dialectical, in the sense of that word that has grown out of recent work on argumentation in informal logic. It is dialectical in that explanation is defined as a speech act within an orderly framework of communication in which two parties take turns asking each other questions, presenting arguments to each other, and presenting explanations to each other. The term 'dialectical', as used here, means conversational. According to (Grice, 1975), a conversation can be viewed as an orderly goal-directed sequence of verbal exchanges with various rules indicating how one party should respond to the various moves made by the other, what sorts of moves are regarded as permissible and relevant, and other matters of the same sort. Hamblin (1970) constructed formal dialectical models in which such moves, permissible rules, and other matters are precisely defined by both participants before any exchanges in the dialogue begin. Harking back to the ancient term *dialectikos* (conversation), Hamblin used the term 'dialectical' in roughly the same way that Plato and Aristotle had used it. 'Dialectic' in this ancient sense refers to a kind of argumentative conversation in which a questioner, like Socrates, probed into a controversial issue by examining the views of others and criticizing the arguments on both sides (Robinson, 1962). In short, the dialectical model is highly suited to modeling conversational explanation sequences in question-reply dialogues.

Analyzed as a speech act, an explanation should be seen as an answer to a previous question in a dialogue. The asking of the question is the preparatory condition of the speech act. The type of question indicates the type of explanation. For example, a why-question is different from a how-question (Hamblin, 1970; Bromberger, 1966; van Fraassen, 1993). But within question categories, there can be other types of explanations. For example, there can be causal why-questions and causal how-questions. Types of questions can also be classified by the data to be explained. For example, it can be an action or an event that is to be explained. Or it could be the meaning of an unfamiliar term that needs to be explained (as in a lexical definition). Whatever the type of question, the explanation offered in reply to it must meet the pragmatic requirements appropriate for the conversational framework in which the explanation is supposed to take place. The requirements of a dialectical model can be summarized as a set of speech act conditions for explanation. There are three kinds of conditions: dialogue conditions, understanding conditions and success conditions. Each condition stipulates a normative requirement. For something to amount to a good or successful explanation, it must meet all the conditions. The conditions are pragmatic and dialectical, in that they are rules or obligations that apply to the contributions of two parties engaged in a collaborative conversation. The *explanandum*, or thing to be explained, could be anything like an event, a proposition, or even the meaning of a word or phrase. According to the dialectical model, the *explanandum* is defined in a given case by how it initially appears or is expressed in that case. In the dialectical model, it initially appears as the presumption (or presupposition, as it is often called) asked to be explained in the speaker's (explainee's) question. In the speech act conditions as expressed below (Walton, 2004, 83-84), it will be assumed that this presumption can generally be reformulated as a particular statement or proposition. The new dialectical theory does not stand or fall on this assumption, but it is often a convenient way of dealing with cases, because in the new dialectical theory, inference is the basic structure of an explanation.

Speech Act Conditions for Explanation

Dialogue Conditions

Dialogue Precondition: the speaker and the hearer are engaged in some type of dialogue that has collaborative rules and some collective goal as a type of dialogue.

Question Condition: The speaker asks a question of a specific form, like a why-question or a how-question, containing a key presumption.

Presumption Condition: The presumption in the question can be expressed in the form of a proposition that is assumed to be true. The presumption is taken to be "given" or data that is not in question, as far as the dialogue between the speaker and the hearer is concerned.

Understanding Conditions

Speaker's Understanding Condition: the speaker has some kind of special knowledge, understanding or information about the presumption that the hearer lacks.

Hearer's Understanding Condition: the hearer lacks this special knowledge, understanding or information.

Empathy Condition: the speaker understands how the hearer understands the presumption, premises and inferences, understands how the hearer expects things to normally go, and what can be taken for granted in these respects, according to the understanding of the hearer.

Language Clarity Condition: in special cases, the speaker may be an expert in a domain of knowledge or skill in which the hearer is not an expert, and must therefore use language only of a kind that the hearer can be expected to be familiar with and can understand.

Success Conditions

Inference Condition: the speaker is supposed to supply an inference, or chain of inferences (reasoning), in which the ultimate conclusion is the key presumption.

Premise Understanding Condition: the hearer is supposed to understand all the premises in the chain of reasoning used according to the inference condition.

Inference Understanding Condition: the hearer is supposed to understand each inference in the chain of reasoning.

Transfer Condition: by using the inference or chain of reasoning, the speaker is supposed to transfer understanding to the hearer so that the hearer now understands what he previously failed to understand (as indicated by his question).

If a speaker and hearer engage in a conversational exchange that meets some of these conditions, it will be recognized that an explanation attempt is being made. If all of the requirements are met, then the explanation will be successful, to some extent. But how successful an explanation is, in a given case, should depend on how well understanding is transferred from the speaker to the hearer. This factor can only be judged from the particulars of the given case.

But is the dialectical model suited to modeling scientific explanations? Many would think that the DN model is much better suited to modeling scientific explanations, and that the dialectical model is less useful for these applications. But actually the dialectical model seems to do better in cases where dynamic reasoning in scientific testing and refinement of an explanation is taken into account. Take a scientific explanation that is tested as a hypothesis, and then improved by adding refinements, before undergoing further experimental testing. A good explanation could get better, through such a process. Such cases call for a more sophisticated analysis of how the process of reasoning works as an explanation is improved. Thus the dialectical can offer a fuller analysis, because it is a dynamic model showing how an explanation can improve along a sequence of reasoning, whereas the DN model is a less sophisticated, static, one-step inference model.

7. Evaluating Explanations as Better or Best

There is a distinction to be made between identifying something as an explanation and judging how good an explanation it is. The first task could be called explanation identification, while the second task could be called explanation evaluation. The evaluation task is typically phrased in the literature as a process of finding the so-called "best" explanation. Part of the task, presumably, also involves the comparative evaluation of explanation so that it can be said that one explanation is "better" than another. How then does this process work? How are explanations selected out from sets of competing explanations so that one is rightly said to be better or best? There have been empirical studies of how such a procedure of evaluation is typically carried out in the sequence reasoning from given evidence to the formation of an explanation that can function as a hypothesis. These studies are quite interesting from a point of view of coming to understand the structure of logical reasoning that evaluation of explanations is based on. Empirical research on how reasoning is actually carried out in practical argumentation, for example in scientific problem-solving, can be useful in leading to normative insight in how such reasoning ought to be evaluated as instrumentally rational. From a pragmatic point of view, what is vital is to analyze the sequence of reasoning as a series of stages leading ideally towards some goal that can be identified and stated clearly.

Surveying research from various fields in which human diagnostic reasoning has been studied, Peng and Reggia (1990, pp. 6-7) describe a characteristic sequence of inferences that is used, called hypothesize-and-test reasoning. Peng and Reggia, along with many other studies of diagnostic reasoning in AI like the Josephsons (1994), see the process as abductive in nature, because the sequence of reasoning is based on inference to the best explanation. The first stage in the sequence is the raising of a question or a problem. In medical diagnosis this stage is called "disorder evocation", in which a "disorder" is evoked through observing a "newly given manifestation" (Peng and Reggia, 1990, p. 6). The next stage, in which a hypothesis is formed to explain the given manifestation, is called "hypothesis generation"(p. 6). The third stage, called "hypothesis testing", consists of updating an existing hypothesis by coming up with a new hypothesis on the basis of newly available information. The whole process of hypothesis-and-test reasoning (HAT reasoning) takes the form of a cycle. The given data leads to the formulation of a hypothesis, which is then tested. The test expands the data, which may simply confirm or refute the hypothesis. But the expanded data base may suggest refinements in the hypothesis, leading to an improved version of the existing explanation. The sequence of reasoning in such a case is a circular process of refinement of a hypothesis through a continuing cycle of observing, explaining and testing. The process can be described as abductive, because the basic unit of reasoning used is that of inference to the best explanation. Josephson and Josephson (1994) have shown how abduction machines have been constructed using this model of reasoning, for example in medical diagnosis.

What is particularly interesting about this account of HAT reasoning is that it is a definite sequence in which steps of inference of a recognizable kind are identified. Another interesting characteristic is that the reasoning is based on explanation, combining argumentation with explanation. Another interesting aspect, from a logical point of view, is that the process is circular. But the circle is virtuous rather than vicious, as long as the process of HAT reasoning leads to better and better hypotheses as it proceeds through the various loops. The circular process as a whole is useful, or has value as a process of reasoning, if it refines and tests a hypothesis, leading to a more refined hypothesis based on better and better evidence. But what should the goal of the process be, as a whole? It would seem that the goal is to produce the best hypothesis to explain the given facts, and thereby to solve the original problem by explaining the given disorder as well as can be done. But there is also another goal, or at least a subgoal connected to the main one. That goal is to keep collecting relevant information that can be used to keep testing out the successive hypotheses, so that the hypothesis is as strong as possible, and as well-based on available evidence as possible. To put it in slightly different terms, the goal should be to produce the best explanation. But what should 'best' be taken to mean?

Using the covering law model, 'best' could be taken to mean not only an explanation that fits the facts as well as possible, but that is comprehensive enough to fit as many of the facts as possible. Peng and Reggia (1990, p. 7) report that the empirical research on HAT reasoning suggests that the process is based on resolving a conflict between two conflicting goals. The *covering goal* is the goal of explaining all the manifestations that are present. The *parsimony goal*, sometimes identified with "Occam's razor", is the goal of minimizing the complexity of the explanation. According to their view, the notion of best explanation as the goal outcome of HAT reasoning involves the twin goals of comprehensiveness, as the covering goal is better and better realized, and refinement, as the parsimony goal is better and better realized. These reported findings of empirical research seem to be based on a covering law view of what makes an explanation good, better or best. But there are other factors to be considered.

In medical diagnosis, where the aim is treatment, a satisfactory diagnosis may be one that finds a factor that can be used for treatment. Finding such a causal factor could be called a low-level explanation even if, at a theoretical level, it is not clear yet how the treatment works exactly. Nevertheless, citing this particular factor could be called an explanation of the problem. A better explanation would link the thing to be explained to some scientific theory that could show better how the process works that connects the explanation to the thing to be explained. A best explanation could reduce key steps in the process to basic units of scientific explanations, like molecules or genes. What makes the one explanation better than another is not just that one covers more data than the other, or that one is simpler than the other. The better one is the one that gives more depth of scientific understanding, relative to a scientific field or discipline, relative to the basic theories of that field, and the basic entities recognized in that field. According to this view, two explanations could cover the same data, and be equally parsimonious, and yet one could be better than the other. One could be better than the other because it is deeper than the other, going into more depth by relating what is to be explained to the scientific models and fundamental entities in a given field. In short, one explanation is better because it yields greater understanding than another. This view of best explanation is pragmatic, because it is based on understanding and is field-dependent.

An analysis of how the process of discovery moves forward in scientific and medical reasoning has been presented by Thagard (1999). Thagard uses the case of the hypothesis that peptic ulcers are caused by the *h. pylori* bacterium. Thagard shows (p. 54) how the process of discovery in such a case proceeds from data to a hypothesis, but also requires conceptual changes through the formation of new concepts. The sequence of discovery by hypothesis formation characteristic of explaining a disease scientifically is seen by Thagard as based on cognitive processes of questioning and searching (p. 55). The sequence of HAT reasoning is dynamic, because it leads to better explanations as new data come to be known, and new hypotheses are generated.

Another characteristic of HAT reasoning is that its goal is most favorably seen as a process of satisficing rather than maximizing. The goal should not be seen as one of producing the best possible explanation. Instead, the process should be seen as one that, in principle, can go on and on, as more information is collected. It never stops at some clear point where it can now be said the best possible or ultimate explanation has been produced. The process should be seen as open-ended, as the search for new information continues. For practical purposes, the goal should be seen as achieved when a good enough explanation has been reached to make a practical decision for action. This decision, in a case of medical diagnosis for example, would be one with generally two options. One is the option of going ahead and taking action in the form of treatment now. The other is the option of continuing the hypothesis-and-test cycle with the aim of getting a better hypothesis, or at least of getting more evidence to support or refute the existing hypothesis. In other cases, there can be competing explanations for the same data. For example, the given symptoms in a case may suggest two different diseases. In this kind of case, the best or better explanation may be the one that differentiates successfully between the two hypotheses, for example, by ruling out one. In general, the expression 'best explanation' should not be taken to refer to the maximal explanation that is better than any other possible explanation. Instead, by 'best explanation' should be meant one that is good enough to do the job at hand, whatever that job is. The job may be one of treating a patient, or it may be one of helping to guide a further search by ruling out avenues that appear to be less useful to improve the existing hypothesis.

8. Different Kinds of Understanding

There is a common tendency to see understanding as a psychological notion (Trout, 2002). And this assumption poses a barrier to the further analysis of explanation as a logical or structural notion. For if understanding is merely an "aha" feeling of insight or feeling of being right, it could be wrong, even if the feeling of grasping something is very strong. Von Wright's remarks (1997, p. 1) on understanding explanations are helpful to clarify this point. He makes the distinction between the existence of reasons for action and the efficacy of reasons for action. According to his account (p. 1), something can be a reason for an action even although it may turn out that the action was not performed for that reason. Thus understanding, in this sense, is not necessarily based on a determination of the psychological motive an agent had for carrying out an action. It is based on the reasons the agent presumably had, given the assumption that he was acting on reasons. It is possible that this meaning of the concept of understanding could be analyzed as dialectical notion. It could be based on Collingwoods' theory of reenactment, and on the technology of plan recognition. If so, the prospects for a dialectical theory of explanation would be quite promising. But there seems to be a problem, because understanding is best seen as relative to the person. It seems to be subjective in an important way. Understanding, it would seem, can only properly be defined in terms of what an individual is familiar with or not. For example, suppose Bob is a plumber, but not an electrician. Then you can presume that Bob is quite familiar with how drains, sewer pipes, taps and toilets work. But suppose Ed is not a plumber, or any kind of expert on pipes and toilets, or has any more knowledge of such matters than the average homeowner. Then you can presume that Ed is not going to have the same level of expertise or familiarity with matters of plumbing that Bob does. In short, understanding should be seen as relative to the knowledge, skills and expertise of the individual to whom an explanation of something is to be provided. But can such an individualized relativity be modeled systematically in a dialectical framework? There is some evidence that it can be. Work on plan recognition (Carberry, 1990; Mayfield, 2000) is based on domain-dependent routines, or familiar ways of doing things that agents can be familiar with. In other cases, one agent might be an expert, and familiar with a certain domain, while another agent might not be an expert. Work in expert systems, and on the form of argument called appeal to expert opinion, has modeled argumentation and explanation in kinds of conversational exchanges between expert and non-expert. It does seem possible that these technologies and dialectical framework could be extended to include consideration of explanations as well as arguments based on shared and unshared understanding.

These fairly recent developments in computer science have opened a new way of modeling the kind of reasoning used in explanations of human actions (and machine actions as well). The logical empiricist view that there are only two kinds of reasoning that are significant in explanations, deductive and inductive, has become less and less plausible. We now not only have single-agent models of practical reasoning, but also multi-agent models in which agents can engage in practical reasoning with each other. The Collingwood-Dray notion of one agent explaining the action of another agent by a process of mental reenactment or empathy can no longer be dismissed as obscure or merely subjective. It has now become implemented in planning recognition technology. Its basic ideas, along with their implementations and extensions in planning recognition technology, are presenting possibilities for developing a new and distinctive model of explanation based around the idea of reenactment. This kind of reasoning, in which one agent reaches a conclusion by thinking about what another agent is (presumably) thinking about, is now called simulative reasoning (Barnden, 1995). The resources offered by the logical structure of practical reasoning used in multi-agent systems and planning theory open up the prospect of working up an agent-based simulative practical reasoning model of explanation that is a serious alternative to the old DN model.

Explaining human actions, as typically occurs in history or law, and explaining events not involving actions, as typically occurs in physics or chemistry, seem to involve two different kinds of explanation. The human action kind of explanation typically proceeds by linking an agent's goals (intentions) with the agent's knowledge of the situation. As noted, much of the resistance to the DN model of explanation came from its apparent failure to represent explanation in history very well. Dray (1964) argued that explanation in history is not based on the DN model, but on explaining the actions of a human agent by reconstructing the thinking that presumably went on in the agent's mind. According to this approach, explanation of an action is based on a kind of empathy or understanding in which the explainer mentally re-enacts the past action of the historical agent. Dray's theory of explanation in history was inspired by Collingwood's (1946, pp. 282-283) theory of history as the reenactment of past experience (Dray, 1995). According to Collingwood's theory, in order to explain the past action of a person, the historian needs to engage in a simulative act of understanding the actions of another agent. He needs to imagine himself as confronting the same problem that the past person saw himself facing, by seeing the possible alternatives and the reasons for choosing one possible solution to the problem rather than another. In Collingwood's view, historical problems arise from practical problems: "We study history in order to see more clearly into the situation in which we are called upon to act."(p. 114). Dray (1964, p. 11-12) explained this process of empathetic reenactment as one in which the explainer enters into the practical deliberations of the agent whose action is to be explained. The explainer has to get a picture of what the agent's picture of the facts were at the past time when the agent carried out her action. The explainer also has to get some picture of what the agent's purposes were in so acting. Dray (p. 12) described Collingwood's theory of reenactment as presupposing a process of "vicarious practical reasoning on the part of the historian." It is this shared or empathetic understanding of the practical reasoning used by an agent in a given case that enables the reenactment by another agent to take place. This theory of reenactment of action is opposed to the DN model proposed by the logical empiricists. They saw historical explanation as a process of logical deduction from historical laws, and saw the reenactment idea of explanation as obscure or subjective.

There have been many supporters of the view that explanation should be defined in terms of understanding, even among philosophers of science. Scriven (1962; 2002) made clear and forceful statements of the view that a successful explanation should be judged by a process of reduction of what is not understood to what is understood. According to his view, (2002, p. 49), "Explanation is literally and logically the process of filling in gaps in understanding, and to do this we must start out with some understanding of something". Finocchiaro (1975; 1980) offered case studies of scientific discovery showing that scientific explanation is most accurately seen as a process of growth of understanding. He presented Newton's theory of gravitation and Galileo's achievement of making motion subject to mathematical analysis as cases of a scientific discovery that were successful explanations because they produced better scientific understanding. Other noted philosophers of science have gone on record as stating that scientific explanation should be linked to understanding. Achinstein (1983, p. 16) stated that there is a "fundamental relationship between explanation and understanding". According to Salmon's view of scientific explanation (1998, p. 77), scientific understanding fits phemonena into a comprehensive world picture that reveals the "inner mechanisms" of the way things work in nature. Kitcher (1988, p. 168) also held the view that scientific explanations should be judged in relation to how they advance scientific understanding. All these statements acknowledge the view that explanation should be accompanied by an increase of understanding. But as Trout (2002, p. 215) noted, none of them commits to the view that increase of understanding is a required criterion of a successful explanation, and none of them has "much to say about the precise nature of understanding". How the notion of understanding is to be modeled in scientific explanations remains an open question.

Friedman (1974) defined understanding in terms of reduction. For example (1974, p. 18), he argued that it can be explained why heated water turns to steam by reducing the process to an account of molecular motions. Dieks and de Regt (1998) agreed with Friedman that the notion of understanding is the key to scientific explanation, but argued that reduction is not a good way to define understanding. The most popular current view is that understanding can be defined in terms of unification. Schurz (1999) argued that unification is a main goal of science that can be used to analyze scientific explanations and evaluate them as successful or not. Halonen and Hintikka (1999) are leading critics of this view, arguing that unification is important for integrating one scientific explanation with another, but that it is not an essential factor in the process of explanation itself. Instead, they argue (p. 27), scientific explanation is best seen as based on a derivation process using two kinds of steps – logical inferences and question-answer steps. Their view of explanation fits very well with the IP model proposed above. In addition to the *Araucaria* model representing a chain of inferences, their model requires the interposition of question-answer dialogue sequences at each node of the diagram. Weber and van Dyck (2002) have offered what they take to be counter-examples to both of these competing claims. They propose a pluralistic approach in which explanations sometimes consist in unification while in other cases different factors are involved.

9. Understanding and the Clarifying Function

Explanation may be defined dialectically as a species of speech act or verbal exchange in a dialogue, where some given datum is presumed by the two parties in the dialogue. This datum is the "Given" cited by the Josephsons. The given is the presupposition or presumption in the question asked by the party who requested the explanation. Let us call the two parties the explainer and an explainee. The explainee asks a question that is a request for an explanation. The explainer is supposed to answer the question, by either giving the requested explanation or giving some reason why no explanation can be given by him at this time. But what is it that the explainer is trying to give and that the explainee is asking him to give? What is it that the explainer is supposed to be doing when he gives a successful or adequate explanation to the explainee? What is it that the explainee lacks that the explainer is supposed to provide? The best answer is the one already argued for at length by von Wright (1971). The thing that is lacking and that needs to be provided by a good explanation is understanding (*verstehen*). The explainee lacks understanding about the given, and the explainer has the goal of providing it. But what is understanding?

Von Wright (1997) described a special type of explanations of actions that makes reference to reasons. He calls these explanations "understanding explanations". His view is that there is a special type of explanation that is connected to the notion of having a reason for doing something and that is tied to the notion of understanding. This notion of an understanding explanation can be expanded. It is not just the understanding of an individual agent that is always involved. It can be the understanding in a scientific field, based on the methods of the field, and on what is recognized as knowledge in it. Von Wright (1997, p. 2) mentioned two types of scientific explanations of this kind that involve understanding and the giving of reasons. In both, it is not individual understanding that is involved. One type he called the medical explanation. In this kind of explanation that action is traced back to an illness of an agent, perhaps caused by a physical defect or disturbance in bodily function. Another type of explanation he cited is the kind called sociological. These explanations refer to special categories of actions that an agent is capable of carrying out. For example, such an explanation might state that a person is incapable of performing a particular kind of act because of his economic circumstances, lack of schooling, or membership in a particular social class. His notion of the understanding type of explanation, or reason-based explanation as he sometimes calls it, can be seen as the basis of the explanation in such cases.

One very large problem discussed above is that of drawing a bright line between the concept of an argument and that of an explanation in a way that is generally acceptable for all purposes. In addition to this one, there is another very large problem with the new dialectical theory of explanation that is hard to solve, and that cannot be solved in the scope of any single paper. It is to define the notion of understanding in philosophy of science in a way that is adequate for a theory of scientific explanation. Even so, in order to make any theory of explanation a contender, some way of dealing with these problems must be offered. We will now comment briefly on the latter problem.

My main goal in presenting the new dialectical theory (Walton, 2004) was to offer a theory of explanation that can be part of a theory of abductive reasoning of a kind that is useful to analyze the concept of evidence in law. In work on legal evidence, it is very common to use the language of abductive inference, or inference to the best explanation of a given set of facts. A theory of abductive reasoning is extremely useful to help explain what evidence is in legal cases. But of course, in philosophy, writing on explanation is dominated by work in scientific explanation. And philosophers will probably never accept any general theory of explanation unless it can be convincingly applied to scientific explanations. Thus the problem posed here is how to define scientific understanding. But this is not an easy question to answer. For one thing, it is highly controversial, and subject to "culture wars", and different philosophies of science defended by their advocates. For another thing, on the new dialectical theory, scientific understanding varies with different scientific fields and disciplines, It depends on the methods used in a science at any given time, and on the basic units a science accepts in its methodology, as well as on the standards of proof they accept. So although it is necessary to make some statement about what scientific understanding is, in general terms, there should be no illusion that this problem can be solved in one shot.

The goal of an explanation is to be sought in a transaction between the two parties involved, the proponent or "explainer" and the "explainee", the party to whom the explanation is directed. The explainee has asked a question, or has otherwise shown evidence that he does not understand something. But once again we come to the philosophical question of how to define understanding. In cases in everyday discourse, understanding is what is achieved when someone figures out how or why something works, so that he can have an "Aha!" experience and can say, "Yes, now I get it!" To understand what understanding is, it is important to realize that things in everyday life work in normal routinized ways that are familiar to all of us as agents. Such domain-dependent routines have also turned out to be the basis of the technology of plan recognition. For example, if you ask me why my cup is broken, I might reply that I knocked it off the desk. I understand what you are saying because I am familiar with cups, gravity, the hardness of floors, the breakability of cups (assuming it is a china cup), and how a cup can easily hit the floor when accidentally knocked off a fairly high platform like a desk. The situation resonates with familiarity. I grasp right away that a cup can easily be knocked off a desk, fall to the floor, and break because of the impact with the floor, especially if the floor in uncarpeted. So when I say, "I knocked it off the desk." you understand how the cup got broken, without having to probe for more details.

Understanding in one agent can be achieved or invoked successfully by an explanation when the explainer inserts herself imaginatively into the mind of the explainee, to base the explanation on how the explainee understands things. What is required is an act of empathy, because the understanding of the explainer may be quite different from that of the explainee. Explanations frequently take place in an asymmetrical context where the level of knowledge and understanding of the explainer is quite different from that of the explainee. For example, in teaching, the teacher may have an advanced knowledge of the subject while the student may be a beginner. The teacher cannot speak to the student as an equal, or colleague who also has advanced knowledge of the subject. If she did, the student simply would not understand what she is saying. Or the expert, who must explain something to a layperson, say in legal testimony, or as a financial counselor, cannot assume that the listener has an equal knowledge of the specialized matter being discussed. In such cases, the explainer has to try her best to look at the matter from an average layperson's point of view, and express the matter simply and in clear non-technical language. Some experts are quite good at this task, while others are not. What the explainer should be aiming to do is to clarify the proposition in terms that the respondent already understands. The goal is to take some fact or situation (proposition) that appears unclear to the respondent, and relate it to other facts or situations (propositions) that do appear clear or comprehensible to him. Each of the two parties has a goal. And the explanation itself, as a sort of verbal act, also has a goal. Its goal is to make clear what was previously unclear, or thought to be so. This speech act of explanation uses what could be called a clarifying function of discourse, as contrasted with the probative function of discourse used in an argument that is meant to give reasons to support a claim. How the clarifying function works is to increase the understanding of the respondent. The respondent begins with a certain level of understanding when he asks for an explanation of something he does not understand, or does not understand very well. Conversational postulates of Grice (1975, pp. 45-46) include the injunction to make your contribution informative (maxim of quantity) and the maxim of manner, which includes the injunction to be "perspicuous". Van Eemeren and Grootendorst (1992, p. 50) have a conversational maxim of clarity, expressed in the injunction, "Be clear." But to see how to follow this injunction, it is important to recognize that an explanation could be clear in one context of dialogue but unclear in another. A scientific explanation may be clear to readers who are specialists in a field, for example, but unclear to nonspecialist readers.

There are various ways an explanation can fail to meet the pragmatic requirements stated above. One of the most common is the failure to be clear, by using obscure terms, or specialized terms that the respondent is not familiar with. Another interesting phenomenon in this connection is the circular explanation. For example, in a television interview on cancer statistics (CBC National, September 25, 2000), a physician was asked to explain why statistics for cancer deaths were so high in the maritime provinces. His answer was that so many people die of cancer there. Formally speaking, this answer is a correct causal explanation. The deaths do cause the statistics to be higher, because the findings are accurately collected and recorded by Statistics Canada. But such an explanation fails the pragmatic requirement of increasing the understanding of the explainee as to why the statistics are so much higher in this region than in other regions, like British Columbia or Utah. A circular argument can be fallacious, even though formally valid, because it fails to fulfill the probative function, as used in a given case. Comparably, a circular explanation could be a formally valid sequence of logical reasoning, but could be unhelpful as an explanation because it fails to communicate genuine enlargement of understanding to the questioner.

10. Main Features of the New Dialectical Model

According to the new dialectical model, the purpose of an explanation as used by one party in a dialogue should be to get the other party to come to understand something he did not understand before. This aim is achieved by using connections, and especially logical reasoning, to connect things together in the thinking of the other party. In explanations of events not involving human actions, logical reasoning is important for linking specific facts to various kinds of generalizations. Even more often than absolute generalizations of the kind stressed in deductive logic, defeasible generalizations are used. These are generalizations about how things can normally be expected to go in a familiar kind of situation, subject to exceptions. In explanations of human actions, practical reasoning is the glue that holds the explanation together as a functionally coherent whole. Because one agent can grasp the practical reasoning of another agent by simulative reasoning, the one agent can increase the understanding of the other by clarifying something.

How does the clarifying function work in a successful explanation? The answer has to begin with the familiarity of the respondent. A successful explanation takes something that the questioner is unclear about, or does not understand, and then relates it to things he is familiar with, and does understand, or thinks he understands, in a way that now enables the respondent to understand that thing. How does such a process work? It works as follows. The questioner asks the respondent to explain something, X, that the questioner is unclear about. The question might be about the meaning of a word, or it might be about how something works, like a machine, or it might be how something happened. There are all kinds of different questions that might pose requests for different kinds of explanations. No matter what type of question it is, the respondent must take X and relate it in some way to something else, Y, that the questioner is familiar with. It could be a causal relationship, a logical relationship, or a comparison. It could be the relation of having the same meaning or synonymy. No matter what the relationship, it is always one between X and Y - between something that is familiar to the respondent and something that he, at present, does not understand very well, or is unclear about.

There can be various kinds of explanations. One kind works by fitting the thing to be explained into a coherent story, or so-called anchored narrative (Wagenaar, van Koppen and Crombag, 1993). Another kind of explanation uses goal-directed practical reasoning to clarify the reasons for an action. Another kind can be deduction of a proposition to be explained from a set of laws (general propositions) and antecedent facts. A common element of arguments and explanations uses reasoning, and is based on an underlying sequence of reasoning. An assumption made here is that there is a distinction to be made between the concept of reasoning and the concept of argument. A useful way of making the distinction (Walton, 1990) is to postulate that reasoning can be defined as the chaining together of inferences, while argument is the directing of the chain towards a conversational goal. On the dialectical approach, the difference between argument and explanation is then to be sought in how they use reasoning for different purposes. The key comes back to the central notion of the "Given" cited by the Josephsons. An explanation presumes the Given is true, or may be taken by both parties to be true, or represent what is really the case, as far as they know. The Given is not questioned by either party (at least for the moment). An argument is all about questioning. It is about something that is in question, or subject to doubt, and about trying to resolve or settle such doubt. An argument is properly used to bring reasoning to bear on an unsettled issue, or that is subject to doubt as to whether it is true or not. An explanation is properly used to increase understanding of something that is settled as a given fact, or at least is not doubted as being something that is true. What is vital to the distinction between argument and explanation is that each is used for a different purpose in a conversational exchange. Thus the distinction between the two types of speech acts is inherently dialectical. If so, a dialectical theory is the best approach to not only analyzing both, but to providing criteria for distinguishing between them.

The six main characteristics of the dialectical (dialogue) view of explanation cited by Moore, (1995, p. 1) can be summarized as follows.

1. *Dialogue-Based.* Explanation is based on a dialogue between two parties that is "incremental" as the dialogue proceeds: "Explanation is an inherently incremental and interactive process, requiring a dialogue between the advice giver and the advice seeker."
2. *Information-Seeking.* During the dialogue, new information comes in that is related to what the information seeker already knows and that facilitates understanding and learning.
3. *Simulation-Based.* The two parties in the dialogue do not have perfect information about what the other party thinks. Therefore, explanation requires "making assumptions about the listener's beliefs, plans and goals." The term 'simulation' is often used to indicate reasoning based on what another party is assumed to think or believe. Often the term 'empathy' is also used to describe this characteristic.
4. *Feedback.* Feedback is involved in explanations as dialogue proceeds. By feedback one party can test whether the other party has understood his explanation correctly or not.
5. *Question-Reply.* Explanation is a dialogue process of asking and answering questions. When one party presents an explanation to the other, he expects the other "to ask further questions, request clarification, or provide some kind of indication when something is not understood."

6. *Enough Information.* Through questioning and feedback, the explainer can provide more information or clarification until the other party is satisfied.

The dialogue view is a much more robust view of explanation than views like the DN model that see explanation purely in terms of reasoning or as based on a covering law. The dialogue view can still accommodate the view that explanation is based on reasoning, or is based on laws or rules that support inferences. But it goes well beyond these more narrowly inferential theories of explanation. It sees explanation as a dialogue process in which both parties are reasoning, but each has to try to reason about the reasoning and understanding of the other. The dialogue process is not a one-step model. It involves a connected sequence of moves. It sees the explanation as going through various stages of being asked for, being presented, questioned, being improved, and so forth, as the dialogue proceeds. The dialogue view represents a much richer and more natural model of explanation than previous views that tried to see explanation in purely logical or semantic terms without taking the dialogue aspect into account.

Various types of dialogue can be involved. The role of information-seeking dialogue is highlighted above. But Moore (1995, p. 2) has also indicated that advisory dialogues are best viewed as a negotiation process in which the two parties negotiate not only the problem, but also the solution that the advice seeker can understand and accept. As indicated above, the analysis of explanation given is also dialectical in that it requires essential reference to questioning and answering in a dialogue between two parties. Following these dialectical lines, the different types of explanations can be studied and classified in relation to how they function as appropriate replies to different types of questions in a dialogue exchange between two parties. For example, it has often been shown in the literature on explanation how a how-question prompts a different type of explanation from a why-question (Bromberger, 1966; van Fraassen, 1993). The pragmatic accounts of explanation given by Bromberger and van Fraassen highlight the important notion that the given on which an explanation is based is equivalent to the presupposition of the question that the explanation is supposed to answer. Both these pragmatic accounts emphasize the importance of the logic of questions. But from a viewpoint of the IP model, neither goes far enough to investigate how formal dialectical models, of the kind constructed by Hamblin, are necessary to represent the structure of how question-reply sequences work in explanations.

Hamblin based his dialectical theory of argument around the basic notion of the set of commitments held by an arguer in a dialogue. This dialectical approach can be extended to the notion of an explanation. As well as a commitment set, a participant in a dialogue can be thought to have an understanding of the way things normally work in that commitment set. There will be a set of generalizations and other propositions that are "given" or presumed to be true by that participant. These are the things he understands, or can be taken to accept without further questioning. They can be used to clarify things that he asks about, because he understands them. They can be used to fulfill the clarifying function by the other party in the dialogue.

A fundamental point raised carefully by Hamblin (1970, pp. 271-274) is that why-questions are ambiguous in a significant way. In some cases a why-question functions as a request for an explanation. In other cases a why-question functions as a request for an argument. In this latter sense, the question 'Why *A*?' is a request by the respondent to furnish some good reasons that should lead the questioner to come to accept *A* as a true proposition. This pervasive and fundamental duality of function of why-questions is a continuing source of confusion between arguments and explanations. The dialectical approach, as suggested by Hamblin's insightful remarks (1970) on the subject, provides quite an attractive solution to this practical problem. The function of an argument is to transfer the commitment of the respondent from the premises to the conclusion by using reasoning. The function of an explanation is to transfer understanding. The dialectical approach can also clarify the fundamental role of reasoning as used in explanations. The role of reasoning in explanations has often been overlooked, because short examples of explanations are often cited in the literature, as opposed to more lengthy examples of the kind cited by Cawsey. As von Wright and others have often emphasized, practical reasoning of the kind associated with the Aristotelian practical syllogism is closely tied in with explanation.

Typically in a given case, it may be difficult to judge exactly how successful the explanation should be taken to be. The reason is that much information, both factual and contextual, might be missing. The best that can be done in such cases is to comment on what information is known about the case. Thus the evaluation of many cases will, inevitably, be partly hypothetical or conjectural. This incompleteness of many actual cases is not an inherent problem in the new dialectical model however. It is simply a result of reality. If more evidence is available in the case, then a much better assessment of the success or failure of the explanation can be made. In judging an explanation in any real case, all the information the evaluator has is what has been given in the text of discourse comprising the case. Even so, the new dialectical model can be used to spot specific problems or missing aspects of a given explanation attempt in any real case. The best part of the new model is that it can use the text of discourse of a dialogue to judge success of an explanation attempt. The success of the explanation needs to be judged in relation to the feedback and information exchange that occurred, or did not, between the two parties in the dialogue. Both parties have roles to play, and have obligations on how they make moves in the form of speech acts. The respondent is supposed to ask questions if he does not understand the explanation. Then an assessment can be made on how successful the speaker's response was in answering the question. Thus the assessment of the success of any explanation will be based on the evidence from the dialogue. It will be not just one speech act or move, but a whole sequence of connected moves in which one party asks questions and the other provides information and answers.

It is important to emphasize that in judging an explanation in a given case, the basis of an evaluation should be the conversational framework in which the explanation is supposed to be performed. For example, a scientific explanation in a group of specialists in a field of knowledge will be quite different in nature, and in its requirements for success, from an explanation offered by such a scientist to a layperson in that field. In general, an explanation, to be successful, must be designed to increase the understanding of the questioner. In cases of scientific explanation, understanding of the participants must always be seen in light of what is accepted as the theories and explanatory concepts in that field. For example, in physics an explanation might be acceptable if it reduces the phenomenon to electrical charges between particles of a kind physicists are familiar with and accept as entities. In biology, an explanation in terms of genes might be successful, because genes are things that biologists accept as fundamental. Whatever the context, the questioner and the respondent who offers the explanation must be seen as taking part in an orderly goal-directed dialogue. Whether the questioner's understanding is increased or not should be judged differently depending on what point the dialogue has reached in the question-reply sequence. In particular, whether a proposed explanation should be judged to be successful or not, by meeting the requirements of the clarifying function appropriate for a type of dialogue, should be taken to depend on how prior and posterior questions were asked and answered in the given case. The new criteria for explanation classification and evaluation proposed above are not purely inferential, as they supposedly are in the DN model. They depend on features of the dialogue exchange as known from the given text of discourse in a particular case.

The set of speech act conditions given above is still in need of much further fleshing out to see how it can be applied to actual cases successfully. The logical reasoning involved in different kinds of explanations varies greatly. In empathetic explanations of human actions, the reasoning is practical goal-directed reasoning. But how it is used in explanations depends on plan recognition. Typically, an anchored narrative is presented by one party, in which an action is described by posing a problem and describing how an agent tried to solve the problem by practical reasoning (Wagenaar, van Koppen and Crombag, 1993). The explanation can often take the form of an account or "story" that can be very complex. The other party can then question parts of the story that don't seem to be plausible or consistent. There is a chain of logical reasoning involved in such a case, but there appear to be a lot of other factors involved as well. It would take us too far afield to try to examine these kinds of cases, and many other kinds of explanations, to show how a chain of logical reasoning is centrally involved. But that is the hypothesis in the version of the dialectical model put forward above. It will turn out that many features of the model will need extensive revisions and additions as the theory is applied to more realistic cases and becomes more sophisticated. For the moment, the theory has been expressed in a relatively simple form that is amenable to further study and possible improvements of formulation.

Chapter 7: Argument Invention for Proof Preparation

Chapter 7 builds on the methods developed in the previous chapters by showing how they fit as components into a broader framework of legal argumentation. From this basis it is shown how a program of research can be assembled that shows great promise in solving the problem of argument invention. When building a case, for example in law in preparation for a trial, can one use such argumentation methods to search around to discover the best arguments that might be potentially used to support the claim one needs to prove or refute? [1] This question can only be answered by consolidating the gains of the previous chapters and by advancing to the development of new technology. As shown in the previous chapters, argumentation methods are applicable to analyzing a mass of evidence in a case, once that case has been decided. But could they potentially be applicable to proof construction in trial preparation methods of the kinds developed by Palmer (2003)? The existing tools for argumentation analysis have not yet been applied to large sets of evidential facts of the kind typical of evidence in a legal case at trial, with one notable exception.[2] Still, the question keeps coming back, as an issue of theory, and one of future directions for research in artificial intelligence and law. Can the bridge be crossed from evaluating a given argument as evidence for an ultimate *probandum* in a case to discovering new lines of argumentation that could be used as evidence for it?

The transition from argument evaluation of a given text of discourse to the argument invention is a difficult leap to take, conceptually speaking. It is the ancient gap from logic to rhetoric. Since Plato, there has been a quarrel between these two subjects, and it is difficult to reconcile them, even though some authors, notably Aristotle, saw them as closely connected (Hohmann, 1989; 1990). It will be argued that the key to making the transition is the notion of dialectical relevance, as analyzed in chapter 4. In that chapter it was shown how relevance is important in

---

1 The question was asked when the author visited University of Miami Law School in 2004. Professor Terence Anderson asked whether these tools could be applied to invention of arguments in cases of marshaling legal evidence. I didn't know how to answer this question, because such a project had not yet been attempted, but I ventured the opinion that carrying out such a project should be possible in principle.

2 The exception has been the application of Wigmore charts to large bodies of evidence in cases by Anderson and Twining (1991).

trial rules, like the Federal Rules of Evidence (Callen, 2003)[3]. The hypothesis put forward in chapter 7 is that argument diagramming can be used to discover new arguments by searching through a database of facts in a case, and, using them as premises, along with schemes, seek out relevant chains of argumentation that aim at the ultimate *probandum*. A main concern is to provide a precise structure for the formalization of argumentation schemes, and deal with the problem of burden of proof posed in chapter 1. Chapter 7 develops a unified structure for a formalization of legal argumentation that provides a framework for solving this problem and for developing a system of argument invention in law. Ten basic components of legal argumentation are identified in this structure.

1. Argument Invention as a Search Process

A process called a search in computing is one in which an agent considers possible sequences of actions to realize a goal (Russell and Norvig, 1995, p. 85). A search is always a solution to a problem. The search is always built around the following three components. There is an initial state, an end state, and a procedure that can be applied to the initial state, over and over again, so that each time the initial state changes to an intermediate state. Reaching the end state is the goal. Thus the search is successfully concluded when an intermediate state reached by applying the procedure is the same as the end state. The problem has been solved when this point in the search has been reached. In other words, a solution to the problem is a path of intermediate states between the initial state and the end state. In real life, many problems are ill-defined, but with some problems, given analysis, the problem can fit the search model, and be solved by it. In this section we will show how argument invention represents a kind of problem that can be solved by analyzing it using a search model. We begin with some historical remarks about what argument invention was taken to be historically. Systems of rhetorical debate based on Aristotle's *Topics* have used sets of commonplace arguments or so-called "topics" that help a beginner to look around for arguments that might help to win a debate. Perhaps because Aristotle developed his method of argument invention in his *Topics* alongside his use of the same topics as a device to help criticize arguments, historically there has been much confusion about what the purpose of his method was supposed to be and whether it was of any value. The reason is that logic took no interest in the notion of argument invention, seeing it as rhetorical, and twisted the topics around to try to make them a method of proof. This twisting of the topics merely confused the matter. However, if we examine the structure of the topics in their proper context as part of a system of argument invention, as well as being part of a system that could also be used for argument criticism, they can begin to make sense once again.

---

3 The most up to date version of the rules can be seen at the web site listed in the references section: Federal Rules of Evidence – Rules in Effect (2002).

Kienpointner (1997) analyzed systems of argument invention in antiquity, medieval and early modern times, and found that even though they were designed for different reasons, they have a common structure based on three central characteristics.

1. The purpose of the system is to find new arguments, where an argument is taken to be a statement brought forward to confirm or attack a controversial claim (Kienpointner, 1997, p. 225). Central to this characteristic is that all the arguments sought are meant to be useful to support or attack this central claim.
2. The finding process looks not for all conceivable arguments, but only all plausible ones (p. 225). A plausible argument is one in which the audience accepts the premises, and accepts some general rationale for drawing a conclusion from these premises.
3. Different kinds of systems can have stronger or weaker requirements on what counts as an argument that fits the requirements in characteristic 2. For example, a system with very strong restrictions might require that all conclusions must follow from a set of premises by valid deductive reasoning only. A weaker system might admit forms of argument like argument from analogy, or argument from expert opinion, that are not deductively valid, but instead represent inconclusive forms of argumentation.

The third feature suggests that there could be different systems for inventing arguments for different contexts of argument use. For example, Kienpointner (1997, p. 231) cited creativity techniques for so-called "brainstorming" and "associative thinking".

This way of looking at argument invention as based on these three central characteristics suggests that a practical system of invention could be built by analyzing the system as a search process. The claim to be proved can be identified as a proposition to be proved or refuted by the argumentation in the system. That proposition, designated prior to the search, is the end state of the search process. The initial state is the set of premises given in the case in point. The procedure to be applied to the initial state to try to reach the end state is represented by the argumentation schemes. Such a system is quite general, and could be fairly flexible, the way Kienpointner describes it. It could be used in science, for example, in a different way than it could be used in law. For example, argument invention could potentially be used in abductive reasoning to discover new hypotheses at the discovery stage of scientific inquiry. Argument invention could also be used in legal argumentation in the preparation stage for a trial by building a case on the evidence and devising a proof strategy. Each of these contexts is different, since it would have different kinds of restrictions on what kinds of inferences can be drawn, and on how strong an inference must be to derive a conclusion from a set of premises. There would also be different requirements on what are regarded as acceptable premises.

So conceived, a system of invention needs to have three basic components. The first is a set of statements S that are regarded as acceptable premises for arguments. Some could be particular statements while others could be generalizations.

The second is a set of rules of inference *R* that can be used to draw conclusions from these premises. The third is a device *Ch* for constructing chains of argumentation from the first two components. How such a chaining device works can be illustrated as follows. The argument inventor takes a set of premises and applies *R* to them singly, pairwise, or using triples of premises, or whatever is required by the rule of inference. This procedure, when applied once, generates a conclusion. This conclusion is added to the set *S*. Then the argument inventor repeats the process, this time possibly using the newly accepted conclusion as one of the premises in the inference she draws. The particular statement formerly drawn as a conclusion in the first round has become a premise in the next inference drawn to a new conclusion. Hence this process is recursive. As the argument inventor draws a conclusion at one step, she can use that conclusion as a premise at the next step in the process of argument invention to draw a new conclusion. The new conclusion may then be used itself to draw another new conclusion at the next step of the process.

The diagram below represents argument invention as a search process.

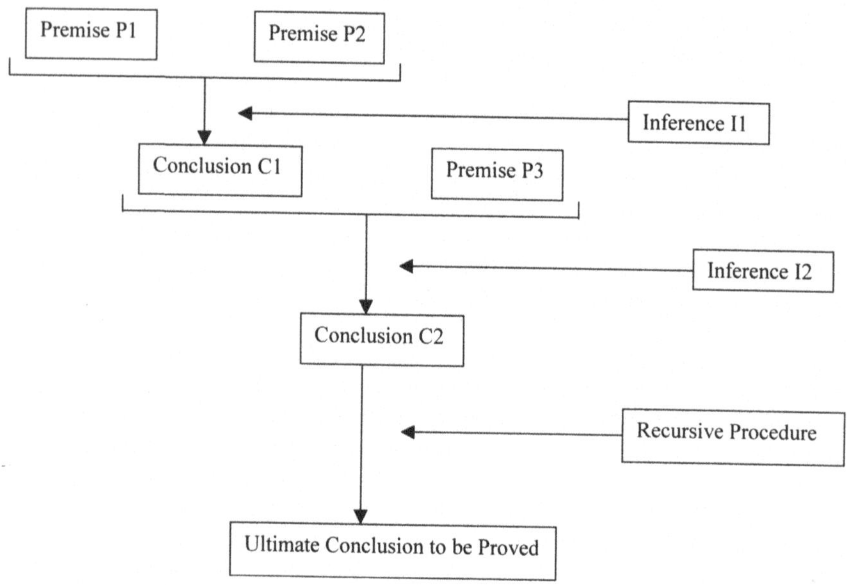

Fig. 7.1. Search Process of Argument Invention

In this search process, the end state is to reach the ultimate conclusion, represented at the bottom, by finding a chain of argumentation that leads to it from the initial premises by applying the rules of inference to them. At the first step, inference I1 is applied to premises P1 and P2 to derive conclusion C1 (by some unnamed rule of inference). Then in a next step, conclusion C1 is itself used as a premise to derive conclusion C2 (a step that may be based on the same rule of inference or a different one). The search process is carried out in the same way at each step. Thus it is a recursive procedure in which rules of inference are applied over and over again both to the set of original premises and to the new ones generated as conclusions and then added to the set at each step. The procedure is applied over and over again until one of two things happens. Either it hits the ultimate conclusion as the outcome of the search, or it does not. If it hits that proposition as a conclusion generated by the system, it has successfully plotted out a sequence of argumentation that can be used for argument invention.

Even if the search process of argument invention did not succeed in proving the ultimate conclusion set as the proposition to be proved, it could still be useful. If it fails to prove this proposition, it has shown that this conclusion cannot be proved by the facts given in the case. This type of failure to prove finding, a negative outcome of the search process, can be very important in argumentation. For example, as emphasized many times before, it is important in lack of evidence arguments, of the kind traditionally called arguments from ignorance. Also, if the path of argumentation from the initial premises falls short of the ultimate conclusion to be proved in a given case, but goes some way toward it, knowing about that path could be very useful. It could show an arguer what steps she now needs to take to find additional premises or rules of inference needed to move the chain of argumentation further along toward proving that conclusion. This negative finding can be very important, as shown by the examples considered in chapter 1 of cases of legal evidence where the given item of evidence is not sufficient by itself to prove the ultimate *probandum* in a case. Taken along with other evidence, that needs to be searched for, this item of evidence could be useful as part of a larger body of evidence.

It is proposed here as a hypothesis that the method of argument diagramming can be used as a search engine for developing systems of argument invention based on the three components attributed to Kienpointner above. This method has gained increasing acceptance in recent years, both inside logic and without. It has recently been fairly widely advocated as a method for analyzing a mass of evidence in legal cases (Friedman, 1986; Schum, 1994; Lodder, 1999). It is also more and more commonly used in logic textbooks to identify premises and conclusions of arguments (Copi, 1982; Hurley, 2003). As noted in chapter 1, the method has also come to be widely used in artificial intelligence as applied to legal argumentation (Wigmore, 1931; Friedman, 1986; Anderson and Twining, 1991; Schum, 1994; Gordon, 1995; Reed and Norman, 2003; Verheij, 2003; Prakken, Reed and Walton, 2003). In the normal kind of case of argument analysis shown at work in the previous cases studied, the argument is found in a text of discourse, and interpreted through a process of analysis. We identify the premises and conclusion, determine what type of argument it is, and judge by criteria whether the given argument is strong, weak or fallacious. But can the same skills and methods set out and applied in the previous cases be used to invent new arguments?

The hypothesis proposed here is that it can be used as the basis for a method of argument invention by following three steps. First, as applied to a case, the argument diagramming method begins with a set of statements in a given case regarded as the acceptable premises for arguments in the case. These are provided by the key list for the case. Second, it has a set of rules of inference that can be used to draw conclusions from this set of premises, namely the argumentation schemes. The schemes might be supplemented with common sense and domain-specific generalizations, like those studied in chapter 2, as devices used to draw inferences from the premises using SMP, DMP, and other rules of inference. It has a device for constructing chains of argument from these two components. This is provided by applying the rules to the premises, using an argument diagram to visualize the full chain of argumentation produced by applying the rules to the premises. Third, it has a goal that can be carried out by applying these two components over and over. That goal is to prove the conclusion of the argument, as specified in the case, from the premises and the argumentation schemes.

2. An Easy Case of Argument Invention

In hard cases of argument invention, the argument is still at an initial stage of a discussion. And so it is very hard to judge, at that point, where it might lead. It often happens in legal argumentation in a trial, that the argument to be evaluated occurs at an early stage, before each side has had a chance to present much of its evidence. In such a case the judge is not yet in a position to determine where the lawyer's argument is likely to go. In such cases, as will be shown below, there are problems about conditional relevance. An argument might be conditionally admitted as relevant on the assumption that one of its required premises can later be proved as the trial proceeds. But there are also lots of easy cases, where an argument is clearly relevant or irrelevant. In some cases of forensic evidence used in trials, the structure of the argumentation is fairly clear (Keppens and Zeleznikow, 2002). For example, expert testimony could be relevant if DNA was found at the crime scene, and a forensic scientist who has tested the DNA sample is called to testify.

Let's begin with an easy case. The following case is taken from a column in the *Miami Herald* in which a questioner asks a lawyer for advice and the lawyer reports the advice given. In this particular case, a health aide who had looked after an elderly woman before she died was found to possess some valuable jewelry that the woman had owned.[4] Family members questioned whether the aide had a right to keep the jewelry. The case involves a shift in the burden of proof, and so is interesting in line with the discussion of this topic in chapter 1. The shift in the burden of proof is readily apparent in the question-answer format of the summary (Segal, 2004, p. 8) quoted below.

---

[4] The column describing this case (Segal, 2004) can be found at the following web site: http://www.miami.com/.

The Undue Influence Case

Q: Our elderly mother recently died, and my two brothers and I are the heirs of her estate. During probate we were shocked to learn that some valuable jewelry was missing. We were even more upset when we learned it was in the possession of the health aide who was caring for her, who claims it was a gift from mother. Now to be fair, that lady who we'll call Alice took care of mother for a long time, was very nice, and our mother spoke well of her. And even though our mother was physically frail at the end, she was still sharp mentally. We just don't know what happened, but it sure looks like there was some funny business. Do we have any legal recourse?

A: Your situation involves the legal doctrine called "undue influence," which typically is claimed by heirs of an elderly or ill donor of assets that would otherwise be inherited. The giver appears weak and vulnerable and the transaction has the appearance of impropriety. But since the heirs were not present at the time of the alleged gift, they don't have first-hand knowledge of the donor's motivation. Since in most civil litigation the parties who want to cancel the transfer have the burden of proving their case by a preponderance of the evidence, the heirs normally would not prevail as plaintiffs because they really don't know the true facts.

It would therefore appear that you can't legally complain. But the answer is the opposite due to another one of those legal areas where a fairness doctrine will protect you. Here's how it works. The plaintiff heirs (you) only have to prove:

1. A special relationship of trust and confidence exists between a dominant and weak party, or legal fiduciaries such as attorney-client, doctor-patient or financial advisor-customer.
2. The stronger party or fiduciary (Alice) received a benefit.

The relatively easy proof of these two elements raises a legal presumption of undue influence and shifts the burden of proof to the benefited party to prove he or she was innocent of the offense.

In this case, it initially seemed to the questioner that there was no case, i.e. no argument that stood a chance of winning in court, the reason being that she had no first-hand knowledge of the donor's motivation. Given the facts as stated, argument invention could not, it would seem, have any way of applying to the case. How did the lawyer invent an argument that fit the case? The answer is that he knew of a law concerning special relationships of trust and confidence that would fit the case. Once this law was applied, it reversed the burden of proof, placing it on it the person who received the benefit. Once this rule was applied to the facts of the case, it produced an argument that raised a presumption of undue influence. The raising of this presumption shifted the burden of proof to the other side, who now had to prove the voluntary nature of the gift.

An *Araucaria* diagram can be drawn representing an analysis of the argumentation in the undue influence case, provided two implicit premises (shown in the diagram below) are inserted.

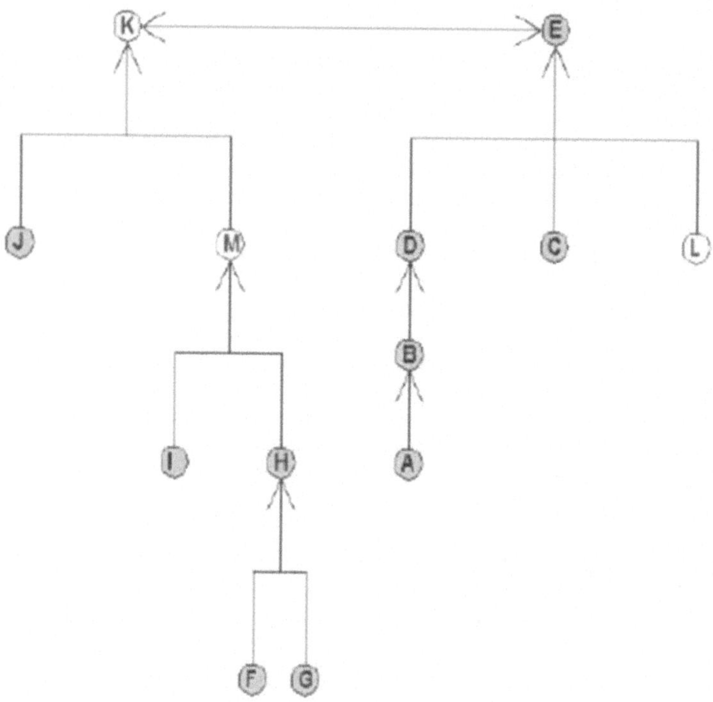

Fig. 7.2. Diagram of the Argumentation in the Undue Influence Case

Key List for the Undue Influence Case

(A) The heirs were not present at the time of the alleged gift.
(B) The heirs do not have first-hand knowledge of the donor's motivation.
(C) Since in most civil litigation the parties who want to cancel the transfer have the burden of proving their case by a preponderance of the evidence, the heirs normally would not prevail as plaintiffs.
(D) The heirs really don't know the true facts.
(E) Therefore, the heirs would not prevail as plaintiffs.
(F) If a special relationship of trust and confidence exists between a stronger party who received a benefit from a weaker party, a presumption is raised that the stronger party exerted undue influence over the weaker party.
(G) In this case, there was such a relationship and the stronger party, Alice, received a benefit from the mother.
(H) Therefore, Alice (it may be presumed) exerted undue influence over the mother.

(I) If Alice exerted undue influence over the mother, there is an appearance of impropriety in the transaction.
(J) If there is an appearance of impropriety in a transaction, the heirs transferred might prevail as plaintiffs.
(K) Therefore, the heirs might prevail as plaintiffs.
(L) The heirs are the parties who want to cancel the transfer.
(M) There is an appearance of impropriety in the transfer.

The double arrow in the diagram represents refutation. E is the initial conclusion, supported by the arguments under it, and leading to it as conclusion. K is a refutation of E, and K is supported by the arguments shown under it, and leading to it as conclusion. The case is interesting in what it shows about argument invention. The lawyer invented an argument that generated a conclusion that made it possible to take the case to court, whereas previously it has not been possible to do so. The invention aspect of the case is made apparent by the observation that premise F came from the lawyer's knowledge of the law, and was applicable to G. Once the two premises were put together, they led to the derivation of conclusion H. This argument, in turn, led through the chain of argumentation pictured above to conclusion K. This chain of argumentation provides relevant evidence, based on the facts and law of the case. It is strong enough to provide a refutation of E and reverse the burden of proof in the case. L is needed as an additional premise to prove conclusion E from premises C and D. M is needed as an additional premise to prove conclusion K from premise J.

In this case then, argument invention can be applied, once the knowledge base that can be applied was expanded to comprise fairness laws known by the lawyer.

If a special relationship of trust and confidence exists between a stronger party who received a benefit from a weaker party, a presumption is raised that the stronger party exerted undue influence over the weaker party.

In this case, there was such a relationship, and the stronger party, Alice, received a benefit from the mother.

Therefore, Alice (it may be presumed) exerted undue influence over the mother.

The first premise is a rule of law (known to the lawyer). The second premise is a fact of the case. A secondary premise supporting this premise is the proposition that legal fiduciaries such as attorney-client, doctor-patient or financial advisor-customer, are the kinds of special relationships that fit cases of undue influence. Thus it is easy to construct an argument diagram showing how the burden of proof is reversed.

This case is an easy one, meaning that once the law concerning special relationships of trust and confidence is known, it can easily be applied to the facts of the case. The conclusion drawn is a presumption that has the effect of reversing the burden of proof, in advance of taking the case to court. The reversing of the burden of proof in this case did not seem problematic. The new evidence shown in the analysis of the argumentation above was relevant, and thus it shifted the burden to the other side without causing any indecision over a burden of proof issue.

The problem now to be faced is that search processes of the kind used in computing are known, in many cases, to be very costly, to involve huge calculations, or to be difficult to apply to real cases for a variety of reasons. Thus many techniques have been developed to shorten the search, or otherwise make it less costly and more practical to use (Russell and Norvig, 1995, pp. 55-119). When applying AI to legal argumentation, the problem is often that the evidence needed to prove the conclusion is incomplete. For example, we might be at the beginning of a trial, or even at the beginning stages of proof preparation. What is needed is a direction for the search. In typical cases, this kind of search is based on the notion of relevance. As indicated in chapter 1, not all problems of evidence are this easily solved. Let's turn to a case that poses a harder problem of argument invention.

3. The Breach of Contract Case

Some cases are harder to evaluate than others. As always, there are the easy cases and the hard cases. Applying the schemes to premises that represent the facts (given statements) in a case, argumentation chains can be built up that can potentially be used to prove the ultimate *probandum* in the case. Hard cases require judgments of relevance based on incomplete data. If such a chain either arrives at the ultimate *probandum* as its end point, or at least seems to be moving toward it, then the argument that started out as part of the chain is relevant. Thus, as shown in chapter 4, the problem is to take individual cases, and make some judgment whether the chain of argumentation is leading towards the ultimate conclusion to be proved or away from it. In law the judge is supposed to use the trial rules to make such determinations (Morgan, 1929). But as shown in chapter 4, there are logical problems inherent in using this method, like the problem of conditional relevance (Ball, 1980; Friedman, 1994; Tillers, 1994; Nance, 1995), and the problem of enthymemes in logic (Ennis, 1982; Burke, 1985; Hitchcock, 1985; Walton and Reed, 2004). How you diagram an argument is typically subject to interpretation and analysis (Friedman, 1986), and whether a premise can be inserted as an implicit assumption is often a problem (Gough and Tindale, 1985). Thus building a search process that applies to an argument in a given case depends on how the argumentation in the case is diagrammed, and this in turn depends on how the original argument in a natural language text was analyzed. Diagramming is merely a tool to help the analysis. Hence a system of argument invention based on diagramming is itself merely a tool that helps the argument analyst find new arguments.

In an argument diagram representing evidence in a legal case at trial, there will be many premises and conclusions connected to each other by inferences. One final conclusion or ultimate *probandum* represents the claim on the one side or the other that is to be proved or to be shown doubtful. It is this final claim that determines what is relevant or not in a case. The following is a hypothetical case, but has many of the features of another kind of case that is very common. There tend to be a lot of facts in any real case, but let us consider a simplified hypothetical case as an example.

Facts of the Breach of Contract Case

Alice signed an agreement to deliver a package to Bob on a certain date. The package contained widgets. The widgets were green. She failed to deliver the package to Bob on that certain date. There was a written contract describing the agreement by Alice to deliver the package. Bob kept two copies of the contract in his desk drawer. The contract contained Alice's signature, and showed she agreed to deliver the package by the date indicated.

Based on these facts, Bob sued Alice for breach of contract. Bob has made a charge against Alice, which puts the various facts above into an argumentation framework. The proposition 'Alice is guilty of breach of contract' is claimed by Bob to be true. This proposition can thus be described as Bob's claim or ultimate *probandum* in the case.

Now we can look over the facts of the case and make a determination of which facts are relevant, in light of Bob's *probandum*, and which are not. But what do we mean by 'relevant'? A proposition is relevant in the desired sense if it can be used to prove or disprove Bob's claim. In other words, it is relevant if Bob can use it as evidence to support his contention that his claim is true, or if Alice could use it to argue that his claim is not true (or can't be proved to be true). As we look over the facts in the case, we can see that some are relevant in this sense, while others are not. The fact there were widgets in the package is not relevant. The fact that the widgets were green is not relevant. The fact that Bob kept two copies of the contract in his desk drawer is not relevant. These facts could turn out to be relevant as the case develops later, but at the moment they do not provide any part of the evidence that could be used or is needed to prove or disprove Bob's claim.

But how could it be proved that these facts are not relevant or that the remaining facts of the case are relevant? It could be done by showing how each of the relevant propositions has a place in the chain of argumentation used to provide evidence for Bob's claim. Let's begin by making a list of these propositions.

Key List for the Breach of Contract Case

(A) Alice is guilty of breach of contract.
(B) There was an offer made by someone for Alice to carry out some action.
(C) Alice accepted that offer.
(D) Alice failed to carry out the action.

(E) Alice signed an agreement to deliver a package to Bob on a certain date.
(F) Alice failed to deliver the package to Bob on that date.
(G) Bob showed a written contract describing the agreement by Alice to deliver the package.
(H) The contract contained Alice's signature, and showed she agreed to deliver the package by the date indicated.

The next step in the analysis of the argumentation in the breach of contract case is to see how inferences are drawn from the facts, making up a chain of argumentation supporting Bob's claim. In order to prove that there was a contract in law, you have to prove that there was an offer and an acceptance. In this case, Bob has to prove that he made an offer to pay something for Alice to deliver the package by a specified date, and that she agreed to deliver the package by that date. To prove breach of contract, he has to prove that she failed to deliver the package by that date. That's Bob's side of the case. The chain of argumentation is represented in the *Araucaria* diagram below.

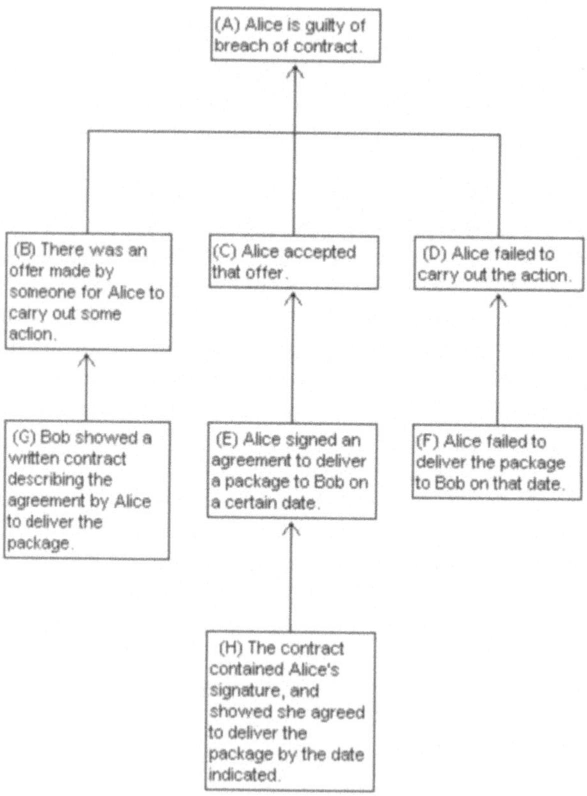

Fig. 7.3. Full Text Diagram of the Breach of Contract Case

What this case (or any one like it) shows is that in law, once a well-defined charge, like breach of contract, is made, the charge is defined in a standard way so that the elements needed to prove it are specified. Here there are three elements. There has to be a contract, which means there has to be an offer and an acceptance. Third, there has to be to be some breach of the contract by one of the parties to it. In order to fulfill burden of proof, i.e. to prove breach of contract, the complainant has to prove all three of the elements or subsidiary propositions. Thus in the *Araucaria* diagram above, as in any breach of contract case, there is one proposition at the top, the ultimate conclusion that there has been breach of contract. Then there are the three element propositions forming a linked argument just beneath this top one. Under each of these three nodes will be a connected mass of premises and conclusions making up the detailed facts of the case. The argument diagram shows how each of the arguments, represented by an arrow joining a set of premises to a conclusion on the diagram, is relevant. Each is relevant because it leads either directly or by a chain of connecting argumentation to the ultimate *probandum*. The diagram shows how each argument represented is logically relevant, meaning that it can be used as evidence that supports the ultimate *probandum* when taken along with all the other subarguments representing other bits of evidence in the case.

How was this determination made? The method put forward in chapter 4 was called *argument extrapolation*. To determine relevance, the argumentation given in a text of discourse in a case is extrapolated forward to judge whether it is leading toward the ultimate *probandum* in the case or not. Applying the method begins by using an argument diagram to fill in the missing premises and conclusions needed to get a grasp of the direction of the argumentation as a whole. We found in previous cases from chapter 1 onward, however, that many legal arguments are based on unstated premises, or even unstated conclusions that need to be made explicit in order to show how the conclusion was arrived at from the given evidence. Using argument extrapolation to carry out such tasks has already taken us some ways toward developing an automated method of argument invention. To see how to advance further, some understanding of what is expected of such a method is needed.

4. Relevance and Invention

How does relevance relate to invention? The theory employed here to answer this question is that when an advocate is in the discovery stage of seeking arguments to prove a target conclusion, she will restrict the search to those arguments that are relevant. She will begin with a set of so-called facts, a set of propositions she takes to be the data of the case, and try to use all the different kinds of arguments she can that takes these propositions as premises. How will such a search work? As suggested by the method of invention outlined above, she will take all the argumentation schemes she has, and try to apply them to the facts, one at a time, pairwise, or whatever is required to make a scheme fit the premises needed for it.

Then once she gets a fit, she takes this new conclusion and uses it as an additional premise. Once again she scans through the facts and tries to find a premise there that will fit with this new premise so that the two together will form an argument by fitting one of the schemes. This search process is the basic method of finding new arguments. But this kind of search could be time-consuming, and even then it might not take the agent all the way to the ultimate conclusion. Still, guidance at this point could be useful. Is there a better way to guide the search?

The bidirectional search is a method that has been developed in computing: "The idea behind bidirectional search is to simultaneously search both forward from the initial state and backward from the goal, and stop when the two searches meet in the middle' (Russell and Norvig, 1995, p. 80). The method of chaining both forward and backward to get the chain of argumentation to match up in the middle was a characteristic of the method proposed in (Walton, 2004) to determine relevance of argumentation in a given case.

The argument inventor casts around for a chain of relevant argumentation that would lead toward the ultimate conclusion to be proved. How would she carry out such a bidirectional search by chaining both forward and backward during the same process of argument invention? Three tasks are required. The first is chaining forward from the given set of facts known to the agent in order to construct a chain that has the ultimate conclusion as its end point. The second is finding gaps in the chain that need to be filled. The gaps are propositions that are not in the set of given facts, but such that, if added to them, would provide premises needed to fit into the argument required to complete the chain. In real cases, this process tends to be quite complex. Not only is the given set of facts quite large, but it can change rapidly as new information comes in. But in principle, the process is a relatively simple one, provided we close the set of facts, seeing them as fixed, and the set of argumentation schemes used to draw inferences form these premises is not too large. The third task is that of chaining backward from the ultimate *probandum* to determine which other statements are needed to prove it. This third task was well illustrated in the breach of contract case displayed in the full text diagram above. It is established in law that in order to prove breach of contract, you need to prove three things: offer, acceptance, and a failure to carry out an action. This information enables you to chain backward to see what is needed to prove the ultimate *probandum*.[5]

The process as a whole is recursive. Essentially the argument inventor repeats the process of applying the schemes to the facts over and over again, generating new conclusions that are then added to the original set. The argument inventor's goal is to find a chain of argumentation leading from the facts to the ultimate *probandum*. But she can also work backward, by judging what premises are needed to prove the ultimate *probandum*. Working both forward and backward, the aim is to match up the two chains of argumentation somewhere in the middle. To carry out this task, implicit premises will need to be inserted in both chains of argumentation. In some cases, there may be more than one way to match up the two chains.

---

5 David Godden, in commenting on this chapter, pointed out the necessity and importance of the third task.

In other cases, they can't be matched up, showing that the original argument is not relevant. In still other cases, they can be matched up only if additional premises not in the original set of facts can be inserted. This outcome represents a finding of conditional relevance. But there is simply no space here to go further into the controversial notion of conditional relevance described in chapter 4 (Nance, 1995; Callen, 2003). There are many problems to be worked out, but the structure of the method for determining relevance is established.

An example can be given to show how such a system needs to be built on components for managing dialogue systems of various kinds, argumentation schemes, enthymemes, argument diagramming, and discourse analysis. It can show how the system of argument invention is technically possible as a search process, based on search methods currently in use in computing and diagramming methods currently in use in argumentation studies. The argument inventor would always have to pose the problem by asking the following questions. How do I get some chain of argumentation from the given set of facts that moves toward the conclusion to be proved by going at least some way in its direction? How is the ultimate conclusion to be proved by proving some other premises that are required to support it? How can I match these two chains of argumentation together so that one leads into the other, perhaps with additional implicit premises? Can these additional premises be proved or supported? What new evidence do I have to seek out to prove or support them? These questions are the basis of the search process for argument invention. They are answered by beginning with a set of facts and schemes and using argument diagramming to recursively chain the argument forward, constructing a chain that leads towards the ultimate *probandum*. At the same time, the argument inventor must chain backward from premises needed to prove the ultimate *probandum*.

To give a simple and short example of how such a system works, let's go back to the breach of contract case. Now let's add another fact to the case. An acquaintance of Alice, named Cassie, had gone on record as saying that Dragut, a known gangster, threatened to burn down Alice's shop if Alice did not sign the agreement. Alice did not dispute any of the facts alleged in Bob's argument above. She agreed that she failed to deliver the package by the specified date. This new fact opens up a potentially relevant line of argumentation for Alice's lawyer. He knows that as a rule of law, a contract is not valid if one of the parties was forced to sign it.[6] He also knows that if Cassie would testify to this effect in court, such testimony would be considered relevant evidence to refute Bob's claim that there was a valid contract. Of course, any lawyer would know that these facts are relevant, and could be used in trial. But how could a system of invention model such a chain of argumentation to show how it could be invented or constructed from the facts? Here it is shown how the outlines for a system of invention can be applied to the case using argumentation schemes and *Araucaria*.

6 This statement, listed as J in the key list, is called a generalization in the sense of Anderson and Twining (1991). As shown in chapter 2, such generalizations in legal argumentation have been studied and classified by Anderson (1999).

To see how such a chain of argumentation can be constructed in *Araucaria,* we must add a new fact to the case.

(I) Cassie said that Dragut, a known gangster, threatened to burn down Alice's shop if she did not sign the agreement.

Also, we must add another proposition in the form of a rule (having the form of a conditional statement).

(J) If one of the parties was forced to sign a contract, it is not valid.

These propositions are clearly relevant, but to see why, we have to add some implicit premises to the case. Each is a plausible assumption that would be hard to contest.

(K) If Dragut, a known gangster, threatened to burn down Alice's shop if she did not sign the agreement, then Alice was forced to sign the contract.
(L) Alice was one of the parties to the contract.
(M) Cassie is a witness.

Using argumentation from witness testimony, from M and I another conclusion can be drawn.

(N) Dragut, a known gangster, threatened to burn down Alice's shop if she did not sign the agreement.

From these propositions, taken all together, a conclusion can be drawn.

(O) Alice was forced to sign the contract.

From J and O, another conclusion follows.

(P) The contract is not valid.

This last proposition is the negation of Bob's ultimate *probandum* in the case. Thus clearly, in this set of propositions there is a chain of argumentation that can be used to argue against Bob's claim that Alice is guilty of breach of contract. This chain of argumentation is displayed in the *Araucaria* diagram below.

The final step in representing all the evidence in the case is to join the two diagrams into one large diagram. In this large diagram P is shown as a refutation of A. We won't present a picture of this large diagram here, but at the top of it, P and A are joined by a double arrow. Under P the diagram just above will be shown, and under A the diagram in section 1 above, representing the prosecution's argumentation in the breach of contract case, will be shown.

In the model, it is shown how the defense invents its argument strategy by casting around among the known facts of the case to try to provide a chain of argumentation that will refute the prosecution's argument. In this case, the generalization J is the key, along with the new fact about the threat that was made.[7] Once the argumentation has reached this stage, the defense searches for some supporting evidence to prove the threat was made. Since there was a witness who said this, the argument from appeal to witness testimony can be applied, thus generating a chain or argumentation represented by the diagram above. Of course, in this case, the chain of argumentation needed to find the relevant argument is obvious, and the invention does not seem very creative. But in principle, this process represents the structure of how a system for invention can be constructed using relevance, argument diagramming and argumentation schemes. The application of such a process would seem creative, it can be conjectured, if it required a lengthy recursive search using an extensive set of argumentation schemes applied to a large set of facts and generalizations.

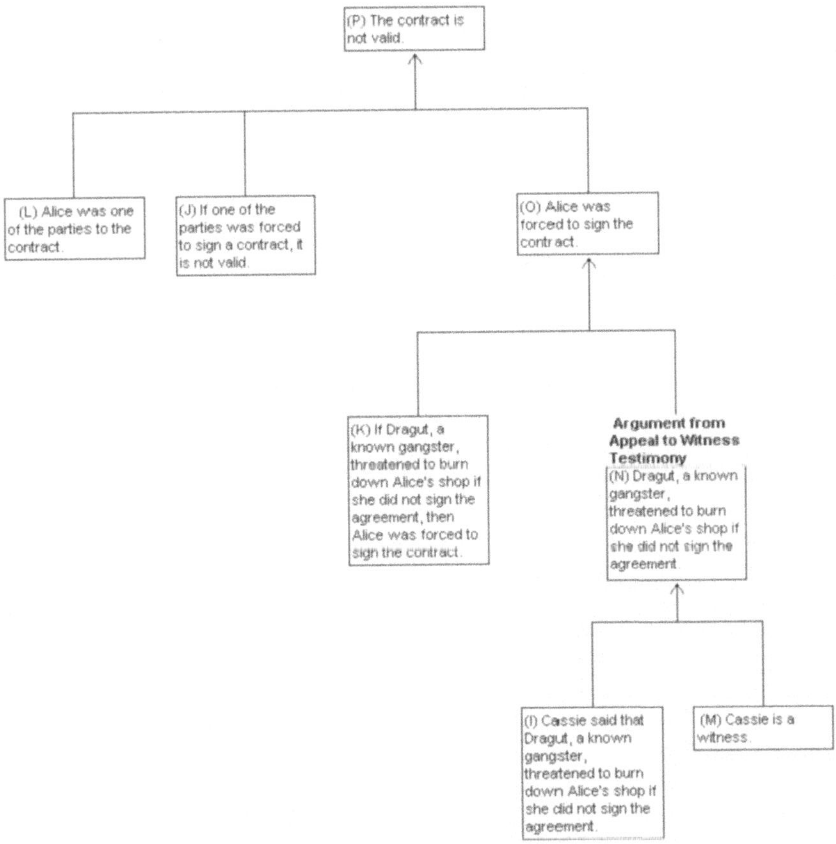

Fig. 7.4. Full Text Diagram of the Gangster Case

7 The importance of generalizations in legal argumentation as means of supporting inferences, as shown in chapter 2, should be stressed again here – see Twining (1999).

5. Building a Method of Argument Invention

The key to solving the problem of bridging the gulf between argument evaluation and argument invention has been shown to rest in large part on the development of argumentation schemes. The schemes are the engine used to draw the inferences from the given facts and legal rules, thereby building up chains of argumentation aiming to prove the ultimate *probandum*. Generalizations, both legal ones and other kinds of common-sense generalizations of the kinds studied by Anderson and Twining (1999), as well as schemes, need to play their part in generating conclusions by inferences from the given set of facts and rules. It is clear that two things are needed for invention. One is a set of schemes that can represent the kinds of arguments commonly used in law. The other is the application of such a set of schemes in a recursive search procedure to a set of facts and laws. These are the basic tools needed for the job. Another is a method of argument analysis that can fill in missing premises creating a chain of argumentation that can be visualized by marking it up using an automated method of argument diagramming. It is this method of argument diagramming that enables the argument inventor to chain the given set of facts and rules forward toward the target conclusion to be proved in a case.

Even with such tools, the task of discovering new arguments that can be used as evidence to prove a conclusion is not easy in legal cases. The kinds of arguments studied so far in everyday argumentation tend to be relatively simple ones with only a few premises and conclusions, with perhaps one or two missing premises. These cases can be problematic, to be sure, but the existing methods have proved to be helpful, even if the task of analyzing the argument by identifying the premises, conclusions and inferential links is a substantive skill that has to be developed. There can often be more than one way of interpreting a text of discourse, requiring two diagrams representing two different interpretations. Still, the method of diagramming has proved to be helpful.

There are also some problems about how burden of proof is defined in Anglo-American law, where a distinction is often drawn between two kinds of burden of proof called burden of production and burden of persuasion. Wigmore (1940, p. 270) drew a distinction between two meanings of 'burden of proof'. The first one is called risk of non-persuasion. Wigmore offers the following example (p. 271) from "practical affairs". Suppose A has a property and he wants to persuade M to invest money in it, while B is opposed to M's investing money in it. A will have the burden of persuasion, because unless he persuades M "up to the point of action", he will fail and B will win. Wigmore then goes on to show how the burden of persuasion works in litigation, in a way similar to that of practical affairs, except that the prerequisites are determined by law (p. 273), and the law divides the procedure into stages (p. 274). The second meaning is called the burden of production. It refers to the quantity of evidence that the judge is satisfied with to be considered by the jury as a reasonable basis for making the verdict (p. 279). If this is not fulfilled, the party in default loses the trial (p. 279). According to Wigmore (p. 284), the practical distinction between these two meanings of burden of proof is this: "The risk of non-persuasion operates when the case has come into the hands of the jury, while the duty of producing evidence implies a liability to a ruling by the judge disposing of the issue without leaving the question open to the jury's deliberations." Wigmore gives a number of good examples, and goes on to discuss shifting of the burden of proof (p. 285). He says that the risk of non-persuasion never shifts, but the duty of producing evidence to satisfy the judge does have this characteristic often referred to as a shifting (pp. 285-286).

Strong (1992, p. 425) cited what appears to be the same distinction, contrasting the burden of producing evidence and the burden of persuasion. He describes the first as follows: "The burden of producing evidence on an issue means the liability to an adverse ruling (generally a finding or directed verdict) if evidence on the issue has not been produced"(p. 425). The burden of persuasion (p. 426) means that if the party having that burden has failed to satisfy it, the issue is to be decided against that party.

Park, Leonard and Goldberg (p. 88) cite two meanings of burden of proof – burden of persuasion and burden of production. They say that the burden of production involves two things – the amount of evidence required to establish the ultimate question of fact, and the allocation of the risk of non-persuasion to that degree. The burden of persuasion (p. 89) defines the degree to which the factfinder must be persuaded in order for the ultimate claim to be proved, and which party must meet that burden. There are various degrees, like "more likely than not", "beyond reasonable doubt" and so forth.

The problem is that it is not altogether clear that these three ways of drawing the distinction between the two types of burden are entirely consistent with each other. They do indicate that at least two distinct meanings of the concept of burden of proof are recognized in Anglo-American law. However, they don't seem to agree exactly on what these burdens should be called, how they should be defined precisely, and how they might be applied to problematic cases where burden of proof is an issue. We won't try to legislate terminology for law by ruling on how these three definitions should be integrated. All we can do is to reiterate that the notion of legal burden of proof is legally problematic, in some important respects, as well as being problematic as a concept for argumentation and AI, as indicated in chapter 1. Below, in section 9, we return to the problem of defining the concept of burden of proof more precisely by facing the problem of how it should be formally modeled so it can be applied to hard cases.

There are other problems using argument diagramming methods to apply to the evaluation of argumentation to legal cases. In any realistic case, as the two cases Wigmore (1931) worked out to illustrate his chart method show, there will be a large mass of evidence making for quite large diagrams. Also, to usefully represent such argumentation, the system will have to contain a large number of generalizations and legal rules. Many kinds of arguments can be used, and hence the set of argumentation schemes to choose from may also have to be quite large. The system will have to do a lot of computation to build chains of argumentation from such a mass of data with such a potentially large number of rules. Lengthy case studies of evidence trials, like those worked up by Anderson and Twining (1991) need to be worked up. Developing a formal theory of invention, or a software package that could be used to aid invention in these kinds of cases, are projects that lie in the future. In this book, we have made no pretense of trying to build a realistic system with this capacity, or of trying to apply it to a real case of argument invention of a kind that was used or could be used in a trial. The main problem is to cut down the avenues of potentially useful chains of argumentation to those that are most promising, given the evidence currently known in a case.

It can be argued that a very useful way of approaching this task is to utilize the notion of relevance. Relevance can guide the process by cutting down the search procedure, winnowing the irrelevant facts and rules not needed to prove the conclusion from the needed premises that are relevant. Relevance, as shown in chapter 4, is a notion already central to evidence law, and is prominent in widely adopted rules of evidence like the federal rules of evidence. Relevant arguments, as defined above, are those fitting into argumentation chains that move toward the target conclusion to be proved. Irrelevant arguments are those that show little promise of moving along such a line of advance, or even move away from any chain of argumentation leading toward the ultimate conclusion, in some cases leading to a different one that may resemble the one to be proved. Thus, according to the model proposed here, the way to discover productive lines of argumentation, that are likely to prove useful to prove a conclusion that has been designated in advance, is to judge alternative chains by relevance.

The question asked and answered in chapter 7 represents a big interdisciplinary leap, from logic to rhetoric, two subjects that have in the past often been seen as at loggerheads. Despite this gulf between the two subjects, and the size and scope of the question, it was argued that there are resources for offering an affirmative, if speculative answer to the question. Although *stasis* theory is well established in traditional rhetoric (Hohmann, 2001), there has never been any theory of invention based on it that is well enough structured to be developed into a precise formal model of a kind that might be used in computing, for example, or for constructing software for argument invention.[8] That such a system is possible demonstrates that there is a close connection between rhetoric, seen as a method of argument invention, and dialectic, seen as a method of argument identification, analysis and evaluation. It has been shown that even though the purpose of the one field is different from that of the other, the two share many components and techniques. It has been shown how a method of argument invention and discovery is possible, building on tools and techniques already widely in use for identifying, analyzing and critically evaluating argumentation. Steps have been taken to argue that the leap from here to there isn't as big as it looks. By showing a way to bridge the gap from argument evaluation to argument invention, the promise for productive future interdisciplinary research on invention in legal argumentation has been shown.

---

[8] It might be noted once again here that stasis theory had its origins in the study of legal argumentation (Hohmann, 1989; 1990).

6. Classifying and Formalizing Schemes

In the formalization of Reed and Walton (2005), the set of schemes in a given system is composed of a set with three elements. One is the name of the scheme, like 'argument from consequences'. One is a designated proposition representing the conclusion. The other is a set of premises. Thus each scheme is uniquely named, and is associated with a conclusion type and a set of premise types. An instantiation is an argument based on one of the schemes, identified as a triple <*name, conclusion, premises*>. Given this mechanism for the representation of schemes in a formal system, how could one build an automated mechanism for reasoning with schemes? The answer, presented in Reed and Walton (2005) is to add a binary operator of a kind called a connective in logic that corresponds to the operation of implication in logic. The set of implications defined by this connective includes not only those of classical deductive logic but also those fitting any given set of presumptive argumentation schemes. In other words, the chaining of arguments in the system can be based not only on deductively valid forms of argument like strict *modus ponens* (SMP) used as rules of inference, but also on defeasible schemes like defeasible modus ponens (DMP). Acceptability of argument in the system can then be defined by closure under this new operator, bringing the representation of schemes into standard models of defeasible argumentation of the kind applied to legal reasoning by Prakken (2001) and Verheij (2003).

This type of formal system can be implemented in a simple one-agent structure by using argument diagramming techniques like *Araucaria*. The underlying representation language of *Araucaria* is an XML language called AML (argument markup language). A basic AML component called a PROPTEXT is made up of a proposition, its owner (telling us which party advocated that proposition), and an INSCHEME element, which allows the analyst to mark a given PROP as belonging to a particular scheme. Each scheme has a unique name, allowing the specification of the formal structure of a scheme and its accompanying set of critical questions. Using this formal system, a particular bit of legal evidence, like say an instance of witness testimony used as evidence in a trial, can be visually represented by an argument diagram. The diagram displays its premises, its conclusion, and the name of the scheme representing the kind of inference that joins the conclusion to the premises. Bex, Prakken, Reed and Walton (2003) have shown how diagrams of this kind can be used to represent single instances of common examples of legal evidence of many kinds. And even more significantly, larger masses of evidence of the kind commonly found in trials, like those represented by Wigmore charts are used in analyses of evidence in trials by Anderson and Twining (1991) and Schum (1994).

The system for formalizing schemes outlined above provides a framework for argument invention by chaining arguments using argumentation schemes as the inferential device that can be applied over and over again to a database of premises and conclusions in a given case. Research on schemes is showing that quite a variety of different presumptive schemes representing kinds of argument that are commonly used in law have been identified and analyzed. Some schemes are subspecies of others. For example, argument from expert opinion is a special type of argument from position to know. It would therefore be useful if a system of classification for schemes could be developed. This is a project for the future. However, many of the most common kinds of schemes have been identified in the literature on logical fallacies, and a tentative classification of these schemes under three main categories (below) is useful.

I. REASONING

1. Practical Reasoning
   Argument from Consequences
   Argument from Alternatives
   Argument from Waste
   Argument from Sunk Costs
   Argument from Threat
   Argument from Danger Appeal

2. Abductive Arguments
   Argument from Sign
   Argument from Evidence to a Hypothesis

3. Causal Reasoning
   Argument from Cause to Effect
   Argument from Correlation to Cause
   Causal Slippery Slope Argument

II. SOURCE-BASED ARGUMENTS

1. Arguments from Position to Know
   Argument from Witness Testimony
   Argument from Expert Opinion
   Argument from Ignorance

2. Arguments from Commitment
   Argument from Inconsistent Commitment

3. Arguments Attacking Personal Credibility
   Arguments from Allegation of Bias
   Poisoning the Well by Alleging Group Bias
   Ad Hominem Arguments[9]

---

[9] A set of argumentation schemes for the argument against the person (*ad hominem* argument) is given in (Walton, 1998a, pp. 248-263), along with a proposed system of classification for them. A useful proposal for developing a method of formalizing this set of schemes is given in (Verheij, 2003, pp. 172-174).

4. Arguments from Popular Acceptance
   Argument from Popular Opinion
   Argument from Popular Practice
   Ad Populum Arguments

III. APPLYING RULES TO CASES

1. Arguments Based on Cases
   Argument from Example
   Argument from Analogy
   Argument from Precedent

2. Defeasible Rule-Based Arguments
   Argument from an Established Rule
   Argument from an Exceptional Case
   Argument from Plea for Excuse

3. Verbal Classification Arguments
   Argument from Verbal Classification
   Argument from Vagueness of a Verbal Classification

4. Chained Arguments Connecting Rules and Cases
   Argument from Gradualism
   Precedent Slippery Slope Argument
   Sorites Slippery Slope Argument

In principle, any set of schemes can be used in an automated system of argument invention. In *Araucaria*, the user can use the existing scheme sets that can be loaded into the system, including one that comprises the original set of twenty-six presumptive schemes from (Walton, 1996). Or the user can add new schemes to any of these given sets. Any system of argument invention of the kind described above will become more and more powerful for representing legal argumentation as more and more schemes representing common kinds of legal arguments, like those listed above, are added to the set. A scheme set can also include deductive and inductive schemes as well as the presumptive schemes listed above. Among the most common forms of legal argumentation are those representing causal reasoning. At the same time, studying causal reasoning in law has proved highly problematic. To carry us a step further with the study of the prospects for automated argument invention in legal argumentation we now turn to causal argumentation schemes.

7. Studying Causal Schemes

In the simplest and most basic argumentation scheme for argument from cause to effect (Walton, 1996, p. 73), the variables *A*, *B*, *C*, ... stand for "states of affairs", or statements describing events.

Argument from Cause to Effect (Walton, 1996, p. 73)

Generally, if *A* occurs, then *B* will (might) occur.

In this case, *A* occurs (might occur).

Therefore in this case, *B* will (might occur).

The conditional in the first premise is not an absolute one, like the material conditional of deductive logic, but a defeasible one, saying that if *A* occurs in a particular context an agent is familiar with, then the agent can reasonably expect *B* to occur as well, subject to possible exceptions as the agent comes to learn new information. Thus Perelman and Olbrechts-Tyteca (1969, p. 262) described argumentation from cause to effect in defeasible terminology as "tending to show the effect which must result from a given event". Van Eeemeren and Kruiger (1987, p. 74) recognized the same kind of argumentation scheme based on the supposition of a causal relationship. Grennan (1997, p. 187) formulated an argumentation scheme for what he called cause to effect argumentation. It is based on a so-called "warrant backing" stating that generally, events of one kind cause events of another kind. This formulation explicitly recognized the defeasible nature of argumentation from cause to effect.

Argument from cause to effect can be defeated by the asking of any one of the following three critical questions (Walton, 1996, p. 74).

Critical Questions for Argument from Cause to Effect

CQ1: How strong is the causal generalization (if it is true at all)?

CQ2: Is the evidence cited (if there is any) strong enough to warrant the generalization as stated?

CQ3: Are there other factors that would or will interfere with or counteract the production of the effect in this case?

So conceived, argument from cause to effect needs to be evaluated in a dialogue format. The proponent makes a move by putting forward an argument. If the proponent's argument meets all the requirements of the argumentation scheme for argument from cause to effect, and the respondent is committed to all the premises, then the respondent must either commit to the conclusion at his next move or ask one of the appropriate critical questions. Unless the proponent offers an adequate answer at the move in the dialogue, the argument defaults in favor of the respondent.

Prakken and Renooij (2001) modeled the causal reasoning on both sides of a causation case using facts and rules in a real case. In this case, (Prakken and Renooij, 2001, pp. 132-133), driver and passenger were returning home when the driver lost control of the car on the highway. In the resulting crash, the passenger was injured. The passenger sued the driver claiming he had lost control. The driver argued that the passenger had suddenly pulled the handbrake, and that had caused the accident. In this Dutch Supreme Court case (HR 23 October 1992, NJ 1992, 813), the police found that the accident took place just beyond an S-curve where skidmarks were found. The handbrake was in the pulled position when the car was found. Prakken and Renooij began with a set of causal rules and a set of presumed facts as representing arguments of each side. They used a double arrow to represent a causal rule. For example, according to Rule 1, if skidding occurs then an accident might occur.

Rule 1: *skidding* $\Rightarrow$ *accident*
Rule 2: *skidding* $\Rightarrow$ *tire marks present*

Each rule warrants a forward-moving defeasible inference, meaning that if the antecedent holds in a case, then the consequent might plausibly also hold, subject to the conditions in the case. But each rule can also be seen as warranting a backward-moving defeasible inference as well, which could be seen as based on abductive reasoning. For example, if there is an accident in a given case, depending on other circumstances, skidding might be a best explanation of the accident. Or if there were tire marks present, skidding could be a best explanation of them. To analyze the argumentation in the case, Prakken and Renoij constructed an argument diagram showing the forward-moving sequence of reasoning in the case. The sequence of causal argumentation on the one side led to the conclusion that the driver's loss control caused the car to crash. The sequence on the other side led to the conclusion that the passenger's pulling the handbrake caused the car to crash.

The same sequence of argumentation in the car crash case was reconstructed (Walton, 2004) as a backwards-moving sequence of abductive reasoning, based on the following argumentation scheme. Using the new dialectical theory of explanation presented in chapter 6, which offers a way of judging whether an explanation is satisfactory, we can now implement useful argumentation schemes for abductive reasoning, including the abductive causal scheme below.

Abductive Argumentation Scheme for Argument from Effect to Cause

F is a finding or given set of facts in the form of some event that has occurred.

E is a satisfactory causal explanation of *F*.

No alternative causal explanation *E'* given so far is as satisfactory as *E*.

Therefore, *E* is plausible, as a hypothesis for the cause of *E'*.

This scheme appears to resemble the invalid form of reasoning called affirming the consequent, but when seen as a form of abductive reasoning it represents a correct type of defeasible argumentation. The advent of this scheme, and other causal schemes like it (Walton, 2002) presents an extremely useful toolkit for the analysis and evaluation of legal argumentation. We can now view causal reasoning as providing evidence in law, based on defeasible argumentation structures.

Of course, it is all very well to formulate such argumentation schemes, but it has long been known in law that the notion of causation is extremely hard to define. Indeed, this notion has been subjected to such severe attacks in the past that it has been generally assumed that no precise analysis of it can be given. Nor is there much skepticism about the notion in law; but in philosophy as well, there is no widely agreed on theory of causation that has been accepted. Sometimes the term 'cause' is taken to represent a necessary condition of the occurrence of an event, while in other cases it is taken to represent a sufficient condition. According to the but-for test, the most widely used criterion for judging causation in tort law (Wright (1985, p. 1775), "an act (omission, condition, etc.)" is said to be "a cause of an injury if and only if, but for the act, the injury would not have occurred." This test assumes that a cause is a necessary condition. The view of the causal relation as a necessary condition of the occurrence of an event is the basis of the following definition of the casual relation (Kienpointner, 2002, p. 1).

Event *A* is the cause of event *B* if and only if

1. *B* regularly follows *A*
2. *A* occurs earlier than (or at the same time as) *B*
3. *A* is changeable/could be changed
4. If *A* would not occur, *B* would not occur (*ceteris paribus*)

The Kienpointner analysis could be offered as a working criterion of the but-for test.

The problem with the necessary condition criterion for causation is that it does not take cases into account where causation arises from sufficient conditions rather than necessary conditions for an event. In an often-cited type of example (Wright, 1985, p. 1777-1778), two persons each start separate fires, each of which by itself is sufficient to burn down a house, and then the fires converge and burn the house down. Pick one fire. It's false that but for that fire, the house would not have burned down. Thus that fire was not a necessary condition of the burning down of the house. Hence causation in law cannot be analyzed only by citing necessary conditions. Sufficient conditions must also be taken into account.

To provide a more widely applicable analysis of causation, Scriven (1964, p. 408) proposed a criterion requiring that a set of necessary conditions, taken together, be sufficient for the occurrence of the outcome. This test implies that the remainder of the set, apart from the designated necessary condition, is not sufficient for the outcome (p. 408). Mackie (1965, p. 245) formulated the so-called INUS Condition test, based on these requirements.

If *C* is a cause of *E* (on a certain occasion) then *C* is an INUS condition of *E*, i.e. *C* is an insufficient but necessary part of a condition which is itself unnecessary but exclusively sufficient for *E* (on that occasion).

Hart and Honore (1962), after examining many legal cases of causation, came to the skeptical conclusion that the INUS test cannot capture the notion of causation in all cases. On their view, an adequate analysis of legal causation must incorporate two apparently subjective notions: the voluntariness of a human action, and abnormality of an event in some context in which human expectations about what is normal or plausibly expected play a role. In opposition to this view, Wright (1985) argued that an analysis of legal causation based on INUS conditions can be rescued from all the difficulties posed by the problematic legal cases cited by Hart and Honore.

Causal arguments of the kind so often subject to dispute in tort law, are often best analyzed as based on a kind of abductive reasoning that is defeasible. The conclusion of the argument represents a hypothesis that offers causal explanation of the facts presented in a case. But the other side in the dispute presents a competing causal explanation of the same facts, even though, at the same time, there can be disputes about what the facts of the case really are. Thus in typical disputed cases, there are lengthy arguments and counter-arguments on both sides, for example arguments about the supposed effects of medical treatments. So-called "toxic tort" are cases involving personal injury allegedly caused by exposure to toxic substances (Alberts, 2001, p. 34). Because the injury is often a syndrome that may be hard to define or diagnose, and because the symptoms arguably shown in the case are not unique to the disease, proving causation of a toxic tort can often be a "challenging prospect" (Alberts, 2001, p. 34). Some famous and highly controversial cases of this sort have been studied by (Huber, 1991) and are associated with the term "junk science", because the arguments have been so dubious. In evaluating scientific evidence about causation in legal argumentation, it must be noted that judges, lawyers and juries are not generally themselves expert scientists. They cannot scientifically test the evidence on which two opposed causal theories or explanations are arguably based. As shown in previous chapters, the evaluation rests on argument from expert opinion, the critical questioning of the argumentation that takes place during examination of testimony, and the burden of proof. For these reasons, causal arguments of the kind disputed in torts cases are best seen as defeasible, resting on rules and causal generalizations that are subject to critical questioning. The application of defeasible causal argumentation schemes to such cases is therefore a potentially useful area of investigation.

8. Ten Components of Legal Argumentation

The methods set out in the previous chapters apply to all kinds of problems of legal reasoning, but the one problem central to the others is to see how an argument can be reconstructed in a given case. The paradigm is an argument that has been put forward as evidence at some stage of a trial. The problem is to put forward a set of rational standards that can be used to identify, analyze and evaluate such an argument. So, for example, one particular argument of this sort might be evaluated as strong because the premises have probative weight, and the inference from the premises to the conclusion conforms to the requirements of a known argumentation scheme. But then the other side in the trial may ask an appropriate critical question revealing that the argument has a weakness its proponent does not or cannot fix by answering the question adequately. The primary goal of using argumentation in such cases is to criticize the argument by finding its weak points. To do that, the argument first has to be identified and analyzed.

As noted above, logic has been seen historically as the tool of argument evaluation and criticism, while rhetoric was seen as the tool for invention of new arguments needed to persuade an opponent or audience to accept the conclusion one is arguing for. The problem was that, apart from Aristotle, a long tradition has sharply separated these two subjects. The idea that logic could be used for the purpose of argument invention has simply never been felt to be feasible. Now, with the advent of argumentation schemes, all that has changed. Informal logic has built up a new system for argument criticism based on argument diagramming and argumentation schemes. The new method is proving to be successful as a tool that is extremely helpful for evaluating arguments of the kind used in everyday conversational disputes, as well as for analyzing these arguments and identifying their components. This method is now also showing promise as applied to analyzing problems of evidence in law, like the problem of burden of proof.

It has been argued in chapter 7 that the problem of argument invention can be solved by applying the same method, but in a different way. One takes the set of propositions given as premises in a case, identified by the key list, and uses the argumentation schemes (along with generalizations) to draw conclusions. This process is applied over and over, producing an argument diagram that either reaches the ultimate conclusion in the case or not. The diagram represents the evidence that can be used to determine whether the argument, or any parts of it, are relevant in the case or not. This recursive process of applying rules of inference to premises given in a case can also be used for argument invention. At least, the examples studied so far show how relevance can be determined and invention carried out in relatively easy cases. The real test of applying the system to a hard case will not be carried out in this book, and will not be until the set of argumentation schemes set out above has been expanded and the schemes formalized. Only then will practical automated systems of legal argument invention be feasaible. But to prepare the way for the development of such systems, a more general account of the structure and components of the method needs to be given.

In order for the method to be applied, any argument must be seen as having ten components that can be identified in the given case.

1. There will be a set of premises and a conclusion that can be identified as specific propositions, although implicit premises and conclusions may be recognized as well. These are represented by the key list for the case.
2. The argument, in the minimal case, has only one proposition designated as its conclusion, but as identified in a typical case, it will be a chaining of arguments. The same proposition that is a conclusion of one subargument may function as a premise in another one.
3. An argument diagram, with linked and convergent argument structures represented, can be used to analyze the structure of a chain of argumentation in a given case of this sort.
4. Argumentation schemes, including deductive ones like SMP, inductive schemes like statistical syllogism, and defeasible ones like DMP, can be labeled as specific linked arguments represented in the diagram.
5. Generalizations and rules of various kinds can also link a set of premises to a conclusion, providing a warrant on which an argument is based. Some of them are domain-specific. Some of them are common sense generalizations. Some of them are legal rules based on statutes or court rulings.
6. In addition to generalizations and rules, there will be some propositions accepted by both sides in the case, and not challenged by them. There will also be precedents set by rulings in prior similar cases.
7. The set of propositions described in 1, 5 and 6 act as what is called a knowledge base, or set of premises from which conclusions can be drawn by arguments that fit the requirements of an argumentation scheme.
8. In each case there will be a designated ultimate *probandum* of the argument specific to the case at issue.
9. There are criteria that can be used to determine whether an argument, as put forward so far in a case, is relevant or not in that case.
10. An argument can be assessed as logically irrelevant under the right conditions in some cases, and that determination can be used as part of the justification for the claim that the argument should be judged inadmissible as evidence in that case.

These ten components, when applied to any case that might be considered at any stage of a trial, or during the collection of evidence or proof preparation prior to a trial, or in any other context of legal argumentation, can be used as a framework for various purposes. These purposes include determining relevance and invention of relevant arguments.

It must be emphasized, however, that when applied to any complex or hard case at law, the knowledge base, cited as component 7 above, would be quite large. Consider trying to apply the ten components to a real case being disputed, in order to invent some arguments that could be used on one side or the other. The knowledge base would include the set of laws (legal rules) that apply to the case, the precedent cases, and possibly other similar cases, as well as the evidence known in the case. Using *Araucaria* to apply component 3 would therefore be problematic, if for no other reason than the sheer size of the knowledge base. Another problem is that there would be unresolved issues of burden of proof, like those studied in chapter 1. Even so, it is a hypothesis put forward here that the ten components can be used as a framework for not only making judgments of relevance, but also for building a mechanized system of legal argument invention.

9. Future Problems for Research

Argument invention is only at the beginning stage of its development. In this book, the formal structure of argument invention and its main components have been described in a systematic way. Implementing working systems of argument invention based on this model depends very much on the analysis and classification of argumentation schemes as a research project that has only just begun. As schemes representing the most common and important kinds of legal arguments are formalized, and built into formal systems that can be expressed in machine readable languages, these automated systems will become more and powerful devices of argument invention in helping with legal tasks like trial preparation. In collaboration with Chris Reed and Fabrizio Macagno, I have undertaken a current research project with the aim of analyzing schemes and classifying the known schemes into a general system. These are future problems for research. The constants and variables used to specify the logical form of each of the known schemes, as they have been defined so far, has admitted of variations. The variables mainly range over propositions and predicates, and thus the format of the schemes roughly resembles predicate logic in general outline. But there are also variables for agents, events, actions, and other factors that recur in many schemes but do not appear to be easily reducible to systematization. In this work, some 60 schemes have been identified from the work of Walton on argumentation and fallacies. Several attempts were made to provide systems of classification for this set of schemes, but none so far has proved to be very successful.

Verheij (2003) has formulated several specific problems arising from any attempt to formalize schemes, and has proposed some ways of moving ahead to solve these problems. Each of the schemes has a premise-conclusion form, but there seems to be three different kinds of arguments (Verhiej, 3002, p. 170). Some fit familiar deductive argument forms like DMP. Others fit familiar inductive forms like statistical syllogism. These two types of schemes appear to be applicable apart from the context of a given case. Others, the defeasible schemes, appear not to fit any deductive or inductive forms very well, and require the context of a case to be taken into account. These schemes are best analyzed and evaluated by seeing them as subject to critical questioning and to counter-arguments in a dialogue format. When using such schemes to apply to cases of legal argumentation Verhiej (2003, p. 171) noted, domain-specific rules and various kinds of generalizations also need to be taken into account. Despite the potential usefulness of applying such defeasible schemes to legal argumentation in dialogue formats, there are several specific problems that need to be addressed.

Three of the problems that have recurred frequently in the analyses of arguments in this book are those of relevance, enthymemes and burden of proof. To build a more practical working system of argument invention, better results on solving all three of these problems need to be achieved. The way the comparatively crude mechanism developed so far in this book works is that one of two outcomes of an argument invention attempt is achieved by a search. One is that the search finds a path of argumentation connecting the given argument by a chain of intervening reasoning to the target (ultimate) conclusion. But in by far the more common kind of outcome, the search falls somewhat short of proving the ultimate conclusion. What does this outcome mean? It could mean that the system didn't work, and that no argument can be invented from the given data that could be used to support that conclusion. Or it could mean that a relevant path was found, but it just doesn't go all the way. Here the problem of relevance comes in. But the problem of enthymemes could also quite likely come in. For what might be indicated by the failed search is that implicit premises or conclusions need to be added in at key points in the argument diagram in order to help the chain of argumentation move forward toward the ultimate conclusion. And here too, the problem of burden of proof comes in, for it may be that only a weak argument can be generated that gives some support to the target conclusion, but not a strong enough argument to be worth much as evidence. But does the conclusion have to be proved by the chain of argumentation generated by the search, or would it be a good result if the search gave an argument that only weakly offered support? Or could the search be a success if it suggested some critical questions that could be used to cast some doubt on the conclusion, reversing a burden of proof?

It will be recalled from chapter 1 that there are harder cases of reversal of burden of proof. Here is one to consider (Weast v. Schaffer, 41 IDELR 176, 4th Cir. 2004). In this case, parents of a special education student sued a school district for reimbursement for private school tuition costs on the grounds that the individualized education program (IEP) the district provided for their son was inappropriate for his needs. The district claimed their program was appropriate, and the issue was which side should have the burden of proof. The 2nd, 3rd, 8th and 9th Circuit Courts placed the burden on the school districts in cases where a procedural deficiency is alleged. The 4th Circuit Court of Appeals reversed this decision, ruling that the burden belonged on the parents, saying that it found no reason to depart from the general rule that the party wanting change should have the burden. We won't go into further details here[10], but merely note that this is a hard case of a burden of proof problem. The arguments concerning burden allocation on both sides were deadlocked, as indicated by the splitting of opinions in the court rulings.

---

[10] The 4th Circuit Court argued that placing the burden on the district was inappropriate on the grounds that the basic policy of the Individuals with Disabilities Education Act is to rely on the expertise of local educators. The other side used the same grounds to argue that the district should have the burden.

To deal with hard cases, a formal protocol for two-party burden of proof disputes has been devised and applied to several of these cases, including that of the school tuition case of Weast v. Schaffer by (Prakken, Reed and Walton, 2005). The formal dialogue structure in a case assigns a level to each move. In a case where a dispute about burden of proof cannot be resolved by other means, as in the case above, the dialogue moves to a higher level. At this level, there are rules for resolving the burden of proof dispute. A mechanism is in place in the formal system for assigning each move in a dialogue a level, for moving to a higher level, for making a decision at that level, and for jumping back to the lower level. How the actual mechanism works is not so important here as the recognition that such hard cases of burden of proof deadlocks exist, and are not all that uncommon in legal argumentation. Such hard cases, as shown in chapter 1, do not only exist in law, but also in argumentation theory and AI, concerning how to represent undercutters, defeaters, rebuttal and critical questions in argument diagrams. Whether an argument is stronger than a counter-argument, or can be defeated by the asking of a critical question, is a matter of determination of burden of proof in such cases. It is a matter of which side has the burden of proving a claim made. Thus the important lesson is that the strength of an argument in such cases depends on the dialogue framework of the argument. The importance of this lesson for the analysis and evaluation of legal argumentation generally cannot be emphasized too strongly. It tells us that defeasible argumentation of the most common and typical sort in law, cannot (in many cases) be properly analyzed and evaluated using only the framework of argument diagrams, i.e. as a set of propositions joined by inferential links representing arguments. One must also take the context of dialogue into account. This lesson can be applied to the methodology that has been adopted throughout this whole book. The investigation of any case or problem has started with structuring the analysis as an argument diagram, and then gone on to address the problem of how to extend the analysis by adding factors, like missing premises or relevance, that require a dialectical component.

10. A Procedural Model of Legal Argumentation

An important qualification that needs to be added to chapter 7 is that the model of relevance put forward in chapter 4, used as the basis for argument invention, has been artificially restricted. Relevance is defined in relation to the ten components above, in a framework in which only argumentation from a set of propositions to another proposition is considered. This framework does not take relevance of other kinds of moves in a dialogue into account. For example, a reply to a question may be said to be irrelevant if it fails to answer, or even address the question asked at the previous move (Walton, 2004). The problem that faces legal logic now is to move beyond the narrow structure defined by the ten components above, and to fit this structure into the broader framework of computational dialectics. This task takes us back to some of the hard issues about burden of proof discussed in chapter 1, as indicated in the school tuition case studied in the previous section.

In addition to modeling an argument as a set of propositions and inferences as displayed in an argument diagram, we need to confront the issue of how the asking of critical questions in a dialogue should impact on the evaluation of an argument.

What is most novel in the approach of this whole book, or will seem so to those trained mainly in formal logic, is the assumption that an argument should be judged to be good or bad at two levels. At the first level, it needs to be evaluated as good reasoning or not by standards for good reasoning fitting the framework of the ten components above. At the second, it needs to be evaluated dialectically on the basis of whether it contributes to a certain conventional type of goal-directed conversation of the kinds outlined in chapter 1. Adding a dialectical level of argument evaluation to the more familiar semantic level of formal logic offers a new procedural model of rationality that is extremely useful for applying logic to cases of legal argumentation. Unless we are ready to work with and develop such a dialectical viewpoint on argument analysis and evaluation, there is little prospect that we can fully carry out the important jobs set for this field. One is the job of providing useful criteria for evaluating arguments of the kind found in trials and other legal settings. Another is the job of developing tools for argument invention.

The posing of the problem of invention, and the other problems of legal argumentation and evidence discussed in this book, like that of enthymemes, formulated new problems that can't yet be solved. They can be solved, as indicated, within the narrower framework of the ten components. But that is just a beginning. What can be done, at this point, is to make a general statement in the form of a hypothesis on how to proceed, taking a computational dialectics approach to rationality. Solving the problem of enthymemes, and various other problems of legal argumentation, requires the two levels of rationality to be taken into account, and thus requires meta-rules that bridge the two levels. Of course, the missing statements in an enthymeme can only be determined by reconstructing the chain of reasoning in the case. Thus analyzing cases at the reasoning level is necessary. But such a reconstruction is only possible through the use of dialectical conversational rules like those postulated by Grice (1975), or like the principle of charity. Thus moving to a dialectical level is also necessary. The reasoning level and the argument level need to be combined, in order to move towards fully solving these problems.

The reasoning level has been dominant in logic for so long because, in many cases of arguments and enthymemes, the text of discourse in the given case can be incomplete or ambiguous. Real arguments may even contain deceptions, fallacies, and intentional ambiguities. A real argument, as used in a particular case, can rarely be judged, using dialectical methods, as absolutely correct or incorrect – end of story. Because the dialectical viewpoint is aware of these messy aspects of real argumentation, it appears to be in agreement with the postmodernist viewpoint. From this viewpoint, the best that can be given is often a conditional evaluation of an argument. This means that the argument is judged as correct or incorrect, depending on what we can take the speaker to have meant, judging by the evidence furnished by the text of discourse in the case. From a dialectical viewpoint, the best an argument critic can say is that an argument, as used in a given case, should be judged as correct or incorrect relative to the textual data in that case. Arriving at this judgment must take place at the dialectical level. The argument is no longer viewed just as a set of statements connected in a chain of reasoning. Where the reasoning is supposedly going is now important. What is the reasoning being used for? That is now the question. The argument needs to be judged at this level as a speech act that contributes collaboratively (after the fashion roughly indicated by Grice, 1975) to a conventional type of dialogue exchange with a respondent. The six conventional goal-directed types of dialogue that are the basic normative models in which arguments need to be evaluated are summarized in the table in chapter 1: persuasion dialogue, negotiation, inquiry, information-seeking dialogue, deliberation and eristic dialogue (quarrelling). Many problems of how such types of dialogue can be formalized, and how the formal models can be applied to legal argumentation, now need to be solved.

Judging the worth of an argument in relation to its conversational context of use takes us to a new procedural level of rationality. It is a step that many are unwilling to take, precisely because it takes them out of the semantic comfort zone of logical inferences and reasoning. To take it seems to the cautious logician to risk involvement in problems of computational dialectics that seem impossible to solve using only context-free semantic methods. Taking this step leads to the view expressed by Toulmin (1958) that the same argument may need to be evaluated by different standards in one field than another. For example, an argument from expert opinion may need to be evaluated differently as evidence as used in law than it was when used in a scientific context. For example, the burden of proof for it may have to be set differently. Such a dangerous abandonment of the old and safe context-free view of rationality stems from the admission of contextual dialectical considerations in interpreting a text of discourse, and in judging the worth of an argument. But the methods presented in this book have shown that the step to the dialectical level can be taken without leaping to the relativistic conclusion that one argument is always as good or bad as another one. This conclusion does not need to follow as long as there are normative standards for evaluating arguments at the dialectical level, over and above the viewpoints of the participants in an argument. For the dialectical view sets normative standards in place that can be used to judge whether a given argument is strong or weak, reasonable or fallacious. Even though it makes a place for the context of dialogue of an argument, it still provides rules and standards that can be used to evaluate arguments at the dialectical level.

Does adopting the procedural view of rationality make anyone who holds it a legal pragmatist? Perhaps it does, with some qualifications. What is required by the dialectical viewpoint is that the strength or weakness of an argument needs at least partly to be judged by how it contributes to a dialogue exchange between two parties. This dialectical view is sharply at odds with the purely semantic view adopted by logicians over the last two thousand years or so. The purely semantic view sees an argument as a set of propositions to be evaluated by essentially calculative, mathematical criteria like the propositional calculus and quantification theory. Supplementing this purely semantic method, it is possible to maintain the dialectical view that an argument is a dialogue between two parties - not just a solitary or objective set of propositions. According to the dialectical approach, each argument needs to be considered in relation to the text of discourse in which it was used, insofar as enough information is given by the actual text of discourse in the case. The dialectical method does confront the problem of interpreting real cases of argumentation in a natural language text of discourse, with all its attendant problems. On this method, the evaluation of an argument is partly judged as a function of the context of use in a given case.

As we have seen in this book over and over again, the reason we need to move to the dialectical level to analyze and evaluate so many common cases of legal arguments it that these arguments are defeasible. Their conclusions can be only accepted provisionally as hypotheses or assumptions that carry probative weight but are subject to critical questioning and examination in a dialogue. According to Verheij (2003, p. 183) a dialectical tool called DEFLOG is used to keep track of the sequence of moves and counter-moves in a dialogue in a given case. The usefulness of such a dialectical approach paves the way for a new procedural view of legal reasoning. The procedural view of rationality permits an argument to be analyzed not just as a set of premises and a designated conclusion, but as a record of moves made and commitments incurred by two parties who take part in the argument. This framework enables us to not only analyze arguments as premises and conclusions, but to question and correct them, and to see such questioning and correcting as part of the argumentation to be evaluated in a case.

In the previous chapters, many examples illustrating the ten components of an argument (set out in section 8 of chapter 7) were used to study and analyze them. It has been established roughly how they fit together into a general structure representing rational argumentation of the kind commonly used in law. Specific problems in analyzing the components and determining how they fit together into such a structure have been formulated. And it was shown how each of the components has been formally analyzed, revealing formal patterns and characteristics of legal reasoning. Each of these components has been shown to be useful for gaining greater understanding of legal reasoning. Indeed, the analyses of them has provided strong evidence for the thesis that a legal logic is now within our reach. A question now is whether the components can be fitted into a formalized structure providing the basis for a unified logical structure that is useful for applications in AI and law.

In this book no single attempt to provide a unified formalization comprising all the legal argumentation structures studied was made, although partial formalisms were used to address specific problems. There are four reasons for this reticence. The first is that several of the components were originally intended to be of practical value in representing real examples of arguments in natural language discourse. Thus, in certain respects, they have remained in a rough state of development that is resistant to the simplification needed for formalization. The second reason is that some of the methods, like argument diagramming, become less useful to summarize or simplify the argumentation in case they are made too complex. The third reason is that it remains unsettled yet how some formal methods, like systems developed to study case-based reasoning, fit together with others, like argument diagramming methods and forms of reasoning like argument from precedent and argument from analogy. The fourth reason is the contextual variability of argumentation, and legal argumentation as well. Although the ten main components are clearly visible in the kinds of cases studied in the previous chapters, it has been a thesis of the book that argumentation can occur in various different types of dialogue. Although arguments used in a trial are paradigms, there are all kinds of legal arguments that occur before or after a trial, or even outside the trial setting altogether, that need to be studied from an argumentation perspective. Alternative dispute resolution, especially in the form of online dispute resolution (ODR), is an important case in point. Work in AI and law in the future needs to take the direction of devising and implementing formal models of these types of dialogue of kinds that are applicable to communication between agents in multi-agents systems, to contexts of legal reasoning, and to argumentation generally.

References

Achinstein Peter (1983) *The Nature of Explanation*, New York, Oxford University Press

Alberts Laurie (2001)'Causation in Toxic Tort Litigation', *Villanova Environmental Law Journal,* 12: 33-63

Anderson Barrie, Anderson Dawn (1998) *Manufacturing Guilt: Wrongful Convictions in Canada*, Halifax, Fernwood Publishing

Anderson Terence J (1999)'On Generalizations I: A Preliminary Exploration', *South Texas Law Review*, 40: 455-481

Anderson Terence, Twining William (1991) *Analysis of Evidence: How to do Things with Facts Based on Wigmore's Science of Judicial Proof*, Boston, Little Brown & Co

Aristotle (1928) *On Sophistical Refutations*, Loeb Classical Library, Cambridge, Mass , Harvard University Press

Aristotle (1937) *Rhetoric*, Loeb Classical Library, Cambridge, Mass , Harvard University Press

Aristotle (1938) *Prior Analytics*, Loeb Classical Library, Cambridge, Mass , Harvard University Press

Aristotle (1939) *Topics*, trans Forster ES, Loeb Classical Library, Cambridge, Mass , Harvard University Press

Ashley Kevin D, Rissland Edwina L (2003) 'Law, Learning and Representation', *Artificial Intelligence,* 150: 17-58

Ball Vaughn C (1980) 'The Myth of Conditional Relevancy', *Georgia Law Review*, 14, 435-469

Bench-Capon Trevor (1997) 'Argument in Artificial Intelligence and Law', *Artificial Intelligence and Law*, 5, 249-261

Bench-Capon Trevor (1998) 'Specification and Implementation of Toulmin Dialogue Game', *Jurix 1998: The Eleventh Conference*, ed Jaap Hage et al , Nijmegen, Gerard Noodt Instituut, 5-20

Bench-Capon Trevor (2002) 'Agreeing to Differ: Modelling Persuasive Dialogue between Parties with Different Values', *Informal Logic*, 22: 231-245 Version available (2003) on the web page of the Department of Computer Science at the University of Liverpool: http://www.csc.liv.ac.uk/~tbc/projects/ifl.pdf

Bench-Capon Trevor, Sartor Giovanni (2003) 'A Model of Legal Reasoning with Cases Incorporating Theories and Values', *Artificial Intelligence,* 150, 97-143

Bex Floris, Prakken Henry (2004) 'Reinterpreting Arguments in Dialogue: An Application to Evidential Reasoning', *Legal Knowledge and Information Systems*, ed Thomas F Gordon, Amsterdam, IOS Press, 119-130

Bex Floris, Prakken Henry, Reed Chris, Walton Douglas (2003) 'Towards a Formal Account of Reasoning about Evidence: Argumentation Schemes and Generalizations', *Artificial Intelligence and Law*, 12, 125-165

Bibel Wolfgang (2004) 'AI and the Conquest of Complexity in Law', Invited Lecture, Seventeenth Annual Conference on Legal Knowledge and Information Systems, available on the web site of the JURIX 2004 Conference: http://gi-fg612.fokus.fhg.de/Jurix2004/

Boutlier C, Becher V (1995) 'Abduction as Belief Revision', *Artificial Intelligence*, 77, 43-94

Branting L Carl (2000) *Reasoning with Rules and Precedents: A Computational Model of Legal Analysis*, Dordrecht, Kluwer

Bromberger Sylvain (1966) 'Why-Questions', *Mind and Cosmos*, ed Robert G Colodny, Pittsburgh, University of Pittsburgh Press, 86-111

Burke Michael (1985) 'Unstated Premises', *Informal Logic*, 7, 107-118

Burnyeat Myles F (1994) 'Enthymeme: Aristotle on the Logic of Persuasion', *Aristotle's Rhetoric: Philosophical Essays*, ed David J Furley and Alexander Nehemas, Princeton, N J , Princeton University Press, 3-55

Callen Craig R (2003) 'Rationality and Relevancy: Conditional Relevancy and Constrained Resources', *Michigan State University Law Review*, 4, 1243-1303

Campbell Stephen K (1974) *Flaws and Fallacies in Statistical Thinking*, Englewood Cliffs, Prentice-Hall

Carberry Sandra (1990) *Plan Recognition in Natural Language Dialogue*, Cambridge, Mass , MIT Press

Cawsey Alison (1992) *Explanation and Interaction: The Computer Generation of Explanatory Dialogue,* Cambridge, Mass , The MIT Press

Chakrabarti Kisor Kumar (1995) *Definition and Induction: A Historical and Comparative Study*, Honolulu, University of Hawaii Press

Chandrasekaran B (1986) 'Generic Tasks in Knowledge Based Reasoning', *IEEE Expert*, 1, 23-30

Chorley Alison, Bench-Capon Trevor (2004) 'AGATHA: Automation of the Construction of Theories in Case Law Domains, *Legal Knowledge and Information Systems*, ed Thomas F Gordon, Amsterdam, IOS Press, 89-98

Coffa J Alberto (1974) "Hempel's Ambiguity", *Synthese*, 28, pp 141 - 163

Collingwood Robin G (1946) *The Idea of History*, Oxford, Clarendon Press

Collingwood Robin G (1939) *An Autobiography*, Oxford, Oxford University Press

Collins Allan, Warnock Eleanor H, Aiello Nelleke, Miller Mark L (1975)'Reasoning from Incomplete Knowledge', *Representation and Understanding: Studies in Cognitive Science*, ed Daniel G Bobrow and Allan Collins, New York, Academic Press, 383-415

Copi Irving M (1982) *Introduction to Logic*, 6th ed , New York, Macmillan

Copi Irving M, Cohen Carl (1994) *Introduction to Logic*, 9th ed , New York, Macmillan

Dieks Dennis, de Regt Henk W(1998) 'Reduction and Understanding', *Foundations of Science*, 1, 45-59

Doyle J (1979) 'A Truth Maintenance System', *Artificial Intelligence*, 12, 231-272

Doyle J (1992) 'Reason Maintenance and Belief Revision', *Belief Revision*, ed Peter Gardenfors, Cambridge, Mass , MIT Press, 29-51

Dray William (1964) *Philosophy of History*, Englewood Cliffs, Prentice-Hall

Dray William (1995) *History as Re-enactment: R G Collingwood's Idea of History*, Oxford, Oxford University Press

Dung P (1995) 'On the Acceptability of Arguments and its Fundamental Role in Nonmonotonic Reasoning, Logic Progamming and *n*-person Games', *Artificial Intelligence*, 77, 321-357

Ennis Robert H (1982), 'Identifying Implicit Assumptions', *Synthese*, 51, 61-86

Farley Arthur M, Freeman Kathleen (1995) 'Burden of Proof in Legal Argumentation', *Proceedings of the Fifth International Conference on Artificial Intelligence and Law,* New York, ACM Press

Faye Jan (1999) 'Explanation Explained', *Synthese*, 120, 61-75

Federal Rules of Evidence, Federal Rulemaking – Rules in Effect (2002) The latest versions of the federal rules of evidence as well as other rules can be found on the following web page: http://www.uscourts.gov/rules/newrules4.html

Feteris Eveline T (1999) *Fundamentals of Legal Argumentation: A Survey of Theories of the Justification of Legal Decisions*, Dordrecht, Kluwer

Finocchiaro Maurice (1980) 'Scientific Discoveries as Growth of Understanding: The Case of Newton's Gravitation', *Scientific Discovery, Logic, and Rationality*, ed Thomas Nickles, Dordrecht, Reidel, 235-255

Finocchiaro Maurice (1980a) *Galileo and the Art of Reasoning*, Dordrecht, Reidel

Frank Jerome (1963) *Courts on Trial*, New York, Atheneum

Freeman James B (1991) *Dialectics and the Macrostructure of Arguments,* Berlin, Foris

Freeman James B (1995) 'The Appeal to Popularity and Presumption by Common Knowledge', *Fallacies: Classical and Contemporary Readings*, ed Hans V Hansen and Robert C Pinto, University Park, The Pennsylvania State University Press, 265-273

Friedman Michael (1974) 'Explanation and Scientific Understanding', *The Journal of Philosophy,* 71, 5-19

Friedman Michael (1988) 'Explanation and Scientific Understanding', *Theories of Explanation*, ed J C Pitt, New York, Oxford University Press, 188-198

Friedman Richard D (1986) 'A Diagrammatic Approach to Evidence', *Boston University Law Review*, 66, 571-622

Friedman Richard D (1994) 'Conditional Probative Value: Neoclassicism Without Myth', *Michigan Law Review*, 93, 439-460

Gardenfors Peter (1988) *Knowledge in Flux*, Cambridge, Mass , MIT Press

Gelfond Michael, Przymusinska Halina (1990) 'Formalization of Inheritance Reasoning in Autoepistemic Logic', *Fundamenta Informaticae*, 13, 403-443

Gilbert Geoffrey (1788) *The Law of Evidence*, 5th ed , Philadelphia, John Cruikshank

Goldman Alvin I (1970) *A Theory of Human Action*, Englewood Cliffs, Prentice-Hall

Goodwin Jean (2000) 'Wigmore's Chart Method', *Informal Logic*, 20, 2000, 223-243

Gordon Robert M (1986) 'Folk Psychology as Simulation', *Mind and Language*, 1, 158-171

Gordon Thomas F (1996) 'Computational Dialectics', available at the web page: http://www.tfgordon.de/publications/Gordon1996a.pdf

Gordon Thomas F (1995) *The Pleadings Game: An Artificial Intelligence Model of Procedural Justice*, Dordrecht, Kluwer

Gordon Thomas F (1996) 'Computational Dialectics', *Computers as Assistants – A New Generation of Support Systems*, ed P Hoschka, Mahwah, New Jersey, Erlbaum, 108-123

Gordon Thomas F, Karacapilidis Nikos (1997) 'The Zeno Argumentation Framework', *Proceedings of the Sixth International Conference on Artificial Intelligence and Law,* Melbourne, Australia, 10 18

Gough James, Tindale Christopher (1985) 'Hidden or Missing Premises', *Informal Logic*, 7, 99-106

Grasso Floriana (2002) 'Towards Computational Rhetoric', *Informal Logic*, 22, 195-230

Grennan Wayne (1997) *Informal Logic: Issues and Techniques*, Montreal, McGill-Queen's University Press

Grice H Paul (1975) 'Logic and Conversation', *The Logic of Grammar*, ed Donald Davidson and Gilbert Harman, Encino, California, Dickenson, 64-75

Guthrie WKC (1981) *A History of Greek Philosophy*, Cambridge, Cambridge University Press

Hage Jaap (2000) 'Dialectical Models in Artificial Intelligence and Law', *Artificial Intelligence and Law*, 8, 137-172

Hage Jaap (1997) *Reasoning With Rules: An Essay on Legal Reasoning and Its Underlying Logic*, Dordrecht, Kluwer

Halonen Ilpo, Hintikka Jaakko (1997) 'Unification – It's Magnificent But Is It Explanation?', *Synthese*, 120, 27-47

Hamblin Charles L (1970) *Fallacies*, London, Methuen

Hamblin, Charles L (1971) 'Mathematical Models of Dialogue', *Theoria*, 37, 130-155

Hansen Hans V, Pinto Robert C (1995) *Fallacies: Classical and Contemporary Readings*, University Park, The Pennsylvania State University Press

Hart HLA, Honore AM (1962) *Causation in the Law*, Oxford, Oxford University Press

Hastings Arthur C (1963) *A Reformulation of the Modes of Reasoning in Argumentation*, Evanston, Illinois, Ph D Dissertation

Hempel Carl G (1965) *Aspects of Scientific Explanation*, New York, The Free Press

Hintikka Jaakko (1995) 'The Games of Logic and the Games of Inquiry', *Dialectica*, 49, 229-249

Hitchcock David (1985) 'Enthymematic Arguments', *Informal Logic*, 7, 83-97

Hitchcock David (2004) 'Toulmin's Warrants',: available on David Hitchcock's personal web page: http://www.humanities.mcmaster.ca/~hitchckd/Toulminswarrants.pdf

Hitchcock David, McBurney Peter, Parsons Simon (2001) 'A Framework for Deliberation Dialogues', *Argument and Its Applications: Proceedings of the Fourth Biennial Conference of the Ontario Society for the Study of Argumentation (OSSA),* eds H V Hansen, CW Tindale, JA Blair and RH Johnson, compact disk. Also available on Peter McBurney's web page at the University of Liverpool, Department of Computer Science: http://www.csc.liv.ac.uk/~peter/

Hohmann Hanns (1989) 'The Dynamics of Stasis: Classical Rhetorical Theory and Modern Legal Argumentation', *American Journal of Jurisprudence*, 34, 171-197

Hohmann Hanns (1990) 'The Nature of the Common Law and the Comparative Study of Legal Reasoning', *American Journal of Comparative Law*, 38, 143-170

Hohmann Hanns (2001) 'Stasis', *Encyclopedia of Rhetoric*, ed Thomas O Sloane, New York, Oxford University Press, 741-745

Horacek Helmut (1997)'A Model for Adapting Explanations to the User's Likely Inferences', *User Modeling and User-Adapted Interaction*, 7, 1-55

Huber Peter W (1991) *Galileo's Revenge: Junk Science in the Courtroom,* New York, Basic Books

Hurley Patrick (1991) A *Concise Introduction to Logic*, 7th ed , Belmont, California, Wadsworth

Hurley Patrick (2000) A *Concise Introduction to Logic*, 7th ed , Belmont, California, Wadsworth

Hurley Patrick (2003) *A Concise Introduction to Logic*, 8th ed , Belmont, California, Wadsworth

Jacobs Scott (1989) 'Speech Acts and Arguments', *Argumentation*, 3, 345-365

Johnson Ralph H (2002) *Manifest Rationality: A Pragmatic Theory of Argument*, Mahwah, New Jersey, Erlbaum

Josephson John R, Josephson Susan G (1994) *Abductive Inference: Computation, Philosophy, Technology*, Cambridge, Cambridge University Press

Keppens Jeroen, Zeleznikow John (2002) 'On the Role of Model-based Reasoning in Decision Support in Crime Investigation', *Report of the Centre for Forensic Statistics and Legal Reasoning*, Edinburgh, University of Edinburgh

Kienpointner Manfred (1992) *Alltagslogik: Struktur und Funktion von Argumentationsmustern*, Stuttgart, Fromman-Holzboog

Kienpointner Manfred (1997) 'On the Art of Finding Arguments: What Ancient and Modern Masters of Invention Have to Tell Us About the *Ars Inveniendi*', *Argumentation* 11, 225-236

Kienpointner Manfred (2003) 'Perelman on Causal Arguments: The Argument of Waste', 5th ISSA Conference on Argumentation, *Proceedings of the Fifth Conference of the International Society for the Study of Argumentation*, ed Frans H van Eemeren,

J Anthony Blair, Charles A Willard and Francisca Snoek Henkemans, Amsterdam, Sic Sat, 611-616

Kitcher Philip (1989) 'Explanatory Unification and the Causal Structure of the World', *Scientific Explanation: Minnesota Studies in the Philosophy of Science*, vol 13, ed Philip Kitcher and Wesley Salmon, Minneapolis, University of Minnesota Press, 410-505

Krabbe Erik CW (1995) 'Appeal to Ignorance', *Fallacies: Classical and Contemporary Readings*, ed Hans V Hansen and Robert C Pinto, University Park, The Pennsylvania State University Press, 251-264

Krabbe Erick CW (1996) 'Can We Ever Pin One Down to a Formal Fallacy?', *Logic and Argumentation*, ed Johan van Benthem, Frans H van Eemeren and Frank Veltman, Amsterdam, North-Holland, 129-141

Krabbe Erik CW (1999) 'Profiles of Dialogue', *JFAK: Essays Dedicated to Johan van Benthem on the Occasion of his 50th Birthday*, ed Jelle Gerbrandy, Maarten Marx, Maarten de Rijke and Yde Venema, Amsterdam, Amsterdam University Press, 25-36

Krabbe Erik CW (2001) 'The Problem of Retraction in Critical Discussion', *Synthese*, 127, 141-159

Leenes Ronald E (2001) 'Burden of Proof in Dialogue Games and Dutch Civil Procedure', *Proceedings of the 8th International Conference on Artificial Intelligence and Law*, St Louis, Missouri, ACM Press, 109-118

Lester J, Porter B (1997) 'Developing and Empirically Evaluating Robust Explanation Generators: The KNIGHT Experiments', *Computational Linguistics*, 2, 65-101

Lodder Arno R (1999) *Dialaw: On Legal Justification and Dialogical Models of Argumentation*, Dordrecht, Kluwer

Lodder Arno R (2000) 'Book Review of Gordon (1995)', *Artificial Intelligence and Law*, 8, 255-264

Loftus Elisabeth (1979) *Eyewitness Testimony*, Cambridge, Mass , Harvard University Press

Loui Ronald P (1998) 'Process and Policy: Resource-Bounded Nondemonstrative Reasoning', *Computational Intelligence*, 14, 1-38

Loui Ronald P, GordonThomas F (1994), Call for papers for 1994 AAAI Seattle Workshop on Computational Dialectics http://www.cs.wustl.edu/~loui/comectics.text

Mackenzie Jim (1981) 'The Dialectics of Logic', *Logique et Analyse*, 94, 159-177

Mackenzie Jim (1990) 'Four Dialogue Systems', *Studia Logica*, 49, 567-583

Mackie John L (1965) 'Causes and Conditions', *American Philosophical Quarterly*, 2, 245-264

Mates Benson (1996) *The Skeptic Way: Sextus Empiricus's Outlines of Pyrrhonism*, Oxford, Oxford University Press

Mayfield James (2000) 'Evaluating Plan Recognition Systems: Three Properties of a Good Explanation', *Artificial Intelligence Review*, 14, 351-376

McBurney Peter, Parsons Simon (2002) 'Dialogue Games in Multi-Agents Systems', *Informal Logic*, 22, 257-274

Michael Jerome, Adler Mortimer (1934) 'The Trial of an Issue of Fact: I', *Columbia Law Review*, 34, 1224-1306

Michael Jerome, Adler Mortimer (1934), 'The Trial of an Issue of Fact: II', *Columbia Law Review*, 34, 1462-1493

Moore Johanna D (1991) 'A Reacting Approach to Explanation: Taking the User's Feedback into Account', *Natural Language Generation in Artificial Intelligence and Computational Linguistics*, ed CL Paris, WR Swartout and WC Mann, Dordrecht, Kluwer, 3-48

Moore Johanna D (1995) *Participating in Explanatory Dialogues*, Cambridge, Mass , MIT Press

Moore Robert C (1985) 'Semantical Considerations on Nonmonotonic Logic', *Artificial Intelligence*, 25, 75-94

Morgan Edmund L (1929) 'Functions of Judge and Jury in the Determination of Preliminary Questions of Fact', *Harvard Law Review*, 43, 1929, 165-191

Moulin B, Irandoust H, Belanger M, Desbordes G (2002) 'Explanation and Argumentation Capabilities', *Artificial Intelligence Review*, 17, 169-222

Nance Dale A (1995) 'Conditional Probative Value and the Reconstruction of the Federal Rules of Evidence', *Michigan Law Review*, 94, 419-456

Nissan Ephraim (2001) 'The Bayesianism Debate in Legal Scholarship', *Artificial Intelligence and Law*, 9, 199-214

Nuchelmans Gabriel (1993) 'On the Fourfold Root of the *Argumentum Ad Hominem*', *Empirical Logic and Public Debate*, ed Erik CW Krabbe, Renee Jose Dalitz and Pier A Smit, Amsterdam, Rodopi, 37-47

Palmer Andrew (2003) *Proof and the Preparation of Trials*, Sydney, Australia, Lawbook Co

Park Roger C (1998) 'Character at the Crossroads', *Hastings Law Journal*, 49, 749-754

Park Roger C, Leonard David P, Goldberg Steven H (1998) *Evidence Law*, St Paul, Minnesota West Group,

Pearl Judea (1991) 'Probabilistic Semantics for Nonmonotonic Reasoning', *Philosophy and AI: Essays on the Interface*, ed Robert Cummins and John Pollock, Cambridge, Mass , The MIT Press, 157-187

Pearl Judea (2000) *Causality: Models, Reasoning and Inference,* Cambridge, Cambridge University Press

Peirce Charles S (1965) *Collected Papers of Charles Sanders Peirce*, vol V, 'Pragmatism and Pragmaticism', ed Charles Hartshorne and Paul Weiss, Cambridge, Mass , Harvard University Press

Peirce Charles S (1965II) *Collected Papers of Charles Sanders Peirce*, vol II, 'Elements of Logic', ed Charles Hartshorne and Paul Weiss, Cambridge, Mass , Harvard University Press

Peirce Charles S (1992) *Reasoning and the Logic of Things*, ed Kenneth Laine Kettner, Cambridge, Mass , Harvard University Press

Peng Yun, Reggia James A (1990) *Abductive Inference Models for Diagnostic Problem-Solving*, New York, Springer-Verlag

Perelman Chaim, Olbrechts-Tyteca Lucie (1971) *The New Rhetoric: A Treatise on Argumentation*, trans J Wilkinson and P Weaver, 2nd ed , Notre Dame, University of Notre Dame Press, (First published, as *La Nouvelle Rhetorique*, in 1958)

Pollock John L (1987) 'Defeasible Reasoning', *Cognitive Science*, 11, 481-518

Pollock John L (1995) *Cognitive Carpentry*, Cambridge, Mass , The MIT Press

Prakken Henry (1991) 'On Formalizing Burden of Proof in Legal Argument', *Legal Knowledge-Based Systems: JURIX 99, the Twelfth Conference*, Nijmegen, Gerard Noodt Instituut, 85-97

Prakken Henry (1997) *Logical Tools for Modelling Legal Argument*, Dordrecht, Kluwer

Prakken Henry 'Relating Protocols for Dynamic Dispute with Logics for Defeasible Argumentation', *Synthese*, 127, 187-219

Prakken Henry (2001) 'Modelling Defeasibility in Law: Logic or Procedure?', *Fundamenta Informaticae*, 20, 1-20

Prakken Henry (2002) 'Incomplete Arguments in Legal Discourse: a Case Study', *Legal Knowledge and Information Systems* ed TJM Bench-Capon, A Daskalopulu and R Winkels *JURIX 2002: The Fifteenth Annual Conference,* Amsterdam, IOS Press, 93-102

Prakken Henry (2003) 'Perelman Formalized? On Reconciling the Ideals of Logical Validity and Persuasiveness', *Proceedings of the Fifth Conference of the International Society for the Study of Argumentation*, ed Frans H van Eemeren, J Anthony Blair, Charles A Willard and Francisca Snoek Henkemans, Amsterdam, Sic Sat, 857-860

Prakken Henry, Reed Chris, Walton Douglas (2003) 'Argumentation Schemes and Generalisations in Reasoning about Evidence', *Proceedings of the Conference: The 9th International Conference on Artificial Intelligence and Law*, University of Edinburgh, New York, Association for Computing Machinery (ACM), 32-41

Prakken Henry, Reed Chris, Walton Douglas (2005) 'Dialogues about the Burden of Proof', unpublished paper

Prakken Henry, Renooij Silja (2001) 'Reconstructing Causal Reasoning about Evidence: A Case Study', *Legal Knowledge and Information Systems*, ed Bart Verheij, Arno R Lodder, Ronald P Loui and A Muntjewerjj, Amsterdam, IOS Press, 131-142

Prakken Henry, Sartor Giovanni (1996) 'A Dialectical Model of Assessing Conflicting Arguments in Legal Reasoning', *Artificial Intelligence and Law*, 4, 331-368

Prakken Henry, Sartor Giovanni (1997) 'Argument-based Extended Logic Programming with Defeasible Priorities', *Journal of Applied Non-classical Logics*, 7, 25-75

Prakken Henry Sartor Giovanni (2003) 'The Three Faces of Defeasibility in the Law', *Ratio Juris,* 16, 495-516

Preyer Gerhard, Mans Dieter (1999) 'On Contemporary Developments in the Theory of Argumentation', *Protosociology*, 13, 3-13

Reed Chris (1998) 'Dialogue Frames in Agent Communication', *Proceedings of the Third International Conference on Multi-Agent Systems*, ed Y Demazeau, IEEE Press, 246-253

Reed Chris, Rowe Glenn (2002) '*Araucaria* Software for Puzzles in Argument Diagramming and XML', *Technical Report*, Department of Applied Computing, University of Dundee Available at http://www.computing.dundee.ac.uk/staff/creed/araucaria/

Reed Chris, Rowe Glenn (2003) *Araucaria, Version 2, User Manual,* Available at http://www.computing.dundee.ac.uk/staff/creed/araucaria/

Reed Chris, Norman Timothy J 2003 *Argumentation Machines: New Frontiers in Argument and Computation*, Dordrecht, Kluwer

Reed Chris, Walton Doug (2005) 'Towards a Formal and Implemented Model of Argumentation Schemes in Agent Communication', *Journal of Autonomous Agents and Multi-Agent Systems*, to appear

Reiter Raymond (1980) 'A Logic for Default Reasoning', *Artificial Intelligence*, 13, 81-132

Reiter Raymond (1987) 'Nonmonotonic Reasoning', *Annual Review of Computer Science*, 2, 147-186

Renon Luis Vega (1998) 'Aristotle's *Endoxa* and Plausible Argumentation', *Argumentation*, 12, 95-113

Rissland Edwina L (1990, 1957-1980) 'Artificial Intelligence and Law: Stepping Stones to a Model of Legal Reasoning', *Yale Law Journal*, 99

Rissland Edwina L, Ashley Kevin D, Loui RP (2003) 'AI and Law: A Fruitful Synergy', *Artficial Intelligence,* 150, 1-15

Rescher Nicholas (1976) *Plausible Reasoning*, Assen, Van Gorcum

Robinson Richard (1953) *Plato's Earlier Dialectic*, 2nd ed, Oxford, Clarendon Press

Roth Bram, Verheij Bart (2004) 'Dialectical Arguments and Case Comparison', *Legal Knowledge and Information Systems,* ed Thomas F Gordon, Amsterdam, IOS Press, 99-108

Roth Bram, Verheij Bart (1995) 'Cases and Dialectical Arguments: An Approach to Case-Based Reasoning', *WORM'04: The Second International Workshop on Regulatory On-*

tologies, *Lecture Notes in Computer Science*, vol 3292, ed R Meersman, Z Tari and A Corsaro, Heidelberg, Springer, 634-651

Russell Stuart J, Norvig Peter (2004) *Artificial Intelligence: A Modern Approach*, Upper Saddle River, Prentice Hall

Salmon Wesley C (1970) 'Statistical Explanation', *The Nature and Function of Scientific Theories*, ed Robert G Colodny, Pittsburgh, University of Pittsburgh Press, 173-231

Salmon Wesley C (1989) 'Four Decades of Scientific Explanation', *Scientific Explanation, Minnesota Studies in the Philosophy of Science*, vol 13, Minneapolis, University of Minnesota Press, 3-219

Salmon Wesley C (1992) 'Scientific Explanation', *Introduction to the Philosophy of Science*, ed Merrilee H Salmon et al, Englewood Cliffs, Prentice-Hall, 7-41

Salmon Wesley C (1998) 'The Importance of Scientific Understanding', *Causality and Explanation,* ed Wesley Salmon, New York, Oxford University Press ,79-91

Saunders Kevin W (1993) 'Informal Fallacies in Legal Argumentation', *South Carolina Law Review*, 44, 343-382

Schank Roger C (1986) *Explanation Patterns: Understanding Mechanically and Creatively*, Hillsdale, New Jersey, Erlbaum

Schank Roger C, Abelson Robert P (1977) *Scripts, Plans, Goals and Understanding*, Hillsdale, N J Erlbaum

Schum David A (1994) *Evidential Foundations of Probabilistic Reasoning*, New York, John Wiley and Sons

Schurz Gerhard (1999) 'Explanation as Unification', *Synthese,* 95-114

Scott AC, Clancey WJ, Davis R, Shortliffe EH (1977) 'Explanation Capabilities of Knowledge-Based Production Systems', *Rule-Based Expert Systems*, ed BG Buchanan and EH Shortliffe, Addison Wesley, 338-362

Scriven Michael (1962) 'Explanations, Predictions and Laws', *Minnesota Studies in the Philosophy of Science*, vol 3, ed H Feigl and G Maxwell, Minneapolis, University of Minnesota Press, 171-174

Scriven Michael (1964) 'Critical Study of *The Structure of Science', Review of Metaphysics*, 17, 403-424

Scriven Michael (1976) *Reasoning*, New York, McGraw-Hill

Segal Martin E (2004) 'In Inheritance Case, Try Shifting Burden of Proof', *Ask Doctor Law, The Miami Herald*, December 13, 8

Sextus Empiricus (1933) *Against the Logicians* (*AL*), trans RG Bury, Loeb Classical Library, Cambridge, Mass , Harvard University Press

Sidgwick Alfred (1883) *Fallacies: A View of Logic from the Practical Side*, London, Kegan Paul, Trench and Company

Sidgwick Alfred (1893) *The Process of Argument*, London, Adam and Charles Black

Singh Munindar P (2000) 'A Social Semantics for Agent Communication Languages', *Issues in Agent Communication,* ed Frank Dignum and Mark Greaves, Berlin, Springer-Verlag, 31-45

Singh Munidar P (1998) 'Agent Communication Languages: Rethinking the Principles', *Computer*, 31, 425-445

Snoeck Henkemans A F (1992) *Analyzing Complex Argumentation: The Reconstruction of Multiple and Coordinatively Compound Argumentation in a Critical Discussion*, Amsterdam, SICSAT

Snoeck Henkemans A Francisca (2001) 'Argumentation Structures', *Crucial Concepts in Argumentation Theory*, ed Frans H van Eemeren, Amsterdam, Amsterdam University Press ,101-134

Sterling TD, Rosenbaum WL, Weinkam JJ (1995) 'Publication Decisions Revisited: The Effect of the Outcome of Statistical Tests on the Decision to Publish and Vice Versa', *The American Statistician*, 49, 108-112

Stevenson Charles L (1944) *Ethics and Language*, New Haven, Yale University Press

Strong John W (ed) (1992) *McCormick on Evidence*, 4th ed, St Paul, Minn , West Publishing Co

Thayer James Bradley (1889)*A Preliminary Treatise on Evidence at the Common Law*, New York, Little Brown & Co

Thayer James Bradley (1989) 'Presumptions and the Law of Evidence', *Harvard Law Review*, 3, 141-166

Thomas Stephen N (1981) *Practical Reasoning in Natural Language*, 2nd ed , Englewood Cliffs Prentice-Hall

Tillers Peter (1994) 'Exaggerated and Misleading Reports of the Death of Conditional Relevance', *Michigan Law Review*, 93, 478-484

Toulmin Stephen (1958) *The Uses of Argument*, Cambridge, Cambridge University Press

Trout JD (2002) 'Scientific Explanation and the Sense of Understanding', *Philosophy of Science*, 69, 212-233

Twining William (1985) *Theories of Evidence: Bentham and Wigmore*, London, Weidenfeld and Nicolson

Twining William (1999) 'Narrative and Generalizations in Argumentation About Questions of Fact', *South Texas Law Review*, 40, 351-365

Twining William, Miers David (1976) *How To Do Things With Rules*, London, Weidenfeld and Nicolson

van Eemeren Frans H, Grootendorst Rob (1984) *Speech Acts in Communicative Discussions*, Dordrecht, Foris

van Eemeren Frans H, Grootendorst Rob (1987) 'Fallacies in Pragma-Dialectical Perspective', *Argumentation*, 1, 283-301

van Eemeren Frans H, Grootendorst Rob (1992) *Argumentation, Communication and Fallacies*, Hillsdale, N J , Erlbaum

van Eemeren Frans H, Kruiger Tjark (1987) 'Identifying Argumentation Schemes', *Argumentation: Perspectives and Approaches*, ed Frans H van Eemeren et al , Dordrecht, Foris, 70- 81

van Fraassen Bas C (1980) *The Scientific Image*, Oxford, Clarendon Press

van Fraassen Bas C (1993) 'The Pragmatics of Explanation', *Explanation*, ed David-Hillel Ruben, Oxford, Oxford University press, 275-309

Verheij Bart (1996) *Rules, Reasons, Arguments: Formal Studies of Argumentation and Defeat*, Doctoral Dissertation, University of Maastricht

Verheij Bart (2000)'Dialectical Argumentation as a Heuristic for Courtroom Decision Making', web page of Bart Verheij, Department of Metajuridica, Universiteit Maastricht

Verheij Bart (2000) 'Logic, Context and Valid Inference Or: Can There be a Logic of Law', available on the following web page:www.ai.rug.nl/~verheij/

Verheij Bart (2003) Dialectical Argumentation with Argumentation Schemes: An Approach to Legal Logic', *Artificial Intelligence and Law*, 11, 167-195

Verheij Bart (2005) *Virtual Arguments: On the Design of Argument Assistants for Lawyers and Other Arguers*, The Hague, TMC Asser Press

von Wright Georg Henrik (1971) *Explanation and Understanding*, Ithaca, New York, Cornell University Press

Wagenaar, Willem A, van Koppen Peter J, Crombag Hans FM (1993) *Anchored Narratives: The Psychology of Criminal Evidence*, Hertfordshire, Harvester Wheatsheaf

Walton Douglas N (1984) *Logical Dialogue-Games and Fallacies*, Lanham, Maryland, University Press of America

Walton Douglas (1989) *Informal Logic*, New York, Cambridge University Press

Walton Douglas (1990) 'Ignoring Qualifications (*Secundum Quid*) as a Subfallacy of Hasty Generalization', *Logique et Analyse*, 129-130, 113-154

Walton Douglas (1992) 'Nonfallacious Arguments from Ignorance', *American Philosophical Quarterly,* Vol 29, 381-387

Walton Douglas (1995) *A Pragmatic Theory of Fallacy*, The University of Alabama Press, Tuscaloosa and London

Walton Douglas (1996) *Arguments from Ignorance*, University Park, Pennsylvania, Penn Sate Press

Walton Douglas (1996)*Argumentation Schemes for Presumptive Reasoning*, Mahwah, New Jersey, Erlbaum

Walton Douglas (1997) *Appeal to Expert Opinion*, University Park, Pennsylvania, Penn State Press

Walton Douglas (1998) *The New Dialectic*, Toronto, University of Toronto Press

Walton Douglas (1998a) *Ad Hominem Arguments*, Tuscaloosa, University of Alabama Press

Walton Douglas (1999) 'Rethinking the Fallacy of Hasty Generalization', *Argumentation*, 13, 161-182

Walton Douglas (1999) 'Dialectical Relevance in Persuasion Dialogue', *Informal Logic*, 19: 119-143 Available at www.uwinnipeg.ca/~walton

Walton Douglas (1999) *One-Sided Arguments: A Dialectical Analysis of Bias*, Albany, State University of New York Press

Walton Douglas (2001) 'Abductive, Presumptive and Plausible Arguments', *Informal Logic*, 21, 141-169

Walton Douglas (2002) *Legal Argumentation and Evidence*, University Park, Pennsylvania, The Pennsylvania State University Press

Walton Douglas (2003) 'Argumentation Schemes: The Basis of Conditional Relevance', *Michigan State University Law Review*, 4, 1205-1242

Walton Douglas (2004) 'A New Dialectical Theory of Explanation', *Philosophical Explorations*, 7, 71-89

Walton Douglas (2004a) *Abductive Reasoning*, Tuscaloosa, University of Alabama Press

Walton Douglas (2004) *Relevance in Argumentation*, Mahwah, New Jersey, Erlbaum

Walton Douglas, Krabbe Erik CW (1995)*Commitment in Dialogue: Basic Concepts of Interpersonal Reasoning*, Albany, State University of New York Press

Walton Douglas, Reed Chris (2003) 'Diagramming, Argumentation Schemes and Critical Questions', *Anyone Who Has a View: Theoretical Contributions to the Study of Argumentation,* ed Frans H van Eemeren, J Anthony Blair, Charles A Willard, and A Francisca Snoek Henkemans, Dordrecht, Kluwer, pp 195-211

Walton Douglas, Reed Chris (2004) 'Enthymemes and Argumentation Schemes', *Synthese*, to appear

Weber Erik, van Dyck Maarten (2002) 'Unification and Explanation', *Synthese,* 131, 145-154

Whatley Richard (1836) Elements of Logic, 6th ed, London, B Fellowes

Wick MR, Thompson WB (1992) 'Reconstructive Expert System Explanation', *Artificial Intelligence*, 54, 33-70

Wigmore John H (1913) *The Principles of Judicial Proof*, Boston, Little, Brown and Company (second edition, 1931)

Wigmore John H (1935) *A Student's Textbook of the Law of Evidence*, Chicago, The Foundation Press

Wigmore John H (1940) *A Treatise on the Anglo-American System of Evidence in Trials at Common Law,* 3rd ed, vol 1, Boston, Little, Brown and Company

Wigmore John H (1983) *Evidence in Trials at Common Law*, vol 1a, ed Peter Tillers, Boston, Little, Brown and Company
Woods John (1999) 'Peirce's Abductive Enthusiasms', *Protosociology*, 13: 117-125
Wooldridge Michael (2002) *Reasoning About Rational Agents*, Cambridge Mass , The MIT Press
Wright Richard W (1985) 'Causation in Tort Law', *California Law Review*, 73, 1735-1828

Index

The manufacturer's authorised representative in the EU is Springer Nature Customer Service Centre GmbH, Europaplatz 3, 69115 Heidelberg, Germany. If you have any concerns regarding our products, please contact ProductSafety@springernature.com

Printed and bound by CPI Group (UK) Ltd, Croydon, CR0 4YY
22/09/2026
02221061-0012